Ancient Buddhist Scrolls from Gandhāra

Fragment 2, r

Ancient Buddhist Scrolls from Gandhāra

The British Library Kharoṣṭhī Fragments

RICHARD SALOMON

with contributions by Raymond Allchin and Mark Barnard

Foreword by His Holiness the Dalai Lama

THE BRITISH LIBRARY *London*

First published 1999 by the University of Washington Press,
P.O. Box 50096, Seattle, Washington 98145

This edition published 1999 by The British Library, 96 Euston Road, London NW1 2DB

ISBN 0-7123-4610-4 (cloth)
ISBN 0-7123-4611-2 (paper)

Printed in Hong Kong

All photographs courtesy of The British Library, except the following:
Pls. 5–6, 19–20: Isao Kurita
Pls. 12–14: By the author, with the owner's permission
Pl. 16: By the author
Pls. 17–18: Ashmolean Museum
Fig. 8: From *Journal Asiatique,* ser. 3, vol. 2 (1836): pl. XII.1

Contents

List of Illustrations *ix*

Foreword by His Holiness the Dalai Lama *xiii*

Preface *xv*

Note on the System of Transcription and Citation *xviii*

Abbreviations *xx*

Chapter 1 **The Background: Gandhāra and Gandhāran Buddhism 3**

1.1. Gandhāra: Geographic Setting and Early History *3*

1.2. Buddhism in Gandhāra *5*

1.3. Textual Sources and the Modern Academic Study of Buddhism *7*

1.4. Previous Discoveries of Early Buddhist Manuscripts and Their Significance for the Study of Buddhism *8*

1.5. The British Library Kharoṣṭhī Fragments and Gandhāran Buddhism: A Preview of the Potential Significance of the New Discovery *9*

Chapter 2 **The Contents of the British Library Kharoṣṭhī Collection 15**

2.1. General Description *15*

2.2. Texts and Genres Represented in the Collection *22*

2.3. Catalog of the Fragments *42*

2.4. Summary of Original Scrolls or Scroll Sets *53*

2.5. Summary of Scribal Hands *54*

Chapter 3 **Previous Discoveries of Kharoṣṭhī Manuscripts 57**

3.1. Kharoṣṭhī Manuscripts Found in Chinese Central Asia *58*

3.2. Kharoṣṭhī Manuscripts Found in Afghanistan *59*

3.3. Kharoṣṭhī Manuscripts from Other Regions or of Unknown Origin *66*

3.4. Conclusions *68*

Chapter 4 **Origin and Character of the Collection 69**

4.1. Physical Evidence *69*

4.2. Textual Evidence: The "*Likhidago*" Interlinear Notations *71*

Fragments 16–19 before
unrolling and conservation

4.3. Archeological Parallels *77*
4.4. A "Buddhist Genizah"? *81*
4.5. Additional Comments on the Interment of Manuscripts and Birch Bark Texts *84*

Chapter 5 Format, Material, and Construction of the Scrolls 87
5.1. The Large (Composite) Scrolls *87*
5.2. Construction of the Smaller Texts *98*
5.3. Observations on the Origin and Use of the Scroll Format *100*
5.4. Scribal Materials and Techniques *106*

Chapter 6 Paleographic and Linguistic Features of the Gandhāran Scrolls 110
6.1. The Gāndhārī Language and the Kharoṣṭhī Script *110*
6.2. Paleographic Features *114*
6.3. Orthographic Features *120*
6.4. Phonological Features *124*
6.5. Morphology and Syntax *130*
6.6. Lexicon *133*
6.7. General Remarks and Conclusions 135

Chapter 7 The Date of the Manuscripts 141
7.1. Internal Evidence for Dating *141*
7.2. Dating of the Pots and Their Inscriptions *151*
7.3. Conclusions *154*

Chapter 8 Preliminary Evaluation of the New Corpus 156
8.1. Observations on the Contents of the New Corpus *156*
8.2. Sectarian Considerations: The Dharmaguptaka Connection *166*
8.3. Conclusions: A New View of Buddhism in Gandhāra *178*

Appendix Inscribed Pots and Potsherds in the British Library Collection 183
1. Technical Description and Evaluation of the Pots and Potsherds (*by Raymond Allchin*) *183*
2. Kharoṣṭhī Pot and Potsherd Inscriptions *187*
3. The Inscribed Pots in the British Library Collection *191*
4. The Inscribed Potsherds in the British Library Collection *225*
5. Conclusions: The Functions of the Inscribed Pots *240*

Glossary *249*

References *253*

Index *265*

Pot D

Illustrations

Color Plates *(following page 76)*

1. Fragments 16–19 before unrolling and conservation
2. Fragment 23 before unrolling and conservation
3. Specimen of a deteriorated manuscript fragment after unrolling and conservation: fragment 23, part 2, r
4. Specimen of a relatively well preserved manuscript fragment after unrolling and conservation: fragment 1, part 5, r
5. Pot D with manuscripts inside (1993), viewed from above
6. Earliest available photograph (1993) of fragment 1, removed from pot D
7. Fragment 12, part 1, r
8. Detail of fragment 9, part 3, r
9. Partial colophon text in fragment 3B
10. Detail of fragment 14, r, showing a copyist's notations
11. Detail of fragment 16, r, showing a copyist's notation
12. Pyxis-shaped reliquary in a private collection
13. Contents of the pyxis-shaped reliquary
14. Fragments of a birch bark manuscript found inside the pyxis-shaped reliquary
15. Fragment 2, r
16. A monastery cell at Jauliāñ (Taxila) with fragments of a pot in which a birch bark manuscript was found
17. Clay pot decorated with ink drawings of monks
18. Detail of decorated pot in pl. 17
19. Traces of the inscription on the decorated pot in pl. 17
20. Decorated pot in pl. 17, showing the bones found inside it
21. Fragment 1, part 2, v
22. Pot A
23. Pot A, viewed from above
24. Pot B
25. Pot B, viewed from above
26. Pot C
27. Pot C, viewed from above

28. Pot D
29. Pot D, viewed from above
30. Pot E
31. Pot E, viewed from above
32. Potsherds 1–9
33. Potsherds 10–18
34. Potsherds 19–26

Figures

1. Fragments 25–7 before unrolling and conservation *14*
2–6. Mark Barnard and Mike Chambers unrolling fragment 24 *16–7*
7. Fragment 24 after conservation *18*
8. Kharoṣṭhī manuscript discovered by Martin Honigberger at Shiwaki stūpa *63*
9. Fragment 1, part 2, r, detail of separated juncture between segments *93*
10. Fragment 1, part 5, r, detail of intact juncture between segments *95*
11. Original segments of the Khotan Dharmapada scroll *97*
12. Chart of Kharoṣṭhī script, as written by the scribe of fragments 1, 12 + 14, and 16 + 25 (hand no. 1) *111*
13. Genealogical chart of Aśpavarman and his immediate relatives in the line of the kings of Apraca *150*
14. Cross section of pot A, with inscriptions 1 and 2 *192*
15–22. Details of inscriptions 1 and 2 on pot A *193–7*
23. Cross section of pot B, with inscription *200*
24–7. Details of inscription on pot B *201–2*
28. Cross section of pot C, with inscription *204*
29–35. Details of inscription on pot C *204–8*
36. Cross section of pot D, with inscription *215*
37–9. Details of inscription on pot D *215–6*
40. Cross section of pot E, with inscription *217*
41–8. Details of inscription on pot E *220–3*
49. Potsherd 5 *227*
50. Potsherd 6 *227*
51. Potsherd 7 *229*
52. Potsherd 9 *230*
53. Potsherd 12 *232*
54–5. Potsherd 14 *233*
56. Potsherd 17 *235*
57. Potsherd 20 *237*
58. Potsherd 22 *238*
59. Potsherd 26 *240*

Maps

1. Gandhāra *2*
2. Findspots of Kharoṣṭhī manuscripts *56*
3. Findspots of pots and potsherds with Kharoṣṭhī inscriptions *189*

Pot C

THE DALAI LAMA

All Buddhist traditions have been at pains to ensure the authenticity of the teachings they propound. There are several ways to do this. One involves reliance on scriptural sources, many of which originate in the actual words of the Buddha himself, while others involve logical examination and actual application in practice.

There are several classic collections of Buddhist scriptures preserved in the Pali, Chinese, Korean, Japanese, and Tibetan languages. All of them derive from sources that were committed to writing long after the Buddha's parinirvana. Consequently, the Kharoṣṭhī manuscripts that are believed to date from the first century C.E. and that are now in the possession of the British Library are of immense value and interest to Buddhist scholars of all traditions.

These birch bark scrolls are believed to be the oldest surviving Buddhist texts ever discovered. They provide us with the earliest written testimony of the original words of the Buddha. They will provide fascinating insights into how the teachings of the Buddha were studied, preserved, and understood nearly 2,000 years ago. And as such, I believe that they will reinforce and clarify rather than challenge our modern understanding of the fundamental doctrines of Buddhism.

In terms of historical enquiry, these texts also document the importance of Gandhāra as a center of Buddhist literature and scholarly thought. They confirm Gandhāra's key role in the transmission of Buddhism from India, the land of its origin, to central Asia and beyond.

Despite the great respect that Buddhists universally have for their scriptures, there is sometimes a risk of books being venerated from a distance rather than read. This is all the more likely when the manuscripts concerned, like these, are extremely rare and fragile. I am very glad, therefore, that a series of books of which *Ancient Buddhist Scrolls from Gandhāra* is the inaugural volume is to be published. This will make these valuable fragments of ancient Buddhist literature, otherwise necessarily available only to a limited number of professional scholars, accessible to everyone who is interested to read them.

September 30, 1998

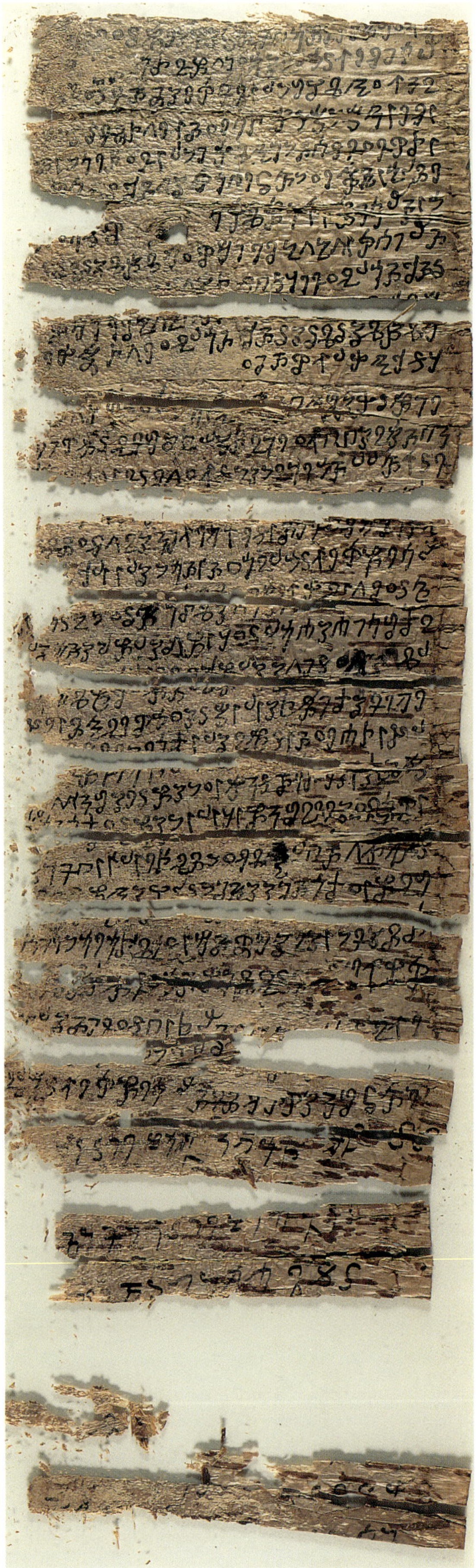

Fragment 1, part 5, r

Preface

In September 1994, the British Library's Oriental and India Office Collections, through the generous assistance of an anonymous benefactor, acquired the collection of twenty-nine birch bark scrolls containing texts in Kharoṣṭhī script that constitute the subject of this volume. It immediately became clear that this was a find of extraordinary interest, among other reasons because these fragments are likely to be the oldest Buddhist manuscripts, as well as the oldest Indian manuscripts, known to date. In June 1996, this discovery came to the attention of the media, and in that and subsequent months numerous reports, inevitably varying in accuracy,[1] appeared in the press and electronic media worldwide. The first scholarly publication on the manuscripts, a brief summary of and introduction to the new materials (Salomon 1997a), was published in July 1997. The present book provides a more detailed description of the new manuscripts and a survey of their contents, in order to evaluate, in a preliminary way, their overall significance and to set an agenda for their further study. It is intended as the first volume of a series of studies of these manuscripts. Subsequent volumes in this series will comprise editions and detailed studies of particular texts within this corpus, and it is hoped that the first of these volumes, an edition and study of the Rhinoceros Horn Sūtra fragment,[2] will appear not long after the publication of this introductory volume. Also projected for a later phase of the project are comparative studies of the Buddhological and linguistic and paleographic significance of these manuscripts.

Because of the wide interest in this discovery that has been expressed outside as well as within the academic community, I have attempted to make this presentation as accessible as possible to the nonspecialist reader, without compromising scholarly standards. Much of the material in chapter 1, for instance, is intended primarily for the nonspecialist, with a view to providing a broader context within which the significance of the new materials can be understood. It is also for the convenience of the nonspecialist audience that a Glossary, providing brief definitions of

1. Among the more accurate reports were those in the *New York Times* (July 7, 1996, p. 3), *Asiaweek* (September 6, 1996, p. 49), and the *Seattle Times* (February 16, 1997, section L, pp. 1–2).

2. See section 2.2.3.

Buddhist words and other technical terms that will be familiar to the experts, has been added (pp. 249–52). Some other sections of the book, such as chapter 6, on the language and script, and the Appendix, on the interpretation of the inscriptions on the pots associated with the manuscripts, may try the patience of the general reader, who should feel free to skip at least parts of them, though in each case the introductory and concluding portions may be of broader interest. Chapter 8, on the other hand, in which the topics introduced in a general way in the first chapter are developed at greater length, is particularly intended for the attention of both categories of readers. It is also with the interests of the nonspecialists in mind that, contrary to standard scholarly practice in this field, I have translated quotations from scholars writing in French and German into English. I hope that in doing so I have not in any way distorted their intended meanings. In the case of longer quotations, the original text is given in a footnote, so that those who wish to check the translation can do so conveniently. I am fully aware that, in trying to write a book that will be of use and interest to both professional scholars and to general readers, one runs the risk of pleasing neither. I can only hope that this is not the case here, but when in doubt I have favored the interests of the former and trust that the latter will understand my priorities.

Inevitably, most of what is said here about the manuscripts, their contents, and their significance is provisional. Much of it will need to be supplemented and modified in the course of future detailed studies, and at least some of it will surely turn out to be incorrect. Nonetheless, I have felt, in view of the unusual degree of interest that this discovery has aroused worldwide, an obligation to bring out this volume as soon as practically feasible, even if this requires some compromise with the degree of certainty and comprehensiveness that is normally desirable in a scholarly publication.

The British Library Kharoṣṭhī fragments are being studied and published under the auspices of the British Library/University of Washington Early Buddhist Manuscripts Project, which supported the preliminary phase of research that has led to the publication of this introductory volume and which is continuing to support the preparation of the individual text studies that are to follow it. I would like to express my sincere gratitude to these two institutions for their generous support, and especially to certain individuals within them who have made these arrangements possible. At the British Library, the efforts of Graham Shaw, Deputy Director of the Oriental and India Office Collections, and Michael O'Keefe, Assistant Keeper, have been invaluable. Not only their practical support but also their keen interest in and enthusiasm for the project have made it a pleasure to work at their institution. Thanks are also due to Mark Barnard, head of the Preservation and Conservation Department of the Oriental and India Office Collections, and to all the members of his staff, both for their skill and expertise in preserving the manuscripts and for their assistance in facilitating their study. I am also indebted to Anne Seawright of the British Museum for her outstanding efforts in preparing the line drawings of the pots and the inscriptions on them. Above all, everyone who is in any way concerned with or interested in this project is profoundly indebted to the sponsor, who prefers to remain anonymous, who not only made it possible for the British Library to acquire this collection initially but also continues to support its study and publication in a most generous manner.

At the University of Washington, special thanks are due to the College of Arts and Sciences and its former Dean, Dr. John B. Simpson, and especially to the former Divisional Dean for Humanities, Dr. Richard J. Dunn, who went to extraordinary lengths and expended great personal effort to arrange support for this project. The current Divisional Dean for Arts and Humanities, Dr. Michael Halleran, has also provided important assistance for the continuation of the project. All concerned are much indebted to the University's Office of Research and its Director, Dr. Alvin L. Kwiram, for providing support for the initial, preliminary phase of this research, which led to the establishment of the joint British Library/University of Washington project, and for subsequent assistance as well.

Equally indispensable, at another level, was the assistance of my colleague Professor Collett Cox and of our graduate students, especially Timothy Lenz and Jason Neelis. The weekly meetings during which all of us have studied and discussed the manuscripts provided insights and ideas beyond counting, and much of what is presented in this volume is the direct result of their contributions. In addition, Collett Cox has provided me with extensive help and suggestions with regard to the preparation of this volume, and I can only hope that her profound knowledge of Buddhism has to some degree provided a balance to my lack thereof.

Other scholars who, in correspondence and conversation, have provided useful insights and information about the materials presented here are, unfortunately, too numerous to mention. But at least a few whose assistance was especially important must be mentioned here by name: Mark Allon, Yael Bentor, Alice Egyed, Fumio Enomoto, Charles Hallisey, Jens-Uwe Hartmann, Oskar von Hinüber, Robert Knox, Isao Kurita, Kazunobu Matsuda, and Robert Senior. I have a special debt of gratitude to Gregory Schopen, who provided a large number of thoughtful comments on, and insightful criticisms of, a draft version of this volume.

The contributions of Pamela Bruton of the University of Washington Press are also deserving of special mention. Her skill and diligence in editing the manuscript of this book at all stages have made the result far better than it would have been without her painstaking efforts.

Finally, on a personal note, I would like to thank my friends Tom Lowenstein and Brigid MacCarthy, whose inexhaustible hospitality during my frequent stays in London over the past three years made those visits a pleasure as well as a success.

Note on the System of Transcription and Citation

In general, the symbols and conventions to be used for the transcription of texts in this volume and in subsequent publications in this series are based on the standards established in Bechert 1990: 14–5 and 1994: lix in connection with the Sanskrit manuscripts from the Berlin Turfan collection. However, they have been modified in some respects to make them more appropriate for use with the Kharoṣṭhī manuscripts.

[ ] An unclear or partially preserved syllable (akṣara) whose reading is not certain.

(*) A lost or completely illegible syllable that has been conjecturally restored on the basis of the context.

< *> A syllable that has been omitted by the scribe and conjecturally restored.

. A missing portion (consonantal or diacritic vowel sign) of a partially legible syllable. For example, *.e* transcribes a syllable in which the diacritic vowel sign *e* is visible, but the consonant to which it was attached is lost or illegible, while *g.* represents a syllable whose consonantal element is legible as *g*, but which is incompletely preserved so that it cannot be determined which vowel diacritic, if any, was attached to it. An *r..* marks a syllable in which the preconsonantal *r* sign is visible but both the consonant that followed it and the vowel of the syllable are illegible. An *a.* indicates an "alif," or vowel carrier sign (𐨀), that is similarly incomplete, so that it cannot be determined if a diacritic sign (indicating the independent vowel *i, u, e,* or *o*) was originally attached to it.

? A visible, but illegible syllable, or one that is completely lost on an otherwise intact part of the manuscript, for example, due to peeling of the surface.

\+ A syllable that would have appeared on a lost portion of the manuscript. A series of these signs indicates the number of lost syllables (actually calculated in verse texts, usually estimated in prose).

/// Beginning or end of an incompletely preserved line.

· A superscript dot indicates a small dot or circle placed on or above the line in the original text as a mark of punctuation, indicating a word, sentence, or verse unit division.

○ A larger circle, a design composed of several circles, or some other such larger symbol used in the original text to mark a major sectional division.

With regard to the transliteration of modern geographical names, an attempt has been made to be as accurate as possible, though in practice it is impossible to maintain complete consistency. In general, toponyms in Afghanistan are spelled according to Ball 1982, and in Pakistan according to Zwalf 1996. But in the case of better-known places for which more or less standard English spellings are established, such as Peshawar and Jalalabad, these, rather than technical transcriptions with diacritics, are used.

All bibliographic citations refer to the list of references at the end of the book. However, citations of Pali texts refer, unless otherwise specified, to the relevant Pali Text Society edition (by volume and page number), and these are not individually cited in the list of references.

Abbreviations

KDhP	Khotan Dharmapada ("Gāndhārī Dharmapada")
MIA	Middle Indo-Aryan
NIA	New Indo-Aryan
OIA	Old Indo-Aryan
r	recto
Skt.	Sanskrit
T.	Taishō Shinshū Daizōkyō
v	verso

Ancient Buddhist Scrolls from Gandhāra

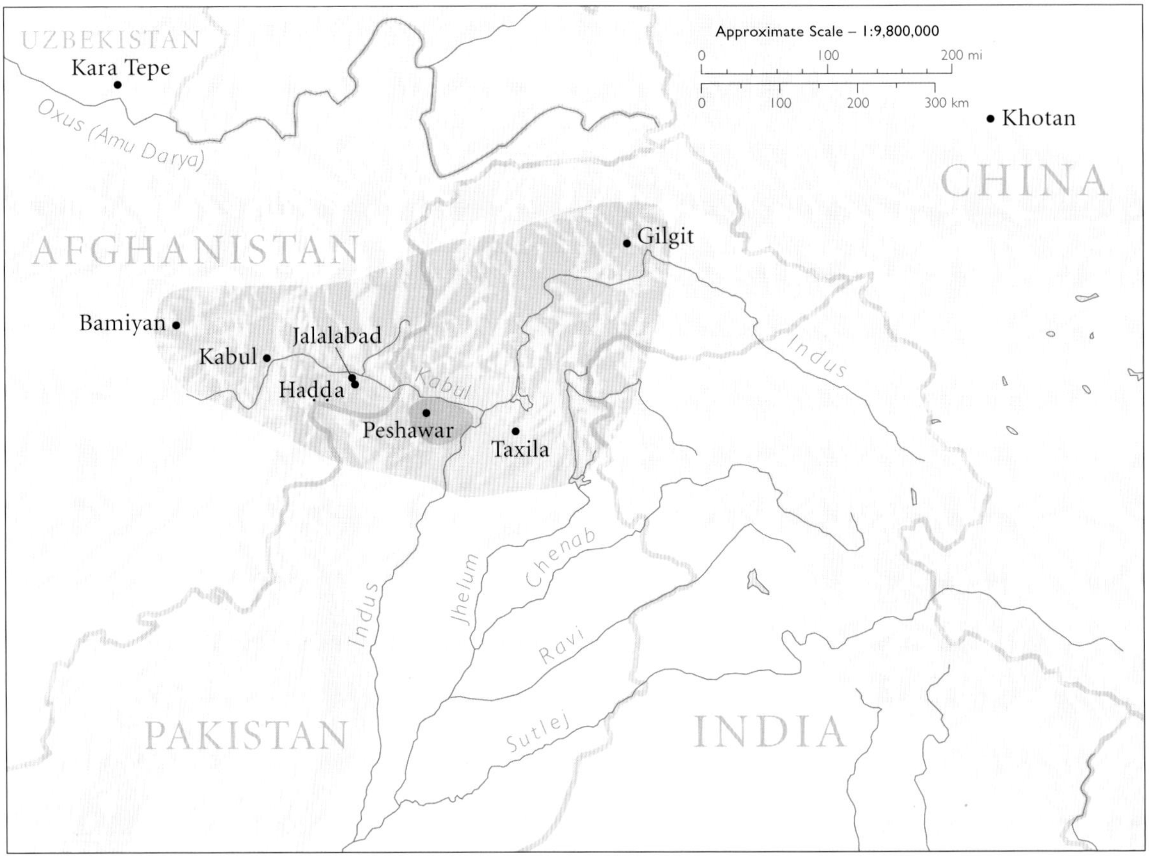

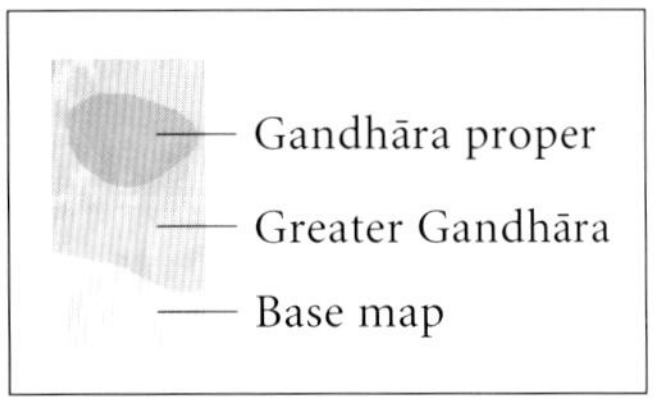

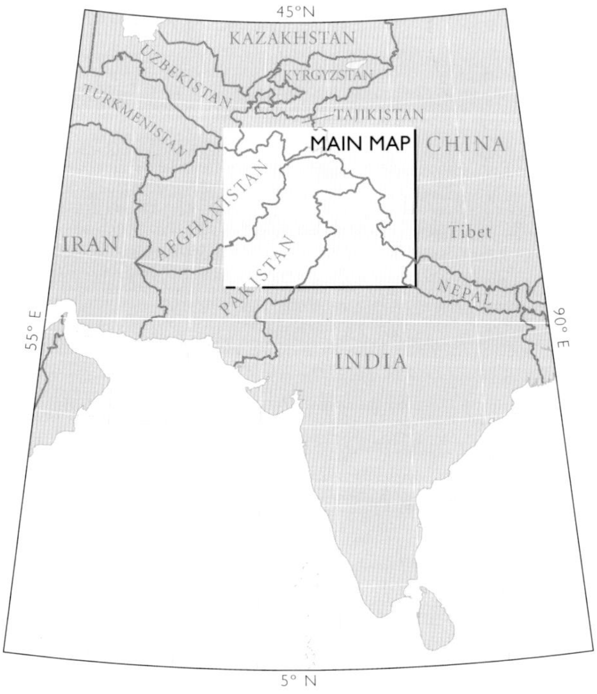

Map 1. Gandhāra

Chapter 1

The Background: Gandhāra and Gandhāran Buddhism

1.1. Gandhāra: Geographic Setting and Early History

Gandhāra, strictly speaking, is the ancient name of the Peshawar Valley region in what is now the North-West Frontier Province of Pakistan, between the Suleiman Mountains along the Afghanistan border in the west and the Indus River in the east (see map 1). The term Gandhāra is, however, also often used in a broader sense to refer to what might be called "Greater Gandhāra," comprising, besides Gandhāra proper, several neighboring regions, particularly the Swat and other river valleys to the north, the region around the great city of Taxila to the east, and the eastern edge of Afghanistan to the west. These, and later on other, more distant regions as well, came under the cultural influence of Gandhāra proper in the period with which we are concerned, namely, the first few centuries before and after the beginning of the Christian era, mainly as a result of being incorporated into the several Indo-Greek, Indo-Scythian, Indo-Parthian, and Kuṣāṇa empires that were centered in Gandhāra proper. The Gandhāran character of the culture of these regions is most clearly attested by their adoption of the distinctive eclectic styles of Gandhāran art and by their use of the Gāndhārī language.

Gāndhārī is one of the Prakrit, or Middle Indo-Aryan (MIA), vernacular languages derived from Sanskrit, or, more precisely, from the Old Indo-Aryan (OIA) dialect group. As such, it is closely related, historically and linguistically, to the other Indo-Aryan languages of India, yet it has a distinct character which sets it off from the rest of them. This special character of Gāndhārī, or of "Northwestern Prakrit" as it is also sometimes called, was conditioned by several factors: by its geographical isolation, on the western fringe of the Indo-Aryan linguistic and cultural area; by its dialectal peculiarities, several of which are unique among the MIA group; and by the fact that it was out of the mainstream of the classical Indian literary tradition, which did not recognize it as one of the principal Prakrit dialects.

But what most effectively sets off Gāndhārī from all other Indo-Aryan and other Indian languages is the fact that it was written in the Kharoṣṭhī script,[1] whereas all the others have been written, from the earliest times, in the Brāhmī

1. See figure 12 for a chart illustrating the basic forms of Kharoṣṭhī script.

script or its several local variants and derivatives. The Kharoṣṭhī script, which developed as an adaptation for an Indian language of the Aramaic script used by the Achaemenian Empire of ancient Iran, is visually very distinct from the pan-Indian Brāhmī script group, especially because it is written from right to left, instead of left to right as are the Brāhmī-derived scripts. Although this and many of the other differences between these scripts are essentially superficial, they are nonetheless emblematic of the distinct flavor of the Gandhāran culture, which, though very much part of the greater Indian cultural sphere, always retained a separate and special identity within it.[2]

Especially in the latter part of the historical period in question, that is, around the second and third centuries A.D., the Gāndhārī language and its constant companion, the Kharoṣṭhī script, spread far beyond even the reaches of Greater Gandhāra as defined above, into the territories of ancient Bactria (comprising modern northern Afghanistan and southern Uzbekistan and Tajikistan) and the oasis cities of the silk routes around the Tarim Basin in central Asia, in what is now the Xinjiang-Uighur Autonomous Region of China. This far-reaching influence of Gandhāra in ancient times is directly attributable to its strategic location at the primary gateway to the Indian subcontinent, a location that has enabled it to play, over and over throughout history, the role of a crossroads and melting pot of cultures. Until relatively modern times, Gandhāra was the principal point of encounter of the Indian world to the east with the Iranian world to the west, and thence with the ever-shifting cultural mosaic of central Asia. On an even broader scale, through these connections Gandhāra has also been the contact zone, usually indirectly but at certain points in history directly as well, with the Western world, including both the Middle East and Europe.

Three great waves of migration and invasion from central Asia that fundamentally shaped the history of the Indian world passed through the gateway of Gandhāra: first, the Indo-Aryan immigrations in, probably, the second millennium B.C.; next, the conquests by the Bactrian Greeks, Scythians, Kuṣāṇas, and associated ethnic groups around the beginning of the Christian era; and finally the series of Afghan, Turkish, and Mongol incursions—the so-called Muslim invasions—between the eleventh and sixteenth centuries A.D. As a result of the first of these three waves, Gandhāra and adjoining regions were for a time a center of Vedic and Brahmanical culture; in ancient times, for example, the Sanskrit spoken in Gandhāra was held to be the purest and most refined form of the sacred language. After the Vedic period, Gandhāra became a rich prize for the great empire builders of the first millennium B.C., being first incorporated into the Achaemenian Empire of Iran by King Darius in the sixth century B.C., then falling briefly into the hands of Alexander the Great

2. For a more detailed introduction to the Gāndhārī language and the Kharoṣṭhī script, see section 6.1.

in 327–326 B.C. These events set the stage for the succeeding series of cosmopolitan kingdoms whose diverse ethnic origins seem to have made them particularly receptive to the Buddhist religion, which was ever ready to accept sympathizers, converts, and patrons regardless of their ethnic and cultural backgrounds.

1.2. Buddhism in Gandhāra

It is generally assumed (though this remains to be confirmed historically and archeologically) that Buddhism was first introduced to Gandhāra around the middle of the third century B.C. under the sponsorship of Aśoka, the great emperor of the Mauryan dynasty and patron of Buddhism, whose control of the region is attested by the sets of his rock edicts engraved in Kharoṣṭhī script at Shāhbāzgaṛhī and Mānsehrā. A second testimony to an early presence of Buddhism in the northwestern edge of the Indian subcontinent is the famous "Questions of Milinda," which purports to record a philosophical dialogue between King Menander, the greatest of the Indo-Greek rulers in the second century B.C., and a Buddhist monk named Nāgasena. Although the presumed Gāndhārī original of this text is lost, it survives in various Pali and Chinese versions and stands as the earliest explicit testimony of the encounter of Buddhism with the cosmopolitan cultures of Gandhāra—an encounter which, in later centuries, is vividly and abundantly illustrated in Gandhāran sculpture with its unique combination of Indian and Hellenistic or Roman themes and styles.

But other than these two sources, we have little direct evidence for this early phase of Gandhāran Buddhism, for it is not until the first century B.C. that we begin to find abundant physical remains, in the form of stūpas and other structural remains, figural and narrative sculpture, and, especially, Buddhist ritual and dedicatory inscriptions. From this point on we can begin to trace the history of Gandhāran Buddhism in relative detail, as Buddhist institutions grew, flourished, and expanded under the patronage of the successive "foreign" dynasties. By the first two centuries of the Christian era Gandhāra had become one of the major centers of Buddhism in India, and it was apparently at some point during this period that Buddhism began to make its way beyond the borders of its Indian homeland and establish footholds in parts of Iran and China.

There is compelling evidence that Gandhāran monks in particular were instrumental in the early expansion of Buddhism beyond India. For example, two Buddhist inscriptions in the Kharoṣṭhī script and the Gāndhārī language, which must have been written by monks from Gandhāra, have been found near the cities of Lo-yang and Chang-an, which were major early centers of Buddhism in China.[3] Furthermore, the abhidharma literature of the influential Sarvāstivādin school, which for the most part survives only in Chinese translations, frequently refers to a Gandhāran

3. See Salomon 1998: 160 for details and references.

tradition, and it is generally agreed by modern scholars that some of the important abhidharma treatises extant in Chinese translations, such as the Abhidharma-hṛdaya, were originally composed in Gandhāra.[4] And finally, linguistic analysis indicates that at least some of the early Buddhist texts rendered into Chinese were translated from originals in, or at least derived from prototypes in, the Gāndhārī language. Thus it was specifically the Gandhāran form (or forms) of Buddhism that was first encountered by other parts of Asia, and here once again Gandhāra's strategic location enabled it to play a pivotal role in the cultural history of Asia, serving, as it were, as the geographical springboard from which Buddhism made the great leaps that enabled it to transform itself from an Indian religion into a pan-Asian and ultimately a world tradition.

But our knowledge of Gandhāran Buddhism has been, until now, curiously skewed. Its archeological remains are very abundant, and these have enabled scholars to reconstruct, in broad outline at least, the historic, artistic, and architectural manifestations of Gandhāran Buddhism. For example, it is primarily the hundreds of dedicatory Kharoṣṭhī inscriptions, which are often dated and sometimes mention the names of contemporary kings and officials, that have made it possible to reconstruct the skeleton of the political and cultural history of this period. But the textual, and hence the doctrinal, content of Gandhāran Buddhism has, until now, remained mostly obscure. Although the aforementioned Chinese translations of abhidharma texts give us some sense of the important doctrinal issues and positions in Gandhāran Buddhism (and in the process prove that Gandhāra was a vital center of Buddhist intellectual activity), we have had virtually no direct, primary records of these matters. Only one specimen of an original Gandhāran Buddhist text has been available to date, namely, the famous "Gāndhārī Dharmapada" scroll (Brough 1962), which was, however, found, not in Gandhāra itself, but near Khotan in the Xinjiang region of China. For lack of anything to compare it to, it has until now been difficult to assess the significance of this unique manuscript with regard to the textual and doctrinal character of Gandhāran Buddhism.

In particular, it has been a matter of controversy whether or not the Khotan scroll (KDhP) should be taken to imply the existence of a hypothetical "Gāndhārī canon" resulting from an organized and concerted project of rendering Buddhist texts into the local language.[5] This notion of a Gāndhārī canon was a priori plausible in light of the traditionally liberal Buddhist attitude toward translation, which encouraged the use of local vernaculars in spreading the dharma, and the new discoveries that are the subject of this book prove that Buddhist texts were indeed

4. See Willemen 1975: xiv, xvi, xxii–xxiii. For connections between various early Sarvāstivādin abhidharma texts and the Gandhāra region, see Nishimura 1982; Nishi 1934; Yamada 1957; and Kawamura 1974: 25ff., esp. 37. (These references provided by Collett Cox.)

5. See chapter 3 and section 8.1.1 for further discussion of the Gāndhārī canon issue.

translated into, and sometimes also originally composed in, Gāndhārī. Thus it is now becoming clear that the abundant physical remains of Gandhāran Buddhism were matched by what was probably a similarly vast corpus of written texts in the local language, of which we now have at least an intriguing sample, if only still a tiny fraction of what must have been the whole.

1.3. Textual Sources and the Modern Academic Study of Buddhism

For some two centuries, scholars have been striving to understand the history of Buddhism, primarily by studying its texts on the one hand, and by observing its modern practice in various parts of Asia on the other. For scholars principally interested in the origins and earlier history of Buddhism, the value of the latter approach is seriously circumscribed, not only because of the obvious difficulties in interpreting the past—nearly two and a half millennia back—on the basis of present practice, but also because Buddhism died out in its Indian homeland many centuries ago. Thus they have tried to seek out the origins of Buddhism mainly from its textual remains, that is, ultimately, from manuscripts. Early modern investigations concentrated on the Pali textual tradition of the Theravāda school, largely because Theravāda Buddhism had survived down to modern times in Sri Lanka, Burma, Thailand, Cambodia, and other parts of Southeast Asia, and so the texts of the Pali canon, or Tipiṭaka, were readily available there. This gave some early scholars the impression, which has since turned out to be illusory, that the Pali Tipiṭaka comprised and represented the sole original textual corpus of Buddhism, preserved more or less intact in its original form and language.

Gradually, however, other approaches and discoveries, and a consequent broadening of the point of view of academic scholars of Buddhism, showed that this was by no means the whole story and that the total picture of the history of Indian Buddhism was far more complex and varied than it had seemed at first. In particular, the discovery, first in Nepal in the later part of the nineteenth century and then in central Asia (mainly in Xinjiang) at the end of the nineteenth and beginning of the twentieth century, of vast numbers of Buddhist manuscripts in Sanskrit or hybrid Sanskrit representing the textual corpus of previously little-known sectarian and doctrinal groups showed that the Pali tradition was by no means the sole authentic representative of Indian Buddhism.

Meanwhile, a gradually increasing awareness of the vast canons of east Asian Buddhism in Chinese, Tibetan, and other east Asian and central Asian languages had a similar effect. In particular, the Chinese translations of Indian Buddhist texts were found to preserve large portions of all three of the main divisions of the canons (sūtra, vinaya, and abhidharma) of the various early Indian sectarian traditions such as the Sarvāstivādin, Dharmaguptaka, and Mahāsāṅghika, among others. Despite the fact that most of these sectarian canons did not survive in any of their original Indian languages, their Chinese versions have in principle an equal claim to authority and originality to that of the Pali canon of the Theravādins, and therefore in this connection it has gradually become clear that the primacy accorded to that tradition by early modern scholars was exaggerated. It was only because Theravāda Buddhism happened to have survived in a more or less uniform and continuous tradition in Sri Lanka and Southeast Asia that it loomed so much larger than other regional, sectarian, and linguistic traditions of Indian Buddhism, particularly the lost traditions of northern India and its heirs in central and east Asia. In short, scholars gradually began to understand Indian Buddhism as a complex of local traditions, none of which could in and of itself be seen as the "original" or "true" form of the religion.

1.4. Previous Discoveries of Early Buddhist Manuscripts and Their Significance for the Study of Buddhism

Original manuscripts naturally provide the best, and in many cases the only, testimony to the earlier stages of development of these various local Buddhist traditions, at least as far as their textual and doctrinal corpora are concerned (though these, admittedly, are by no means completely representative of the traditions' historical reality). In most cases, however, such manuscripts are not of great antiquity, mainly because Indian manuscripts, which are normally written on palm leaf or, in the far north, on birch bark, tend not to survive very long in the hot and humid monsoon climate that prevails throughout the subcontinent. Thus, written text traditions only survive when the manuscripts are copied and recopied with frequency and regularity and are carefully stored and preserved. Such was the case, for example, in the Theravāda tradition of Sri Lanka and Southeast Asia; in these regions, Pali manuscripts survive in very large numbers, but relatively few of them are more than a few centuries old. But in India proper, where Buddhism effectively died out by around the thirteenth century A.D., the tradition of preserving and copying manuscripts died out with it, and relatively few Buddhist manuscripts survive. In Nepal, where Buddhism remained vital, large numbers of Buddhist manuscripts do survive, but there too, the majority are relatively recent, with only a very few specimens more than one thousand years old known.

But in the Tarim Basin in modern Xinjiang, which, as we now know, was an important center of Buddhism in the first millennium A.D., a very different situation prevailed, for there the desert climate was highly conducive to the survival of manuscripts on organic materials such as palm leaf, birch bark, or paper. Thus the explorations undertaken by European, Japanese, and American scholars in this region around the beginning of this century yielded a massive corpus of unprecedentedly early manuscripts from a previously unknown major phase of Buddhism. As mentioned in the previous section, this discovery of thousands of fragments of manuscripts in Sanskrit and various local languages, mostly dating from about the seventh century or later but in a very few cases as old as the second or third century, had a major influence on scholarly views of the history of Buddhism, undermining the old Pali-centered attitudes and precipitating a gradual revision of attitudes which is still continuing today.

Now it is true that older manuscripts are not always or automatically more valuable, authentic, or revealing than later ones. Nevertheless, early manuscripts are always potentially, and usually in practice, of extraordinary value, not only because they tend to preserve more accurate versions of texts, less corrupted by the changes that they inevitably undergo in the course of long-term transmission, but also, and more important, because they provide direct testimony of the textual material that was in use at a remote period. Especially in the case of very early manuscripts such as the ones described in this book, we may find not only forms of previously known texts that may be significantly different from those we know from the later and modern traditions but also texts, and even entire genres and classes of texts, that were previously wholly unknown.

This is particularly important because in Buddhism, as in most institutionalized religious traditions, canons of authoritative texts were eventually established that in effect defined the textual corpora of the various local and linguistic groups, as happened, for example, in the Pali and Tibetan traditions. Such standardized canons inevitably have the effect of obscuring and even completely suppressing earlier texts or even entire bodies of literature. They present, in effect, a censored version of the textual and doctrinal history of their tradition, with the old variations, controversies, and heresies neatly excised from the record. For this reason, in most cases it is only through the discovery and interpretation of old manuscripts that historical scholars can peek behind an established religious tradition's official facade and uncover the complex history that inevitably underlies it. A case in point, from the Western world, is the dramatically altered picture of early Christianity that has been provided by the discovery of the Dead Sea scrolls and the Nag Hammadi manuscripts.

1.5. The British Library Kharoṣṭhī Fragments and Gandhāran Buddhism: A Preview of the Potential Significance of the New Discovery

Although the British Library fragments are comparable to the Dead Sea scrolls and the Nag Hammadi manuscripts in that they give actual samples of the textual corpus of a much earlier phase of Buddhist tradition than had been previously available, they are unlikely to contain anything as radically unfamiliar as appeared in their Christian counterparts. The survey of the new fragments carried out to date, the results of which are summarized in the rest of this book, has revealed nothing that is startlingly at odds with early Buddhist doctrine as previously understood, nor is there much reason to expect that further analysis will turn up anything that will be. The importance of the new collection is on a different and perhaps less spectacular level, though this does not diminish its importance. These fragments give us an unprecedented direct glimpse into the contents of what appears to have been a monastic collection or library of the Dharmaguptaka school in or around the first half of the first century A.D., and they are by far the earliest such sampling of a Buddhist textual corpus that has ever been found. It is likely, though not quite certain, that the British Library fragments are the oldest Buddhist manuscripts yet known,[6] and in any case they are definitely the oldest coherent set of manuscript material.

An important feature of the new manuscripts is the inclusion in some of them of local Gandhāran lore and traditions, which suggests that early Gandhāran Buddhism and, by implication, perhaps the other early regional centers of Indian Buddhism as well were more distinct and localized in their character than has previously been apparent.[7] In particular, the references in some of the new texts to at least two members of the contemporary Indo-Scythian ruling houses of the early first century A.D., who were previously known from coins and inscriptions, are a remarkable and unexpected discovery which enhances the texts' historical value.[8] These references enable us to place the textual tradition of the new manuscripts in a historical context and thereby open up to us the previously obscure formative stage of Gandhāran Buddhism during the Indo-Scythian period. Our view of Gandhāran Buddhism has up to now been colored largely by the dominating effect of the Kuṣāṇa Empire (ca. mid-first to third century A.D.), which, we now begin to suspect, overshadowed and obscured the preceding Indo-Scythian period in later north Indian Buddhist tradition, wherein the Kuṣāṇa period, and especially the reign of Kaniṣka, were portrayed as a sort of golden age. The new manuscripts now bring to light a forgotten but crucial earlier phase in which the Indo-Scythian dynasties played a role in promoting Buddhism and Buddhist institutions around the beginning of the Christian era that was comparable to the better-known activities of the Kuṣāṇas in the succeeding two centuries.

This historical background may be significantly related to another major point of interest about the new manuscripts—namely, their probable connection with the Dharmaguptaka sect. The Dharmaguptakas have until now been a shadowy presence within Indian Buddhism, despite the fact that they are known to have played a leading role in the early dissemination of Indian Buddhism in central Asia and China. The collection therefore promises to provide the missing link, or at least one of the missing links, between Indian Buddhism and its early manifestations in central and east Asia. Moreover, the new material, combined with other recent epigraphical discoveries, suggests that the early success and subsequent decline of the

6. The Gāndhārī Dharmapada from Khotan may be of comparable antiquity, or a little later; the earliest central Asian manuscript fragments are probably a century or more later. For details of the relative and absolute dating of the new fragments, see chapter 7.

7. These and related issues are addressed in sections 2.2.4 and 8.1.4.1.

8. These references are discussed and evaluated in sections 7.1 and 8.3.3.

Dharmaguptakas could have been the result of shifting patterns of patronage as their Indo-Scythian supporters were replaced by the Kuṣāṇas, who were evidently more favorably inclined to the better-known Sarvāstivādin sect.[9]

Another important and surprising feature of the new manuscripts is the amount of unfamiliar material in them. In general, much, though by no means all, of the textual material found in the various later manuscript traditions that have been briefly described above is more or less common to, or at least broadly familiar from, one or more of the extant canonical traditions. For example, many of the central Asian Sanskrit manuscripts contain texts that are essentially variant versions of ones already known in Pali and/or other languages. To some extent this is true of the new Gāndhārī manuscripts as well, but, somewhat unexpectedly, a substantial majority of the approximately two dozen distinct texts represented in them have so far not been identified with known texts in other Buddhist languages and traditions. If this pattern continues to hold as more detailed studies of the individual texts are carried out, it would mean that the textual corpus of the Gandhāran monastery from which they came, and presumably, by extension, of early Gandhāran Buddhism generally, may be considerably more different from the extant corpora than might have been expected. In other words, although the doctrinal positions presented in the new materials are not radically at odds with what is familiar from other traditions, the modes and forms of their presentation and study may be different indeed from what has been known to date.

If this pattern holds true, it has wider, perhaps profound implications for our understanding of the notion of a "Buddhist canon" in general. For example, we may well be dealing here with a stage of development which is still pre- or protocanonical, that is, a stage at which the contents, arrangement, and delimitation of a canon in the stricter sense of the term were not yet fully formed. It is also important to note that these manuscripts come from a time when, if traditional accounts can be accepted, writing had only recently been adopted as a substitute for, or rather as a supplement to, the older techniques of memorization and oral recitation of Buddhist texts. If this is true, we may be dealing with materials from the early phase of an extended period of gradual transition from a primarily oral tradition to what eventually became a largely written one, and examination of this material is likely to clarify the complex issues of the interrelation of these modes of text transmission and of the patterns of canon formation that grew out of them.[10]

One major class of texts which seems to imply structures and genres different from those of the more familiar Buddhist corpora are the commentaries on sets of verses, which are very prominently represented among the British Library fragments.[11] Although the individual verses explicated in these commentaries are for

9. The Dharmaguptaka connection and its ramifications are discussed in detail in section 8.2.
10. See section 8.1.4.2 for further discussion.
11. For further descriptions and a sample of this class of texts, see section 2.2.2.

the most part Gāndhārī translations of material well known in other traditions, the nature, organizational principles, and function of the texts as a whole remain largely obscure. Presumably, they represent local modes of instruction and preaching in the fundamentals of Buddhist teachings, which should provide an interesting counterpart to the well-known Pali commentaries, whose archetypes, now lost, were said to have been composed in the local Sinhalese vernacular language. We may therefore have in these new fragments the earliest surviving original specimens of an ancient tradition of vernacular commentaries.

Such texts, and others as well, may also give us unprecedented insights into the methods of preaching and instruction that were employed in Gandhāran monasteries, and the texts that were preferred for such purposes. For example, a particular subset of texts within the new collection has an intriguing similarity to a list of texts recommended for study by novice monks in a vinaya text preserved in Chinese translation.[12] In view of such indications as these, it seems that the British Library collection provides a representative selection of the works of various types and classes that were studied in the monastery where they were kept, including basic texts, commentaries and explanatory works, and technical treatises. What we have, in other words, is not a set of fragments from a comprehensive, systematized canon of the sort that is often found in later, more developed and standardized traditions but rather a random sampling of texts that were actively used for study and recitation.

Among the more technical texts in the new collection are several abhidharma or abhidharma-related fragments which are likely to be of great interest for the study of the development of Buddhist doctrine. As noted above, we already knew from later traditions, mostly preserved in Chinese, that Gandhāra was an important early center of abhidharma studies. Now, for the first time, we have original and early specimens of Gandhāran abhidharma texts, which are likely to represent a crucial formative period and which therefore have the potential to fundamentally alter and improve our understanding of the history of Buddhist scholastic thought.

Notably absent from the new material is any significant reference to or indication of Mahāyāna concepts and ideals. The origins—historical, geographical, and doctrinal—of the Mahāyāna have long been a matter of fundamental concern and intense controversy in Buddhist studies, and it is believed by many that the Gandhāra region had a crucial role in its development. But it appears that if these new documents are to have any effect at all on this issue, it will be a negative, or at best an indirect, one.[13]

Finally, on a broader scale, the unprecedented discovery of a significant body of Buddhist texts in Gāndhārī may ultimately provide a new standard for evaluating and comparing the previously known corpora of early Indian Buddhist texts

12. See section 8.1.2.1.

13. For further discussion of this issue, see section 8.3.1.

in Pali and Sanskrit, as well as in Chinese and other translations. Just as the discovery and analysis of early Sanskrit manuscripts contributed to a correction of the prevailing Pali-centered view of Buddhism, the new Gāndhārī texts can be expected to shift the balance by providing a new point of reference with which to compare the previously known traditions. In short, although it is impossible to predict at this point the full ramifications of this discovery over the long run, it is probably safe to say that it will open an entirely new chapter in Buddhist studies.

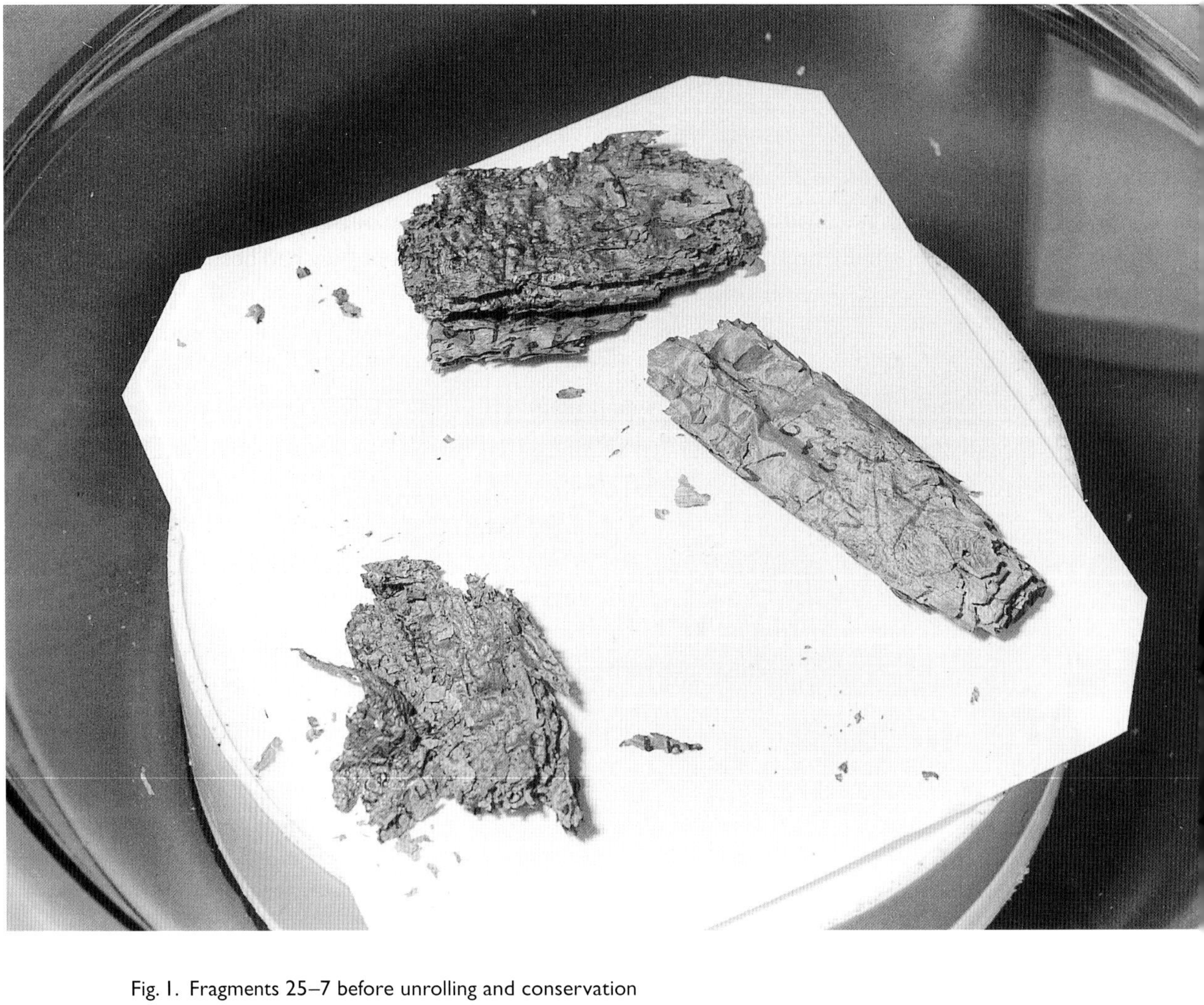

Fig. 1. Fragments 25–7 before unrolling and conservation

Chapter 2

The Contents of the British Library Kharoṣṭhī Collection

2.1. General Description

2.1.1. Arrangement and Initial Disposition

The Kharoṣṭhī manuscripts as originally received in the British Library consisted of twenty-nine fragmentary rolls of birch bark manuscripts (pls. 1–2; fig. 1). Associated with the scrolls were five clay pots and twenty-six potsherds, all bearing dedicatory inscriptions in Kharoṣṭhī. The manuscript rolls were said to have originally been found inside one of the clay pots, but they had been removed from it and placed inside thirteen modern glass jars. Unfortunately, being extremely brittle, they had suffered considerable damage from having been forced into the narrow glass jars.

After being acquired by the British Library, the fragments were moisturized and carefully unrolled by the conservation staff of the Oriental and India Office Collections and mounted in fifty-six glass frames about 30 centimeters wide by 45 centimeters high (figs. 2–7). The delicate process of unrolling and conserving the scrolls is described as follows by Mark Barnard, head of Preservation and Conservation at the Oriental and India Office Collections:

> When first received by the Library, the documents were still in their original format, that is, strips of birch bark rolled up into scrolls some 15 cm wide and 4 cm in diameter. On some of the scrolls writing was visible on the outermost layer of birch bark, in other cases not. The immediate and overwhelming impression was of the extreme fragility of the scrolls. Birch bark is an inherently fragile material, and birch bark of great antiquity even more so. The brittleness of the scrolls was apparent from the fact that minute fragments—some with writing upon them—had fallen off and collected as a layer at the bottom of the modern glass jars in which they had been temporarily placed. It was also observed that some of the scrolls had a shinier appearance than others. At some stage the outer surface of some of the scrolls had been crudely treated, probably with some kind of lacquer spray, no doubt in an attempt to overcome the brittleness, to consolidate the material and to prevent further shedding of fragments. The spray has not yet

Figs. 2–6. Mark Barnard and Mike Chambers of the Preservation and Conservation Department, Oriental and India Office Collections, British Library, unrolling fragment 24

been identified but its adverse effect upon the scrolls is already apparent in the wrinkling or corrugation of the surfaces so treated. It was clear that urgent attention was needed on two grounds: to arrest the process of fragmentation of the scrolls and encapsulate them so that they could be handled more easily, and to enable the written data they contained to be recovered and recorded as soon as possible before more text was lost.

In conservation terms the first task was to unroll the scrolls. Before this could be attempted at all successfully, however, it was necessary to slowly and gently reintroduce some moisture content into the birch bark in order to restore some of its natural flexibility and lessen its brittleness. It was decided to use an ordinary glass bell-jar for this purpose. A layer of slightly dampened blotting-paper was placed over a bowl inside the bell-jar together with some silica gel to ensure that the remoisturization took place gradually and moderately, since too much moisture could have promoted the growth of mold in the birch bark. The scrolls were then placed on top of the blotting paper one or two at a time and left for up to fifteen or sixteen hours in the moist atmosphere created inside the bell-jar (with a relative humidity content of approximately 75%). This method was found to be successful and sufficient pliability was reintroduced to the birch bark to enable it to be unrolled without undue difficulty. Two conservators were required for the unrolling process, one holding the scroll carefully with tweezers while the other slowly teased it open. Throughout the unrolling, further moisture was applied as required with an ultrasonic humidifier supplied by CLE Design Ltd.

Due to the inherent fragility of the birch bark with its horizontal striations, each layer of the scroll tended to form a separate fragment of varying length as it was unrolled, but it was possible to preserve in very large measure the original sequence of layers and their texts. These fragments were

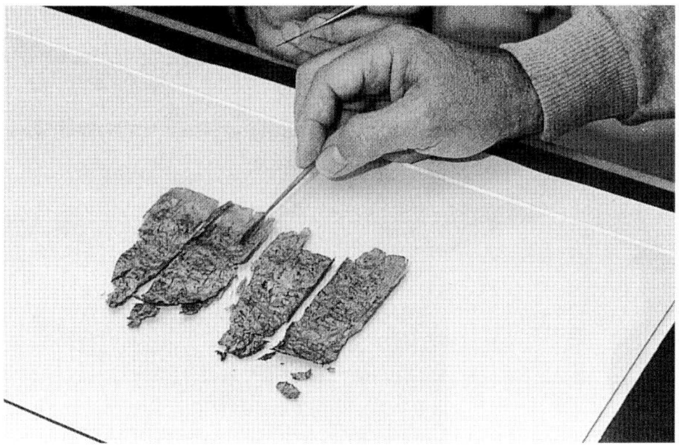

then encapsulated between layers of glass, this being the most suitable storage medium for birch bark (as for papyrus). A special cabinet for the long-term storage of the scrolls has been custom-built by Jezer Conservation Engineers for the British Library. It is made of aluminum and each sheet of glass is housed in its own individual tray edged with plastazote foam to absorb shocks and thus prevent the fragile birch bark from being further disturbed.

It will be obvious from this description that the scrolls have not been conserved in the full modern sense of the word. They have simply been "made safe" until a satisfactory means of preserving birch bark has been developed. The experience of one German library in using an adhesive to consolidate birch bark scrolls has not been entirely successful, as with time the adhesive coating has darkened, rendering the text beneath less legible. The British Library is continuing to monitor research in this field (such as that currently being undertaken at the Wellcome Institute for the History of Medicine into ensuring the long-term stability of such material), and would welcome any expressions of interest in a collaborative program to investigate the problems of birch bark conservation.

After unrolling, the fragments proved to differ widely in size and condition, ranging from small pieces containing only a few badly damaged and incomplete lines of text to large sections of scrolls as long as two meters and preserving several hundreds of lines with most of the text more or less intact. Specimens of the fragments after conservation are shown in plates 3 and 4, as examples of one of the many badly deteriorated pieces (frag. 23, part 2) and one of the best-preserved pieces (frag. 1, part 5),[1] respectively.

1. A sample text and translation from this fragment are presented in section 2.2.3.

Fig. 7. Fragment 24 after conservation

In the preliminary cataloging system that was established when the scrolls were being unrolled, each fragment was labeled according to the number of the glass jar (arbitrarily numbered 1 to 13) in which it was found. Some of these jars contained only one scroll, others as many as four, and the scrolls from jars with more than one scroll were numbered as separate "fragments" within each jar, for example, "J12, fragment 1." However, since the placement of scrolls together in a particular jar was the work of their modern discoverers and hence presumably of no historical or textual significance, the "J numbers" have been dropped here and the fragments are simply renumbered sequentially, following the same arbitrary order. Thus the single scroll in jar 1 has been renumbered as fragment 1, the two in jar 2 (formerly J2, fragments 1 and 2) as fragments 2 and 3, and so on.[2]

The larger fragments are subdivided into "parts," as in "fragment 1, part 5"; in brief references the part numbers are given in parentheses, thus "frag. 1 (5)." These parts represent sections of the larger scrolls that were mounted in separate glass frames, and hence part numbers have no intrinsic textual significance. The division of the parts of the larger fragments among separate glass frames did not involve any actual cutting of the scrolls, because the compression that the rolls were subjected to inside the pot in which they were buried had caused numerous horizontal breaks (see above and sec. 5.3.3), so that the rolls were in effect already divided into smaller pieces. Thus each "part" of the collection as currently arranged contains at least one, and more often several, separated horizontal sections of inscribed bark, depending on the degree of fragmentation of the scroll.

For several reasons, the total number of "fragments" (twenty-nine) does not correspond exactly to the number of original scrolls whose fragments are represented in the collection, nor to the number of texts represented in these scrolls. For example, in some cases (e.g., frags. 16 and 25, and frags. 12 and 14) it is clear that two

2. The following is a concordance of the provisional and final numbering of the fragments, together with the frame numbers in which they are mounted:

Original (Provisional) Number	Final Number	Frame Numbers
J1	1	1–5
J2, frags. 1–2	2–3	6–7
J3	4	8–14
J4, frags. 1–4	5–8	15–18
J5, frags. 1–3	9–11	19–23
J6, frags. 1–3	12–14	24–8
J7	15	29–32
J8, frags. 1–4	16–19	33–6
J9	20	37–41
J10, frags. 1–2	21–2	42–4
J11	23	45–6
J12, frags. 1–4	24–7	47–50
J13	28–9	51–5

fragments were part of the same original scroll, while in other cases (e.g., frags. 20 and 23, frags. 26 and 28) this appears to be so but is not yet definite. Also, some of the fragments proved after unrolling to be composites, in which smaller fragments of what were apparently two or more originally separate scrolls were rolled up together, as in the case of fragment 5, which evidently comprises parts of three originally different scrolls. Depending on how these variables are interpreted, there could have been as few as twenty-one original scrolls involved or as many as thirty-two (see also 2.4).

The number of original texts, as opposed to scrolls, involves further complications, and hence is also indeterminate. For one thing, in several cases a single scroll contains two separate and apparently unrelated texts. In other cases, we find examples of separate scrolls containing what seem to be parts of the same text or similar texts written in the same hand, which may be separate "volumes" of a longer text that was divided up over several scrolls (see 2.2.2 and 5.1.1). Depending on how these cases are interpreted, the possible number of individual texts in the collection could be anywhere from twenty-three to thirty-four. Detailed studies of the individual texts will have to be carried out before their complex interrelationships can be fully clarified.

It is mainly because of these complexities that the original, arbitrary numbering order has been retained, though with modifications as described above. Although it might have seemed desirable to combine fragments that definitely belong to the same original scroll, such as fragments 16 and 25, in practice any such renumbering is likely to cause as many problems as it would solve, as long as the relationships between many of the fragments remain to be determined.

2.1.2. Original Situation and Provenance

No reliable information is available as to the circumstances, location, and date of the discovery of the manuscripts and associated materials. This is highly regrettable, as the loss of a proper archeological context seriously diminishes their scholarly value. To a certain extent, however, this damage can be undone, since some of the missing information can be partly reconstructed through comparative research. A few of the relevant points concerning this are introduced briefly in this section, and these issues are discussed at greater length in the relevant places in the following chapters (3, 4, and 8).

As to the original provenance of the jars and scrolls, oral reports, received indirectly, suggested that they had come from Afghanistan. Although such reports are by no means necessarily reliable, subsequent analysis of these relics has confirmed that they are very likely to have come from eastern Afghanistan. The abundant Buddhist stūpa sites in the Jalalabad Plain (the ancient district of Nagarāhāra) and particularly those in the neighborhood of the village of Haḍḍa (see 3.2.1) have yielded many specimens of both inscribed jars and Buddhist manuscripts in Kharoṣṭhī script that seem to closely resemble the new materials, although few of the former and none of the latter have ever been properly published. Thus, as will be discussed in sections 3.2 and 3.4, the new relics can be presumed to have come from somewhere in this region, possibly from the Haḍḍa area itself. Given the difficult conditions that have prevailed in this area for many years and continue to do so as of this writing, it has been impossible to investigate the matter on-site or even to obtain any kind of reliable information about it, so that for the foreseeable future at least, we must be content with this circumstantial but highly probable hypothesis.

Since the manuscripts had been removed from the clay pot in which they had reportedly been found by the time that they were purchased by the British Library, and since five similar pots were acquired along with them, it was at first not clear which (if any) of the pots had originally contained the scrolls. This was a matter of crucial importance, since the inscriptions on some of the jars contained references to different Buddhist sects (Sarvāstivādin and Dharmaguptaka), while others had references to localities and individuals which could assist in dating the manuscripts and in identifying their original provenance and historical associations. Fortunately, this critical question can be answered by reference to the earliest available photographs of these objects, which were taken in 1993, before these materials were acquired by the British Library. One of these photographs, reproduced here in plate 5, shows what is now designated British Library pot D (also illustrated in pls. 28–9) viewed from above, with the scrolls lying inside it. Although it is remotely possible that the unknown modern discoverers of these relics for some reason removed some or all of the scrolls from another pot or other container and placed them in this one, there is little reason to think that this was the case, and it may be presumed with reasonable certainty that the scrolls were in fact originally found in British Library pot D.

Another of the 1993 photographs, reproduced here in plate 6, shows what is now British Library fragment 1 taken out of pot D. This photograph shows several lines of text on the verso that are no longer preserved; this portion of the outside of the roll was evidently destroyed by mishandling between the time that this photograph was taken and the time that the scrolls reached the British Library (see 5.3.3). A comparison of plates 5 and 6 confirms that this roll is in fact the large one seen inside pot D at the center of plate 5. These identifications in turn confirm that the British Library scrolls were almost certainly originally found inside pot D, which bears a dedicatory inscription labeling it as a donation to the members of the Dharmaguptaka sect (. . . *dhamaüteaṇa [p]arig[r]ahami*, " . . . in the possession of the Dharmaguptakas"), and this in turn means that the manuscripts must have come from, or at least have been associated in some way with, a monastery of the Dharmaguptaka sect.[3] The ramifications of this important point will be discussed in detail in section 8.2.

3. At an early stage in this study, before the information described here had become available, it was thought that the scrolls had been found inside a pot with a Sarvāstivādin dedication and hence were affiliated with this sect. This hypothesis was mentioned in some early media reports and public presentations but is now refuted.

It has, however, been reported that British Library pot A, and apparently some of the other pots as well, also originally contained small fragments of similar birch bark manuscripts. This suggests that at least some of the other pots in the collection were also used, like pot D, as depositories for scrolls, but apparently for some reason these manuscripts did not survive intact to modern times.

2.1.3. Form of the Scrolls

The texts are written with a reed pen and black ink on scrolls consisting of sections of birch bark, which in most cases were glued together to form long strips (see 5.1.2 for details). In general, the texts were written continuously over the recto and verso sides of the scroll, but in a few manuscripts only the recto is inscribed. All of the texts are incomplete and have suffered from varying degrees of loss and damage, in many cases severe (see 5.3.3). This is attributable in large part to the instability of old birch bark, which becomes extremely fragile and usually survives only in favorable conditions such as when it is placed in an airtight container. In all cases the upper parts of the scrolls have been completely lost, since this is the part that is most vulnerable to wear, being exposed on the outside when the scrolls are rolled up from the bottom. Although it is impossible to extrapolate any precise measurements for the original lengths of the complete scrolls, it appears that the largest and best-preserved specimens, such as fragment 15, whose surviving portion is about 115 centimeters long, might represent approximately half of the original scroll (see 5.1.1). The loss of the upper portions of the scrolls is particularly troublesome because it is at the top of the scrolls that we would expect to find titles and/or colophons of the texts, at least in the case of those written continuously on both sides. Due to these circumstances, such colophons are not found (but for one partial exception, discussed in 2.2.6), which renders the task of identifying the texts immeasurably more difficult.

The scrolls also suffer from several other types of damage, including deterioration of one or both margins and peeling and fading of the outer, inscribed layer of the bark, which render them difficult to read in many places and not infrequently all but illegible. Although some of this damage, as noted above, is due to mishandling by the unknown discoverers, it is clear that the scrolls were already damaged, and in some cases badly deteriorated, in ancient times, before they were placed in the clay pot. This, along with certain other indications, which will be discussed at length in chapter 4, implies that the fragments were probably pieces of worn-out texts that had been discarded and were accorded ritual burial in a pot that was interred within the precincts of a Buddhist monastery, probably in or near a stūpa.

2.2. Texts and Genres Represented in the Collection

Since the fragments in the British Library collection appear to represent a more or less random selection of the contents of the library of a Gandhāran Buddhist monastery of about the first century A.D., it is not surprising that virtually all them proved to contain Buddhist religious texts, representing a wide variety of texts, genres, and styles. The best-represented genres are poetic compositions and compilations such as the Dharmapada, the Anavatapta-gāthā, and the Rhinoceros Horn Sūtra; texts in the avadāna and similar genres, relating pious legends of various kinds; and lengthy commentaries on various groups of verses. But for one exception (frag. 8, containing a Sanskrit medical text written in Brāhmī script), all of the texts are composed in the Gāndhārī language and written in the Kharoṣṭhī script invariably associated with it.

At this still preliminary stage of the analysis of the fragments, the number of texts which have been definitively identified is rather small, perhaps disappointingly so. Fewer than a quarter of them have been directly connected with Buddhist texts extant in other languages such as Pali, Sanskrit, Chinese, and Tibetan. Some more identifications may become possible in the course of further studies, but it should by no means be assumed that all of the texts will have parallels elsewhere in Buddhist tradition. On the contrary, it appears that a sizable portion of the new texts may be locally composed material that is unique to the Gandhāran tradition and has not been preserved in other Buddhist literatures.

Moreover, "identifying" a text is not necessarily a simple matter, in that some of the texts have varying degrees of partial correspondences with previously known texts, such that it is not always obvious whether we should speak of an "identification" or simply of parallel or related passages in what may be essentially different texts. Such problems are due, in part at least, to the complex and fluid character of the Buddhist textual tradition, in which textual units seem to have been gradually combined and collected in complex and often overlapping patterns. A good illustration of this type of problem is the text on fragments 12 and 14 (discussed below in 2.2.1), which corresponds in part to sections of the Pali Aṅguttara-nikāya, but in a complex and uncertain relationship. Of course, the unfortunate circumstance that none of the titles of the texts are preserved in the fragments makes it all the more difficult for us to understand their relationships to known works.

Given these problems with regard to the identifications of texts, for purposes of a preliminary presentation the textual material is described here in general terms, that is, under broad headings of genre categories. At this point in the preliminary study of the collection, the majority of the fragments, or at least the majority of the larger and better preserved ones, have been assigned to one of the categories listed below. Those texts which have been more or less specifically identified are described under these general headings. However, the following survey is not meant to be a comprehensive description of the entire contents of the collection but rather presents a representative sampling of the various types of texts and genres as far as they are understood at the present time.

2.2.1. Sūtra Texts and Commentaries

The number of fragments that can be definitively placed in this category is surprisingly small. The most clearly identifiable sūtra text is the relatively long and well-preserved fragment 15, which contains a version of the Saṅgīti-sūtra with an unidentified commentary, which is evidently not the same commentary as the Saṅgīti-paryāya known from a Chinese translation by Hsüan-tsang and from a fragment of the original Sanskrit found at Bamiyan (Lévi 1932: 9–11). The Saṅgīti-sūtra itself, an important sūtra of the numerical listing type, is preserved in Pali as suttanta no. 33 of the Dīgha-nikāya, in Sanskrit fragments from central Asia (Stache-Rosen 1968), and in the Chinese translation of the Dīrghāgama (T. 1 [no. 1], pp. 49b ff.) as well as in a separate Chinese translation (T. 1 [no. 12], pp. 226c ff.). In the new fragment, the ordering of the topics within each of the ten numerical groups agrees most closely with that of the Chinese Dīrghāgama version of the sūtra rather than with the Pali or Sanskrit versions, a fact which has important ramifications that will be discussed in 8.2.2.1. For reasons that will be explained in section 5.1.1, the surviving part of the text can be estimated at a little less than half of the original. A brief sample of this text is presented in section 6.7.3.

The text preserved in fragments 26 and 29 seems to contain a sūtra-type text concerning the four stages of meditative trance (*jana-* = Skt. *dhyāna-*/Pali *jhāna-*). Many of the terms and phrases appearing in these fragments resemble ones preserved in various texts in the Pali canon, for instance in the Sallekha-sutta (suttanta I.8 of the Majjhima-nikāya), but as yet it has not been possible to relate the text as a whole to any specific sūtra in Pali or elsewhere.

A third sūtra-type text is the aforementioned one in fragments 12 and 14, containing a sūtra text that corresponds in part to the Pali Aṅguttara-nikāya. It contains three discrete passages, of which the first consists of a dialogue between the Buddha and the brahman Dhoṇa which corresponds closely to the dialogue with Doṇa in Aṅguttara-nikāya, Catukka-nipāta 36 (Aṅguttara 2.37–9). This is followed by a brief discourse on, apparently, the words of the Buddha (*budha-bayaṇa-* = Skt. *buddha-vacana-*), for which no parallel has been found in Pali. The third discourse, concerning the four *prasaṇas* (= Skt. *pradhāna-/prahāna-*, Pali *padhāna-*), closely resembles Aṅguttara-nikāya, Catukka-nipāta 14 (Aṅguttara 2.16–7). Thus this text has a significant but incomplete correspondence with passages in the Pali Aṅguttara-nikāya; two of its sections are very similar to passages in the same part (the Catukka-nipāta) of the Aṅguttara, though they appear there separately and in a different sequence, while the third is apparently not found in the Pali. These fragments could constitute part of a Gāndhārī compilation equivalent to the Pali Aṅguttara-nikāya and the Sanskrit Ekottarikāgama, but it would be premature to state this outright at this point. The following sample text[4] (frag. 12, part 1, r, lines 8–14; pl. 7) is an extract from the first discourse, the dialogue between the brahman Dhoṇa and the Buddha:[5]

. . . (bha)yavadu teṇa uasakrami uvasakramita bhaya[va]du egha[do] ba[teṇa] ? ? ? (devo bhu bhaviśasi ṇaho bramaṇa de*)v[o] bhaviś[e]˙ ghadhrarvo bhu bhaviśa[si] ṇaho bramaṇa ghadhrarvo bhaviśe˙ yakṣu (bhu bhaviśasi ṇaho bra*)maṇa yakṣu bhaviśe˙ maṇośu bhu bhaviśasi ṇaho bramaṇa maṇośu bhaviśe˙ (devo bhu bhaviśa*)si idi p[r]oṭhu samaṇa ema vadesi naho bra[ma]ṇa dev(o*) bha[viś](e*) ghadh(arvo bhu bhaviśasi i*)di p(r*)oṭhu samaṇa ema vadesi ṇaho bramaṇa ghadharvo [bha]viśe˙ ya[kṣ](o*) bhu bhaviśasi [i]di p[r]oṭh(u*) [sama](ṇa*) [e](ma*) vadesi ṇaho bramaṇa yakṣu bhaviśe maṇosu bhu bhaviśasi [id](i*) p(r*)oṭhu samaṇa (ema vade*)si ṇaho bramaṇa maṇośu bhaviśe k[u] re bhu bhaviśasi budho mi bramaṇa budho ///*

[The brahman Dhoṇa] approached the Blessed One, and after approaching [said these words (?)] to the Blessed One:

["Sir, will you be[6] a god?"

"No, brahman,] I will not be a god."

---

4. Here and in the other preliminary text samples presented in this chapter, the text is presented exactly as it appears in the original manuscript, without detailed apparatus and annotation. Complete critical apparatus and explanatory notes on these passages will be given in the separate editions of the texts to be published in subsequent volumes. The accompanying translations are, of course, also tentative. Thanks are due to Mark Allon for his assistance in the reading and interpretation of this passage.

Note that the broken pieces that make up this fragment (see pl. 7) are out of order. The passage cited here begins in the second line of the larger piece that is the second one from the bottom, then continues in the piece at the top, which originally followed it. Some parts of the text quoted are on the small loose pieces at the bottom.

5. The corresponding Pali text (Aṅguttara-nikāya 2.38–9) reads:

> *Doṇo brāhmaṇo . . . yena Bhagavā ten´ upasaṅkami, upasaṅkamitvā Bhagavantaṃ etad avoca:*
>
> *Devo no bhavaṃ bhavissatīti?*
> *Na kho ahaṃ brāhmaṇa devo bhavissāmīti.*
> *Gandhabbo no bhavaṃ bhavissatīti?*
> *Na kho ahaṃ brāhmaṇa gandhabbo bhavissāmīti.*
> *Yakkho no bhavaṃ bhavissatīti?*
> *Na kho ahaṃ brāhmaṇa yakkho bhavissāmi.*
> *manusso no bhavaṃ bhavissatīti?*
> *Na kho ahaṃ brāhmaṇa manusso bhavissāmīti.*
>
> *Devo no bhavaṃ bhavissatīti iti puṭṭho samāno na kho aham brāhmaṇa devo bhavissāmīti vadesi, gandhabbo no bhavaṃ bhavissatīti iti puṭṭho samāno na kho ahaṃ gandhabbo bhavissāmīti vadesi, yakkho . . . vadesi, manusso no bhavaṃ bhavissatīti iti puṭṭho samāno na kho ahaṃ brāhmaṇa manusso bhavissāmīti vadesi, atha ko carahi bhavaṃ bhavissatīti?*
>
> *. . . Buddho ti maṃ brāhmaṇa dhārehīti.*

6. On the translation of Pali *bhavissati,* etc. (corresponding to Gāndhārī *bhaviśasi,* etc.) in this passage, see Woodward 1952: 44 n. 1.

"Sir, will you be a gandharva?"
"No, brahman, I will not be a gandharva."
["Sir, will you be] a yakṣa?"
["No,] brahman, I will not be a yakṣa."
"Sir, will you be a human?"
"No, brahman, I will not be a human."

"When you were asked, '[Sir, will you be a god?]' you answered thus, 'No, brahman, I will not be a god.' When you were asked, '[Sir, will you be] a gandharva?' you answered thus, 'No, brahman, I will not be a gandharva.' When you were asked, 'Sir, will you be a yakṣa?' you answered thus, 'No, brahman, I will not be a yakṣa.' When you were asked, will you be a human?' you [answered thus], 'No, brahman, I will not be a human.' What, then, will you be?"

"I am a buddha, brahman, a buddha . . ."

2.2.2. *Scholastic Treatises and Commentaries*

A large number of texts, including several of the longest fragments, fall into the category of scholastic treatises and commentaries, which, however, is admittedly something of a grab bag in that nearly all of the texts classified here are essentially unidentified and are probably of rather diverse contents. One particularly interesting text—or perhaps, rather, group of texts—consisting of a commentary on an apparently otherwise unknown collection of verses is represented by several fragments (3B, 7, 9, 13, and 18) that have similar contents and are written in the same hand but that seem to be parts of different scrolls. It is not yet clear whether these fragments constitute part of the same "book," written out in several scrolls (or "volumes"), or whether they are fragments of separate manuscripts of the same text, or of different texts of similar form and content. In these texts, each section of the commentary begins with the citation of the beginning (usually the first quarter) of the verse to be explained, followed by the phrase *sutro tatra nideśo,* apparently meaning "[Thus,] the sūtra; [now,] the explication of it." After this comes a detailed, more or less word-by-word commentary on the entire verse.

Most of the verses cited in these commentary texts correspond to ones found in the Pali canon in various texts of the Khuddaka-nikāya of the Sutta-piṭaka, such as the Sutta-nipāta, Udāna, Dhammapada, Itivuttaka, and Theragāthā, but the order in which they are quoted does not seem to correspond in any way with these Pali works.[7] By way of a sample, the following table shows the sequence of verses quoted on the recto of fragment 9, with their Pali parallels as far as they have been identified so far:

7. The ramifications of this will be discussed in section 8.1.2.2.

Part and Line	Citation	Pali Parallel
1.12	*kameṣaṇa bhaveṣaṇa*	*kāmesanā bhavesanā* Itivuttaka 55 (= Aṅguttara 2.42)
2.19	[illegible]	—
2.23–4	*aṇa va ladhva vasaṇa va kale*	*annañ ca laddhā vasanañ ca kāle* Sutta-nipāta 971 (Sāriputta-sutta, Aṭṭhaka-vagga)
2.32–3	*ṣutva (a*)ha vira agamo agami*	*sutvān' ahaṃ vīraṃ akāmakāmiṃ* Sutta-nipāta 1096 (Jatukaṇṇimāṇava-pucchā, Pārāyana-vagga)
2.40	*ta ? mi[aśa]rosi*	?
2.44	*aṇava[su] . . .*	*anavassutacittassa* Dhammapada 39 (Citta-vagga)
3.14	*ajaro jiamaṇeṇa*	*ajaraṃ jīramānena* Theragāthā 32 (Suppiya thera)
3.21	*paca kadha pariñae*	*pañca kkhandhe pariññāya* Theragāthā 369 (Soṇa Kuṭikaṇṇa thera)
3.27–8	*yasa idriaṇi subhavidaṇi*	*yass' indriyāni bhāvitāni* Sutta-nipāta 516 (Sabhiya-sutta, Mahā-vagga)
3.37	*? ? jama [a] ke[vali] . . .*	*aññena ca kevalinaṃ mahesiṃ* (possibly) Sutta-nipāta 82 (Kasibhāradvāja-sutta, Uraga-vagga)
3.45	*aho prove*	*ahu pubbe tadā n'āhu* Udāna VI.3

The first text on the long fragment 4 (recto) seems to be a commentary of a similar type, but it is written in a different hand than those referred to above, which are all in the same hand. It contains verses that mostly, but not exclusively, correspond to ones in the Pali Dhammapada, but in a sequence that does not correspond at all to that of the extant Pali Dhammapada or of the related collections in other languages.

Thus, these verse commentary texts, which taken together make up a substantial portion of the complete collection, imply the existence of one or more compilations or arrangements of well-known Buddhist gāthās and udānas in Gāndhārī translation that do not follow the organizational principles familiar from similar compilations in other traditions. This may mean that these commentaries, and perhaps also the compilations of verses that presumably underlie them, were of local (i.e., Gandhāran) origin (see 8.1.4.1). The underlying rationale or system of the arrangement of verses is as yet unclear, but a detailed study of the texts of this genre may eventually clarify the matter.

Presented below is a specimen of the commentary on one verse from a text of this group (frag. 9, part 3, r, lines 14–21; pl. 8). The verse in question corresponds, with some variations, to verse 32 of the Pali Theragāthā[8] and 159 of the KDhP (Jara-varga).[9] Only the first quarter of the verse (*ajaro jiamaṇeṇa*) is actually quoted as a *pratīka* at the beginning of the commentary, but the rest of it can be reconstructed from the lemmata in the commentary itself and from the parallel verses, as follows:

> *ajaro jiamaṇeṇa daśamaṇeṇa ṇivudi*
> *ṇimesa parama śati yoakṣemo (aṇutaro*)*[10]

Following the interpretation of the commentary, the translation of this verse would be

> Exchange[11] the decaying, the burning, for the undecaying, [which is] cessation, ultimate calming, supreme peace.

The text of the commentary (with lemmata printed in boldface) reads as follows:

> [line 14, middle] ***ajaro jiamaṇeṇa*** *sutro tatra ṇideśo* [15] ***ajaro*** *aṇuadiśeṣa-ṇivaṇadhadu˙* ***jiamaṇo˙*** *pacau(a*)[da]ṇa-khadha˙ te osirati* [16] *[ṇiva]ṇo˙*[12] *payeṣidavyo˙ ajaribhave˙* ***daśamaṇa˙***[13] *trihi ṇi[ghe]hi tiṣa kṣayo˙ paye*[17]*ṣidav[y]o˙ ya[tra] ṇa kayi˙ daśaṇa˙ eṣa hoso* ***yoakṣemo***[˙] *due ṇivaṇa-dha[d]ue˙* ***ṇ[i][me]sa*** [18] ***parama śati˙*** *dukha yatr[o] osirita griṇa[dha] due ṇivaṇadhadue* [˙] *[ṣa]kṣev[e]* ***jia***[19]***maṇa*** *dukho˙* ***ajare ṇivuti˙*** *ṇiroso˙* ***dajamaṇa˙*** *ṣamudayo* [˙] ***ṇ[i]meṣa˙*** *ñaṇaṇa* [20] *osiridavya˙ aya mago aṣava* ***ṇivudi*** *kileśakṣayo˙* ***ṇimesa*** [21] *kamakṣayo˙* ***ajaro*** *dukhakṣayo* ○[14]

---

8. *ajaraṃ jīramānena tappamānena nibbutiṃ*
nimmissaṃ paramaṃ santiṃ yogakkhemaṃ anuttaraṃ.

9. *ayara jiyamaṇeṇa ḍajamaṇeṇa nivrudi*
nimedha parama śodhi yoka-kṣemu aṇutara.

10. This last word is not cited in the commentary but is tentatively reconstructed on the basis of the reading of the corresponding KDhP verse.

11. The verb *nimesa* is phonetically ambiguous and could be interpreted as a first-person future form equivalent to the Pali *nim(m)issaṃ*, "I will exchange." But the commentary seems to give the plural imperative *griṇadha* (= Skt. *gṛhṇīta*) as its gloss, which would mean that the ending *-sa* was intended to be equivalent to the *-dha* (*-s-* = *-ṣ-* < *-dh-*; see 6.3), presumably imperative, of the KDhP's reading *nimedha.*

12. The expected reading here would be the lemma *ṇivudi*, but this does not seem to be the case, as the third syllable is quite clearly *ṇo.*

13. *daśamaṇa* = Skt. *dahyamāna-;* for Gāndhārī *-ś-* < Skt. *-hy-*, see Brough 1962: 105 (§61). Note also the KDhP reading, *ḍajamaṇa-* (cited here by Brough), and the alternate spelling of

This can be tentatively translated as

> "The decaying for the undecaying . . . ": [Thus,] the sūtra; [now,] the explication of it: "The undecaying" is the element of nirvāṇa without remainder. "The decaying" is the five appropriating aggregates; one [should] abandon[15] them. Nirvāṇa should be sought after; [it is] the state of becoming undecaying. "The burning," [that is, burning] with the three evils.[16] Their elimination should be sought after. Where there is no [such] burning, that has become[17] "peace." [These are] the two elements of nirvāṇa [i.e., with and without remainder]. "Exchange" [means] take up "supreme calm," where suffering has been abandoned. [This too refers to] the two elements of nirvāṇa. In short: "The decaying" is suffering; "undecaying cessation" is suppression; "the burning" is arising; and "exchange" [means that arising] should be abandoned by means of knowledge;[18] [this is] the noble path.[19] Or else: "cessation" is the elimination of defilements; "exchange" [means] the elimination of karma; [and] "the undecaying" is the elimination of suffering.

Another interesting scholastic document is fragment 28, apparently an abhidharma treatise or commentary discussing topics such as the nature of existence in the different times. A representative passage (frag. 28, part 2, r, lines 21–2) reads *sarvakal[o] sarvam asti˙ sarvatra sarvam asti˙ sarvagarena sarvam asti˙*

---

the same word later in this sample text (line 19) as *dajamaṇa*. Here the Pali verse has the variant reading *tappamānena*.

14. The following approximate rendering into Buddhist Sanskrit is offered to help clarify the interpretation of this passage:

> *ajaraṃ jīryamāṇena [iti] sūtram. tatra nirdeśaḥ:* ***ajaram*** *anupadhiśeṣa-nirvāṇadhātuḥ.* ***jīryamāṇaṃ*** *pañcopādāna-skandhāḥ. tān osirati. nirvāṇaṃ paryeṣitavyam ajarībhāvaḥ.* ***dahyamānaṃ*** *tribhir nighaiḥ. teṣāṃ kṣayaḥ paryeṣitavyaḥ. yatra na kiṃcid dahanam, eṣa bhūto* ***yogakṣemaḥ.*** *dvau nirvāṇa-dhātū.* ***niminīta paramaṃ śāntim*** *duḥkhaṃ yatra osiritaṃ gṛhṇīta. dvau nirvāṇa-dhātū. saṃkṣepe:* ***jīryamāṇaṃ*** *duḥkham.* ***ajaraṃ nirvṛtir*** *nirodhaḥ.* ***dahyamānaṃ*** *samudayaḥ.* ***niminīta*** *jñānena osiritavyam. ārya-mārgaḥ. athavā:* ***nirvṛtiḥ*** *kleśakṣayaḥ.* ***niminīta*** *karmakṣayaḥ.* ***ajaraṃ*** *duḥkhakṣayaḥ.*

15. The present tense verb *osirati* is surprising; a gerundive form might have been expected here. For the verb itself, see Edgerton 1953: 75, s.v. *avaśirati*, etc.

16. These are presumably *rāga*, "passion"; *dveṣa*, "hatred"; and *moha*, "delusion."

17. This is a provisional translation for *hoso*, which seems to be a preterite form of the verb *ho-* (= Skt. √*bhū*).

18. *ñaṇaṇa* apparently = Skt. *jñānena;* cf. *tano* = *tena* in the passages cited in sections 6.5.1 and 6.7.3. Apparently in these texts, as in the KDhP, "[n]ot infrequently, an etymological (*i, e*) is omitted in the writing" (Brough 1962: 81).

19. Here the commentator summarizes the verse by equating what he takes as its four main words with the four noble truths.

sarvakara[ne]na (sarvam asti) sarvabhaveha sarvam asti sarvaheduha sarvam asti sarvapacageha sarvam asti* ("Everything exists at all times. Everything exists everywhere. Everything exists with the aspect of everything. Everything exists as the reason for everything. Everything exists as all entities. Everything exists as all causes. Everything exists as all conditions.").[20]

Other substantial remains of scholastic texts include the large fragments 20 and 23, which seem to be part of the same scroll or the same text in multiple scrolls. The contents of these fragments have not yet been closely analyzed, but they seem to treat of a variety of technical topics typical of the concerns of what may best be called "mainstream" Buddhism.[21] This text is the largest one for which no clear textual or genre identification has yet been made.

2.2.3. *Verse Texts*

The category of verse texts, represented by three important fragments, presents much less difficulty than the other categories with regard to the identification of texts. One work of this class is the first of two texts on the long and relatively well preserved fragment 1, consisting of a portion of the Anavatapta-gāthā, or Songs of Lake Anavatapta. This popular text is widely represented in the northern Buddhist tradition, including two separate recensions each in Sanskrit and Chinese. One of these versions appears within the Bhaiṣajyavastu of the Mūlasarvāstivāda-vinaya, extant in Chinese and Tibetan translation and also, in somewhat fragmentary condition, in the original Sanskrit among the Gilgit manuscripts (Bechert 1961; Hofinger 1982). This Mūlasarvāstivādin version consists of the recitations by thirty-six of the Buddha's disciples of their own past lives and karmic histories, which they revealed to an assembly of five hundred followers on the shores of Lake Anavatapta in the Himalayas. The Gāndhārī fragments contain, in part or in full, the recitations by the disciples Nanda, Koṭiviṃśa, Yaśas, Piṇḍola Bharadvāja, Vāgīśa, Nandika, and Kusuma, which correspond to the recitations numbered 26, 6, 11, 8, 7, 10, and 5 in the Mūlasarvāstivāda-vinaya version. This scroll evidently did not contain the entire poem but rather was part (perhaps the first part) of a multivolume text. The discovery of a Gāndhārī version of the Anavatapta-gāthā confirms the popularity of this poem in early northern Buddhist tradition. A comparative study of this Gāndhārī

20. This translation was prepared with the assistance of Collett Cox.

21. By "mainstream" Buddhism I refer to what is otherwise variously known as "traditional," "Śrāvakayāna," "Nikāya," or "Hīnayāna" Buddhism, that is, pre- and non-Mahāyāna Indian Buddhism (see also 8.3.1). It is notoriously difficult to settle on an acceptable term for this tradition that is free of sectarian implications.

version with the other, apparently later recensions in other languages is likely to yield important clues as to the textual and sectarian history of this poem.

The following is a preliminary reading and translation of the recitation by Kusuma (frag. 1, part 5, r, lines 16–29; pl. 4).[22] The point of the story is that, simply by giving a single flower from his hair to a stūpa of the Buddha Vipaśyin, Kusuma (whose name itself means "Flower," as also does the name Sumanas, by which he is known in the Sanskrit version) earned favorable karma that brought him a long series of good births in heaven, culminating in his becoming a human disciple of the Buddha in his present life.

22. The corresponding Sanskrit text of the recitation by Sumanas from the Gilgit manuscript of the Mūlasarvāstivāda-vinaya (V.60–74; partially reconstructed) is reprinted below (from Bechert 1961: 111–4, with minor editorial changes). Sanskrit verses that do not have a correspondent in the Gāndhārī text are put in square brackets; verses that occur in a different sequence in the Gāndhārī are marked with an asterisk at the beginning.

karṇe sumanasaṃ kṛtvā kṛtvā mālāṃ ca mūrdhani/
udyānabhūmiṃ niryāmi vayasyaiḥ parivāritaḥ //60//
vipaśyinaḥ stūpam ahaṃ tatrāpaśyaṃ mahāmuneḥ /
supūjyamānaṃ mahatā janakāyena sarvataḥ //61//
vayasyakā gṛhītāś ca sarve mālāṃ svakāṃ svakām /
tasminn āropayan stūpe prasannena ca cetasā //62//
tān ahaṃ tatra dṛṣṭvātha janam anyaṃ tathā bahu /
karṇād gṛhītvā kusumaṃ stūpe āropaye tadā //63//
[tenāhaṃ kuśalamūlena yatra yatropapannavān /
devabhūto manuṣyaś ca kṛtapuṇyo virocitaḥ //64//]
[ārādhitaḥ sārthavāhaḥ saṃbuddho 'yam anuttaraḥ /
arhatvaṃ ca mayā prāptaṃ śītibhūto 'smi nirvṛtaḥ //65//]
**ekapuṣpaṃ parityajya varṣakoṭiśatāny aham /*
deveṣu paricary' eva śeṣeṇa parinirvṛtaḥ //66//
saced bhadantā ājñāsye saṃbuddhasya guṇān bahūn
bhūyo 'kariṣye satkārāṃ suprasannena cetasā //67//
tasmāt prajānatām asya saṃbuddhasya guṇān bahūn /
kāryaḥ stūpeṣu satkāro bhaviṣyati mahāphalaḥ //68//
**na hi cittaprasādasya svalpā bhavati dakṣiṇā /*
tathāgate ca saṃbuddhe buddhānāṃ śrāvakeṣu vā //69//
etad bhadantās smarāmi yan mayā kuśalaṃ kṛtam /
anubhūtaṃ phalaṃ tasya kāntam iṣṭaṃ manoramam //70//
[tena karmavipākena nāsti jātu punarbhavaḥ /
arhann asmi hatakleśaḥ śītibhūto 'smi nirvṛtaḥ //71//]
[nāhaṃ punarbhavaṃ śayyāṃ saṃsāre śayitaḥ kvacit /
iyaṃ me paścimā jātir anupādāya paścimā //72//]
[tenaiva hetunā cedaṃ nāma me sumanā iti /
mukto 'smi sarvaduḥkhebhya uttīrṇo bhavasāgarāt //73//]
ity evaṃ sumanāḥ sthaviro bhikṣusaṃghāgrataḥ sthitaḥ /
vyākaroti svakaṃ karma anavatapte mahāhrade //74//

[line 16] *kaṇe karita sumaṇa ṇa*[23] *mala [ca] + +* [17] *krida˙*
uyaṇa[ho]mi ṇiasi vayasehi puraskidu˙
tatra daśi [ma][18]*ha thubu vivaśisa śirimad[u]˙*
jaṇaghayu samaghatva satkarisu ma[19]*ma*[24]*hisu [ya*[25]*]˙*
de vayasa samaghatva˙ spa spo malu ghrahi[tvaṇa˙]
[20] *a[r]oaïsu thuvaspi prasaṇamaṇacedasa˙*
teṣu aho dhrispaṇa aña[21]*mañaṇa paśia˙*
kaṇade ghriha sumaṇa thuve aroae spa[e] (˙*)
(*ṇa hi**) [22] *citu prasaṇasa apaa bhudi dhakṣiṇa˙*
tasaghada a sabudha ye ya [b]u[dha][23]*ṇa ṣave[a˙]*
s[ae] aha budha-ghuṇa jaṇamaṇa tasaghad[u]˙
thuve [kariśe] [24] *satkaro bhoya bhaśa ma?[h]io˙*
taspa ho peaṇamaṇeṇa śastara[sa] [25] *baho ghuṇa˙*
thuve kurusa satkaru [ta]da mukṣ[u] sadhrogha[di]˙
(*eko**) [26] *puspu caïtaṇa sahasu barṣakuḍiṇa*
devehi pariarita avaśe[27]*ṣe mi ṇi[b](u*)[d](i*)[˙]*
edaho sparami bha[te˙] e[ko] p[usp]u [caï](t)[va](ṇa*)*
[28] *aṇohodu phal[u] ta[sa] [ṇa h](i*) karmu praṇaśadi˙*
eva kusuma [the][29]*ro bhikhu budhasa ṣa[va]o*
spai karmu viaghaṣe aṇodate maha[sare]

"Putting a flower behind my ear and a garland [on my head], I went out to the park together with my friends.

There I saw the great stūpa of the glorious (Buddha) Vipaśyin. A crowd of people[26] had come together and were worshiping and honoring it.

Those friends (of mine) came together, and each of them took his own garland and placed it on the stūpa, with devoted heart.

Seeing them and watching all the others[27] [as well], I took the flower from my ear and put it on the stūpa myself.

For there is no small benefit from a heart that is devoted to an enlightened Tathāgata and the disciples of the Buddhas.

---

23. This syllable seems to be a dittographic error by the scribe.
24. Here again, there may be a dittographic error; the verse is hypermetric.
25. This akṣara is blurred and may have been canceled or corrected.
26. *jaṇaghayu* = Skt. *janakāyaḥ*. This scribe always writes *gh* in place of *g*; see 6.4.2.
27. *añamañaṇa* = Pali *aññamañña-* and Buddhist Skt. *anyamanya/anyonya*, "various," "different" (not "mutual[ly]"; cf. Edgerton 1953: 42, s.vv.). The word *anyonya* is used in the same way in the Sanskrit Anavatapta-gāthā, VII. 87 (Bechert 1961: 129).

If I had known of the Tathāgata with his Buddha-virtues, I would have worshiped the stūpas all the more; [this would have been most beneficial (?)[28]].

Therefore, knowing[29] the many virtues of the Teacher, worship the stūpas; thence [come] liberation and good future births.[30]

For giving[31] [one] flower, I was served by the gods for a thousand eons and liberated in the end.

This, your reverences, I recall; for (merely) giving one flower, I experienced [this] fruit of that (deed). For karma does not fail."

Thus did the elder Kusuma ("Flower"), a monk and a disciple of the Buddha, explain[32] his own karma at Lake Anavatapta.

The second poetic text in the British Library collection is fragment 5B, which preserves a substantial part of a Gāndhārī version of the famous poem known in Pali as the Khaggavisāṇa-sutta (Rhinoceros Sutta or Rhinoceros Horn Sutta)[33] and in Sanskrit as the Khaḍgaviṣāṇa-gāthā.[34] The Gāndhārī text in general corresponds to the Pali version, which appears in the Tipiṭaka as the third sutta in the Sutta-nipāta and which is repeated twice more in other parts of the Khuddaka-nikāya, once in the Apadāna and again, with commentary, in the Culla-niddesa. However, the ordering of the verses in the Gāndhārī text, and to some extent also their wording and composition, differ significantly from both the Pali and the Sanskrit texts, and there are at least four verses in the Gāndhārī version which do not appear at all in the other versions of this poem. It is interesting, though perhaps not too surprising, to find the Rhinoceros Horn Sūtra represented in the new collection, since it has long been recognized that it holds a special position in the Theravāda

28. The sense of *bhaśa ma?[h]io* is not clear, and a tentative translation is proposed here on the basis of *bhaviṣyati mahāphalaḥ* in the partly corresponding position (verse V.68d; Bechert 1961: 113) in the Gilgit manuscript of the Sanskrit version. This parallel suggests that *bhaśa* could have been miswritten for *bha(vi*)śa* or the like, although this raises metrical problems. The word *ma?hio* might have represented something like Skt. *mahāhitaḥ*. The text may be corrupt here. The second syllable of this word is partly covered by a blob of ink, which may have been a scribal correction.

29. The syntax here is not entirely clear, as the participle (?) *peaṇamaṇeṇa* is in the instrumental, which does not accord with the verb *kurusa*, apparently in the imperative. Compare *prajānamānena* in a similar but unfortunately incomplete verse (IV.11a; Bechert 1961: 107) in a Turfan manuscript of the Sanskrit Anavatapta-gāthā.

30. *sadhroghadi* = Skt. *sādhugatiḥ*.

31. *caïtaṇa* = Pali *cajitvāna* (see Bechert 1961: 110)/Skt. *tyaktvā*.

32. *viaghaṣe* = Pali *vyākāsi*/Skt. *vyākārṣīt* (see n. 26).

33. For a recent review of the old controversy as to the correct interpretation of the term *khaggavisāṇa-*, see Norman 1996. In the translation sample below, I have tentatively accepted his conclusion that "rhinoceros horn," rather than "rhinoceros," was the original sense.

34. This Sanskrit version is preserved in the Mahāvastu (1.357–9 in Senart's ed.).

tradition, as indicated by, among other things, the fact that it is repeated three times in the Khuddaka-nikāya (see Norman 1983: 64–5). Modern scholars have regarded its numerous archaisms in language, form, and content as an index of its antiquity and hence its importance as a record of an early stage of Buddhism (see, e.g., Jayawickrama 1949). A detailed study of the relationship of the Gāndhārī Rhinoceros Horn Sūtra with the Pali and Sanskrit versions thus promises to be of particular significance, and this text has been designated as the first priority for publication in this series.

The following extract from the Gāndhārī version of the Rhinoceros Horn Sūtra is reconstructed from subfragments 7a (lines 2–4) and 7b (lines 1–3) of fragment 5B (see the description of frag. 5B in sec. 2.3). In the translation, the lacunae are supplied in square brackets on the basis of the corresponding Pali text.[35]

ṇago vi yuṣaṇi vivajaita
saṃjadakaṃdho patumaṃ uraḍo
+ + + + + vi + [r.] + + +
+ + + + + + + + + + +

ṇiloluo ṇikuho ṇikaṣayo
ṇimoho ṇidhaṃto kaṣaya[mra]kṣ[o]
+ + + + + + + g(e) bhavitva*
eko car(e) khargaviṣa[ṇa] + +*

catu[d](i)[śo] [a]paḍiho kuhica*
saṃtuśamaṇa itaridareṇa
+ + + + + + h[i]ta achaṃbi
eko care khargaviṣaṇaga +

35. The corresponding Pali verses (nos. 19, 22, and 8 of the Khaggavisāṇa-sutta = 53, 56, and 42 of the Sutta-nipāta) read:

nāgo va yūthāni vivajjayitvā
sañjātakhandho padumī ulāro
yathābhirantaṃ vihare araññe
eko care khaggavisāṇakappo.

nillolupo nikkuho nippipāso
nimmakkho niddhantakasāvamoho
nirāsayo sabbaloke bhavitvā
eko care khaggavisāṇakappo.

cātuddiso appaṭigho ca hoti
santussamāno itarītarena
parissayānaṃ sahitā achambhī
eko care khaggavisāṇakappo.

As a mighty, broad-shouldered, spotted elephant who shuns the herds might move about [at will in the forest, so one should wander alone like the rhinoceros horn].

Free of greed, deceit, faults, and delusion, casting off faults and disparagement,[36] becoming [free of intentions in the whole world], one should wander alone [like] the rhinoceros horn.

At home everywhere, avoiding conflict anywhere, satisfied with one thing or the other, [enduring dangers] without fear, one should wander alone like the rhinoceros horn.

The third poetic composition in the new collection appears as the first of two texts on fragments 16 and 25, which are the right and left halves respectively of the same original scroll. These fragments preserve portions of the last few lines of the end of a text corresponding closely, though not exactly, to the end of the Bhikhu-varga (verses 78–90), which is the second chapter of the KDhP. Therefore, this scroll was probably part of a Dharmapada text comprising several scrolls, of which this was presumably the first (see 5.1.1). The close similarity of this fragment to the corresponding passage in the KDhP makes it likely that it represents a slightly different text of the same recension of the Dharmapada. This text was written by the same scribe who wrote the Anavatapta-gāthā text and the sūtra text in fragments 12 + 14 (2.2.1).

2.2.4. Avadānas and Related Texts

One of the best represented genres among the British Library fragments is collections of stories, apparently of quite diverse content, most of which are explicitly labeled in the manuscripts as "avadānas." The largest and best-preserved specimens of these texts are in fragments 1, 4, 12 + 14, and 16 + 25. In most cases, these texts seem to be secondary ones that were added to scrolls on which the bottom of the recto and the entire verso had been left blank by the scribes who wrote the first texts on the recto only (see 5.1.1). Smaller remnants of what seem to be texts of the same class are found in fragments 2, 3A, and 21, but their original position and relationship to other texts on the same scroll, if any, are unclear due to the very fragmentary condition of these pieces. An unusual feature of the texts of this genre is that nearly all of them are written in the same distinctive large hand. The only exception is the first part of the avadāna text in fragment 4, which is in a hand

36. The phrase *ṇidhaṃto kaṣaya[mra]kṣ[o]* is a semicompound, corresponding to Pali *niddhanta-kasāvamoho,* of a type that is not rare in the Kharoṣṭhī manuscripts and other Gāndhārī texts.

that is not seen in any other texts. However, the latter part of this collection is written by the scribe of the other avadānas,[37] who evidently was a specialist in this genre.

The larger avadāna fragments contain collections of brief recitations which in most cases are numbered sequentially. These numbers in the surviving fragments run as high as sixteen (frag. 4, part 2, v, line 2, *ṣoḍaśo 10 4 1 1*) or possibly seventeen (line 12, *sa(ta*)[daśa]* . . .). In many cases, the individual recitations end with an abbreviation formula such as *vistare sarvo karya*, "The whole [story] is to be done [i.e., recited] in full" (e.g., frag. 25, r, line 26); *vistare janidave siyadi*, "[The story] should be known [i.e., recalled] in full" (frag. 4, part 7, v, line 4); or the frequent but enigmatic *sarva vistare yaṣayupamano siyadi* (frag. 1, part 2, v, line 74) or *vistare jaṇidavo yaṣayupamano siyadi* (frag. 4, part 6, v, line 30), whose interpretation remains to be fully clarified.[38] These notations, which resemble similar formulae in other Buddhist texts in Pali and Sanskrit,[39] as well as the overall brevity, sometimes extreme, of the avadānas give the impression that the texts are merely skeletons or outlines, which were evidently meant to be filled in and expanded by the reader or reciter. In this respect they resemble the similarly abridged avadāna and jātaka texts in the Bairam Ali manuscript from Merv in Turkmenistan (Vorob′eva-Desjatovskaja 1983: 71).

Although many of these avadāna texts resemble avadānas in Sanskrit and other languages with regard to their style and phrasing, in terms of content they appear to represent different traditions from previously known texts of this genre. Thus we find, for example, such stories as the avadānas of Jhādamitra (frag. 1, avadānas nos. 7 and 8), Sārthadāsa (frags. 12 + 14, avadāna no. 7), and an Ājīvika (*āyiviga;* frag. 1, avadāna no. 1), for which no correspondents have so far been found in published texts. Some of the other avadānas, especially those in the large collection in fragment 4, concern more familiar figures in Buddhist tradition such as Gavāmpati, Mahākāśyapa, and Aśoka, but the specific content of these stories does not correspond to any previously known material—or at least so it appears on the basis of preliminary studies.

In at least a few cases, however, there seems to be a possibility of linking an avadāna with stories known from other Buddhist traditions. For example, the first avadāna in the collection in fragments 12 + 14 concerns a person named Puniga, who is associated in some way (which is not entirely clear due to the fragmentary condition of the text) with the householder Anāthapiṇḍika (*anaṣapiḍigasa grahavadisa*) and with King Prasenajit (*p[r]asen[i]g[e]no rayeno*). This Puniga therefore might be connected with the therī (female elder) named Puṇṇā or Puṇṇikā who is mentioned in several Pali commentaries as a servant of Anāthapiṇḍika (Malalasekere

37. See also the description of this fragment in 2.3.

38. See the text sample below and n. 46 for a provisional interpretation of these phrases.

39. Cf. the various formulae with the word *vistareṇa* in Buddhist Sanskrit (Edgerton 1953: 504) and with *peyyāla* in Pali.

1937–8: 2.227–8). But as of this writing, this and other possible connections with other Buddhist traditions remain to be confirmed and further investigated.

At least two of the avadāna-type texts contain references to contemporary historical figures: the mahākṣatrapa Jihonika and Aśpavarman, who can be securely identified with Indo-Scythian rulers of the early first century A.D. and who are well known from coins and inscriptions.[40] These and other peculiar features suggest that, unlike the majority of the avadānas known from Buddhist Sanskrit and other traditions, at least some, probably even most, of the texts labeled "avadāna" do not consist of stories illustrating the karmic results of actions in previous lives. Rather, the term avadāna is apparently being used here in something more like its broader, and not exclusively Buddhist, sense of "pious legend" or "great deed."[41] In general, the avadanas in these texts seem to fall into two classes: those that concern well-known traditional figures of the time of the Buddha Śākyamuni and those that seem to be set in the contemporary world of Indo-Scythian Gandhāra. Curiously enough, avadānas of both types seem to be mixed together within the separate collections on different scrolls. The relationships between the individual avadānas within each collection and the rationale for their arrangement remain to be clarified.

Several of these peculiarities and problems are also exemplified in the second text in fragments 16 + 25. This comprises a particularly interesting series of stories, most of which are similar in form to the avadāna texts and which are written in the same hand but are labeled *provayoge* (Skt. *pūrvayogaḥ*), "past birth(s)," rather than *avadāna.* Unlike the avadānas, these pūrvayoga stories do describe the past incarnations of well-known personages in Buddhist tradition, such as Ājñātakauṇḍinya (*añadakoḍiña*), Ānanda (*anada*), and the Bodhisattva (*bodhisatva/boṣisatva*) himself. Thus, surprisingly, it is these pūrvayoga texts, rather than the ones labeled avadānas, that more closely resemble what are typically known as avadānas in the Buddhist Sanskrit tradition and as apadānas in Pali. Yet, this collection also includes at least one story (the sixth, which is not labeled a pūrvayoga) that is set in Taxila (*takṣaïle*) and concerns the interaction between a monk (*ṣamano* = Skt. *śramaṇa-*) and, apparently, an unnamed Saka (Scythian) (*añadaro . . . sago,* "some Saka"); this evidently belongs to the class of "contemporary" stories alluded to above. As in the other similar texts, the relationship between this story and the other ones in the same collection remains obscure.

The stories of past births in this pūrvayoga collection are also of particular interest because better parallels are available for them than appears to be the case with the avadānas. For example, the second pūrvayoga in this text describes Ājñātakauṇḍinya's past life as a potter (*kulala*).[42] The Mahāvastu contains a previous-

40. See sections 7.1.1–2 for a detailed discussion of these passages and their significance.
41. On the sense of the term avadāna, see Speyer 1906–9: preface, i–iv.
42. This story seems to be repeated, in a shorter form, in fragment 3.

birth story, labeled *jātaka* (Senart's ed., 3.347–8), describing Ājñātakauṇḍinya's life as a potter (*kumbhakāra-, bhārgava-*), and although the plot of the story has little resemblance to the one found in the new manuscripts, there are some intriguing similarities in style and phrasing.[43] But a much closer parallel is found in the "Previous History of Kaundinya" contained in the Fo pên hsing chi ching (T. 3 [no. 190], pp. 813c–814b; translated in Beal 1875: 256–8), a biography of the Buddha that, significantly (see 8.2), is generally considered to be a Dharmaguptaka text (see, e.g., Hirakawa 1990: 263). The very brief story of the previous life of Ānanda told in the fifth story in this group, which is transcribed and translated below, also has a probable parallel in the previous life of Ānanda described at the end of the Fo pên hsing chi ching (T. 3, pp. 930a–931b; not translated by Beal). These parallels suggest that at least some of the lore preserved in this collection, and presumably also in the other avadāna collections, represents Dharmaguptaka traditions that are not otherwise extant in Indian-language materials but for which it may eventually be possible to discover parallels in Chinese translations.[44]

This collection of pūrvayogas also includes, evidently by way of a supplement (apparently labeled *[u]dahara[na]*, "example") to the first story, concerning the Bodhisattva's past life as a merchant, a very brief summary rendition of a story corresponding to the well-known Vessantara-jātaka. The hero, however, is here not called Vessantara as in the Pali and other well-known versions of this story, but *sudaṣa*, that is, *sudaṣṇa;* this evidently corresponds to Sudaṃṣṭra, which is given as the name of the hero of this tale in some northern traditions (e.g., in the Rāṣṭrapāla-paripṛcchā; Finot 1901: 22, line 18).[45] This is the only passage yet found in the entire collection to have any relationship to the jātaka literature as it is known in other Buddhist traditions. But the relationship of this familiar story to the rest of the text in which it is found, and the rationale for its inclusion there, remain to be explained.

The following specimen from fragments 16 + 25 (v, lines 8–11; fifth story) presents, in the extremely terse manner characteristic of the avadāna-type texts, the aforementioned story of the previous life of Ānanda:

> [line 8] *anadasa pr[uva](yo*)ge yaṣayupamano sarvo* [9] *[gadha]badhaǵa iśa jabudive rayo [h](o*)vadi pradeśige tasa duve* [10] *putra hovadi sabrudidrigo co bha[n]o (co.*) [sab](ru*)[didri]g[o] pravayi[d]o ?* [11] *[pra]c.[g.s.]budh[i] prato gatha vi(stare*)* ○ 4 1

---

43. This parallel was discovered by Timothy Lenz, who is preparing an edition of fragments 16 + 25 for publication.

44. See also the further comments on this point in section 8.2.2.3.

45. See also Appendix, n. 38.

The previous birth of Ānanda: The whole [introductory portion is to be recited] according to the usual pattern (?).[46] Gadhabadhaǵa (= Skt. Gandhabandhaka?) was king here in Jambudvīpa. He had two sons, [who were his] regional governors: Sabrudidrigo (= Skt. Saṃvṛtendriya) and Bhano (= Skt. Bhānu). Sabrudidrigo became a mendicant.[47] He attained individual enlightenment.[48] The verse is to be recited in full.[49] [Story number] 5.

2.2.5. Other Genres and Miscellaneous Texts

Fragment 5C is a unique specimen in the British Library collection of a stotra, or hymn of praise, to the Buddha composed in poetic meters such as vasantatilakā, describing him with such epithets as *gunehi guna-parami prataṃ,* "who has attained through his virtues the perfection of virtue"; *soma-sadiśa-[va]dana-,* "whose face is like the moon"; and *sarvasatvutamaṃ,* "supreme among all beings." Unfortunately, the fragment is in particularly poor condition, so that no complete verses can be read. The content is fairly similar to the only directly comparable text, namely, the stotra verses preserved in central Asian Gāndhārī in Niya documents nos. 510 and 511 (Boyer, Rapson, and Senart 1920–9: 2.184–7).

Another unique item is fragment 6, containing a passage from an as yet unidentified medical text. This piece stands out from the others in the collection in form as well as in content; unlike all the others, it is in Brāhmī script and Sanskrit language, and the scroll on which it is written is much narrower (5.5 cm) than the others. These anomalies may mean that this fragment originally came from some source outside the library's collection. The fact that it is written on birch bark, however, means that its original provenance was somewhere in the northwest or far north of India.

Finally, there are several other fragments, such as 5A, 8, 10, 11, 21, and 22, whose contents are as yet completely undetermined. Most of these are very small or very poorly preserved, but it is hoped that, as the contents of the collection as a whole become more familiar, it will eventually become possible to identify these pieces as well, at least with regard to their genre and general contents.

---

46. "According to the usual pattern" is a provisional translation for *yaṣayupamano,* interpreted as equivalent to a Skt. **yathopamānam;* cf. Pali *tath'ūpamaṃ,* "likewise," "in the same way." In this interpretation, the phrase is read as *yaṣa-y-upamano,* with a glide or "sandhi consonant" *y,* which is, however, admittedly not expected in Gāndhārī. See also n. 39 above.

47. *pravayido* = Skt. *pravrajitaḥ;* cf. *[pravaya]di* = *pravrajanti* in KDhP, verse 146.

48. Apparently, *[pra]c(e*)[g](a*)[s](a*)budh[i]* = Skt. *pratyeka-sambodhim.*

49. *Gāthā* here presumably refers to a well-known verse summarizing this legend, which the scribe did not see any need to write down but simply added this reminder to insert it here at the end of the story. Such notes presumably were prompts for use when the story was to be delivered in an expanded, oral form.

2.2.6. A Unique Fragment of a Colophon

As noted above, the loss of the upper portions of all of the scrolls has probably deprived us of the colophons, which would have been of crucial value in identifying the texts and understanding the circumstances of the composition of the scrolls. But there is, fortunately, one partial exception. This is the small fragment 3B, measuring 10 × 4.5 cm, one side of which contains what is clearly part of a colophon (pl. 9). Portions of three lines of text are preserved on it, and below the last line is a blank space about 2 cm in height. The side with the colophon has been labeled as the recto, though this actually only means that it faced the inside of the roll in which it was found. Since the other side of the colophon fragment contains remnants of text in a different hand, the colophon could have been written at the end of a text at the bottom of the recto, and the other text added on to the verso at a later time. But it is also possible that the colophon was written at the top of the verso, that is, at the very end of the scroll, which then may have contained a single text written in two different hands, as was the case, for example, in the second text on fragment 4. But in view of the otherwise consistent pattern of the loss of the upper ends of the scrolls, the former alternative is probably the more likely one. Unfortunately, the remains of the unidentified text on the other side are too fragmentary to permit any conclusive judgment at this point, though further study of it and other texts may eventually clarify its contents. The colophon was rolled up together with fragments of what is almost certainly originally a different scroll (frag. 3A), and hence it seems to have been a loose piece that was put together with other small fragments for interment in the clay pot in which it was found (see 4.1).

Although too little remains of the colophon to permit any identification of the text at this point, its handwriting is not unfamiliar. It is almost certainly the same hand as that of the verse commentaries on fragments 7, 9, 13, and 18 and hence probably—though not certainly—belongs to that text, or perhaps rather to one among that group of texts.[50] Here again, it is hoped that future studies of this important subgroup within the collection will clarify the position and relationship of the colophon fragment with them.

The remaining text of the colophon reads as follows:

1. */// [p.] ///*
2. */// [tv.]a idi ṇavodaśa* ○
3. */// [mi] postaga gaṣa[e]*[51] *pacaviśadi 20 4 1 saghaśravaṣa ṣamaṇaṣa*

The lower part of one syllable preserved in the first line and the first three letters in the second line are presumably part of the end of the text proper. This is

---

50. See the descriptions of these fragments below in section 2.3.

51. There is a blank space between *ṣa* and *e* about the width of one syllable, but no trace of an original akṣara is visible, and it seems that this space was originally left blank.

followed by *idi ṇavodaśa,* "Thus [ends number] nineteen" or "Thus [ends] the nineteenth," which is presumably the label of a section—apparently the last—of that text. The third line, preserving the colophon proper, can be tentatively translated " . . . book; twenty-five (25) verses; of the monk Saṅghaśrava."

The interpretation of this colophon is facilitated by a comparison with the verse that is written at the head of the KDhP manuscript, given below according to Brough's reading and translation (1962: 119 and 177; see also xx–xxi):

budha-varmasa ṣamaṇasa
budhaṇadi-sardhavayarisa
ida dharma-padasa postaka
dharmuyaṇe likhida arañi

This manuscript of the Dharmapada, belonging to the monk Buddhavarman, pupil of Buddhanandin, has been written in the Dharmodyāna forest.

The phrase *dharma-padasa postaka,* "manuscript of the Dharmapada," in this verse suggests that the word preceding *postaga* in our colophon probably contained the name of the text. Regrettably, all that is left of it is part of the last syllable, apparently *mi,* or possibly *me* or *ge.* This could be the end of the title, though *mi* occurs most commonly in Gāndhārī as a locative ending. It is also possible, though less likely, that the syllable *mi* or *me* is the personal pronoun "my," in which case it might agree with the name *saghaśravaṣa* in the genitive; the translation would then be " . . . my book—[in] twenty-five (25) verses—the monk Saṅghaśrava."

Like our colophon, the Dharmapada verse has the name of a monk (*ṣamaṇa*) in the genitive, which Brough takes in its literal sense as indicating ownership of the manuscript. However, since the verse lacks a word in the instrumental to supply the expected agent of the participial main verb *likhida,* "was written," it seems reasonable to understand the genitive phrase as indicating that the monk Buddhavarman wrote it. This interpretation can be justified on technical grounds, since the agentive use of the genitive with participial forms in Gāndhārī is well attested, especially in the central Asian documents, where it is "almost exclusively used for expressing the agent with passives, i.e. the participle in *-taǵa*" (Burrow 1937: 58). By analogy with this, we can suspect that the phrase *saghaśravaṣa ṣamaṇaṣa* in the new colophon gives us the name of the scribe, rather than the owner, strictly speaking, of the scroll.

Finally, the phrase *gaṣa[e] pacaviśadi 20 4 1* has no parallel in the Dharmapada verse quoted above but is reminiscent of similar usages elsewhere in the KDhP manuscript. There, we find at the end of each of the vargas, or chapters, of the text (except for the first two) the letter *ga* followed by a numerical figure corresponding to the number of verses in the chapter. The letter *ga* is presumably an abbreviation for Gāndhārī *gatha* or *gaṣa* (= Skt. *gāthā*), "verse" (Senart 1998: 205), and the same word appears in the new colophon as *gaṣa*-.[52] The number twenty-five, written out both in words and in numerical symbols,[53] must represent the number of verses in the text, or perhaps rather only in its last section. The form *gaṣa[e]*, however, is problematic, since the expected form of the nominative plural feminine would be *gaṣa*, the same as the singular; a nominative feminine plural in *-e* would be difficult to explain. But the reading here is uncertain in any case, as the syllable *e* is not definite, and there may have been another syllable before it that has disappeared (see n. 51).

The sense of the passage, therefore, remains to be completely clarified, but it is nearly certain that it specifies the number of verses in the preceding text. Given the similarity of the handwriting to that of the aforementioned verse commentary texts, we probably have here the end of one such text, or a subsection of it, which contained a commentary on twenty-five verses. Whether this piece actually belongs to one of the specimens of this genre preserved elsewhere in the new collection is unknown at this point, though once again a close study of the manuscripts concerned may eventually provide an answer.

2.3. Catalog of the Fragments

This preliminary catalog is presented in order to give the reader an idea of the scope, character, and variety of the British Library Kharoṣṭhī texts and also to facilitate reference to specific fragments in this and in future studies of the collection. The fragments are listed and described according to the numbers assigned to them as explained in section 2.1.1. The sides of the manuscripts are referred to as "r" and "v" (i.e., recto and verso) respectively; the recto side, which was the original outer surface of the bark, is the inside of the scroll when it is rolled up. References to "right" and "left" (e.g.,"right margin") are made with reference to the recto.

The brief description of each fragment addresses the following points:

1. General form, condition, and degree of legibility.

2. Maximum dimensions (width and length) and number of lines. Most of the figures given here are only approximate because, more often than not, the fragments are incomplete, with ragged or even crumbled edges, and are often broken into several or many pieces, so that it is virtually impossible to give exact measurements. For similar reasons, it is in many cases impossible to give an exact count of lines in a fragment, since many lines are incomplete, overlapping, or illegible.

---

52. The word could also be read as *gadha*, since this scribe (assuming that he was the same scribe who wrote frags. 7, 9, 13, and 18) had the habit of writing *dha* and *ṣa* almost identically. In any case, the meaning would be the same.

53. This is a common practice in Kharoṣṭhī documents, followed, for example, in the dates of some inscriptions. Among the new manuscripts we also find it in the numeration of some of the avadāna collections; see the examples cited in section 2.2.4.

3. Hand(s). A brief, mostly subjective characterization of each scribal hand is provided, particularly with a view to grouping together separated fragments of the same original scrolls. (The results of this analysis are summarized in sec. 2.5.) Other than some observations here and in section 6.2, detailed paleographic and orthographic comments on each hand are not provided in this preliminary survey but will be discussed in the individual editions of separate texts as they are prepared.

4. Contents. Specific textual references are provided where confirmed or probable identifications have been made. In other cases, only brief comments as to the contents and possible genre affiliations are provided, and these should be understood as provisional. For further comments, see also the descriptions of selected texts in section 2.2.

Fragment 1, Parts 1–5 (Frames 1–5)

1. Extensive remains of a single original scroll. Some sections are more or less intact except for slight damage at the left margin. Other portions, especially the upper parts (1 and 2), are more badly deteriorated at the right and especially the left margins. On the whole, fragment 1 is the best-preserved text in the entire collection.

2. 14.5 × 154.8 cm; 130 lines on r, 79 on v.

3. First hand (r, from beginning to part 5, line 29): Medium sized, upright, thick; same hand (no. 1 in sec. 2.5) as in fragments 12 + 14 (first hand) and 16 + 25 (first hand).

Second hand (r, part 5, lines 30–34, and all of v): Large, flowing hand with big spaces between syllables and lines. Same hand (no. 2) as in fragments 2, 3 (second hand), 4 (third), 12–14 (second), 16 + 25 (second), and 21 (first).

4. First text (first hand): Portions of the Anavatapta-gāthā. See section 2.2.3.

Second text (second hand): A collection of avadānas not identified elsewhere. The separate stories are numbered in words and numbers; for instance, the sixth one is labeled *ṣa 4 1 1* (part 3, v, line 45).

Fragment 2 (Frame 6)

1. Small fragment, intact at right edge, but left side lost. The intact portion is clearly legible.

2. 11.2 × 23 cm; 14 lines on r, 13 on v.

3. The large, flowing hand (no. 2) of fragments 1 (second hand), 3 (second), etc.

4. Apparently a collection of avadānas, one of which concerns the mahākṣatrapa Jihonika (*jihonige mahakṣatra(*pe)*, r, line 2; see sec. 7.1.1).

Fragment 3 (Frame 7)

Fragment 3 appears to be a composite, containing small fragments of what were originally two separate scrolls. These are subdivided here into subfragments 3A and 3B.

Subfragment 3A

1. Comprises ten small pieces of (probably) a single manuscript. The larger pieces are intact at the left edge. The smallest fragments contain as little as one akṣara. The intact portions are mostly legible.

2. The largest piece measures 10.5 × 8.9 cm and contains 6 lines on each side. The next largest is 7 × 6 cm, with 3 lines on each side.

3. First hand (only on r of one piece, measuring 8 × 5.2 cm and containing 4 lines, and of another small chip, 2.2 × 0.7 cm, containing parts of 5 akṣaras): A thin, rounded hand (no. 3), apparently the same as that of fragment 8. This part of the text is badly faded and difficult to read.

Second hand (r of the rest of the fragments and v of all of them): The large, flowing hand (no. 2) of fragments 1, 2, etc.

4. The contents of the small remainders of the first text (in the first hand) are undetermined. The larger portion, in the second hand, apparently contains a narrative text of the avadāna class. The verso of the largest piece contains the story of a potter (*kulala*), which is apparently a variant version of the story of Ājñātakauṇḍinya's previous life that also appears in fragments 16 + 25 (see 2.2.4).

Subfragment 3B

1. One small piece and five minuscule chips with a few akṣaras that appear to belong to the same text.[54] The text is mostly legible.

2. 10 × 4.5 cm; 3 lines on r, 4 on v.

3. First hand (r): A small, rounded, precisely written hand. Apparently the same hand (no. 4) as that of fragments 7, 9, 13, and 18.

Second hand (v): A small, thick, upright hand, not noticed elsewhere.

4. The text on the recto (perhaps properly v) is part of a colophon (see 2.2.6). Presumably it belongs to the same or a similar type of commentary text as those in fragments 7, etc., which are written in the same hand. The text on the verso is undetermined, perhaps also a commentatorial text.

Fragment 4, Parts 1–7 (Frames 8–14)

1. Extensive portion of a large scroll containing, apparently, two different texts in three hands. The condition varies; many large sections, especially on the recto,

54. A sixth tiny fragment, containing two akṣaras on the verso, seems, to judge from the handwriting, to be part of fragment 5B (the Rhinoceros Horn Sūtra text).

are fairly legible, though fragmentary. The upper parts (1–5), however, are badly worn at the edges, and part 1 is actually a group of ten small pieces, five of which are flipped over from their proper orientation (i.e., the r text appears on the v side and vice versa).

2. The maximum width of the best-preserved portions, for example, in part 6, which appear to be only slightly damaged at each edge, is about 16.3 cm. The total length of the surviving portions of the scroll is approximately 213.4 cm, with about 204 lines on r and 144 on v.

3. First hand (r, beginning to part 6, line 16): A distinctive squared, upright, bold hand, not seen elsewhere.

Second hand (from part 6, r, line 16 to part 6, v, line 20): A distinctive thin, slanting, vertically elongated hand, also not seen elsewhere.

Third hand (from part 6, v, line 20 through the rest of v): The large, flowing hand (no. 2) of fragments 1, 2, etc.

4. First text (first hand): A commentary on a set of verses which correspond to verses found in the Dhammapada and other Pali texts but which apparently are part of a different and as yet unidentified compilation (see 2.2.2). This seems to be a work of the same genre, but not the same text, as the ones represented in fragments 7, 9, etc.

Second text (second and third hands): Another avadāna collection. Separate sections or stories are numbered in both words and numerical signs; for instance, *du[ve] 2* (part 6, r, line 39), *pac[o] 4 1* (part 6, v, line 20), and *ṇavo 4 4 1* (part 4, v, line 8). There seem to have been at least eighteen stories in the surviving portions (see 2.2.4). Though written in two different hands, the collection seems to be continuous, with the first five stories in the second hand and the rest in the third.

Fragment 5 (Frame 15)

Fragment 5, like fragment 3, is a composite, containing parts of what were evidently three originally separate scrolls, labeled here as subfragments 5A, 5B, and 5C.

Subfragment 5A

1. Small fragment of the right side of a scroll. Intact at the right margin and mostly legible. The fragment is mounted in frame 15 together with fragments 5B and 5C and partly overlaps the former, but it is evidently originally part of a different scroll. However, it might also be the remnant of a separate text which was written on the same scroll as 5B, since both of these, unlike most of the other scrolls, are uninscribed on the verso.
2. 8.2 × 3.5 cm; 4 lines on r; v is blank.
3. Thick, medium-sized hand.
4. Contents unidentified; possibly didactic verses.

Subfragment 5B

1. Badly fragmented section of a scroll which has been divided vertically, probably due to having been bound with a string which cut through the middle portion or to having been folded in half lengthwise while rolled up (see 5.3.1 and 5.3.3). The two resulting vertical sections are reversed from their proper place (see 4.1). The fragment is broken into many smaller pieces, which were jumbled together in the roll in a more or less random order, with several of them placed upside down. The surviving portions are mostly legible, though in many places only with difficulty.

2. 22 × 38.2 cm; 43 lines on r; v is blank.

3. Small, thick hand, with a pronounced diagonal slope toward the lower left.

4. Gāndhārī version of the Rhinoceros Horn Sūtra, generally similar to the Pali Khaggavisāṇa-sutta (see 2.2.3). The verses are written one to each line, with small spaces between each pāda (quarter-verse).

Subfragment 5C

1. Small section of an unusually wide scroll which has been damaged but not completely cut through at the center. The piece is mounted together with fragments 5A and 5B but is evidently part of an originally different text and scroll. The text is fragmentary and only partially legible.

2. 24 × 13 cm; 14 lines on r, 7 on v.

3. Small, carefully drawn hand.

4. A stotra, containing verses in vasantatilakā and other meters in praise of the Buddha (see 2.2.5).

Fragment 6 (Frame 16)

1. A small and exceptionally narrow scroll, apparently complete at the margins. The ink is faded and often only partly legible.

2. 5.5 × 24.6 cm; 25 lines on r, 22 on v.

3. Small, carefully written but somewhat cursive hand (in Brāhmī).

4. Fragment of a medical text in Sanskrit language and Brāhmī script of about the Kuṣāṇa period. The only text in the collection not in Gāndhārī/Kharoṣṭhī (see 2.2.5).

Fragment 7 (Frame 17)

1. Two small pieces, very badly deteriorated, mostly illegible.

2. 11 × 6 cm (combined size); 7 lines each on r and v.

3. Small, rounded, precise hand, apparently the hand (no. 4) also seen in fragments 3B (first hand), 9, 13, and 18.

4. Apparently part of the same text or class of texts (and possibly from

the same scroll) as one or more of fragments 3B, 9, 13, and 18; see fragment 9 for description of contents.

Fragment 8 (Frame 18)

1. Small fragment, fair to poor condition. The recto is mostly legible, verso only partially. The ink is faded.

2. 10 × 9.7 cm; 8 lines on r, 11 on v.

3. Thin, rounded hand, apparently the same (no. 3) as that of fragment 3A (first hand).

4. Contents undetermined.

Fragment 9, Parts 1–3 (Frames 19–21)

1. Large fragment in relatively good condition except for part 1, which is in three pieces and badly broken at both edges. The rest is mostly intact for the entire width. The recto is clearly legible, verso somewhat less so.

2. 14 × 102 cm; 124 lines on r, 120 on v.

3. Small, rounded, precise hand (no. 4); same as that of fragments 3B (first hand), 7, etc.

4. Commentary on an as yet unidentified collection of verses. The verses are partially cited, followed by the phrase *sutro tatra nideśo* and then by the commentary. Most of the verses correspond to ones found in Pali compilations such as Suttanipāta, Udāna, Dhammapada, and Theragāthā (see 2.2.2). This fragment is evidently part of the same text, and possibly but not necessarily of the same original scroll, as some or all of fragments 3B, 7, 13, and 18.

Fragment 10 (Frame 22)

1. Medium-sized fragment, in comparatively good condition. The upper portion is much damaged at both edges, while the lower part is mostly intact. The recto is mostly legible, verso somewhat less so.

2. 10 × 45 cm; 43 lines on r, 38 on v.

3. Small, precise hand, similar to but not the same as that of fragments 3B, 7, etc. Spaces between lines are wider than usual.

4. Unidentified, apparently a scholastic commentary.

Fragment 11 (Frame 23)

1. Small piece, fragmentary and very difficult to read. The verso seems to be blank.

2. 11 × 22 cm; about 18 lines.

3. Tall, thin hand. Possibly the same hand (no. 13), and hence part of the same scroll and/or text, as fragments 21 and 24.

4. Undetermined; possibly a verse text.

Fragment 12, Parts 1–2 (Frames 24–5)

1. Fairly large fragment in reasonably good condition. The upper part (including all of part 1) is very fragmentary, with portions lost at both edges and many small loose pieces, mostly displaced and out of order. The rest of the text, including most of part 2, is intact at the right margin, though the left side is incomplete and damaged throughout. Fragment 14 is a continuation of the same original scroll.

2. 16.5 × 57 cm; 55 lines on r, 22 on v.

3. First hand (r): Medium-sized, thick, upright hand (no. 1), same as that of fragments 1 (first hand), 14 (first), and 16 + 25 (first).

Second hand (v): Large, flowing hand (no. 2), same as that of fragments 1 (second hand), 2, etc.

4. First text (r, first hand): Sūtra text corresponding in part to Pali Aṅguttara-nikāya, Catukka-nipāta, 36 and 14 (see 2.2.1).

Second text (v, second hand): A series of avadānas, including, apparently, the avadānas of Puniga and Sārthadāsa.

Fragment 13, Parts 1–2 (Frames 26–7)

1. Large section of text in relatively good condition. The left edge is mostly intact, but the right side is damaged. The recto is mostly legible, the verso somewhat less so.

2. 14 × 62.5 cm; 71 lines on r, 65 on v.

3. First hand (r and first 20 lines of v): The same small, rounded hand (no. 4) as that of fragments 3B (first hand), 7, 9, and 18.

Second hand (rest of v): A superficially similar hand, but on close analysis evidently the work of a different scribe, since the forms of certain letters, such as *a* and *ṇa/na,* are consistently different from those of the first hand.

4. First text (first hand): Part of the same or a similar commentary text, though not necessarily of the same scroll, as fragments 3B, 7, 9, and 18.

Second text (second hand): Unidentified; apparently not part of the same text as the preceding.

Fragment 14 (Frame 28)

1. The contiguous portion of the same scroll as fragment 12, in good condition except that the left edge is crumbled away. Mostly legible.

2. 14.5 × 27.7 cm; 24 lines on r, 15 on v.

3. First hand (r, lines 1–20): Medium-sized, thick hand (no. 1), same as that of fragments 1 (first hand), 12 (first), and 16 + 25 (first).

Second hand (r, lines 21–4 and all of v): Large, flowing hand (no. 2), same as that of fragments 1 (second), 2, etc.

4. Same texts described under fragment 12. Fragment 14 seems to have followed directly after 12, with no loss of text between them.

Fragment 15, Parts 1–4 (Frames 29–32)

1. Extensive section of a single scroll. Generally in good condition, except for the upper section (part 1 and upper portion of part 2), which is broken into smaller pieces with substantial losses at both edges. The rest of the text is mostly intact except for slight losses at both edges and damage resulting from crushing of the scroll while it was rolled up. This caused the scroll to separate, when unrolled, into sections of about 4 cm each in height, and at the juncture of each section a part of a line is usually lost.

The recto is generally legible except for the damaged portions, especially on part 1. The verso is somewhat less clear but also largely legible.

2. 17.5 × 115 cm; 180 lines on r, 185 on v.

3. The entire text is in a very distinctive hand, somewhat cursive and extremely small, the characters measuring about 0.2–0.5 cm in height.

4. Saṅgīti-sūtra with a previously unknown commentary (see 2.2.1).

Fragment 16 (Frame 33)

1. A narrow, vertical strip of a scroll, which is the right-hand side of the same scroll whose left half is fragment 25. Evidently the original scroll was split in half vertically by a binding string or by lengthwise folding (cf. frag. 5B). The upper portion is very fragmentary, while the lower section is mostly intact. The recto is clearly legible in most places, while the verso is fairly clear in the lower section but faded and difficult to read in the upper part.

2. 10.5 × 40.5 cm; 33 lines on r, 26 on v.

3. First hand (r, lines 1–15): The medium-sized, thick hand (no. 1) of fragments 1 (first hand) and 12 + 14 (first).

Second hand (r, lines 15–33, and all of v): The large, flowing hand (no. 2) of fragments 1 (second hand), 2, etc.

4. First text (first hand): Concluding part of a text corresponding closely to the end of the Bhikhu-varga (verses 78–90) of the KDhP (see 2.2.3).

Second text (second hand): A series of stories of the previous births (*provayoge* = Skt. *pūrvayogaḥ*) of the Bodhisattva (i.e., Śākyamuni), Ājñāta-kauṇḍinya, Ānanda, etc. (see 2.2.4).

Fragment 17 (Frame 34)

1. Small piece in poor condition and very fragmentary. Surviving portions of the text are mostly legible.

2. 11 × 20.5 cm; 19 lines each side.

3. Thick, upright hand.

4. Unidentified text, probably a scholastic or abhidharma text; mentions *paḍicasamupada* = *pratītya-samutpāda* in r, line 2.

Fragment 18 (Frame 35)

1. Small fragment, evidently part of the same text and possibly of the same scroll as fragments 3B, 7, 9, and 13. Condition generally fair; broken into small sections, with losses at both edges and between horizontal portions. Surviving portions of the recto are generally legible, the verso partly so.

2. 12.5 × 17.5 cm; 28 lines on r, 31 on v.

3. Small, rounded hand (no. 4) of fragments 3B, 7, etc.

4. Part of the same or a similar commentary text, though not necessarily of the same scroll, as fragments 3B, 7, etc.

Fragment 19 (Frame 36)

1. Medium-sized fragment, in poor condition. The piece is very badly fragmented and the surface decayed. The recto and lower part of the verso are partly legible in places, but the upper part of the verso is mostly illegible.

2. 13.3 × 44.5 cm; about 37 lines each side.

3. Large, thick, upright hand.

4. Undetermined.

Fragment 20, Parts 1–5 (Frames 37–41)

1. Long section of a scroll, in generally fair condition. The upper and lower sections are fragmentary, but the middle is partly intact, with small portions of each edge lost. Generally fairly legible, but some portions, especially the upper part of the verso, are illegible.

2. 19.7 × 137 cm; about 135 lines each side.

3. Small, neat hand with a distinctive spidery appearance.

4. Unidentified text, probably commentatorial or scholastic. Apparently part of the same text, and possibly of the same scroll, as fragment 23.

Fragment 21 (Frame 42)

1. Medium-sized section of a scroll in poor condition, fragmentary and illegible in many places, especially on the recto.

2. 16.8 × 26 cm; about 9 lines on r, 14 on v.

3. First hand (r): The distinctive large, flowing hand no. 2. Only a few syllables are legible.

Second hand (v): Tall, thin hand, resembling that of fragments 11 and 24 (hand no. 13). All three may be fragments of the same scroll.

4. Undetermined; see fragment 11. This scroll was apparently rolled up back-to-front. What appears as the verso, that is, the outside of the scroll as it was

rolled, was probably the original recto, since the tall, thin hand on it appears on the recto of the apparently matching pieces 11 and 24, whose versos are blank. The large hand (no. 2) on the nominal recto typically appears in the other scrolls on the verso, where it was apparently added to original texts with a blank verso. Possibly, a short text was added that covered only part of the verso of a single scroll, of which fragments 11, 21, and 24 are the remains.

Fragment 22, Parts 1–2 (Frames 43–4)

1. Several small pieces of a scroll in poor condition, very fragmented and crumbling. The scroll was partially broken down the middle, presumably by a binding cord or by folding. The text is only sporadically legible.
2. 15.5 × 28 cm; about 20 lines on each side.
3. Thin, upright hand.
4. Undetermined. Possibly part of the same scroll and/or text as fragment 27.

Fragment 23, Parts 1–2 (Frames 45–6)

1. Very fragmentary remains of a scroll, mostly broken into small pieces. The recto is partially legible, the verso only sporadically.
2. 18.5 × 56.5 cm; approximately 53 lines on r, 42 on v.
3. Small, neat, and precise hand, same as that of fragment 20.
4. Apparently part of the same scroll and/or text as fragment 20.

Fragment 24 (Frame 47)

1. Small fragment, very faded and only partially legible.
2. 11.5 × 16 cm; 10 lines on r; v is apparently blank.
3. Tall, thin hand, apparently same as that of fragments 11 and 21.
4. Undetermined; see fragment 11.

Fragment 25 (Frame 48)

1. Narrow vertical strip of a scroll, in good condition. The recto is legible, verso mostly so. On the lower portion, the original left margin is mostly intact. This is the left-hand side of the same scroll whose right side is preserved as fragment 16.
2. 9.7 × 29.3 cm; 24 lines on r, 19 on v.
3. First hand (r, lines 1–6): The medium-sized, thick hand (no. 1) of fragment 1 (first hand), etc.

   Second hand (r, lines 7–24, and all of v): The large, flowing hand (no. 2) of fragment 1 (second hand), etc.
4. See fragment 16.

Fragment 26, Parts 1–2 (Frames 49–50)

1. Long, thin section of a scroll, with the original right-hand margin intact in some places near the middle but otherwise fragmentary and incomplete. Fair condition. The intact portions of the recto are mostly legible, the verso partly so.
2. 8.2 × 64.5 cm; 49 lines on r, 36 on v.
3. A very distinctive large, angular, thick hand, skillfully written with a calligraphic effect.
4. Apparently a sūtra or some other text, not yet identified, on meditative states (see 2.2.1). Evidently part of the same scroll as fragment 29.

Fragment 27 (Frame 50)

1. Small fragment in poor condition. Only a few small portions are legible.
2. 6.2 × 12.5 cm; about 12 lines each side.
3. Thin, upright hand.
4. Undetermined. Possibly part of same scroll and/or text as fragment 22.

Fragment 28, Parts 1–2 (Frames 51–2)

1. Substantial portion of a relatively well preserved scroll. On the middle and lower sections, both margins are nearly intact. Mostly legible, especially the middle and lower portions.
2. 12.0 × 65 cm; 83 lines on r, 84 on v.
3. Small, neat hand, with closely spaced lines.
4. An unidentified abhidharma text (see 2.2.2).

Fragment 29, Parts 1–3 (Frames 53–5)

1. Large section of a scroll, in fairly good condition. On the lower portion the right margin is intact, but the left edge is lost throughout. Portions near the right margin are generally legible, but much of the center and left side, where preserved at all, is badly decayed and difficult or impossible to read.
2. 13.8 × 127.7 cm; 87 lines on r, 71 on v.
3. Large, angular, calligraphic hand, same as that of fragment 26.
4. Evidently part of same scroll as fragment 26.

Debris

In addition to the manuscripts preserved under glass, there are thirteen small boxes containing loose bits of bark that were collected from each of the glass jars in which the manuscripts were brought to the British Library. Most of these are minuscule pieces without text, but some slightly larger pieces with one or more legible akṣaras are also present. In some cases as many as four or five syllables of a single line are preserved, and in a few others, parts of two different lines are visible. For some of the manuscripts, especially nos. 5B and 15, there is a significant amount of inscribed debris. Thus it may eventually be possible, in the course of detailed studies of the individual texts, to locate the original position of some of these fragments in the manuscripts and thereby put them to use in textual reconstruction.

In addition, there is an extra glass frame (no. 56), labeled "Box 14," containing twenty-six pieces of miscellaneous debris, of which eighteen have at least some traces of writing, in some cases as many as three or four akṣaras. Here too, it may eventually become possible to identify at least some of these fragments with particular scrolls.

2.4. Summary of Original Scrolls or Scroll Sets

In this summary an attempt is made, in a provisional way, to group together the fragments that may originally have been part of the same scroll or set of scrolls. There are, however, several uncertainties involved. In some cases, particularly in connection with small fragments or ones in very poor condition, it is difficult to determine such relationships with confidence (e.g., in the case of no. 12; see below). In other cases, where we find fragments that are written in the same hand and contain similar texts, it often cannot yet be determined whether they are parts of the same original scroll, of separate scrolls constituting "volumes" of a longer text, or even of separate copies of the same or similar texts (e.g., no. 9). All such problematic cases are marked below with a question mark. The total number of original scrolls and scroll sets arrived at here, twenty-one, is the minimum possible, and it is likely that the actual number is somewhat higher because of the uncertainty of several of these associations (see 2.1.1). Conversely, it is also possible that in the course of further study, other linkages may be established between fragments.

Where known, the name of the text or its genre type is also indicated, but some of these identifications are also provisional.

1. Fragment 1: Anavatapta-gāthā plus avadāna collection
2. Fragment 2: Avadāna collection
3. Fragment 3A: Avadāna collection, plus another unidentified text
4. Fragments 3B + 7 + 9 + 13 + 18 (these may actually be parts of the same text but not of the same scroll; that is, they may compose parts of a single long text that was written out on two or more scrolls): Commentary on a verse collection
5. Fragment 4: Verse commentary text plus avadāna collection
6. Fragment 5A: Didactic verses?
7. Fragment 5B: Rhinoceros Horn Sūtra
8. Fragment 5C: Stotra
9. Fragment 6: Medical text in Sanskrit/Brāhmī
10. Fragment 8
11. Fragment 10

12. Fragments 11 + 21 + 24 (?)
13. Fragments 12 + 14: Sūtra text partially parallel to Aṅguttara-nikāya
14. Fragment 15: Saṅgīti-sūtra and commentary
15. Fragments 16 + 25: Dharmapada plus avadāna collection
16. Fragment 17
17. Fragment 19
18. Fragments 20 + 23
19. Fragments 22 + 27 (?)
20. Fragments 26 + 29: Sūtra text?
21. Fragment 28: Abhidharma text

2.5. Summary of Scribal Hands

This list summarizes, again in a preliminary manner, the different scribal hands that appear in the entire collection and the collocations of fragments written by the same scribe. Here too there are several uncertainties, particularly in connection with small or poorly preserved fragments, for which it can be difficult to conclusively identify different hands. Such uncertain cases are indicated by a question mark.

It is not yet possible to determine with certainty who these scribes were. Some vinaya and related texts—for instance, the Bhaiṣajyavastu of the Mūlasarvāstivāda-vinaya from Gilgit (Dutt 1947: 281)—refer to professional scribes (*kāyastha*) who became monks and were permitted, contrary to the general rule, to keep their professional equipment (*bhāṇḍa*). Other related texts, however, such as the Gilgit Cīvaravastu (Dutt 1942: 143, 146), refer to the costs involved in copying manuscripts, evidently suggesting that the work was hired out to persons other than monks. But I would consider it a priori more likely that the British Library scrolls represent the work of monks who were, by specialization, scribes or scholars (or both).

1. Bold, thick, upright hand: fragments 1 (first hand), 12 + 14 (first), 16 + 25 (first)[55]
2. Large, flowing hand with big spaces between letters: 1 (second hand), 2, 3A (second), 4 (third), 12 + 14 (second), 16 + 25 (second), 21 (first)
3. Thin, rounded hand: 3A (first hand), 8
4. Small, rounded, precise hand: 3B (first hand), 7, 9, 13 (first), 18
5. Thick, upright hand: 3B (second hand)
6. Square, upright, bold hand: 4 (first hand)
7. Thin, elongated, slanting hand: 4 (second hand)
8. Thick, medium-sized hand: 5A

55. See figure 12 for a chart showing Kharoṣṭhī script as written by this scribe.

9. Small, thick, diagonally slanted hand: 5B
10. Small, thin hand: 5C
11. Small, slightly cursive hand (Brāhmī script): 6
12. Small, precise hand with unusually large spaces between lines: 10
13. Tall, thin hand: 11, 21 (second hand), 24 (?)
14. Hand similar to, but apparently distinct from, hand 4: 13 (second hand)
15. Very small, cursive hand: 15
16. Thick, upright hand: 17
17. Large, thick, upright hand: 19
18. Small, neat, spidery hand: 20, 23
19. Thin, upright hand: 22, 27 (?)
20. Large, angular, thick, calligraphic hand: 26 + 29
21. Small, neat hand: 28

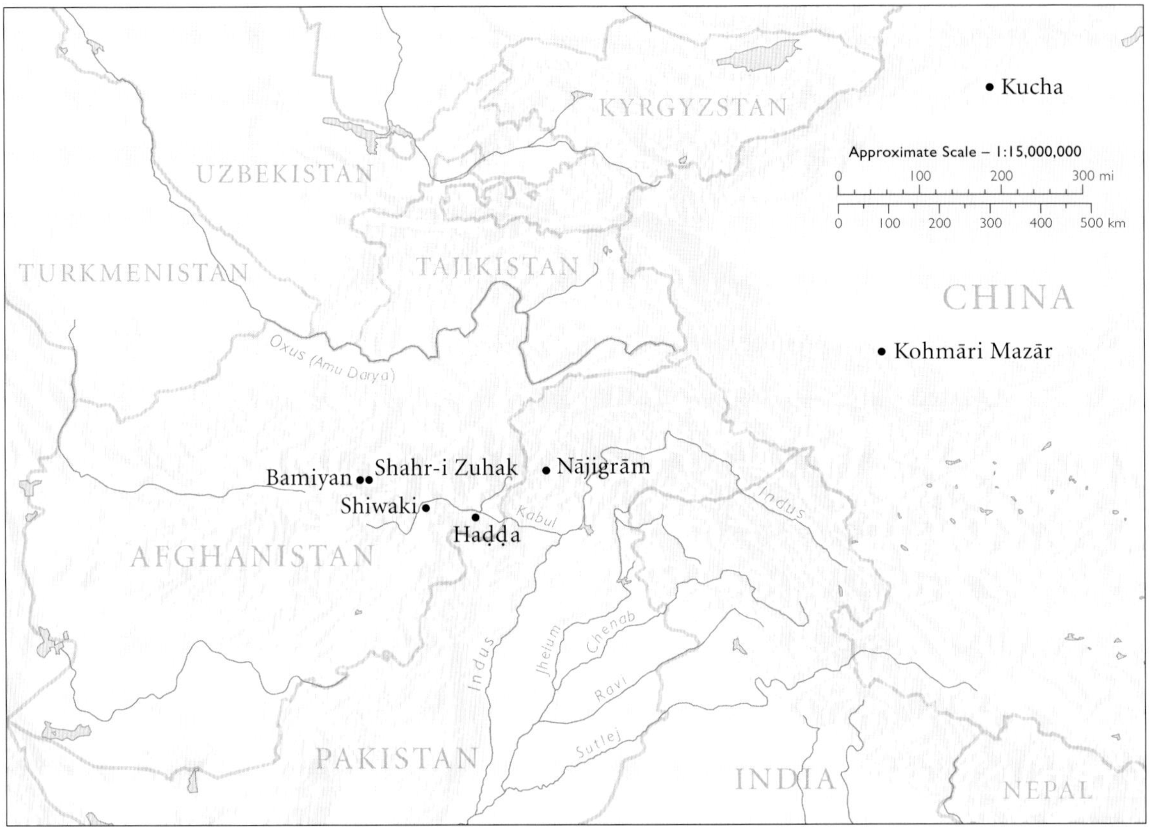

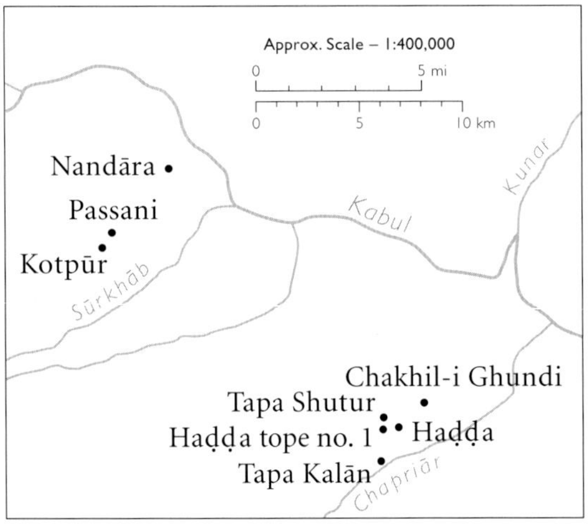

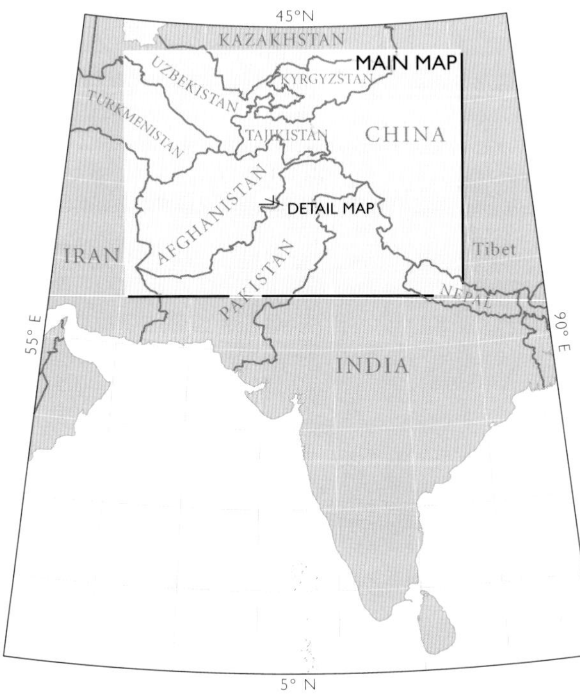

Map 2. Findspots of Kharoṣṭhī manuscripts

Chapter 3

Previous Discoveries of Kharoṣṭhī Manuscripts

Although only one manuscript in the Gāndhārī language and Kharoṣṭhī script—namely, the "Gāndhārī Dharmapada" scroll found near Khotan (KDhP)[1]—has been published until now, a survey of various sources, published and unpublished, reveals that in fact considerable numbers of such texts have been discovered since the early nineteenth century in various parts of Afghanistan, Pakistan, and Chinese central Asia (see map 2). Thus although Kharoṣṭhī manuscripts are scarce in comparison to better-known and better-documented later materials in Brāhmī and Brāhmī-derived scripts, they are by no means as rare as has been generally believed. This impression, however, is easy to understand, since, other than the KDhP, none of these Kharoṣṭhī manuscripts have been properly studied, reproduced, or published, and many or most of them seem to have been lost or destroyed. Moreover, the circumstances of the finds of Kharoṣṭhī manuscripts, including the KDhP, have for the most part not been properly documented.

The apparent—but illusory—uniqueness of the KDhP text has led scholars to question whether it could be taken to imply the existence of a larger body of Buddhist texts that had been more or less systematically translated into Gāndhārī, that is, of what has been referred to in this context as "the Gāndhārī canon"; or whether, on the contrary, it was an anomalous case of one particularly popular text being rendered into the local language on the whim of some individual. In general, scholarly opinion has tended to be cautiously inclined toward the former opinion, as represented, for example, by the authoritative comments of John Brough:

> There are tolerably good grounds for considering that the mere existence of this one text does allow the inference—indeed almost compels it—that there

1. I have chosen to refer in this book to this manuscript as the "Khotan Dharmapada," rather than the "Gāndhārī Dharmapada," as it is usually known after the title of Brough's definitive edition. I do so in order to avoid confusion with the fragmentary remains in the new collection of another manuscript of what is essentially the same Gāndhārī version of the Dharmapada (frags. 16 + 25), since the term "Gāndhārī Dharmapada" is now no longer a distinctive one. In earlier publications, the Khotan text was referred to by various names, such as "ms. Dutreuil de Rhins" and "Prakrit Dhammapada."

> did exist a more extensive canonical collection of texts belonging to the same school. It seems to me very difficult to believe that a group of monks might have possessed a Dharmapada . . . without at the same time possessing at least some stock of Sūtra and Vinaya works.
>
> I should therefore not hesitate to say that the existence of this Dharmapada does imply the existence of a canon of which it formed a part. (1962: 43)

As the material presented in this chapter will show, even before the discovery of the new British Library collection the large number of previously known Gāndhārī manuscripts could have produced more confidence in the hypothesis of a "Gāndhārī canon," had they been properly brought to the attention of scholars. In any case, the new collection shows beyond any doubt that there was a large—perhaps very large—body of Buddhist texts that were translated into, and in some cases probably also originally composed in, Gāndhārī. In this sense, then, we can say that the Gāndhārī canon hypothesis has already been confirmed, although it must be stipulated that this is only true with reference to a loose sense of the word "canon" as referring to a sizable body of scriptural texts in a single language.[2]

3.1. Kharoṣṭhī Manuscripts Found in Chinese Central Asia

3.1.1. The Khotan Dharmapada ("Gāndhārī Dharmapada")

The KDhP first came to light in 1892 when part of it was acquired by J.-L. Dutreuil de Rhins and F. Grenard in Khotan. Another portion was acquired by N. Th. Petrovskii at about the same time, but the missing third fragment of the manuscript has never been located. John Brough's definitive study and edition of this text has shown that in the original intact form in which it was apparently discovered (it seems to have been torn into fragments by its unknown modern discoverer) it was a single birch bark scroll, approximately 20 cm wide and 5 m long. According to information reported by Grenard (1898: 142), the manuscript was found in a cave at Kohmārī Mazār, twenty-one kilometers southwest of Khotan, which has been identified with the ancient Gośṛṅga- or Gośīrṣa-vihāra mentioned by Hsüan-tsang and other Buddhist writers. But this reported provenance is doubtful, especially as Aurel Stein visited the cave in question in 1900 and found it "distinctly improbable that the antiquarian relics now in Paris and St. Petersburg [i.e., the KDhP manuscript] were actually discovered within the cave" (Stein 1907: 188; see also Brough 1962: 2 and n. 3). The remarkably good condition of the scroll, as compared to all other specimens of Kharoṣṭhī manuscripts, including the new ones that are the subject of this volume, indicates that it must have been preserved in some secure and airtight

2. Some further comments on the complex problem of precisely what kind of "canon," or perhaps rather protocanonical collection, the British Library texts actually represent will be offered in section 8.1.

container. This container might have been the "bowl of well-finished pottery" (Stein 1907: 188) which was said to have been found "next to the manuscript" ("à côté du manuscrit"; Grenard 1898: 143), since, as will be seen below, several other manuscripts of this and similar types have been found inside pottery vessels. Since the description of the circumstances of the find was based on unreliable secondhand reports, it seems more likely that the manuscript was actually inside, rather than "next to," the pot with which it was allegedly found, for if it had lain exposed over the centuries, it could hardly have remained in such excellent condition.

3.1.2. Other Kharoṣṭhī Manuscripts from Chinese Central Asia

According to M. I. Vorob'eva-Desjatovskaja, the S. F. Oldenburg Collection in the Institute of Oriental Studies of the Russian Academy of Sciences in St. Petersburg includes "[a] small fragment of palm leaf bearing a text in the Kharoṣṭhī script in Gandhārī, and evidently an excerpt from the Hinayana version of the *Mahāparinirvāṇa* sutra" (in Litvinsky 1996: 435). The findspot of this important fragment, as yet unpublished, is unknown, but it may be presumed to have come, like the other texts in the Oldenburg Collection, from Chinese central Asia.

Numerous other fragments of Kharoṣṭhī manuscripts, mostly as yet unpublished and little understood, have been found in various places in Chinese central Asia. Among these is an unpublished fragment of an unidentified text in Sanskrit written in Kharoṣṭhī on palm leaf, which was found in the region of Kucha and is now in the Bibliothèque Nationale, Paris. Some specimens of texts written on slips of wood in what appears to be a late variant or derivative of Kharoṣṭhī script are illustrated in Filliozat 1958: pl. VII. A small fragment of a paper manuscript with a text in Kharoṣṭhī is described and illustrated, with a tentative reading by E. J. Rapson, in Conrady 1920: 140, 191, and pl. 38 (no. 36). Further references to central Asian Kharoṣṭhī manuscripts are provided by Lin (forthcoming).

3.2. Kharoṣṭhī Manuscripts Found in Afghanistan

3.2.1. Kharoṣṭhī Manuscripts from Haḍḍa and Other Sites around Jalalabad and Kabul

Several specimens of fragmentary birch bark manuscripts in Kharoṣṭhī script were discovered in eastern Afghanistan as early as 1834 by the explorer Charles Masson, as described in his "Memoir on the Topes and Sepulchral Monuments of Afghanistan" (chap. 2, pp. 55–118, of Wilson 1841). Masson reported that he found in reliquaries and other containers from several sites in the region of Jalalabad "twists of tuz-leaves, inscribed internally with characters" (Wilson 1841: 59–60). Here Wilson explained in an editorial note that "[i]t seems likely that what Mr. Masson denominates 'tuz-leaves' is the inner bark of the bhurj or birch tree, which was very commonly used for writing upon by the Hindus in early times" (1841: 60 n. 1; see also 41–2). Masson added that "it is peculiarly unfortunate that they have become so decayed as to have crumbled away, or to do so when handled. In one or two instances only have we obtained twists in better preservation, their leaf being of coarser texture, and consequently more durable than the finer specimens generally employed. The characters on these leaves are invariably those found on the native legends of our Bactrian and Indo-Scythic coins" (i.e., Kharoṣṭhī) (p. 60). From his sketchy descriptions, it is difficult to be sure of the exact nature of Masson's "twists," but I consider it most likely that they are manuscripts in scroll form, similar to the ones that are the main subject of this book, as opposed to, for example, smaller amulet-type texts on birch bark of the type discussed in section 4.5.2.

The first of the birch bark texts described by Masson was found by him in the relic chamber of tope (i.e., stūpa) no. 1 at Nandāra, where he discovered "fragments of tuz-leaves, . . . completely pulverized, but which clearly had been originally formed into a twist, and bound with thread. These contained Bactro-Pali [i.e., Kharoṣṭhī] characters, but the state in which the faithless [*sic*] record was found rendered it impossible to do any thing with them, even to copy them" (Wilson 1841: 84). Interestingly, these manuscript fragments were found in the relic chamber together with "a box of bark of tree, enveloped with tuz-leaves, formed into a twist at the top, and bound with a thread. These originally fragile materials had become so decayed as to crumble on being touched" (p. 83; illustrated in Wilson's pl. IX, between pp. 118 and 119).[3]

Masson also mentions, among the relics he found in tumulus[4] no. 2 near the "topes" of Passani, a human skull, a large steatite vase divided into five compartments, and "a twist of coarse tuz-leaf inscribed with Bactro-Pali characters" (Wilson 1841: 94). Similarly, he found inside a steatite vase in the nearby tope no. 1 at Hidda (= Haḍḍa) "a twist of tuz-leaf . . . inscribed with Bactro-Pali characters, but I fear it is too much to expect that it could be unrolled and deciphered" (p. 106). In tope no. 2 at the same site, Masson also found "the fragments of a casket of bark of tree" (p. 106), presumably similar to the one he found at Nandāra, as quoted above.

At Hidda tope no. 13 Masson discovered, inside a "small earthen jar," "a stone wrapped in tuz-leaves" (Wilson 1841: 111), though he does not refer to any inscription on them.[5] Similar examples of stone wrapped in bark, but again evidently

3. Masson also refers to "a box of bark of tree" (in Wilson 1941: 76), presumably a similar object, found by J. M. Honigberger at Bīmārān tope no. 5.

4. According to Simpson (1881: 189), "[Masson] made a distinction between topes and tumuli, which my experience leads me to reject." Simpson felt that what Masson called "tumuli" were simply decayed "topes." Some of Masson's comments—for instance, "[t]opes are always accompanied by inferior structures, which may be called tumuli. . . . no tope, however remotely situated, is without its dependent tumulus" (in Wilson 1841: 58)—suggest that at least some of his "tumuli" are actually what were later referred to as "votive stūpas," that is, the small subsidiary stūpas that usually surround a large one

5. Although this is not very clear in his report, the "Bactro-Pali inscription, written with a pen," that Masson refers to in the next sentence is evidently the inscription on the earthen jar itself; this is the "Hidda inscription of the year 28" published in Konow 1929: 157–8 and Konow 1935–6.

uninscribed, were noticed by Masson inside Hidda tope no. 8, where he found "a huge boulder, covered with tuz-leaves, which I carefully examined, but found no characters upon them" (p. 107), and at tumulus no. 7 of Passani, where he found "a large stone covered with layers of plain tuz leaves, or perhaps the smooth internal bark of some tree" (p. 95).

In figure 11 of plate III in Wilson 1841 (between pp. 53 and 54) is illustrated "[a] piece of birch-bark, with characters, such as has been found in several topes, but in fragments too small and brittle to offer any continuous and legible inscription" (p. 53). No information is provided as to its exact provenance; presumably it is part of one of the "twists of tuz-leaves" referred to above, but there is no way to know which one. In the sketch itself, portions of two lines are visible. Of the upper line, only the nondistinctive bottoms of the syllables are preserved, but in the lower line, the first two syllables can be read clearly enough as *midha,*[6] followed by a fragment of a third unidentifiable letter.[7] This is presumably one of the specimens "of coarser texture" (p. 60)[8] that survived at least partially, unlike the others, which appear to have disintegrated completely.

Georg Bühler examined some fragments of birch bark in the British Museum that were said to belong to Masson's "twists" but reported that they "show no letters" (1904: 18 n. 6). However, I had occasion in October 1996 to examine a small box of birch bark fragments from Masson's collections in the British Museum, which are presumably the fragments seen by Bühler, and found, among the hundreds or perhaps even thousands of minuscule fragments, one fragmentary akṣara (perhaps the tip of a *ya*) on a piece of bark about 0.5 cm in diameter. Meager as this result may be, it does confirm that at least some of the fragments belonged to an inscribed piece of bark.

This, sad to say, is all that is known of the Kharoṣṭhī manuscripts found by Masson in the stūpas of the Jalalabad Plain. But other specimens of texts of similar types were found by John Martin Honigberger, who explored the Buddhist remains of eastern Afghanistan in 1833 (i.e., just before Masson), as described in Jacquet's accounts (1836, 1838) of his discoveries. The most striking of Honigberger's finds came from "Bourdj i takht i minâreh siâh Tchekeri bâlâ," that is, what is known in later archeological literature as the Shevaki (Wilson 1841: 114) or Shiwaki (Ball 1982: 1.253–4, no. 1087) stūpa, on the southwestern outskirts of Kabul, where in 1833 he found inside a stone reliquary "a papyrus, fairly well preserved, folded in several

6. Since the compound *thīna-middha* (Pali)/*styāna-middha* (Sanskrit), "sloth and drowsiness," is very common in Buddhist texts, it is likely that the word that preceded this was the Gāndhārī equivalent of *thīna/styāna,* perhaps *stina.*

7. Bühler (1895: 87 n. 1) read the third letter as "*ya* (?)." He refers to these birch bark fragments as probably "the oldest MSS., actually found" (p. 87).

8. This "coarser texture" probably refers to pieces of bark with a relatively large number of component layers; see section 5.4.1.

layers, on the reverse of which were drawn in black some Bactrian characters" (Jacquet 1836: 260).[9] From this description and the excellent drawing of the object in the accompanying plate XII.1 (reproduced here in fig. 8), it appears that this text may have had the form, not of a scroll, but rather of a small single sheet (see 5.2) that was folded repeatedly into a small packet so that it could be fitted inside the small (four inches high; Jacquet 1836: 259) reliquary, though it is also possible that it was originally a larger scroll that had been folded up for the same reason. Despite Jacquet's description of it as "papyrus," it can be assumed that the material was in fact birch bark. Judging from the illustration, the object seems to have been remarkably well preserved, and Jacquet adds a suitable note of caution that it would be "the most precious of objects discovered until now in the *topes* if one could succeed in opening it without damaging either the material of the sheet itself or the characters drawn upon it; this material has indeed become so fragile that it will be necessary to resort to chemical procedures to soften and open it" (1836: 260–1).[10] Unfortunately, this was apparently never actually done, and the fate of this potentially very important text is unknown. In his memoirs, Honigberger reported that "the only Bactrian manuscript which has ever been found" (Honigberger 1852: 59) lay for fifteen years in the custom-house in Vienna, after which it was sold for "about three pounds" at auction to persons unknown, whereby "in all probability, the invaluable contents of the Bactrian scroll will be lost forever to the scientific world!" (1852: 60).

Among Honigberger's other discoveries was "a very fine and fairly well preserved fabric, folded in several layers which were stuck together by the liquid which had penetrated them" (Jacquet 1838: 184–5),[11] found inside a silver box in Kotpūr stūpa 1 (cf. Wilson 1841: 64–5). Jacquet commented that "one can assume from the start that this strip of material had been covered with writing and deposited in this box with the same intention as the papyrus in the one from the *tope* of *Tchekeri bâlâ*" (p. 185 n. 1).[12] Again, nothing further is known of this object.[13] Also, in the stūpa at Bourdj i Kemri (= Masson's Kamari; Wilson 1841: 114), Honigberger found a bronze bowl containing, among other relics, "pieces of bark" (Jacquet 1836: 266); these too were most likely fragments of an inscribed piece of birch bark.

9. " . . . un papyrus assez bien conservé, plié en plusieurs doubles, sur le revers duquel sont tracés en noir quelques caractères bactriens."

10. " . . . le plus précieux des objets jusqu'à présent découvertes dans les *topes,* si l'on peut réussir à le déployer sans altérer ni la substance même de la feuille, ni les caractères qui y sont tracés; cette substance est en effet devenue si friable qu'il sera nécessaire de recourir à des procédés chimique pour l'amollir et l'étendre."

11. " . . . un tissu très fin et assez bien conservé, plié en plusieurs doubles, agglutinés par le liquide qui les avait pénétrés."

12. " . . . on peut supposer d'abord que cette band d'étoffe avait été couverte d'écriture et déposée dans cette boîte avec la même intention que le papyrus dans celle du *tope* de *Tchekeri bâlâ.*"

13. Iourkevitch comments that Honigberger "lost many things, including some manuscript rolls" (1974: 81), but it is not clear whether he is referring to the objects mentioned above or to others, or what his source of information is.

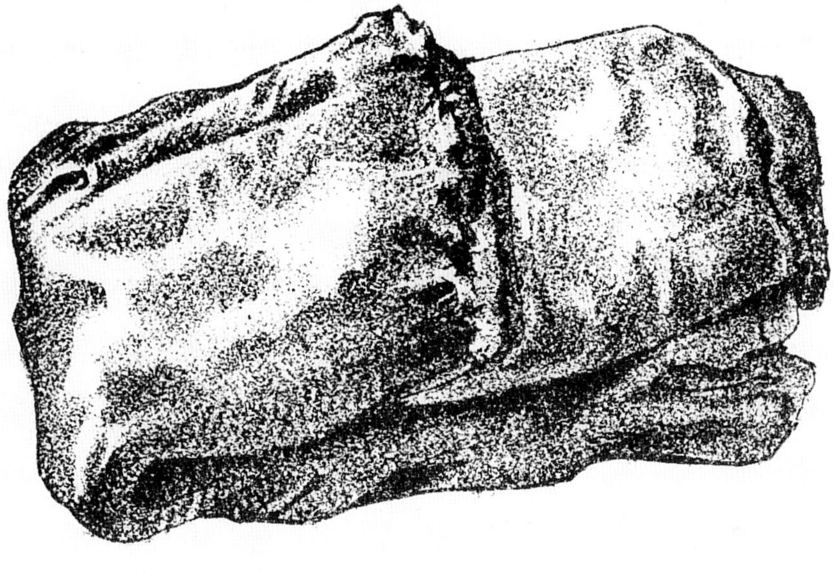

Fig. 8. Kharoṣṭhī manuscript discovered by Martin Honigberger at Shiwaki stūpa

Several more examples of Kharoṣṭhī texts on birch bark from the same region were discovered nearly a century later by J. Barthoux in the course of his excavations at Haḍḍa. He refers, for example, to some pots which contained "debris of manuscripts (bark paper)" (1933: 60), presumably referring to Kharoṣṭhī texts, and also, more specifically, to "some fragments of a manuscript (bark paper) in Kharoṣṭhī characters, with the color, appearance, and fragility of papyrus" (p. 61). One such manuscript, "the size of a fist" (p. 61), was found rolled up in the ruins of Chakhil-i Ghundi under stūpa C, 8. According to Barthoux, "the text reproducing the sermon at Benaras was unfortunately without interest for the chronology of the structures" [!] (p. 61), and he provides no further information about it. It would have been particularly interesting to know on what grounds he identified the contents of the text as the "sermon at Benares," but apparently no further information about this important text has been published. Elsewhere, however, Barthoux refers to what is presumably the same manuscript "reproducing the sermon at Benares" (p. 63) as having been found at Tapa-i Kāfarihā, which is a separate site located some four kilometers to the southeast of Chakhil-i Ghundi. Barthoux's apparent confusion about the findspot does not increase the reader's confidence in his vague description and undocumented identification of the manuscript.

Barthoux also mentions fragments of another, coarser ("plus grossier") manuscript found in chamber K 19 at Tapa Kalān. These fragments, "very deteriorated and incomplete, did not permit any exact reconstruction of the texts" (1933: 61). Barthoux then goes on to describe further discoveries of such manuscripts:

> Others, very fine, bearing prayers, were met with in the rubble of the rooms. Finally, others were also found in holes in the walls where they had been deposited, but most often, they were placed in the hands of meditating Buddhas, the depression between them and their bodies being admirably suited for such a deposit. It is in this way that they turned up in the stūpas T[apa] K[alān] 23, 119, and 122 within the hands of isolated statues dressed in yellowish white robes.
>
> These fragments, very fragile, had already been crushed by the rubble, and in removing them, despite all the precautions that were taken, one managed to destroy them. (1933: 61)[14]

Only the specimen found in TK 122 is mentioned further, described as "a prayer on bark paper, carefully folded . . . [and] placed between his [the meditating Buddha's] hands" (p. 103).

Despite the frustrating lack of detail, it is at least clear from Barthoux's brief descriptions that he found numerous Kharoṣṭhī manuscripts on birch bark at Haḍḍa. Two in particular seem to have been substantial scrolls similar to the KDhP and the new British Library texts. Masson's description of the texts that he found at Haḍḍa and other nearby sites as "twists," in one case (Nandāra) tied up with thread, seems to imply that they too were rolled-up scrolls of the same type. But some of the other texts found by Barthoux, referred to by him vaguely as "prayers," such as the one that was "carefully folded" and placed in the hands of a Buddha figure, appear to have been of a different format, apparently written on smaller sheets of bark and folded, rather than rolled up as scrolls. The intact manuscript found by Honigberger at Shiwaki also appears to have been of this class, and another possible example is described below in section 3.3. The smaller-format texts in the British Library collection (see 5.2) seem also to belong to a similar type of text. It is impossible to tell how many of these smaller texts Barthoux found, but his vague references to "others" might be taken to imply that they were fairly numerous.

It is also not clear what has become of the Kharoṣṭhī manuscripts discov-

14. " . . . très déteriorés et dont il manquait une partie, n'ont permis aucune reconstitution précise de textes. . . . D'autres, très fins, portant des prières, ont été rencontrés dans les décombres des chambres. D'autres enfin se trouvaient encore dans les trous des murs où ils avaient été déposés, mais le plus souvent, ils étaient placés dans les mains de Bouddhas en méditation, la dépression située entre elles et le corps du personnage convenant admirablement à un tel dépôt. C'est ainsi qu'ils se présentaient dans les *stūpa* TK, 23, TK, 119 et TK, 122 entre les mains de statues isolées et vêtues du manteau blanc jaunâtre.

"Ces fragments, très fragiles, étaient déjà broyés par les décombres, et en les retirant, malgré toutes les précautions prises, l'on achevait de les détruire."

ered by Barthoux at Haḍḍa. He admits that the smaller pieces were destroyed in the process of removal, but the fate of the larger ones, especially the one tantalizingly identified as the sermon at Benares, is not known to me, and I have not been able to locate any illustration, publication, or further reference to any of them.

Apparently similar materials were also found at Haḍḍa during the more recent Afghan excavations at the Tapa Shutur site. One such manuscript, found during the fourth season there, was described by Mustamandi:

> Another and headless figure made of stucco has aroused our deep interest in the rear part of the statue containing a small booklet, with a size of 3 × 2.3 cm, embedded in it. The booklet is probably made of date-palm bark or peepul-tree bark. . . . What the booklet mean[s] is difficult to say. . . . [N]o definite opinion can be expressed unless and until the booklet is opened and i[t]s contents deciphered. (1970: 71; see also Stwodah 1980: 7)

Another, evidently similar item was found in the fifth campaign at Tapa Shutur:

> [T]he mission was able to find two heads of a Bodhisattva. . . . made of unbaked mud. . . . Inside their heads there are holes in which rolls of "Ficus Religivsa" [*sic*] leave[s] were stuffed. On the leaves is some writing. Due to this fact the leaves are very important, but unfortunately neither these nor the [roll] of leaves, found last year, has been s[t]udied so far. It is rather hard to separate the leaves from each other here in Afghanistan. (Mustamandi 1971: 131)

In light of the other inscribed objects previously reported from Haḍḍa, it is likely that the material in question is birch bark rather than date-palm bark or *Ficus religiosa* leaves as reported here, and that the writing on it is Kharoṣṭhī. Judging from the placement of these texts inside statues of Buddhas or Bodhisattvas, we can surmise that they were more in the nature of the "prayers" found by Barthoux in the hands of Buddha figures, that is, short votive texts rather than complete scrolls. However, I have not been able to find any further information about or description of these texts. As with the other materials from Haḍḍa described above, their present location and fate are unknown, but there is reason to fear that they have been lost, since, according to Ball, "[t]he Tepe Shutur remains and museum were completely destroyed in the fighting in 1980" (1982: 1.116).

3.2.2. Kharoṣṭhī Manuscripts from Other Parts of Afghanistan

Besides the abundant examples of Kharoṣṭhı manuscripts on birch bark found by Masson, Barthoux, and Mustamandi in the area of Haḍḍa and the other Buddhist sites in the Jalalabad Plain, numerous specimens of Kharoṣṭhī manuscripts have been found elsewhere in Afghanistan, mainly in the Bamiyan area in central northern Afghanistan. These were noted by Sylvain Lévi, quoting Joseph Hackin's description of the "large quantity" of birch bark manuscripts found in a cave thirty-five meters east of the great Buddha of Bamiyan, among which "some rare manuscripts are in Kharoṣṭhī" (Lévi 1932: 1). As far as I have been able to determine, these Kharoṣṭhī texts have never been published, but I have seen a photograph (kindly supplied by Dr. Lore Sander) taken many years ago in the Kabul Museum that shows a small manuscript fragment with three lines of text on each side in Kharoṣṭhī, with about twelve characters per line; this may be one of the Bamiyan fragments found by Hackin.

Four small fragments of Kharoṣṭhī manuscripts from Shahr-i Zuhak, twelve kilometers east of Bamiyan, were illustrated by Pauly (1967: pl. IV.E–H), with the comment that "not knowing this script, I leave it to those who are more capable to take the effort to decipher them" (p. 283). As far as I am aware, no further mention has been made of these fragments in subsequent publications.

I have also recently seen in a private collection a substantial group of small fragments of Kharoṣṭhī manuscripts on palm leaf which are believed to have come originally from somewhere near Bamiyan. This collection comprises seventy fragments in all, representing parts of twenty-three original manuscripts. Their contents remain to be analyzed and identified, but in general they seem to be somewhat later in script and style than the British Library fragments, as suggested, for example, by their Sanskritized orthography.

3.3. Kharoṣṭhī Manuscripts from Other Regions or of Unknown Origin

Another interesting specimen of remnants of a Kharoṣṭhī text on birch bark was recently observed by me in a private collection. These fragments were found inside a pyxis-shaped reliquary of green schist (illustrated here in pl. 12), measuring 10.5 cm in height and 37.1 cm in circumference and bearing traces of red pigment around the knot on the lid. Around the outside of the base there is a "Kharoṣṭhī" inscription in two lines, but this is patently a modern forgery, presumably added on to enhance the antiquarian value of the piece. Nonetheless, the reliquary itself and its contents are clearly genuine. These contents (pl. 13) are the following:

1. A round silver casket, 3.6 cm in diameter and 1.5 cm in height, containing seventeen small flower-shaped pieces of gold leaf about 1 cm in diameter, and thirty-two similar pieces in silver.
2. A small round gold casket, 1.7 cm in diameter and 0.9 cm in height.
3. Two pins, in brass and iron, 5.2 and 5.3 cm long respectively.
4. Two brass (or gold?) earrings.
5. A circular copper lid with a loop at the center, 4 cm in diameter and 0.9 cm in height.

6. Nine bronze rings, 1.7–2.0 cm in diameter.
7. Two heart-shaped bangles of turquoise-colored glass, 4.8 cm wide.
8. One broken iron bangle, 5.9 cm wide.
9. Fourteen beads of various forms.
10. Ten bow-shaped ivory necklace pieces, each with two holes, 1.6 cm wide.

Besides these items, the bottom of the reliquary was covered with tiny fragments, apparently numbering in the thousands, of birch bark. The largest of these fragments was about 0.9 cm in diameter, but most were smaller and many were completely decomposed, hardly larger than a speck of dust. Nonetheless, on many of the larger fragments it was possible to discern parts of Kharoṣṭhī akṣaras. No complete akṣaras were found, but in a few cases parts of two syllables were visible on the same fragment (pl. 14, lower left and lower right fragments), and in rare instances it was possible to identify a partial akṣara, for instance, *rma* (perhaps part of the word *dharma*) on the upper right fragment in plate 14.

Although there is no possibility of identifying or reconstructing the text that was contained on these minuscule fragments, it is clear that they are the remnants of a birch bark manuscript. Given the similar discoveries by Honigberger of small pieces of inscribed birch bark placed inside reliquaries, this might have been another "small-format" text consisting of a single folded piece of bark, though once again it could also have been a complete scroll that was folded up to fit inside the small casket. If this was a small piece of bark containing a short text, the contents, at a guess, might have been a sacred formula, quite possibly the *pratītya-samutpāda*, for this formula was added as a supplementary text to the donative inscription on the Kurram relic casket (Konow 1929: 155) and also seems to have been the text written in Brāhmī script on a birch bark strip similarly found inside a reliquary at Lauṛiyā-Nandangaṛh (see 4.5.2).[15]

The findspot of the reliquary examined is unfortunately unknown, but given its general resemblance to other objects found in the Gandhāra and Swat regions of Pakistan, it could well have come from that general area. There is also some evidence of a similar item having been found in the Swat Valley; Tucci refers to the discovery at one of the stūpa sites near Nājigrām in lower Swat of "a well-preserved casket in steatite which was found among their ruins, containing a small golden box with some relics, and also it seems a birch-tree leaflet which has since disappeared: according to what I was told the casket was given to the Wali Saheb" (1958: 317). No further information or description of this object is provided, but given its character and provenance it is more than likely that the "birch-tree leaflet" was yet another example of a birch bark manuscript in Kharoṣṭhī.

15. For further references to this practice; see Bentor 1995: 251–2.

3.4. Conclusions

Sketchy as most of the reports cited here may be, they suffice to show that Kharoṣṭhī manuscripts on birch bark must have been very numerous in ancient Gandhāra and surrounding regions.[16] No doubt many more of them have been discovered but subsequently lost or destroyed by mishandling; hopefully, more also remain to be discovered. They seem to have been especially common in the numerous stūpa sites in the Jalalabad Plain of eastern Afghanistan but are also attested in other areas, such as Swat and Chinese central Asia, that were under the cultural influence of Gandhāra. The relative rarity of surviving specimens is no doubt due to their extreme fragility, such that even those which survived until modern times have, more often than not, been destroyed by their discoverers, as shown by the confessions of Masson and Barthoux quoted above.

As far as can be deduced from the scanty information available, it would appear that there were (at least) two main types of birch bark manuscripts in wide use in Buddhist Gandhāra. The first type consists of scrolls containing continuous texts for use in Buddhist monasteries and monastic libraries, and is exemplified by the KDhP manuscript, the new British Library texts, and also, presumably, the longer of the texts found by Barthoux at Haḍḍa and at least some of Masson's discoveries. The second type, even less well documented, consists of small pieces of inscribed bark used, apparently, as charms or amulets, which were placed in or on stūpas, statues, or reliquaries. In the latter case, they seem to represent supplementary offerings, or *dharmaśarīra* ("bodily relics of the dharma"; Bentor 1995: 251), to go with the bodily relics (*śarīra* or *dhātu*) contained in the reliquaries, or perhaps in some cases to substitute for them (see also 4.5.2). But as yet, no intact specimen of this latter type of text from the period in question has come to light for scholarly examination, so that this remains in part a matter of speculation.[17]

Finally, the large number of birch bark manuscripts that have been found at Haḍḍa and other nearby sites in the Jalalabad Plain makes the hearsay reports that the new British Library manuscripts came from Haḍḍa more plausible. Moreover, Haḍḍa is known to be very rich in its yield of funereal clay pots, often decorated and/or inscribed in Kharoṣṭhī, and we know from Barthoux's reports, sketchy and unsatisfactory though they are, that these sometimes contained remnants of birch bark manuscripts.

16. Bühler noted that even in his time (the late nineteenth century), "[t]he Himâlaya seems to contain an inexhaustible supply of birch-bark. . . . To give an idea of the quantities which are brought into Śrînagar, I may mention that on one single day I counted fourteen large barges with birch-bark on the river" (1877: 29). Similarly, commenting on a birch bark manuscript of the complete Ṛg Veda in 191 folios, Müller noted that "there was no difficulty in producing from the bark of the birch tree thousands and thousands of pages of the largest quarto or even folio-size, perfectly smooth and pure, except for the small dark lines peculiar to the bark of that tree" (1880: 159). Presumably in ancient times, too, birch bark was a cheap and abundant material for writing and other uses, and one can easily envision monastic libraries with very large numbers of bark scrolls.

17. See also the further discussion of the format of birch bark manuscripts in 5.1–2.

Chapter 4

Origin and Character of the Collection

This chapter addresses the question of why this particular set of manuscripts was placed in a clay pot and buried, apparently, in the precincts of a Buddhist monastery. Specifically, it focuses on the search for some common factor—not necessarily a textual one—among the scrolls, which are very diverse with regard to their contents and physical form. This search is very seriously hampered by our ignorance of their original archeological context and also by the fact that the scrolls had already been removed from their container by the time they were first subjected to scholarly examination, so that their original positions and relationships cannot be reconstructed. Largely as a result of this unfortunate situation, the hypothesis presented here—namely, that the collection represents a ritual interment of worn and discarded manuscripts—cannot be conclusively proven. Nonetheless, for reasons that will be presented below in detail, it seems to me the best explanation, given the limited evidence that is available to us.

4.1. Physical Evidence

There are several indications that the fragmentary character of these manuscripts is only partly due to the decay that must have affected them during the nearly two thousand years in which they lay buried and/or to further damage that may have been inflicted on them between the time that they were unearthed and their acquisition by the British Library. It is certain that at least some of the manuscripts were incomplete and otherwise damaged even before they were assembled and deposited in a clay jar.

An extreme example is fragment 5, which actually consists of parts of what were evidently three originally separate scrolls containing different texts in different handwritings, which had been put together into a single roll. Of these, fragment 5A is a small piece, preserving only parts of four lines. Fragment 5B is a larger piece, which seems to preserve most of an original small-format scroll (see sec. 5.2), but in very decrepit condition, as will be explained below. Fragment 5C is another very decrepit fragment, larger than 5A but smaller than 5B, of yet another separate scroll, probably also originally of the smaller format.

The remnants of fragment 5B, which contains the text of the Gāndhārī recension of the Rhinoceros Horn Sūtra, are divided vertically into two parallel columns. This probably resulted from the original scroll having been cut in half lengthwise by a tying cord or having been folded in half lengthwise (see 5.3.3). However, when the fragment was unrolled, it became apparent that it was arranged with these two vertical columns reversed left to right from their original position; this was obvious from the fact that the verses were written one to a line, and the refrain which is the last quarter of each verse in this sūtra (*eko care khargaviṣaṇagapo*, "One should wander alone like the rhinoceros horn") appeared in the fragments in the right-hand column, rather than in its proper position at the left (since Kharoṣṭhī script is written from right to left). This proves that the splitting of the scroll into two vertical columns took place in ancient times, before the scroll was deposited in the pot. At that point it must have already been in pieces, which were carelessly rolled up together without regard for their proper positions. This is confirmed by the fact that the two columns of text themselves are composed of several smaller fragments, fourteen in all, and these too are randomly arranged with no regard to their original sequence. Many of them, moreover, are placed upside down.

Thus one gets the impression that fragment 5 was a composite roll put together from scraps of at least three originally separate and already badly fragmented scrolls. There is at least one other case of such a composite scroll—fragment 3—which combines pieces of at least two originally separate fragments (see 2.2.6). Here too we seem to be dealing with a set of miscellaneous small fragments that were rolled up together before being interred.

In several other cases, there is evidence that longer scrolls that had been constructed by gluing shorter pieces of birch bark together (see 5.1.2) had separated into their component parts before they were interred. This is evidently the case, for example, with fragments 12 and 14, whose textual contents show that they are contiguous sections of the same original scroll, but which were found rolled up separately. In other cases, such as fragment 29, a subfragment about 1.9 cm in length was found to be oriented upside down within the larger scroll of which it is a part. This too must have been a component section, or a part of one, that had separated from the scroll, and, as in the case of fragment 5B, the separate remnants of this already fragmented scroll were evidently rolled up together for ritual disposal without special attention as to their proper sequence or orientation.

In these examples, there is incontrovertible evidence that the scrolls were already fragmentary before they were buried (or otherwise disposed of). In several other cases, the evidence is less clear, but there is at least some reason to think that the situation was similar. This is so, for example, in several instances where sections of what seem to be the same or a similar text written in the same hand were found in separate scrolls. In most of these cases we do not know yet whether we are dealing with separated fragments of the same original scroll or of distinct scrolls of a long text written out in multiple "volumes." Another interesting case is that of fragments

16 + 25, which are the right and left sides respectively of the same original scroll, which, like fragment 5B, had been cut in half lengthwise. In this case, however, it is not clear whether the scroll had been completely divided before it was put in the pot, or whether it broke in two during the long period that it lay buried. Had it been possible to examine the manuscripts in their original position in the pot, the positions of the fragments probably would have made this clear, but as it is we can only guess. Given the indications from the previously mentioned examples, I would say that there is a good possibility that the original scroll that comprised fragments 16 + 25 had in fact already been broken in two before it was deposited, but this cannot be proven with the evidence now at hand.

These examples of scrolls which were evidently worn out and damaged before being placed in the pot raise the possibility that all of the scrolls were in some sense defective, and that this is the common factor which caused them to be interred together. It must be admitted, however, that such cases are not representative of the entire collection, which also includes several less fragmentary specimens. In the case of the more complete and better preserved scrolls, such as fragments 1, 4, and 15, we have the remains of scrolls whose lower portions, at least, seem to have been mostly intact when they were first unearthed. In these examples, the damage consists principally of the loss of a substantial part of the upper part of the scrolls, which was the outer, and hence most vulnerable, part of the scroll when it was rolled up from the bottom, and which is missing to a greater or lesser extent in all the fragments (see 5.3.3). At least some of this loss, which in the three relatively well preserved examples under discussion here seems to amount to roughly half of the original length of the scroll, must have resulted from gradual decomposition during the nearly two thousand years of interment, and some more was undoubtedly caused by mishandling of the scrolls by their discoverer (2.1.1 and 2.1.2). But there is no way to know for sure how much, if any, of the upper part of these and other scrolls had already been lost before they were placed in the pot. It is possible that some of them were complete and more or less wholly intact when they were deposited, but they might equally well have already suffered this type of damage before that time. On the physical evidence, there is no way to prove either alternative, and if this were all we had to go on, the nature of the manuscript deposit would have been largely indeterminate. Fortunately, however, there is also textual evidence which supports the hypothesis that the collection as a whole consists of discarded texts.

4.2. Textual Evidence: The "*Likhidago*" Interlinear Notations

This textual evidence consists of a series of secondary interlinear notations observed on several of the manuscripts, including some of the well-preserved specimens such as fragment 1.[1] For example, fragment 14 has two such notations on

1. For a list of these annotations, see the summary at the end of this section.

the recto (pl. 10). The first of these is written between the middle of the third and second lines from the bottom (lines 22 and 23), which are the fourth and fifth lines respectively of the second text on the fragment, namely, the avadāna collection that commences near the bottom of the recto. The inserted word slants downward to the left, so that the bottoms of its letters overlap with the tops of the letters of line 23 of the text proper. This first annotation reads *likhidago,* "[it is] written." The second annotation commences at about the middle of the last line (24), following a large circle which served as a punctuation sign in the original text, marking the end of the first avadāna in the collection. The space in which the annotation was written was therefore originally a blank half-line left by the scribe at the very bottom of the scroll before he commenced the next avadāna at the top of the verso. Like the other one, this annotation slants downward toward the left. It reads *likhidago sa[rvo]* "[it is] all written."

The term *likhidago* and its graphic variants appearing in the other interlinear notes described below can be interpreted as an extended past participle form, that is, as meaning "written," by comparison with the frequent use in the central Asian Kharoṣṭhī documents of the corresponding word *likhitaǵa/likhidaǵa/lihitaǵa/lihidaǵa,* etc. both as a noun, "(written) document," and, as here, as a past participle with a pleonastic suffix *-ga* (< **-ka*), which is common generally in the central Asian Kharoṣṭhī documents (Burrow 1937: 53–4). An example of the latter function is found in document no. 586, undertablet, obverse, line 8, *eṣa pravaṃnaǵa likhidaǵa mahi,* translated by Burrow as "This receipt was written by me" (1940: 124). In the label on the cover tablets (obverse, lines 1–2) of the duplicate texts 431–2, the word is used in both senses, as noun and as participial adjective: *eṣa likhidaǵa yav́e av́anaṃmi masu prace[ya] likhidaǵa,* which Burrow renders "This document is written concerning the wine in Yav́e av́ana" (p. 87).

A similar scribal annotation is found at the top of the verso of one of the several small pieces that make up fragment 3A: *lihidaǵa sarve,* "[it is] all written." Presumably, this note was originally placed between this line and the one preceding it, which is now lost. Curiously, though, this note is written upside down in relation to the rest of the text on the fragment. Whatever may be the reason for this, it confirms that the phrase is an incidental addition rather than part of the original text.

In fragment 16, we find on line 18 of the recto (the third line visible in the detail photograph in pl. 11), which is the fourth line of the second text on the scroll, the phrase *likhitage aca avadane,* apparently meaning "the avadāna has been written."[2] The upper right corner of the first akṣara of this phrase slightly overlaps the upper left end of the preceding syllable, *va,* of the main text, confirming that it is a secondary annotation. The phrase is written on the level of a line of the original text, rather than between or across the lines as in fragment 3A and the first annota-

2. The meaning of the uncertain word *aca* is discussed below.

tion on fragment 14 respectively. In this respect, its position resembles that of the second notation on 14, which was written on what had been a blank space at the very bottom of the scroll; the place where the notation on fragment 16 was written was also almost certainly originally a blank space in the text. For one thing, a similar blank space appears at the right end of the line two lines above (line 16), apparently marking the transition between the first and second texts on the scroll. Second, the annotation on line 18 is followed (on fragment 25, which is actually the left half of the same scroll; see 4.1) by a large punctuation mark originally consisting of (probably) nine circles arranged in three rows of three circles each,[3] and then by the words *boṣisatva provayoge* ("The previous life of the Bodhisattva"), introducing the first of the series of pūrvayoga ("previous life") stories that are the theme of the second text on fragments 16 + 25. Thus the space where the annotation *likhitage aca avadane* was written on fragment 16 was almost certainly originally a blank between sections of this text, probably coming between a prefatory introduction and the first of the pūrvayoga stories.

Since fragment 1 resembles fragments 12 + 14 and 16 + 25 in containing two texts written in the same two hands, namely, nos. 1 and 2 (see sec. 2.5), we should not be surprised that it too had such interlinear notations. The second and more evident of the two interlineations in fragment 1 appears on the verso of part 4, where it is written across the middle of the scroll, between lines 23 and 24, and reads clearly *likhidago aco sa[rvo]*, "[it is] all written." The first interlinear notation on fragment 1 is at the very bottom of the recto (part 5), which is badly fragmented and difficult to read. However, it is possible to discern at the center of the upper edge of the short (approximately 1 cm high) separated segment at the very bottom of the scroll the lower portions of what are fairly clearly the syllables *dago,* and before them also a curl which could easily be the very bottom of *kh(i*)* (see pl. 4). From this, we can securely reconstruct, on the basis of the parallels presented above, the familiar word *likhidago.* The word was evidently written sloping downward to the left, as was the case with the corresponding word in fragment 14, which explains why the lower portions of only the left-hand letters are preserved below the horizontal break.

Finally, fragment 2 also has what seems to be an interlinear note between lines 8 and 9 of the recto (pl. 15). The notation, which is broken off at the left, seems to read *sarva ime avadasa [a] ?,* but the last complete character could perhaps be read as a slightly unusual form of *na* rather than as *sa.* Although at first glance it looks more like a *sa,* it is in fact quite different from the *sa* at the beginning of the phrase,

3. The small stroke at the edge of line 18 on fragment 16, to the left of the word *avadane,* may be a remnant of one of these circles. Four of them survive at the right edge of the corresponding line of fragment 25, arranged in a vertical row of three circles at the left, plus a fourth at the right of the bottom one. The complete set thus seems to have originally consisted of nine circles arranged in three rows of three.

with a bigger head and a curve rather than an angle leading into the vertical stem; thus *na* is at least a possible reading. If this is correct, the full notation might have been *sarva ime avada[na] [aca] (likhidaga*)*, "all these avadānas have been written," similar to the notation on fragment 16 (*likhitage aca avadane*).

Thus we have seven examples on five separate scrolls of this kind of secondary notation. In all five of these scrolls at least part of the text is written in the distinctive hand no. 2. Three of the five (frags. 1, 14, and 16) each contain two separate texts written by the same two hands (nos. 1 and 2). A fourth, fragment 2, has only a text in hand no. 2, but since only a small part of this scroll survives, it may originally also have had another text, perhaps again in hand no. 1 as in the other three scrolls. The fifth interlineated fragment, 3A, also had two texts, one again in hand no. 2, but the other in a different hand (no. 3). Thus the manuscripts with the secondary notations fall into a distinct separate group within the entire collection in that they all have at least one hand in common, and in at least three of five cases the same two hands. This is clearly a significant link, since the collection as a whole contains the work of about twenty-one different scribes.

As to the hands of the notations themselves, all but the notation on fragment 2 are the same hand, which superficially resembles hand no. 1 of the texts proper but which on closer examination is revealed to be a different one, not seen elsewhere in these or any other texts in the entire collection. This is confirmed by the fact that the annotator uses the consonant *ga*, whereas hand no. 1 never writes *ga* but always uses *gha* in its place (see 6.4.2). Only the annotation on fragment 2 seems to be in yet another hand, and in this case we also find a slightly different phrasing (according to the conjectural reconstruction suggested above), *sarva ime avada[na] [aca] (likhidaga*)*, in contrast to the other constructions such as *likhitage aca avadane* (frag. 16) and *likhidago sa[rvo]* (14).

Thus five scrolls, which seem to have been in some sense part of a set, contain seven secondary notations that were made (with one exception) by the same hand and that label them as having been "written." What could the point of this have been? One explanation might be that the notations were the work of an inspector or supervisor of the original writing of the manuscripts whose task was to certify their correctness and completion. But if this were the case, why were the notes written in such a haphazard fashion, between and even across the lines of the text (frag. 14) or upside down with respect to it (frag. 2)? For these reasons I think it is more likely that the secondary annotations were added, not by an inspector or editor, but by a subsequent copyist. According to this theory, the scribe who had been assigned to make new copies of the texts contained in our scrolls would have marked them, after he had finished recopying them, as "written" (*likhidaga*), that is, "copied," to indicate that they could be discarded. The casual placement of the notations is much easier to understand in such circumstances.

Such a theory would also help to clarify the different formulations of the notations, and particularly of the double notations in fragments 1 and 14. In 14, we find first *likhidago* and then, a few lines below, *likhidago sa[rvo]*. Perhaps this indicates that the first notation was made after the copying of the first text (a sūtra-style text, written in hand no. 1) had been completed, while the second one was added after the second text, a collection of avadānas written by hand no. 2, had also been copied, whence the added word *sarvo*, "all," referring to the contents of the entire scroll. In fragment 1, we find a similar pair of notations. The first one, reconstructible as *likhidago*, is written at the very bottom of the recto, just after the beginning of the second text, an avadāna collection, while the second notation, reading *likhidago aco sa[rvo]*, is written on the verso, approximately 100 cm up from the bottom of the scroll. Except for the addition of the word *aco* and the different location of the second note, this pair of annotations is virtually identical to those on fragment 14. Thus, here too this pattern probably indicates that the contents of the scroll had been recopied in two separate stages. The difference in the position of the second notations on these two scrolls—at the bottom of the recto in fragment 14 and well up on the verso in 1—is probably of no particular significance, since, as we have seen, these notes seem to have been placed more or less randomly.

In fragment 16, we have a situation similar to that of 1 and 14, with the two original texts on the scroll in the same two hands, but here only a single annotation by our hypothetical copyist, reading *likhitage aca avadane*, is preserved. Here *avadane* obviously refers to the second text, which as in the case of fragments 1 and 14 is written by hand no. 2 and comprises a collection of avadāna-like texts (actually, pūrvayogas). In view of the patterns noted above, it is conceivable that there may have also been a previous annotation reading *likhidago* written further up on the recto of fragments 16 + 25, of which only a small piece from the bottom of the scroll is preserved. If this were the case, we would have a reasonably close parallelism between the pairings *likhidago/likhadago (aco) sarvo* in fragments 1 and 14 and a hypothetical pair *(likhidage*)/likhitage aca avadane* in 16 + 25. Given the similar contents of all three scrolls (a first text followed by an avadāna or avadāna-like text), the phrases *likhidago (aco) sarvo* and *likhitage aca avadane* would in effect indicate the same thing.[4]

One remaining problem is the explanation of the word *aca* (frag. 16)/*aco* (frag. 1). It can be assumed that these are simply variant spellings for the same word, since an alternation between final *a* and *o* is well attested among the new texts (see 6.5.1). Given its position and apparent syntactic function, it seems most likely that

4. Of course, this interpretation depends on a hypothetical lost first annotation in fragments 16 + 25. If this never existed, the single annotation *likhitage aca avadane* might indicate that the entire scroll, including both texts, had been copied in one stage, rather than two, as seems to have been the case of fragments 1 and 14. Alternatively, it could mean that the copyist who inserted the annotation had copied only the avadāna text, and that the first text (a portion of the Dharmapada) was for some reason not copied, or at least not by him.

aca/aco is an adverbial particle of some sort. Some connection with *ca,* "and," is conceivable—for instance, a contracted form of *api ca* or the like—in which case *likhadago aco sarvo* and *likhitage aca avadane* would mean something like "and [it is] all written" and "and the avadana has been written" respectively. It is also tempting to think of *aca/aco* as a derivative of Sanskrit *adya,* "today," in place of the expected *aja* (i.e., *ajja*). But the devoicing of *j* would be difficult to explain; according to Burrow, "internal *j* never becomes *c*" (1937: 72). Although he does note certain exceptions elsewhere (p. 5), these seem to reflect misspellings by native speakers of non-Indian languages in central Asia and hence are not relevant to the problem being addressed here.

Alternatively, *aca/aco* could be, not an adverbial particle, but a demonstrative pronoun; this is suggested, perhaps, by the variant annotation reconstructed as *sarva ime avada[na] [aca] (likhidaga*)* in fragment 2. But there are phonetic and etymological problems here. A derivation from a pronominal stem *aya-*, for example, is hardly likely, for although the change of intervocalic *c* to *y* is well attested in Gāndhārī, a development in the opposite direction would not be expected. In short, the word *aca/aco* remains to be clarified.

However this may be, the close linkages among the subset of texts containing these secondary copyists' marks suggest that the process not only of the original writing of the scrolls but also of their storage and recopying was orderly and controlled. This was evidently not the case, however, with their disposal. It would appear that, once they had been recopied and marked for disposal, the old and damaged scrolls were consigned to some sort of discard pile whose contents were assembled more or less at random and placed in clay pots for a ritual burial.

Summary of the "*Likhidago*" Annotations

1. Frag. 1, part 5, r, between lines 33 and 34	*(li*)kh(i*)dago*
2. Frag. 1, part 4, v, between lines 23 and 24	*likhidago aco sa[rvo]*
3. Frag. 2, r, between lines 8 and 9	*sarva ime avada[na] [aca] (likhidaga*)*
4. Frag. 3A, v, at top edge of the largest fragment	*lihidaǵa sarve*
5. Frag. 14, r, between lines 22 and 23	*likhidago*
6. Frag. 14, r, line 24	*likhidago sa[rvo]*
7. Frag. 16, r, line 18	*likhitage aca avadane*

Pl. 1. Fragments 16–19
before unrolling and conservation

Pl. 2. Fragment 23 before unrolling and conservation

Pl. 3. Specimen of a deteriorated manuscript fragment
after unrolling and conservation: fragment 23, part 2, r

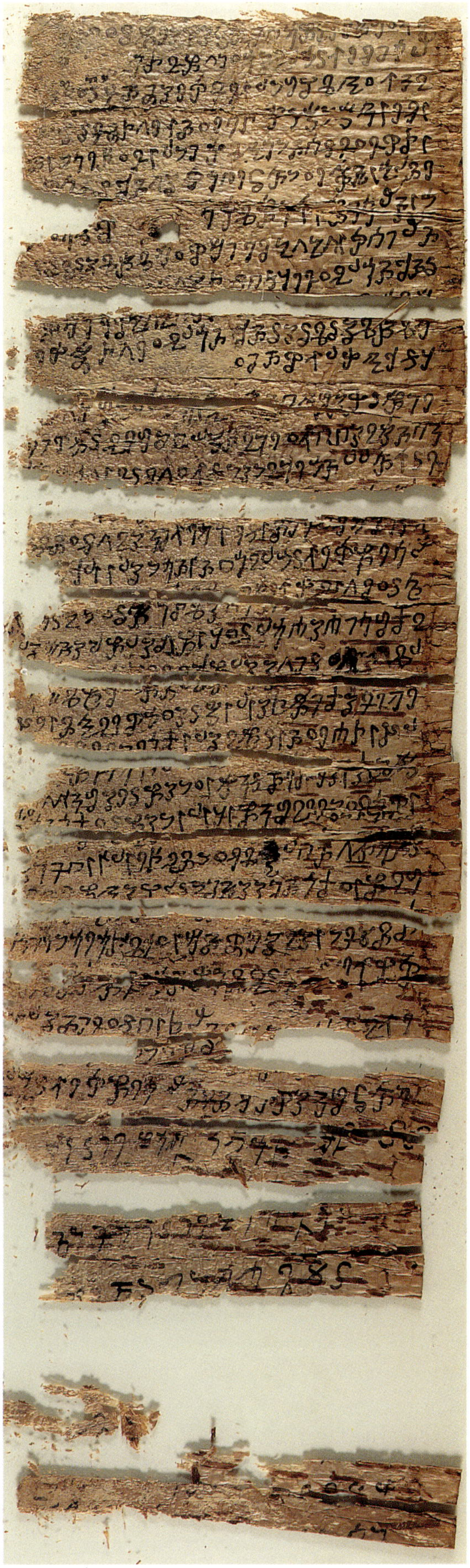

Pl. 4. Specimen of a relatively well preserved manuscript fragment after unrolling and conservation: fragment 1, part 5, r

Pl. 5. Pot D with manuscripts inside (1993), viewed from above

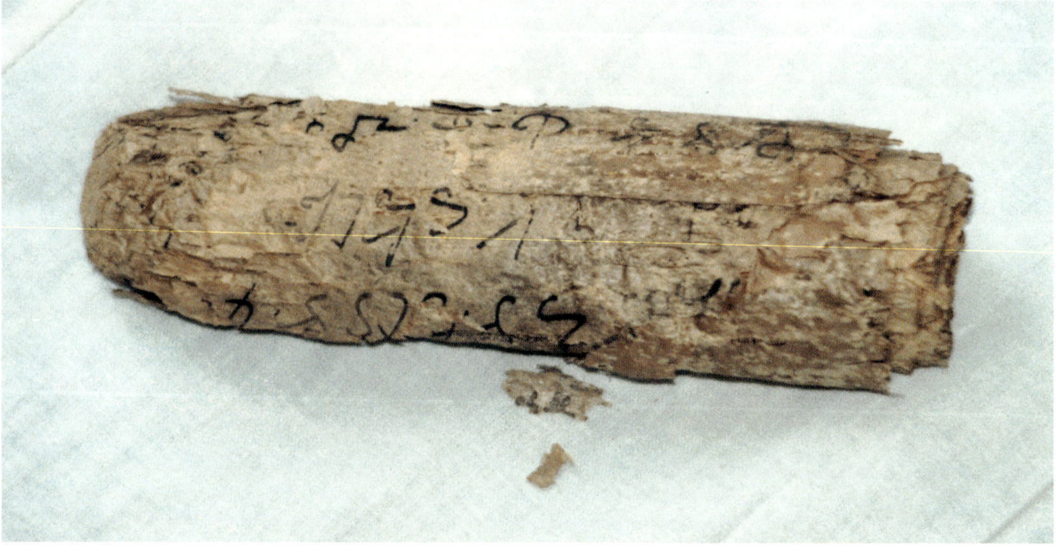

Pl. 6. Earliest available photograph (1993) of fragment 1, removed from pot D

Pl. 7. Fragment 12, part 1, r

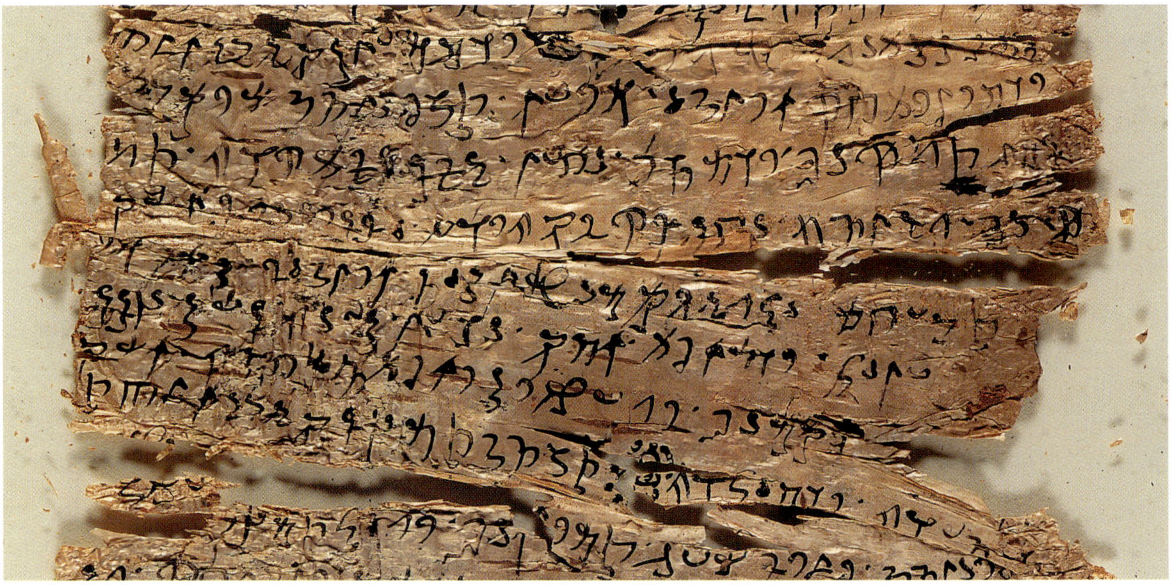

Pl. 8. Fragment 9, part 3, r: detail of passage transcribed and translated on pp. 28–9

Pl. 9. Partial colophon text in fragment 3B

Pl. 11. (*opposite*) Detail of fragment 16, r, showing a copyist's notation

Pl. 10. Detail of fragment 14, r, showing a copyist's notations

Pl. 12. Pyxis-shaped reliquary
in a private collection

Pl. 13. Contents of the pyxis-shaped reliquary

Pl. 14. Fragments of a birch bark manuscript
found inside the pyxis-shaped reliquary

Pl. 15. Fragment 2, r

Pl. 16. A monastery cell at Jauliāñ (Taxila)
with fragments of a pot in which a birch bark
manuscript was found

Pl. 17. Clay pot decorated with ink drawings of monks

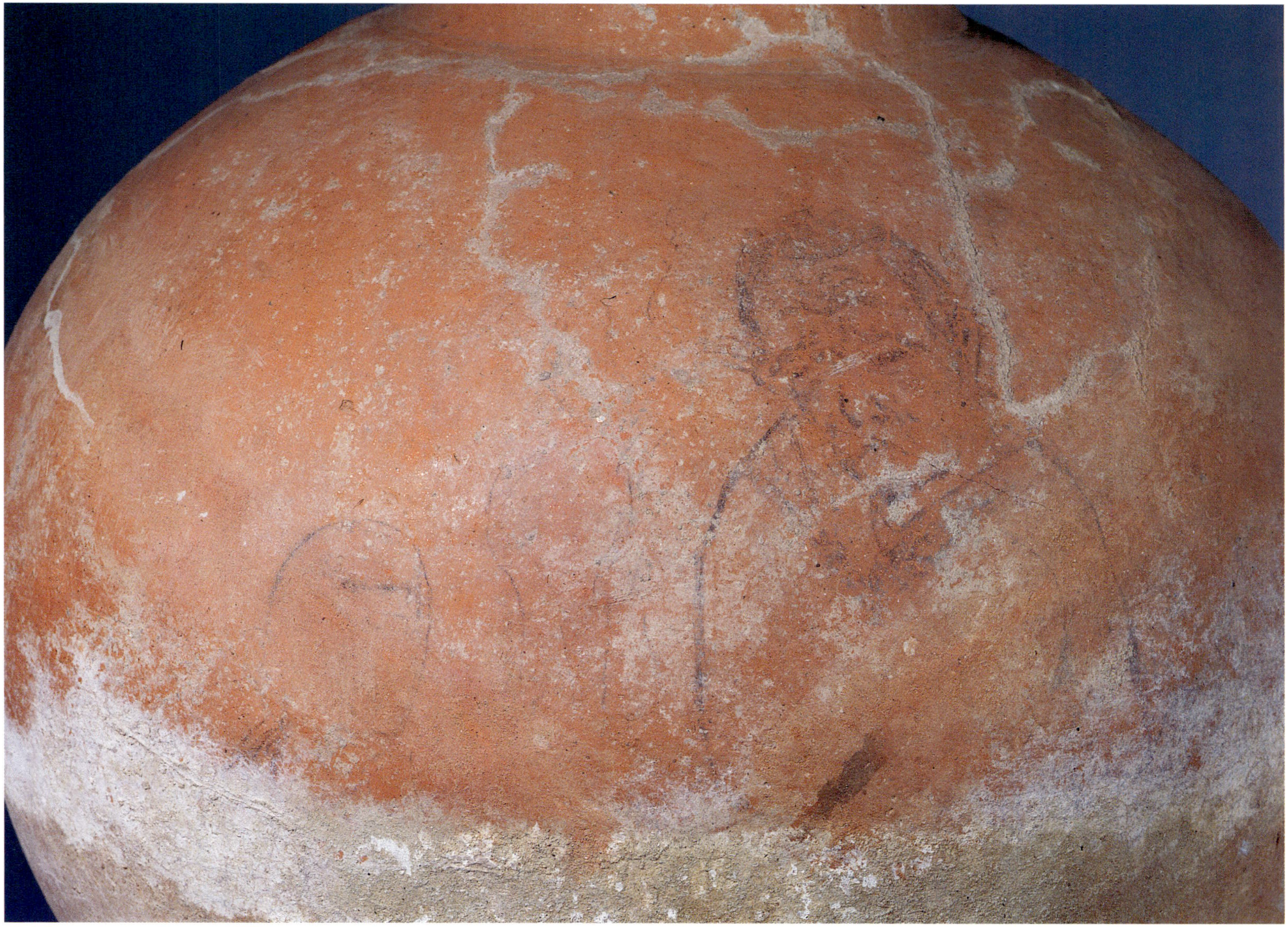

Pl. 18. Detail of decorated pot in pl. 17, showing an aged monk and a younger monk bowing before him

Pl. 19. Traces of the inscription
on the decorated pot in pl. 17

Pl. 20. Decorated pot in
pl. 17, showing the bones
found inside it

Pl. 21. Fragment 1, part 2, v

Pl. 22. Pot A

Pl. 23. Pot A, viewed from above

Pl. 24. Pot B

Pl. 25. Pot B,
viewed from above

Pl. 26. Pot C

Pl. 27. Pot C, viewed from above

Pl. 28. Pot D

Pl. 29. Pot D, viewed from above

Pl. 30. Pot E

Pl. 31. Pot E,
viewed from above

Pl. 32. Potsherds 1–9

Pl. 33. Potsherds 10–18

Pl. 34. Potsherds 19–26

4.3. Archeological Parallels

The hypothesis that Gandhāran Buddhists ritually interred old manuscripts in clay pots is well supported by data from other discoveries. For example, at least one of the pieces of birch bark with Kharoṣṭhī inscriptions discovered by Masson at Haḍḍa (tope no. 13; see 3.2.1) was found inside a "small earthen jar." Barthoux also described, in somewhat vague terms, "some pots"—he does not tell us how many—containing "a sort of earth among which was mixed the debris of manuscripts (bark paper)" (1933: 60).[5] We have also seen (3.1.1) that there is reason to believe that the KDhP scroll may have been preserved in the clay pot which was reported to have been found along with it.

Finally, there is at least one similar discovery that has been well documented and described in detail, unlike the previously mentioned ones. This is the fragmentary birch bark manuscript of an unidentified Buddhist text written in Sanskrit in late Brāhmī script that was found in the course of Marshall's Taxila excavations at the Jauliāñ site (Marshall 1951: 1.387; Chanda 1921). The pot in which the manuscript was found was located in the northeast corner of cell 29 in the Jauliāñ monastery. When I visited this site in January 1996, some remnants of this pot were still visible under a pile of rubble, and it appeared that it had been partially buried in the soil with the upper part and neck left exposed (pl. 16). The cell in which the pot was found is the one immediately adjacent to the entrance to the monastery, and the outer wall of this cell has the largest of the several sculpture alcoves in the monastery complex, containing a terra-cotta figure of the Buddha with several attendant figures (Marshall 1951: 1.380–1). Thus cell 29 seems to have had some particular importance that made it stand out from the twenty-eight other cells. Several of these other cells also contained clay pots, but none of them contained manuscripts or any other remains deemed worthy of note by Marshall (p. 380). In short, it would seem that the pot containing the manuscript was placed in a location of some special significance. Although the Jauliāñ manuscript reflects a late phase of Gandhāran Buddhism in which the Kharoṣṭhī script and Gāndhārī language had been, or at least were being, supplanted by Brāhmī and Sanskrit, we are still, broadly speaking, within the same cultural tradition whose earlier phase is represented by the British Library manuscripts, and there is no reason to doubt that similar ritual practices concerning the storage or disposal of old manuscripts were current throughout the entire period.

Further clues about the intention and significance of the interment of old manuscripts in pots are provided by several cases where similar pots in similar locations were found to contain human remains. The following is a longer extract from Barthoux's description of the contents of the pottery he found at Haḍḍa, part of which was already quoted above:

5. ". . . une sorte de terre à laquelle étaient mélangés des débris de manuscrits (papier d'écorce)."

> All of these pots were covered with a slab of schist that protected their contents from dust and wind.[[6]] In the interior [was] found debris of semi-calcinated bones . . . among which were distinctly discernible vertebrae, the bases of ribs, and clavicle joints. . . . Most often, the bones had completely disappeared through calcination and the contents of the pots were nothing more than a sort of earth among which was mixed the debris of manuscripts (bark paper) . . . or coins. (1933: 60)[7]

What is particularly striking in Barthoux's report is the suggestion of a juxtaposition of human bones and manuscript fragments in similar situations, and possibly even in the same pot, though it is not exactly clear from his comments whether this was actually the case. However this may be, the discovery of bones, presumably human, in Gandhāran clay pots was already well attested—for instance by A. Foucher's description of "a round earthen vase with the usual form of Indian jugs (*gharrah*, Skt. *ghaṭa*) . . . it contained, besides a small quantity of clay, 'fragments of cinders and carbonized bones'" (1905: 52).[8]

A group of what would seem to be similar relics was found by Masson, who reported, in connection with the many jars he saw in the Haḍḍa area:

> Large numbers of funereal jars may be found in a mound behind the village of Hidda, near Tappa Kelán. . . . They vary much in size, from a depth of three feet to six inches: they . . . generally are marked with some ornamental lines around the head and shoulders. Some of them are further adorned with flowers of varying colours. . . . They contain merely ashes and bones in greater or less quantity, and their mouths are invariably covered with stones. . . . They have been deposited sometimes in regular succession . . . resting on a common line of cement. . . . On one an inscription was scratched. (Wilson 1841: 112–3)[9]

6. This and similar comments on finds from Haḍḍa and elsewhere (cited below) show that it was standard practice to seal the mouths of the buried pots with a stone or other covering. Although no trace of any covering material has been preserved with the British Library pots, they must have been similarly sealed or the manuscripts could not have survived. Unfortunately, none of the relevant reports contain illustrations or detailed descriptions of these covers, so that it is not possible to form any clear idea of how they looked and functioned.

7. "Toutes ces poteries étaient recouvertes d'une dalle de schist préservant leur contenu de la poussière et des vents. A l'intérieur, se trouvaient des débris d'ossements à demi-calcinés . . . parmi lesquels se distinguaient nettement des vertèbres, des têtes de côtes, des articulations de clavicules. . . . Le plus souvent, les os avaient complètement disparu par calcination et le contenu des poteries n'était plus qu'une sorte de terre à laquelle étaient mélangés des débris de manuscrits (papier d'écorce) . . . ou des monnaies."

8. "[U]n vase de terre ronde de la form habituelle des cruches indiennes (*gharrah*, Skt. *ghaṭa*) . . . il contenait, outre une petite quantité d'argile, 'des fragments de charbons et d'os carbonisés.'"

9. The inscription referred to by Masson is presumably the one reproduced in Wilson 1841: pl. IX, along with four of the jars, but nothing can be made of it from this rough eye-copy.

The arrangement of such jars "in regular succession" brings to mind a group of four pots that were found "standing in a row from north to south, each covered with a flat stone" (Marshall and Vogel 1902–3: 163), outside the square courtyard in the southeast portion of the Pālāṭū Ḍherī mound at Chārsada. In size and form the Pālāṭū Ḍherī jars resemble the other ones under discussion here, including the new British Library jars; they are roughly spherical with a wide neck (see Marshall and Vogel 1902–3: fig. 24, no. 19), and the largest of the four is three feet, four inches in circumference. Unfortunately, no mention is made in the report of what, if anything, was found inside these jars. Three of the four jars had dedicatory inscriptions in Kharoṣṭhī, which have been edited by Konow (1929: 120–2). These are typical brief dedicatory inscriptions, with no reference to the intended function of the jars (see Appendix, sec. 2).

A better-documented instance of clay jars containing bones from the Haḍḍa complex is presented in Tarzi 1990: 715–7. Tarzi describes two funeral urns "containing fragments of human bones mixed with ashes" (p. 715) that were discovered along the outside walls of chapels I and V adjoining the central stūpa courtyard at the Tapa-e-Top-e-Kalān site.[10] Their situation on the outside of a square central courtyard matches that of the Pālāṭū Ḍherī jars, and it would seem that such a location, adjoining but not within the central precincts of the stūpa compound, was a favored one for the burial of funereal vessels. The jars, which are not inscribed, are illustrated in Tarzi 1990: 720, fig. 13. They are squat, roundish vessels with wide mouths, rather different in form from most of the inscribed Gandhāran pots.

Fussman (1969) has also published a well-preserved inscription on a broken clay jar from Haḍḍa that closely resembles the similar objects described by Masson and Barthoux and that, according to a subsequent note by Fussman, was probably the one from the Chakhil-i Ghundi site mentioned by Barthoux in 1933: 175 (Fussman and Le Berre 1976: 46 n. 1).[11] Judging from the neck and upper part, which are all that remain of this pot, it seems, unlike the ones mentioned in the previous paragraph, to have resembled the newly discovered inscribed pots in the British Library collection. The label in the Kabul Museum describing it reads, according to Fussman's translation from the Persian, "comes from Haḍḍa, found in a large jar with earth and bones" (1969: 5). Fussman offers the following interpretation, which seems plausible, of this note: "I think . . . that the Persian inscription only means that the inscribed potsherd had been found inside the jar, that is to say that the jar had been crushed and its neck [bearing the inscription] had fallen inside it. In our opinion there never was any other jar than this one, which contained the

10. Not to be confused with Tapa Kalān, which is a different subsite in the complex of Buddhist monuments in and around the village of Haḍḍa; see Tarzi 1990: 708.

11. Further information on funereal jars from Afghanistan is provided in Fussman and Le Berre 1976 and in Fussman 1974: 61.

bones" (1969: 9).[12] Thus, it seems likely that this jar too was used as a funereal vessel, although more recent discoveries show that Fussman was probably not correct in thinking that the pot "was intended for the inhumation of the monk" (p. 9) whose name appears in the inscription.[13]

Finally, another clay jar (pl. 17), which contained bones, now in the Ashmolean Museum, Oxford (accession no. EA 1995.158), was apparently found at about the same time as the pots that are now in the British Library collection and may have come from the same site. This jar differs from the others, however, in that it is decorated with drawings in ink of several figures. The best-preserved figure is that of, apparently, an aged monk, before whom one, or perhaps two, younger monks are bowing (pl. 18). About 90° to the right of this there are traces of another indistinct figure facing to the right and, apparently, yet another figure facing him. Also visible in the earliest available photograph, taken in 1993, are traces of a Kharoṣṭhī inscription (pl. 19), in which, however, only a few akṣaras are legible.[14] Inside the pot were found pieces of charred bones (pl. 20), presumably human.

To sum up the information provided here: there have been numerous finds, particularly from Haḍḍa and other sites in the Jalalabad Plain of eastern Afghanistan but also from sites in Gandhāra proper, of large earthen pots, generally resembling ordinary waterpots of a type still used widely in south Asia today. Some of the pots bear Kharoṣṭhī inscriptions recording their dedication to the Buddhist community by pious lay followers; in several such inscriptions, the objects are explicitly labeled as "waterpots" (*pani-ghaḍe,* etc.; see Appendix, sec. 5.1). Several of the pots, including both inscribed and uninscribed examples, contained human remains, while others contained fragments of Kharoṣṭhī texts written on birch bark. Thus such waterpots were evidently sometimes put to secondary use (see Appendix, sec. 5.2) by the inhabitants of the monasteries for the disposal of sacred relics, which included the ashes and bones of deceased monks or other persons and also, it now appears, the remains of old and worn-out manuscripts of Buddhist texts.

In some places—for example, at Tapa Kalān (Haḍḍa) and Pālāṭū Ḍherī—several such pots were found arranged in a neat row. This is reminiscent of similar situations at Buddhist sites in western India such as Sudhāgaṛh, Naḍsur, and Pitalkhoṛā, in southern India at Guṇṭupalle, and in the northeast at Lauṛiyā-Nandangaṛh, where stūpas containing bodily relics are arranged in "orderly rows" (Schopen 1991: 304). Abundant epigraphical and archeological evidence for the practice, evidently current from early Buddhist times, of burying the faithful "ad sanc-

12. "Je crois . . . que l'inscription persane signifie seulement que le tesson inscrit a été trouvé à l'intérieur de la jarre, c'est-à-dire que la jarre était écrasée, et que son col était tombé à l'intérieur. A notre avis il n'y a donc jamais eu qu'une jarre et cette jarre, contenait des ossements."

13. The interpretation of this inscription and related matters are discussed in detail in the Appendix, section 5.2.

14. This inscription is discussed in detail in the Appendix, section 5.3.

tos," that is, in the vicinity of the main stūpa of their monastery, has been collected and analyzed by Schopen (1987, 1991, 1994b). Various types of containers for the remains of the deceased have been found at Buddhist sites in many parts of India, including conventional relic caskets, special recesses at the top of stūpas (Schopen 1991: 294, 304), and earthenware vessels.[15] In the northwest the last type seems to have been preferred, to judge from the numerous examples found there.[16]

But the most important point with regard to our main topic, namely, the significance of the placement of the old scrolls in pots, is that they not only were deemed to be worthy of ritual interment but were evidently treated in the same way as the bodily relics of monks. This implies that written texts were perceived to have some sanctity or spiritual power comparable to that of the relics of deceased holy persons; or rather, that they were considered as a sort of relic themselves. Although it might seem strange that relics (bodily and textual) were interred in such humble containers as old waterpots and that no explicit inscriptional or textual record of this act was provided, this pattern is nonetheless consistent with the archeological and epigraphic record of Gandhāra: although monks' relics were often labeled by inscriptions in other parts of Buddhist India, in Gandhāra inscriptions seem to have been used only in connection with the relics of Śākyamuni himself (Schopen 1987: 198).

4.4. A "Buddhist Genizah"?

Several traditional cultures around the world have developed rules or customs that prohibit treating old written texts, especially holy scriptures, as ordinary refuse and that mandate some sort of ritual interment or disposition. Probably the best known manifestation of this phenomenon is the Jewish institution of the genizah, a storeroom in a synagogue in which worn-out books and ritual objects were placed. The original rationale of this institution was to avoid destroying the name of God written in religious texts, but eventually the practice was extended to the point where all written materials, regardless of their contents, were disposed in the genizah, in order to avoid even a remote possibility of obliterating God's name. In Islam too, it is common practice to avoid destroying written materials, again for fear of obliterating the name of God, and storerooms, analogous to the Jewish genizah,

15. E.g., several clay pots containing bones were found at Ratnagiri in Orissa; see, e.g., Mitra 1981–3: 1.29 and pl. XVIIA.

16. Although the burial of bones in and around stūpas is thus established as a widespread practice in early Indian Buddhism generally, it is nonetheless tempting to speculate that the particularly large number of human bones which seem to have been interred at Haḍḍa might be connected with the local cult of the Buddha's skull, which according to the Chinese pilgrims Fa Hsien (Legge 1886: 36–8) and Hsüan-tsang (Beal 1884: 95–6) was kept in a vihāra at "He-lo" (i.e., Haḍḍa) and was an object of great veneration there. Moreover, as was first suggested by Cunningham (1871: 38–9), the name Haḍḍa itself seems to be derived from the Sanskrit/Prakrit word *Haḍḍa*, "bone," and the name of the place itself may have promoted this association.

for discarded books, especially Korans, are also found in some old mosques (Sadan 1986: 42). The question of the proper procedures for the disposal of worn-out holy books was also a matter of concern among Muslim theologians (Sadan 1986).

A similar reverence for written materials has also developed in Asian cultures, though presumably not for the same reason. Thus in Tibet, according to Y. Bentor, "decaying holy scriptures are deposited in stupas and especially in edifices called tsha-khangs (tsha-tsha khang-pa or tsha-tsha house) that house both relics deposited in tsha-tshas [clay votive tablets] and decaying holy books" (private communication, August 1997). In China too, it was traditional to avoid throwing away any papers with written characters. "Orthodox persons would erect stone receptacles by the roadside where one could deposit unwanted scraps of inscribed paper . . . so as to prevent them from becoming soiled or being trodden upon in the street" (van Gulik 1956: 52).

In some cultures, a "dead book" is explicitly compared with, and treated analogously to, a dead human being. Sadan notes that "certain figures in Islamic jurisprudence . . . have drawn a parallel between the burial of the body of a deceased person . . . and the burial of worn-out sacred books" (1986: 39) and that, in Jewish practice, "[i]n many communities, once the Torah scroll has become worn-out and difficult to read, a 'funeral' is arranged to bury it" (p. 39). In India, the same concept seems to be reflected in Hoernle's report that "[i]n India, e.g. in Benares, it is the practice, when manuscripts have become old and damaged, to prepare a fresh copy, and consign the old one to the waters of the sacred river Ganges" (1916: 1). Hoernle also mentions the practice in eastern Turkestan "of giving to old and damaged manuscripts an honoured burial in the relic chamber of a stūpa" (p. 1).

The new material presented above suggests that the Buddhists of ancient Gandhāra may have followed practices analogous to those of Jewish, Islamic, and other traditions, in respect to both the general concept of ritually depositing old scriptures in the precincts of the place of worship and the specific idea of burying them in the same way as dead persons. Although there does not appear to be any direct textual reference to such a practice in Buddhist tradition, Bentor, in a study of the treatment of Buddhist books as relics in India and Tibet, does consider it "possible that Buddhist scriptures were deposited in stûpas in a practice analogous to the Jewish *geniza* . . . , that is to say, damaged books were 'buried' in a stûpa" (1995: 251 n. 18). It is true, however, that the actually attested examples of books treated as relics in the Buddhist world, including some of the Gilgit manuscripts as well as the stūpa burials of early Buddhist Japan and the abundant modern examples such as those described by Bentor (1994, 1995), involve complete and intact, rather than "dead," books (see also 4.5.1.).

All in all, the best explanation of the British Library Kharoṣṭhī fragments seems to be that they are a collection of old, worn-out or damaged texts that had been recopied and then ritually buried like dead monks. If this is correct, what we have is, in effect, a scrap heap of "dead" manuscripts from the library, or perhaps rather from the scriptorium, of a Buddhist monastery, probably of the Dharmaguptaka school, dating from around the first century A.D. and apparently located in eastern Afghanistan. As such, the contents of the scrolls could be expected to reflect a more or less random sampling of the contents of the library from which they came, and the detailed analysis of the texts, to be undertaken in years to come, should provide us with unprecedented insights into the corpus of texts that were set in writing by a community of Gandhāran Buddhists in this formative period.

Although the selection of the pieces that have survived is a matter of chance, there is internal evidence to suggest that the process of the recopying and disposing of old texts was an orderly and planned activity. As discussed in section 4.2, the manuscripts with the later copyists' notations form a coherent group in that not only were they originally written by the same two scribes but also the later annotations on them are, in six out of seven cases, in an identical third hand. This means that these manuscripts not only originally constituted a distinct set of texts but also were recopied as a unit. This in turn suggests that they constituted part of a "library" in the proper sense of the term, that is, of an orderly and systematic collection of written texts, as opposed to a more or less randomly accumulated pile of manuscripts.[17] Furthermore, the fact that they were evidently recopied as a group indicates that the preservation of written texts was also an organized and systematic activity.[18] Although we should not assume that the existence of what seems to be an orderly corpus of written scriptures means that the Buddhists of ancient Gandhāra maintained a formal and comprehensive written canon in the strict sense of the term, it does show that they used writing as an important, if not exclusive, means for preserving their traditions.[19]

Finally, it must be conceded that the explanation presented here of the British Library fragments as a cache of discarded manuscripts is not the only possible one, nor is it completely beyond doubt. As mentioned previously, it is possible that some of the scrolls could have been more or less intact when they were placed in the pot. Thus, it is conceivable, though I think less likely, that the collection as originally interred in ancient times was a mixture of intact and fragmentary scrolls. If this were the case, a different explanation would have to be found. Such a situation, for instance, could reflect a practice parallel to that followed in contemporary

17. Virtually nothing can be said at this point about the physical form, location, and arrangement of such a (still hypothetical) monastic library, though some possibly relevant hints appear in the vinaya literature (see Schopen 1994a: 530–1).

18. If we are correct in thinking that all the scrolls were to some extent damaged or fragmentary before they were interred, the question arises as to how satisfactory copies could have been made from them. The copyists might have accomplished this either by referring to other, better-preserved copies of the same texts and/or by reconstructing the missing portions from memory.

19. This point will be discussed further in section 8.1.4.2.

Tibet, where learned lamas are said to be buried together with their books. If such a practice was current in ancient Gandhāra, we would expect to find cases in which remains of both human bones and manuscripts were found together in funereal vessels. Unfortunately, none of the available reports clearly document such a case, and there is no indication that the pot that contained the British Library fragments also had any traces of human remains; but since we have no reliable report of its complete original contents, it is possible that this was the case. In view of these uncertainties, it may not be possible to definitively determine the nature and purpose of the deposit of the British Library manuscripts, unless similar materials should happen to come to light, under more favorable circumstances, in the future. But for the time being, I consider the genizah model the most likely explanation.

4.5. Additional Comments on the Interment of Manuscripts and Birch Bark Texts

4.5.1. The Burial of Books in Later Buddhist Practice

The practice of storing or interring written texts, particularly sacred texts, in earthenware containers was widespread in the ancient world, although the motives for doing so were probably quite diverse. The Nag Hammadi codices and the Dead Sea scrolls, for example, were, like the Gandhāran manuscripts, found in clay jars. In the Buddhist world, numerous Sanskrit manuscripts in Brāhmī-derived scripts, all somewhat later than the ones with which we have been concerned here, have been found in more or less similar circumstances in diverse regions. For instance, birch bark manuscripts dating from about the fifth and sixth centuries A.D. were found inside painted clay vases buried in the stūpas at Merv and Bairam Ali[20] in Turkmenistan (Vorob′eva-Desjatovskaja 1983: 69–85; Frumkin 1970: 147–8; Bongard-Levin 1975–6: 78–80). The so-called Gilgit manuscripts are another outstanding example of the interment of manuscripts in stūpas (though not in earthenware containers). The manuscripts comprise a large group of Buddhist texts on birch bark which, according to Joseph Hackin's report, were found "deposited in the chamber arranged in the interior" of the largest of a group of four stūpas at Naupur, near Gilgit in northern Pakistan (quoted in Lévi 1932: 14).

There is, however, an important difference between the circumstances of the interment of the British Library manuscripts and of these later texts. Whereas the British Library scrolls were evidently already damaged and fragmentary before the time of their interment, the later deposits usually consist of texts that were more or less intact and complete, and sometimes, as in the case of some of the Gilgit manuscripts, even in excellent condition. And the ritual deposit of intact manuscripts, though better attested in later centuries, may also be reflected in the case of the

20. On the Bairam Ali manuscript, see also section 2.2.4.

KDhP scroll, which is at least approximately coeval with the British Library scrolls. If it is true, as I have provisionally surmised (3.1.1), that the KDhP scroll was actually kept inside a clay jar, it must have been placed there while still relatively new and intact, since it seems to have been complete and in good condition when it was discovered in the late nineteenth century. Unfortunately, the circumstances of the discovery of the KDhP are too poorly documented to permit any definite conclusion on this point, but if the KDhP is in fact a case of ritual interment of an intact text, this would establish a much earlier origin for this practice.

Thus, it remains to be determined how the hypothetical practice of ritually disposing of "dead" books might relate to the practice, better attested in later times, of depositing written texts as *dharmaśarīra* ("bodily relics of the dharma"), or even whether there is in principle any difference between them; and further, whether and how either or both of these practices may be historically related to the Mahāyāna "cult of the book" (Schopen 1975). The ramifications of these questions, however, go far beyond the scope of the present study, and this issue is merely raised here by way of a suggestion for future discussion.

4.5.2. Birch Bark Texts Found in Reliquaries

Besides the several cases of texts written on birch bark in Kharoṣṭhī and other scripts and preserved in earthen funereal vessels, examples are also known of small inscribed pieces of birch bark placed in conventional stone or metal reliquaries. One such example—remnants of a Kharoṣṭhī text on bark found inside a pyxis-shaped stone reliquary—was described above in section 3.3. Another specimen is a "long strip of thin birch-leaf manuscript" with an inscription in Brāhmī script of about the fourth century A.D. that was found inside a "tiny copper vessel with a lid fastened to it by a wire" (A. Ghosh in *Archaeology in India* 1950: 60) in the loose soil near a small stūpa at Lauṛiyā-Nandangaṛh. The strip was "so fragile that it was impossible to spread it out thoroughly. The bits that could be extricated were sufficient to show that the manuscript was that of a Buddhist text (probably the *Pratītya-samutpāda-sūtra,* as the word *nirodha* could be read a few times)" (Ghosh 1989: 2.255; see also Ghosh 1966: 23). If this guess as to the contents of the text (which unfortunately seems to be the only information available on it) is correct, the find is reminiscent of the dedicatory Kharoṣṭhī inscription on the Kurram casket, which includes, as a sort of postscript, a text of the *pratītya-samutpāda* in Gāndhārī (Ghosh 1967). The Kharoṣṭhī text on the hopelessly fragmented piece of bark that was placed along with relics and other objects in the aforementioned pyxis-shaped reliquary cannot be reconstructed at all, but it too might have contained a *pratītya-samutpāda* or similar formulaic text. The same might also have been the case with the "prayers" found by Barthoux on small pieces of bark at Haḍḍa (see 3.2.1), as well as with some of the inscribed pieces of bark found by Masson, such as the one inside a steatite vase at Haḍḍa tope no. 1.

Small birch bark texts of this type also sometimes contained dhāraṇīs. A dhāraṇī text from Tunhuang cited by Hoernle recommends that it be copied onto, among other materials, birch bark (*bhūrja-patre vā vastre vā kalke vā kāyagate vā kaṇṭhagate vā likhitvā;* Hoernle 1911: 475), and several actual specimens of dhāraṇī texts on small scrolls of birch bark were found inside reliquaries at Naupur, near Gilgit (von Hinüber 1981: 166–7). But some of the birch bark texts found inside reliquaries may also have been ordinary manuscripts intended to accompany, or even to substitute for, the bodily relics. This could be the case, for example, with the one found by Honigberger at Shiwaki (see 3.2.1 and fig. 8). In any case, this is all more or less guesswork, since none of these smaller birch bark texts has been satisfactorily studied and published.

It is clear, however, that birch bark texts were used as amulets, in both Buddhist and Hindu practice, for many centuries. Bentor (1995: 255) quotes a late Buddhist text recommending that one should write the "Buddhist creed" (*ye dharmā hetuprabhavāḥ,* etc.) on a piece of birch bark and wrap it around a relic, and Bühler reported that in the late nineteenth century "the use of birch-bark for writing still survives in India, though the fact is little known. *Mantras,* which are worn as amulets, are written on pieces of Bhûrja. . . . The custom prevails in Bengal, as well as in Gujarât" (1877: 29 n. 4). R. Mitra also described "a piece of birch-bark about a hundred years old, which on a space of ten inches by eight, contains the whole Bhagavadgītā, written with letters so small that they are illegible to the naked eye. . . . It was evidently intended to be worn as an amulet enclosed in a locket of gold or copper" (cited by Janert 1955–6: 71).[21] It thus appears that birch bark had, or eventually developed, a ritual function well beyond the geographical and temporal boundaries of ancient Gandhāra. Although these later remains involve different practices from those motivating the interment of the British Library manuscripts, it is nonetheless possible to see a broad continuity with regard to a certain sanctity granted to texts written on birch bark.

21. I have not been able to trace the original text cited by Janert.

Chapter 5

Format, Material, and Construction of the Scrolls

5.1. The Large (Composite) Scrolls

5.1.1. Format and Dimensions

All of the fragmentary manuscripts in the new collection are in the form of scrolls composed of strips of birch bark. From the fragmentary colophon in fragment 3B and from the verse written at the top of the KDhP scroll (see 2.2.6), we know that these scrolls were referred to as *postaka* or *postaga*, an Iranian loanword which appears in Sanskrit as *pustaka*, "book." The majority of the scrolls are composite pieces made up of several pieces of bark cut to an appropriate size and glued together to form long strips of continuous writing surface. The scribes would begin writing at the top of the recto side, which was the outer surface of the bark, and continue to the bottom. Then, in most cases, the strip would be turned over and the writing continued in the reverse direction on the verso, from the bottom of the scroll back up to the top. The writing on the verso is thus upside down in relation to that on the recto, and both the beginning and the end of the text (assuming that the verso was completely filled up) would have been at the top of the scroll. The inscribed scrolls were rolled up from the bottom with the recto on the inside. In theory, then, a colophon at the end of the scroll (i.e., the top of the verso) would be visible when the scroll was rolled up, enabling a reader to identify the contents of the scroll without having to unroll it. However, for reasons that will be discussed below, the tops of the scrolls have not survived, except for one apparent exception (see 2.2.6). In all the texts, the writing is across the scroll, that is to say, parallel to its narrow dimension, so that the scrolls would have been held vertically when read.

In several scrolls, however, instead of a single text written continuously from top to bottom on the recto and then, on the verso, back again to the top of the scroll, we find that a text was written on the recto only (e.g., frags. 1, 5A, 5B, 14, and 16 + 25), and the scribe stopped writing at or near the bottom. Evidently the recto, that is, the soft white outer side of the bark, was the preferred writing surface, and some scribes did not like to use the verso at all. In writing longer texts, they apparently preferred to use several scrolls inscribed on the recto only to make up a single text in multiple "volumes." In several of these cases, however (e.g., frags. 1, 14, and 16 + 25), the blank spaces remaining at the bottom of the recto and on the whole of the verso were filled in, presumably at a later date, by another scribe writing what seem to be unrelated texts.[1] In most such examples, the same two hands (nos. 1 and 2 in the list given in 2.5) are involved, so that this might have been an arrangement peculiar to this particular set of scrolls; but I think it likely that this was common practice, in part because similar usages are well attested in other parts of the ancient world—for instance, in Egyptian, Greek, and Roman papyri (Diringer 1953: 130, 138). Likewise, many of the Chinese rolls found at Tunhuang have secondary texts added on the verso.

The width of the scrolls varies considerably, and for most of them it is impossible to provide precise figures because one or both of their vertical edges are broken off. The maximum widths observed are 24 cm (frag. 5C), 22 cm (5B), and 19.7 cm (20), but in each case the margins are damaged, so their original widths must have been somewhat greater. The widest scroll for which precise measurements can be given, that is, whose edges are intact at one or more points along its length, measures 14.5 cm (frag. 1), but this is actually one of the narrower scrolls, which tended to suffer less damage to their edges. The narrowest scroll with intact margins measured only 5.5 cm, but this one (frag. 6) is the unique and anomalous Sanskrit medical text in Brāhmī script, which should not be taken as representative. Otherwise, the narrowest intact scroll is the comparatively well preserved fragment 9, whose width varies between 13 and 14 cm. The original width of the majority of scrolls whose margin(s) are damaged is impossible to establish with precision, but it is noteworthy that several of the present widths fall within the range of 16–20 cm; for example, fragment 20, with both margins lost, measures a maximum of 19.7 cm, and the maximum width of fragment 23, whose left margin is intact in a few places and whose right margin is broken off, is 18.5 cm. Thus, the original width of the majority of the scrolls probably ranged from about 14 to 25 cm, or 5–9½ inches. This agrees with the dimensions of the only comparable piece, namely, the KDhP scroll, whose present width, according to Brough, "varies for the most part between 19 and 19.5 cm., but occasionally approaches 21 cm. Allowing for some slight loss through wear, the average width in its original state may be taken as approximately 20 cm. or 8 inches" (1962: 18).

The original length of the scrolls is more difficult to determine. The longest surviving sections are 213.4 cm (frag. 4), 154.8 cm (1), 127.7 cm (29),[2] and 115 cm (15). But all of these and the other scrolls are incomplete, and the amount of material missing can only be estimated, in a very rough way, from textual indications. This can be done in connection with scrolls bearing texts for which parallel or re-

1. It is, however, possible that the second texts, which are invariably avadāna or similar collections, were in some way linked to the first texts, perhaps by way of serving as commentarial material or illustrative examples, but no firm evidence of this has yet been found.

2. Fragment 29 seems to be part of the same text and scroll as 26, which is 64.5 cm long, but it is not yet clear whether the two fragments originally followed one after the other or were the right and left halves of a scroll split vertically like fragments 16 + 25 (see 5.3.3).

lated texts are available in complete form from other sources, enabling us to estimate the proportion of missing text. This applies, for example, to fragment 15, which contains the Saṅgīti-sūtra with a commentary. The Saṅgīti-sūtra consists of lists of sets of items or categories grouped according to the number of items in each set, from one to ten; that is to say, the first section is a list of single items, the second is a list of paired items, the third, groups of threes, and so on. The Saṅgīti-sūtra is extant in several different versions, in Pali, Sanskrit, and Chinese, which diverge considerably from one another, but the number and ordering of the items in the new Gāndhārī recension agree most closely with the Chinese Dīrghāgama version (see 8.2.2.1), so that version is used as a basis for comparison here.

The Gāndhārī text of the Saṅgīti-sūtra, like most of the larger scroll fragments, preserves only the lower part of the original scroll, which contains the middle of the text, since the beginning and end would have been at the lost top of the scroll, on the recto and verso respectively. The preliminary examination of the text carried out to date has located the sets corresponding to sets III.16 through V.6 of the Chinese version. Since the Chinese text has a total of thirty-seven triads in section III and thirty-six tetrads in section IV, this means that the total number of items discussed in the surviving portions of the scroll should be approximately sixty-four, that is, the last twenty-two triads of III (37 minus 15) plus all thirty-six tetrads in IV and the first six pentads of V. The total number of sets in all ten sections of the complete Chinese text is 139, which would mean that the extant portion of the Gāndhārī scroll, comprising about sixty-four sets, should be slightly less than half of the complete text.[3] Therefore, since the surviving portion of fragment 15 is 115 cm long, the length of the complete scroll would probably be slightly more than double that, or in the neighborhood of 230–50 cm (≈90–100 inches).

Using the same principle, an estimate may be made of the length of another original scroll, portions of which are preserved as fragments 16 and 25, which are actually the right and left halves respectively of the same original piece. The surviving portion of the larger fragment, 16, is 40.5 cm long, of which, on the recto side, the lower 26 cm are taken up by a second text that was evidently added to the blank space left at the bottom after the first text was completed. The first text consists of fragments of verses that correspond closely to the last thirteen verses of the Bhikhu-varga (nos. 28–40 = nos. 78–90 of the text as a whole) of the KDhP. Since

3. This estimate depends on the following assumptions:

a. That the total number of topics was similar in the Chinese and Gāndhārī texts: this is very likely, in view of the close parallels in their sequences for the extant portion of the latter (as documented in 8.2.2.1).

b. That the length of the commentary on each of the topics in the Gāndhārī text is on average approximately equal: preliminary studies of the text seem to bear this out.

c. That the text began and ended at or near the lost top of the scroll, without any lengthy blank space at the end: this cannot be determined but seems to be the most likely assumption.

the Bhikhu-varga is the second chapter of the KDhP, it is likely that the first text on this fragment contained the first two vargas of the same or a similar recension of the Dharmapada and constituted the first scroll of a multivolume manuscript of this text. This assumes, of course, that the sequence of vargas was the same in both texts, but the close (though not perfect) correspondence in the order of the surviving verses makes this fairly likely. In any case, if this assumption is correct, the missing upper portion of the scroll would have contained the fifty verses of the first chapter (Brammaṇa-varga) plus the first twenty-seven verses of the Bhikhu-varga. Since the thirteen surviving verses in the new fragment take up about 15 cm of the scroll, the entire text of the Brammaṇa- and Bhikhu-vargas, comprising ninety verses, should have covered about 100 cm. This, added to the remaining 26 cm at the bottom of the scroll, which had apparently been left blank by the original scribe of the Dharmapada and filled in later by a different scribe writing a different (avadāna) text, yields a total length for the entire scroll of roughly 125 cm (≈50 inches).

An estimate of the total length of the KDhP scroll was made by Brough on similar grounds, though his results are likely to be considerably more accurate, since a greater portion of that scroll is preserved than is the case with the new ones discussed here. Brough's calculations yielded a total original length of "some 5 metres or 16 feet 6 inches" (1962: 19), with a maximum margin of error of about 1 foot. Thus, unlike the case of the width, where the comparison of the new scrolls with the KDhP produced similar results, the calculated lengths of the two new fragments in question are much less than that of the KDhP; slightly less than half in the case of fragment 15 and only one quarter in the case of 16 + 25. Therefore, if the estimates proposed here are even remotely close to correct, they would indicate two significantly different techniques of constructing scrolls. In the case of the KDhP, it was clearly the intention of the scribe to write the complete text on a single long scroll, as explained by Brough (1962: 13). But at least some of the scribes of the new texts preferred to divide longer texts onto two or more scrolls. This is presumably the case, for example, with fragments 16 + 25, where the first text ends with the last verse of the second chapter (of twenty-six chapters) of the KDhP. If we are correct to assume that this was the first of a set of scrolls containing a complete Dharmapada, and if we can further assume that the text as a whole was similar in extent and sequence to that of the KDhP, the complete set would probably have comprised six scrolls of similar size, since these two chapters (the longest in the collection, whose sections are generally arranged according to the number of verses they contain in descending order) have ninety verses in all, while the complete KDhP is estimated by Brough (1962: 23) to have had about 540 verses.

One reason for dividing a single text among several scrolls is an evident distaste for writing on the verso side, at least on the part of the scribe (hand no. 1) who wrote the first text on fragments 16 + 25, as well as on two other manuscripts (1 and 14) that also have different texts on recto and verso. The scribe in question has a neat and precise hand and seems to have been a careful writer who was particular about his materials and disliked writing on the rougher texture of the inner surface of the bark. Another possible motivation for writing multivolume texts is that several shorter scrolls may be more convenient to read than a single long scroll (see Brough 1962: 12). In fact, the practice of using multiple scrolls is well attested in other parts of the ancient world (see, e.g., Diringer 1953: 130–3) and accounts for the modern term "volume" (from Latin *volumen*, "a roll"), as well as for the use of "book" to refer to a subsection of a long text that, in modern practice, may actually be printed in a single volume.

But whatever his motivations might have been, it is virtually certain that this scribe in particular, and presumably others as well, divided single texts over multiple scrolls. This is confirmed, for example, by fragment 14, where a passage that corresponds approximately to section 14 of the Catukka-nipāta of the Pali Aṅguttara-nikāya ends after the detailed description of the third of the four *pradhānas* (*saṃvara, anurakṣaṇa, bhāvanā,* and *prahāṇa*) that were introduced earlier in the text. The text breaks off in the middle of a discrete section and certainly must have been continued on another scroll, which unfortunately has not been preserved. In some other cases, however, such as that of the Saṅgīti-sūtra manuscript described above, a single text was evidently written out in full on a single scroll, recto and verso, as was the KDhP. The extremely small handwriting of the scribe of fragment 15 evidently facilitated fitting the entire text on one relatively short scroll.

But beyond the two cases discussed above, we can only guess the original lengths of the new scrolls. Further detailed study and identification of the texts of some of them might make additional estimates of this type possible, but such indications as are available at present suggest that most, if not all, of the new scrolls were much shorter than the KDhP. It could be that the latter scroll, at about five meters, was an anomalously long one in the Gandhāran tradition, but comparisons with other parts of the ancient world show that scrolls of this and greater length were not unusual. For example, Pliny the Elder, who lived at around the same time (A.D. 23–79) as the probable date of the new manuscripts, described standardized papyrus rolls being sold in Rome with a length that seems to correspond to about fifteen feet (Diringer 1953: 129), and much longer Egyptian and Greek scrolls are known. Diringer concludes that in the classical world, "[g]enerally speaking, the length of the rolls seems to have varied according to taste and convenience" (p. 133), and this seems to have been the case in the Gandhāran cultural sphere as well. Nonetheless, it is striking that, as far as we can tell from the surviving fragments, the newly discovered scrolls appear to have been considerably shorter than the KDhP scroll. This is one of several indications, which will be discussed in this and the following chapter, that although the Khotan scroll comes, broadly speaking, from the same Gandhāran cultural milieu as the new Kharoṣṭhī texts, it nonetheless seems to represent a separate tradition with different scribal, paleographic, and linguistic habits.

5.1.2. Construction

Scrolls several meters long, like the KDhP, and even the relatively shorter ones in the new collection, at least some of which were probably two to three meters long, were not constructed out of a single sheet of bark. The technique of construction of the KDhP scroll has been a matter of uncertainty in the past, but the new scrolls now enable us to clarify the matter. Brough does not directly address the question of the construction of the long scroll, only referring rather vaguely to "the whole strip, held together by stitching down both edges" (1962: 18). Also, in discussing the total length of the scroll, he speculates that "the scribe normally takes the obvious precaution of continuing to extend his strip until he is a little beyond half-way in the text" (p. 13), but he fails to explain exactly what a scribe might have done to "extend his strip." In earlier descriptions of the Khotan scroll one finds comments such as "[t]he strips of bark on which this manuscript is written, measure about 8 inches (or 20 centimeters) in width and one yard, more or less, in length" (Hoernle 1900: 126). But this figure of one yard, and the 1.23 meters reported by Senart (1898: 199), seem to refer to the pieces into which the complete scroll was torn after its discovery in the late nineteenth century and have no relevance to its original components. Kaye seems to come closest to a correct understanding of the composition of the KDhP scroll in supposing that "[t]he scapus was made by joining pieces of unknown depth together," though he adds, "[B]ut I can see no evidence of this in the illustrations given in the *Journal Asiatique* (1898, p. 308)" (1927: 10 and n. 1).

In several of the new scrolls, however, the method of construction is readily apparent. In fragment 1, in particular, we can clearly see places where separate strips of bark have been overlapped and glued together to form the long compound scrolls. This becomes even clearer in some places where the separate strips have come apart, as for example in part 2 of fragment 1 (fig. 9). Here the joint has separated and a gap appears between the two component sections as they have been set in the glass frames. On the recto, the lower piece has a blank space about 3 cm high below a neatly trimmed straight edge at the top, while on the verso there is a similar blank at the bottom of the upper piece (upper piece of verso = lower piece of recto). These empty spaces represent the area that was originally overlapped and glued to another section before the composite scroll was inscribed. Part 4 of the same scroll has a similar separated joint, and the distance between these two joints is approximately 45 cm. Farther down the scroll, on part 5, at almost exactly the same distance (44 cm) from the joint on part 4, there is a joint that is still intact but easily discernible in the form of a heavy horizontal line with a notably different texture in the bark surface above and below it (fig. 10). The line of text immediately above this juncture line is incomplete, ending halfway across the scroll, and the text resumes at the beginning of the next line. The scribe has apparently done this in order to avoid having to write across the juncture line, which he otherwise could not have avoided because he had written the preceding line with a pronounced downward slope.

Fig. 9. Fragment 1, part 2, r, detail of separated juncture between segments

Thus in fragment 1, the continuous scroll, of which 154.8 cm is preserved, was evidently pieced together from separate strips about 45 cm in length, except for the bottom strip, which seems to have been about 30 cm long and hence may have been trimmed to size. Similar junctures are visible in several other of the better-preserved scrolls, though nowhere as clearly as in fragment 1. For example, there is a partially separated joint at the middle of fragment 12, part 2, and another one at the bottom of the same fragment.[4] In this case, the two junctures are separated by only 21 cm, so that 12 + 14 was apparently made up of shorter sections than fragment 1.

The margins of the composite-scroll manuscripts were usually sewn along each vertical margin about 0.5–1 cm in from the edge (see also Kaye 1927: 10). In the KDhP these margin threads are well preserved and clearly visible. In the new manuscripts they have mostly disappeared, although a few remnants of them are preserved, for example, in fragment 25, where a frayed piece of dark brown, almost black thread about 4.5 cm long is visible lying across the upper right corner of the verso. But in most of the scrolls where parts of one or both margins are preserved, the needle holes through which the edging string had been threaded, typically about 5 mm apart, are still clearly visible, as also are the vertical bruises left by the thread itself between the holes.

The purpose of sewing the margins was probably not so much to protect the edges themselves as to guard against the horizontal cracks that birch bark is prone to develop when it is rolled up for long periods (see 5.3.3). The binding would serve both to retard the process of horizontal splitting and also to hold together those pieces of scrolls that had split apart. Although the margin threads may have helped to reinforce the joints between the sections of the composite scrolls, this was evidently not their primary function, as seems to be suggested by Brough's reference to "the whole strip, held together by stitching down both edges" (1962: 18), for if this were the intention, there would be no reason to stitch the entire length of the margins. As will be shown below, in the KDhP scroll the joints were reinforced by two separate, additional rows of stitching, nearer the center than the continuous margin threads, but this was not done in any of the scrolls in the new collection.

A few of the scrolls appear to have had unsewn edges. This is clearly the case, for example, in the small fragments 2 and 3A. Fragment 6 is also unsewn, but this manuscript is anomalous in several respects, being the only text in the collection in Sanskrit and in Brāhmī script, as well as being much narrower than all the others, so that it cannot be considered representative. Finally, fragments 11, 21, and 24, which are tentatively attributed to the same original text and/or scroll, are also unsewn. If

4. This latter joint was originally connected to the top of fragment 14. The identical hand and textual continuity (see pp. 48, 70) show that fragment 14 is actually the next component section of the same original scroll as fragment 12, although the juncture between them had separated before they were interred, so that they were rolled up and placed in the pot separately (4.1).

Fig. 10. Fragment 1, part 5, r, detail
of intact juncture between segments

these pieces, including the relatively large fragment 21, are in fact part of the same scroll, this would establish that even longer scrolls were sometimes left unsewn.

5.1.3. Comparisons with the Khotan Dharmapada Scroll

In light of this new information, it is now possible to have another look at the KDhP with a view to finding evidence of a similar composite structure. A close study of the published photographs in Brough's edition led me to suspect that this scroll too has similar junctures, hitherto unnoticed, and this was confirmed by a direct examination of fragments A, B, and C, which are kept in the Bibliothèque Nationale, Paris, in December 1996. My inspection revealed that the long KDhP scroll is actually made up of twelve separate strips, ranging from about 13 to 47 cm in length, each joined to the next with an overlapped section from about 2.5 to 4 cm long. Each juncture is reinforced by two small rows of thread, from 1.7 to 3.5 cm long, double-stitched vertically over the overlapped portion at a point anywhere from 3.5 to 6.5 cm in from each margin. These joint-reinforcing threads are visible, with varying degrees of clarity, in the plates in Brough 1962 (e.g., in pl. II at the lower left), but they are more clearly reproduced in the plates in Senart 1898 (e.g., pl. III, center). On the original fragments they are well preserved and easily visible, though they seem to have escaped the attention of the several scholars who have studied the scroll.

Fig. 11. Original segments of the Khotan Dharmapada scroll, based on Brough 1962: 11, with the divisions between the segments added. Solid and broken lines (after Brough) mark the pieces into which the scroll was torn after its discovery. Dotted lines (added to Brough) mark the junctures between the original segments of the scroll, and lines of x's mark such junctures hypothetically posited in the missing parts of the scroll.

Below each pair of reinforcing threads, the line of juncture between the separate sheets of bark is visible as a horizontal line, which is sometimes discernible in the photographs (e.g., in Brough's pl. IX, between lines 198 and 199) and which is unmistakably clear in the original fragments. In most cases, the normal amount of space is left between the lines of writing above and below the juncture line, but in one case, on the verso of fragment C, a vertical space about 5.5 cm long has been left blank. This blank area corresponds more or less to the overlapping junction of the two joined sections, and the surface here shows several anomalously wrinkled portions. (These are virtually invisible in Brough's pl. XX but clear in Senart's pl. IV.) Here Brough suggests that "the reason seems to have been an unusually rough piece of bark" (p. 14), but I think it more likely that the wrinkling resulted from an excessive application of glue to the juncture.

Contrary to what Brough believed, it can be established that the composite scroll of the KDhP was made up in full before the scribe began writing on it. The clearest indication of this is that, in numerous places, a larger than normal space is left between letters located on either side of one of the vertical joint-reinforcing threads. For instance, in lines 217–9 of fragment C, the space between the second and third akṣaras of the fourth pāda in each line (*viha-ramu, viha-ramu, putre-ṣu*) is considerably wider than normal because of the presence of the joining thread between them (see Brough's pl. X). This and many other similar examples throughout the manuscript show that the entire scroll was prepared before writing began and that Brough was wrong to think that the scribe would "extend his strip" (1962: 13) as

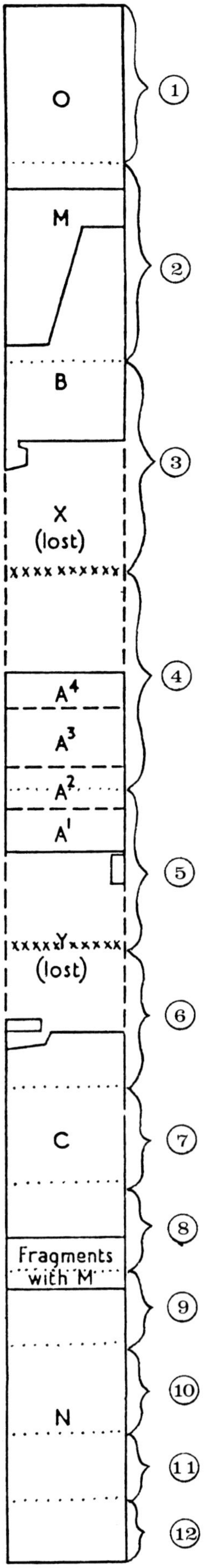

he went along, estimating the length (though wrongly, according to Brough 1962: 13) that he would need to fit his full text on the scroll. Actually, instead of a cumbersome and time-wasting procedure of building up the scroll section by section as the scribe proceeded in writing the text, we may think, in light of the larger number of scrolls now known, of a system of manufacturing birch bark scrolls in advance, whether with a specific text in mind or, perhaps more likely, through production en masse in a separate workshop. In this scenario, a scribe might have chosen from an available store of blank composite bark scrolls what appeared to him to be an appropriately sized prepared piece for the text he intended to write or copy.

Now that it is possible to positively locate the junctures in the KDhP scroll, its component sections can be identified and measured with reasonable accuracy. The results of such an analysis, carried out on the basis of a direct examination in the case of the Paris fragments and from published photographs of the sections now in St. Petersburg, are presented below and in figure 11:

Number and Extent of Section	Length (cm)[5]
1. From beginning (top) of the scroll to line 28 (frag. O)	40.6 + ?[6]
2. From line 29 to line 116 (frag. B)	46.9
3. From line 117 to (hypothetical) juncture in the lost fragment X	26.9 + ?
4. From juncture in fragment X to line 175 (frag. A^2)	? + 35.8
5. From line 176 to (hypothetical) juncture in the lost fragment Y	13.1 + ?
6. From juncture in fragment Y to line 198 (frag. C)	? + 13.8
7. From line 199 to line 219 (frag. C)	23.5
8. From line 220 to line 82/90 ("fragments with M")[7]	20.4
9. From line 83/89[8] to line 249 (frag. N)	20.0
10. From line 250 to line 269 (frag. N)	23.1
11. From line 270 to line 283 (frag. N)	17.5
12. From line 284 to end of the scroll (frag. N)	13.1

5. Measured directly from the originals in the case of the Paris fragments. A comparison with these measurements shows that Brough's plates are about 80% of actual size, so that approximate measurements for the actual size of the St. Petersburg fragments were derived by multiplying their sizes in Brough's plates by 1.25. Given these and other variables such as the unevenness of the junctures between sections, the measurements provided are approximate but should be accurate within about 1 cm.

6. Brough's plate I does not show the complete extent of the blank space at the top of the scroll, so the actual length is somewhat (but probably not too much) longer than 40.6 cm.

7. This designation (following Brough) refers to several loose fragments that were arranged and photographed in St. Petersburg together with fragment M (at the upper portion of the scroll) but that textual studies have shown to actually belong between fragments C and N, near the end of the scroll. Here and throughout, the numbering of the lines of the KDhP scroll is dependent on

This chart shows that the component sections of the KDhP scroll were arranged approximately in order of size, with the largest pieces at the beginning and the smallest at the end. This situation could have resulted from a process whereby the scribe, or perhaps rather the artisan whose task it was to construct the scrolls, would choose from a stock of precut pieces of bark the largest and best pieces first and then resort to gradually smaller sections until he had reached the desired length for the complete scroll. The construction of the British Library scrolls, particularly that of fragment 1 as discussed above, indicates a similar pattern of shorter sections toward the bottom of the scrolls, although their incomplete condition does not permit a complete analysis like the one presented above for the larger and better-preserved KDhP. It is also striking that the length of the sections in the KDhP and in the new scrolls is closely comparable, particularly with respect to the maximum attested size, namely about 47 cm in the KDhP and 45 cm in British Library fragment 1. This is perhaps not coincidental but may be governed by factors such as the size of the largest vertical section of bark that could be safely and conveniently peeled from a birch tree (see 5.4.1).

In conclusion, a comparison of the techniques of construction of the KDhP scroll and the new British Library scrolls shows that they are essentially similar, differing only in detail. In both cases, the long scrolls were built up of strips of bark that were joined together, but the method of juncture differs. In the KDhP, the strips were sewn and (apparently) also glued together, whereas the British Library scrolls seem to have been glued only, as no traces of the type of reinforcing threads seen in the KDhP have been found in them.

5.2. Construction of the Smaller Texts

Although the long composite-scroll format predominates among the new manuscripts (and hence, presumably, among Gandhāran manuscripts generally), the British Library collection also contains a few smaller pieces that seem to have been constructed in a different manner. The clearest example of this is fragment 5B, the Rhinoceros Horn Sūtra text. The remaining fragments of this unfortunately very fragmentary and poorly preserved text cover an area about 22 cm wide and 38 cm long. The width is exceptionally large compared to most of the scrolls. The length, on the other hand, is unusually short, but there is reason to think that

their placement in the photographs rather than their proper position in the original scroll, which was only determined gradually later on through the efforts of various scholars who worked on them, culminating in Brough's definitive edition. This explains the anomalous and seemingly illogical ordering of many lines (e.g., in this case, line 82 following line 219). The double line numbers here ("line 82/90") represent cases where parts of the same original line were separated and numbered differently according to their positions in the photographs.

8. Line 89 follows line 90 because the small fragment that contains these lines was placed upside down in the photograph; see the preceding note.

the fragment, despite its poor state, contains most of the original text. This is established mainly on the grounds of a comparison with the corresponding Pali text, the Khaggavisāṇa-sutta, which contains forty-one verses, while the remaining fragments of the Gāndhārī text preserve parts of about forty-three verses, at least thirty-five[9] of which correspond to verses in the Pali version (though in a largely different order). This indicates that the two versions of the poem were approximately similar in contents and scope, although the Gāndhārī one was slightly longer, and this in turn suggests that the complete Gāndhārī text was probably only slightly longer than the part of it that has survived. If this is correct, the poem was written on a relatively small, single, noncomposite piece of bark, unless it was part of a longer composite scroll containing two or more texts. But this is not likely, since the multitext scrolls that are attested in this collection seem to involve secondary texts added to uninscribed portions of preexisting composite scrolls rather than collections of short texts on a long scroll originally prepared for such use. Thus, it seems that some brief texts were written on small, single sheets of bark, much shorter but perhaps somewhat wider than most of the long, composite scrolls.

The Rhinoceros Horn scroll has other features that set it apart from most of the other manuscripts, though these features are not necessarily characteristic of the shorter format. For instance, the verses are written one to a line, with a space about 1.5 cm in length between each of the quarter-verses. This agrees with the arrangement of the KDhP but not with the other verse texts, such as the Anavatapta-gāthā (frag. 1), in the new collection, where the lines are written continuously without regard to verse divisions or pāda breaks. Also unlike most of the other new manuscripts, the verso of the Rhinoceros Horn scroll was left blank, being used neither for the primary text nor for a secondary text, as was done with many of the longer scrolls with originally blank versos. But this is readily understandable, since the blank verso portion was probably too small to be of much use to a later scribe in search of a free writing surface.

However, another specimen of the short-roll format in the new collection does use both recto and verso for one continuous text. This is the stotra text (frag. 5C), which was rolled up with the Rhinoceros Horn text, but which was evidently part of a different original manuscript. It too is exceptionally wide (at least 24 cm), and it is perhaps for this reason that the two fragmentary scrolls were rolled up together. Although the text is incomplete and very fragmentary, it appears to be part of a relatively short collection of verses, and like the Rhinoceros Horn Sūtra was probably written on a single, noncomposite sheet.

These smaller texts thus may be similar to the small birch bark texts that have been found at various sites, folded up and tucked into holes in statuary

9. Only four of the Gāndhārī verses do not correspond at all to a verse in the Pali version. Another four are too fragmentary to be judged either way.

or rolled up in reliquaries (see 3.2.1, 3.3, and 4.5.2). However, it is impossible to make any direct comparisons, since no specimens of this latter class of documents have survived intact. In any case, despite their small size, these small-format texts in the new collection were evidently still "scrolls," at least in the sense that they were stored in rolled-up form. In the case of the two new texts discussed above, this is evident from the fact that they have been broken in two (the Rhinoceros Horn scroll) or at least damaged in the middle (the stotra fragment) by a tying string or by lengthwise folding. This damage could not have resulted from the manuscripts' having been tied or folded immediately before they were placed in the pots and interred, because the two columns of text in the Rhinoceros Horn text as it was found had been switched from their original, proper positions before interment. Thus the manuscript had already broken in half while it was being stored, rolled up, in the monastery library, and therefore this must have been the usual method of storing the small-format texts as well as the larger, composite scrolls.

5.3. Observations on the Origin and Use of the Scroll Format

It therefore appears that all of the texts, including the small ones, in this collection, and by extension in the hypothetical monastery library from which they came, were treated as scrolls. This may have been, in part at least, a matter of convenience for storage and retrieval purposes; although no archeological or textual evidence survives, one can imagine some structure of wood or other material in which large numbers of scrolls could be efficiently stored in a relatively small space on shelves or in cubbyholes.

In any case, the discovery of these new manuscripts removes the doubts that have hitherto lingered as to the original format of the KDhP text. Old theories like that of Kaye that "[m]ost probably it was never intended that the manuscript should be rolled up; possibly it was to be hung on a wall" (1927: 10) are easily rejected. But it has still remained uncertain until now whether the strip was indeed rolled up or was perhaps rather folded in some fashion. Senart referred to long leaflets (*feuillets*) which, "once they were inscribed . . . were folded over themselves in such a way as to have the appearance of booklets 20 centimeters long and 4½ to 5 centimeters high. Given the condition in which the fragments have reached us, we cannot further determine if and how they were originally intended to be attached to each other" (1898: 199–200).[10] It was apparently these folding marks at intervals of about 4.5–5 cm that also led Brough to state that "though it is possible that it was originally intended to be a roll . . . it seems certain that at a later date it was folded

10. "Une fois écrits, ils étaient repliés sur eux-mêmes de façon à se présenter sous l'aspect de cahiers de 20 centimètres de long sur un hauteur de 4 centimètres et demi à 5 centimètres. Étant donné l'état où nous sont parvenus nos fragments, nous ne pouvons d'ailleurs décider si et comment ils étaient primitivement déstinés à être rattachés les uns aux autres."

into the concertina-form" (1962: 12). But in view of what we now know from the new British Library manuscripts, all of which were rolled up as scrolls, as well as from clues provided by descriptions of now-lost specimens of what seem to be similar items, such as Masson's "twists" (see 3.2.1), there can no longer be any doubt that the original format of the KDhP was also that of a roll or scroll. Brough's idea that the KDhP scroll was at some point folded concertina-fashion may be correct, but as Brough correctly observed, this could hardly have been the original arrangement; quite possibly it was the work of the modern discoverers of the manuscript.

5.3.1. Evidence for the Use of Rollers

Brough observed in connection with the KDhP that, "if a roll was the original intention, it must be assumed that it was wound round a cylinder, possibly of wood, since the end of N, which would have been the innermost part, shows no signs of the tight folding which is characteristic of most paper strips which have been rolled without a centre-piece" (1962: 12). It should also be noted that there is a narrow horizontal strip missing from the otherwise well-preserved fragment N just above the blank space at the very bottom of the KDhP scroll (see Brough's pl. XIII, bottom, and pl. XIV, top). This damage could have been inflicted when the scroll was separated from such a rolling cylinder to which it had been pasted or otherwise attached. No direct evidence of such a cylinder was found among the new scrolls, which were simply wound around themselves with nothing in the center, but it may be that their rollers were removed for reuse when the fragments were marked for disposal, according to the hypothesis developed in chapter 4. There are in fact a few cases where we can detect at the bottom of the new scrolls what could be traces of an original attachment to a central roller, as in the case of the KDhP. In fragment 14, for example, there are two small circular holes just above the bottom margin (pl. 10), which could have been left by pins that fastened the bottom of the scroll to a roller. In this case, as in other similar ones such as fragment 1, part 5, the first scribe ended his text a few inches from the bottom, a practice which would be consonant with the use of an attached roller. However, in both of these cases the secondary text that was added on by another scribe is written down to the very bottom of the recto side and then continued from the very top of the verso. Thus, even if the scroll had originally been fixed to a roller, it could not have been so when the secondary texts were added to it. Thus the evidence for the use of a central roller in the new scrolls, as in the KDhP, remains inconclusive; there are some features that could be taken as indicative of its use, but no direct evidence.

5.3.2. Theories on the Origin of the Scroll Format

Perhaps because the scroll format of the KDhP scroll seemed so untypical of other early Indian books, which almost always are in some variety of the long, narrow "*poṭhī*" format based on the shape of palm leaves, several scholars have suggested that it was constructed under the influence of non-Indian traditions. Thus, Hoernle drew a comparison to "Greek manuscripts of papyrus" (1900: 126), while Kaye suggested directly that "the Khotan manuscript . . . seems to have been shaped in imitation of the western papyrus roll" (1927: 8). But Janert, commenting on Hoernle's comparison, pointed out differences in format between the KDhP and Greek papyrus scrolls, noting in particular that in the former (and this is true of all the new scrolls as well) the text is written across the scroll, that is, parallel to its narrower dimension, instead of in columns parallel to the long side, as was the usual practice in Greek scrolls.[11] Janert therefore concluded that "the birch bark manuscripts were *not* similar to the Greek papyrus rolls" (1955–6: 73 n. 57).

An alternative suggestion for the inspiration of the scroll format was offered by Schlingloff, who referred to the KDhP's "divergent form, perhaps imitated from Chinese books" (1956: 121). Although he did not present any further evidence for the Chinese model, Schlingloff referred (p. 121 n. 8) to the arguments by Konow (1914) on linguistic grounds in favor of the view that the KDhP scroll was actually written in Khotan rather than imported from the Gāndhārī-speaking regions of India. Presumably, Schlingloff had in mind here the fact that Khotan was on the fringe of the Chinese sphere of influence in the period in question. It may also be noted that some later Sanskrit manuscripts written in central Asian Brāhmī script in scroll format have been found at sites on the northern edge of the Tarim Basin in Chinese central Asia (Waldschmidt 1959; Bechert 1995: 89–90).

However, now that we know that many Kharoṣṭhī texts in scroll format existed in Gandhāra proper and in adjoining regions of what are now Pakistan and Afghanistan, the theory of a Chinese inspiration looks less persuasive. Moreover, at least some of Konow's linguistic arguments for a Khotanese origin have been cast into doubt by subsequent and recent discoveries (see 6.4.3). Questions about the alleged central Asian origin of the KDhP also arise in connection with its material, namely, birch bark. Although it has been clearly established by Schlingloff (1956: 121–2; see also Sander 1968: 27–8) that birch bark was used as a writing material in the ancient sites on the northern rim of the Tarim Basin (contrary to the previously prevailing assumption that all birch bark texts must have been imported from India), there is still, to my knowledge, no other case of a birch bark manuscript from Khotan or any other of the southern Tarim sites.

If the new discoveries of numerous birch bark scrolls from the greater Gandhāra region weaken the hypothesis of a Chinese background for the scroll format, they support the argument for a Hellenistic source. The Khotan manuscript appears no longer as a unique specimen of its class but rather as an isolated case

11. Janert also cites as a difference from Greek papyri the fact that "the birch bark was . . . not glued together but consisted of a *single* piece" (1955–6: 73 n. 57), but it is now clear that this is not correct (see 5.1.2).

from the most distant limits of Chinese influence, whereas we now can see that the birch bark scroll was the standard book format in a time and place—that is, in Gandhāra in the early centuries of the Christian era—which was still under a strong influence of late Hellenistic culture. For example, the discovery of a hybrid figure of Herakles-Vajrapāṇi at Tapa Shutur (Tarzi 1976: 396–7; Mustamandi 1984) illustrates the Hellenistic atmosphere of the Haḍḍa area itself, which is likely to be the original provenance of the new manuscripts. Thus, the Greek papyrus scroll must be considered a priori the more probable inspiration for the Gandhāran scrolls, despite the differences in details of their construction noted by Janert. It is of course also conceivable that the scroll was an indigenous Gandhāran development, since the scroll format has been developed, apparently independently, in various parts of the world, including, for example, Egypt, China, and central America. But all in all, in view of the pervasive Hellenistic influence in Gandhāra during the Indo-Scythian period, it seems only reasonable to assume that the Gandhāran scrolls arose as an imitation, or rather an adaptation, of the Greek papyrus scrolls that must have been familiar to its inhabitants.

A Hellenistic origin for the scroll format is also supported by the depictions of similar scrolls in Gandhāran sculpture. One example is in a relief from Swat in the British Museum (OA 1904.12-17.43-4), showing a man seated on a stool and holding in his left hand a half-rolled scroll. To his right stands a female figure holding what Tissot (1985: 109 and fig. 257) identifies as a covered box intended to contain the scroll. The identification of the scene is problematic. Zwalf suggests that it may be an unusual rendition of the schooling of the Bodhisattva in which "a Western model, perhaps one of the poet and Muse, has replaced the usual iconographies among which a woman may occur carrying the Bodhisattva's writing board" (1996: 1.232), whereas Kurita (1988–90: 2.fig. 859) identifies it as a scene from the Mahā-ummagga-jātaka. But Tissot compares the theme with that of a similarly composed mosaic portrait from Hadrumetum (Tunisia) showing Virgil holding a half-rolled scroll in his left hand (Bianchi Bandinelli 1971: 236, fig. 218). Although the resemblance between these two renditions is striking and presumably not coincidental, there is an important difference with regard to the present discussion: in the Hadrumetum mosaic, the poet is holding the scroll horizontally across his lap, reading the text (which is actually legible on the mosaic) as written in the European fashion, that is, in columns parallel to the long dimension of the scroll, while in the Swat relief the man holds the scroll vertically, reflecting the now well attested Gandhāran pattern in which the lines are written across the scroll, parallel to its shorter dimension. Thus, the Swat relief is, in a sense, emblematic of the Indo-Hellenistic culture of Gandhāra, in that the scene is evidently based on a Western theme, but with a significant element, namely, the arrangement of the scroll, adapted to local custom rather than slavishly imitated from the Western model. Therefore, although this relief is in no sense a direct proof of a Hellenistic origin for the Gandhāran scroll format, it reinforces the impression that the use of scrolls reflects the cosmopolitan and semi-Hellenistic environment of ancient Gandhāra.

Another Gandhāran relief, whose current location is unknown but which was briefly described by Taddei (1983: 338 and pl. IIb), shows three monks seated around a table, each holding a partially unrolled scroll. Here too the scrolls are held vertically, in the Gandhāran fashion. Yet another relief, found at Shnaisha Gumbat in lower Swat (Rahman 1993: 95, pl. XLIa), shows a man, described by Rahman as a "state functionary" (p. 28), sitting in front of two standing figures and holding a partly opened scroll, once again placed vertically in the Gandhāran manner.

An unusual gold object, possibly a headdress ornament, said to be from Kashmir and dated to the first century B.C. or A.D. (Errington and Cribb 1992: 138–40), shows a winged female divinity holding a small scroll. The scroll bears an inscription which can be interpreted as the Greek word θεα, "goddess" or "divine." Here, the direction of writing follows the pattern seen in metal scrolls with Kharoṣṭhī relic dedication inscriptions (see, e.g., Salomon 1986, 1996b: 233–8), which, unlike the manuscript scrolls, are always inscribed across the longer dimension.

There are also several Gandhāran sculptures (listed in Quagliotti 1990: 105–9) showing a bodhisattva holding what is variously described as an Indian-style book (e.g., Foucher 1918: 238, "en forme de manuscrit indien sur feuilles de palmier") or as a "book or scroll" (Ingholt 1957: 123). It is indeed difficult to determine from the available photographs whether the object in the bodhisattva's hands is intended to represent a rolled-up scroll of the type with which we are concerned here or rather a conventional Indian folio manuscript, though a direct examination of the originals might clarify the issue.[12]

5.3.3. Patterns of Damage Conditioned by the Scroll Format

The scroll format provides a clear explanation for the patterns of damage which affect all of the manuscripts in the British Library to a greater or lesser degree. The fact that all of them are missing a substantial part—in many cases, apparently, the majority—of their upper portion is explained by the practice of rolling such scrolls up from the bottom, so that the upper part is most subject to wear and tear. Especially in the case of as fragile a material as birch bark, which becomes extremely brittle when old and dried out, it is inevitable that the outer layers of the scrolls will be lost unless they were treated with exceptional care or deposited in a secure con-

12. Two of the specimens of such "books" have what appear to be inscriptions in Kharoṣṭhī, but Quagliotti (1990: 110) is probably correct to observe that in the example with which she is primarily concerned (in the Victoria and Albert Museum, London), "[t]he inscription does not seem to have any specific meaning. . . . the artist drew the signs just in order to show that the object held by the bodhisattva was a book." The writing on a similar object in the Indian Museum, Calcutta, may also be merely a pseudo-inscription, notwithstanding the interpretation proposed in Sawoo 1983: 58.

tainer while still intact. Bühler noted that even among birch bark manuscripts of much lesser antiquity, which, in the Kashmiri fashion, were bound together between leather covers like modern European books, "[t]he friction of the leather invariably destroys the first and last leaves in a very short time, and hence many Sanskrit works from Kaśmîr have neither beginning nor end" (1877: 30).

At least some of this damage to the upper sections of the new scrolls had probably taken place in antiquity, before the already worn scrolls were interred, and further damage no doubt was inflicted during the nearly two millennia in which they lay underground. Furthermore, a comparison of the earliest available photograph of one of the fragments (no. 1), taken in 1993 (pl. 6), shows that it then had four or five more lines of writing on the verso than it did by the time it reached the British Library. This means that a further section of the scroll which may have been as long as 7 or 8 cm was lost during this interval (see 2.1.2).

As noted above (4.3.1), most of the scrolls, when unrolled, show a pattern of regular horizontal cracks or, very often, actual breaks at vertical intervals of about 3–4 cm, resulting from compression of the brittle rolls. Here too, the damage was probably inflicted gradually at different times. Some of the scrolls may have already been cracked in this way before they were interred, but part, perhaps most, of this damage probably resulted from their lying atop each other for many centuries inside the clay pot; this is indicated by the superior condition of fragment 1, which we know from the early photograph reproduced in plate 6 to have been at the top of the pile. Although the lower (i.e., inner, more tightly folded) parts of fragment 1 are cracked in the usual manner, its upper sections, unlike nearly all the other manuscripts in the collection, are relatively intact.

All of the manuscripts also suffer, to a greater or lesser degree, from deterioration of one or both of the edges. Only rarely do we find, in a few manuscripts, some lines that are preserved completely or nearly completely at both margins. Here once again the damage is probably a combination of deterioration before interment, gradual crumbling during the long period of burial, and mishandling after the discovery. Not surprisingly, the widest texts have tended to suffer the most in this respect, while the edges of narrow scrolls tend to be better preserved. Thus the best-preserved specimen in this respect is the anomalously narrow (5.5 cm) fragment 6, which, alone among all the other scrolls, retains both of its margins completely intact. In many of the scrolls, one margin is more or less intact while the other is badly deteriorated. This is probably the result of one end of the scroll having been in contact with the inner surface of the pot, causing it to absorb excessive moisture from the ground.

As mentioned previously, several scrolls are damaged along a vertical line throughout their length, or are even broken into two separate columns. This type of damage could have resulted from the action of a binding string that gradually cut through the middle of the rolled-up scroll, but it is more likely that it results from a habit of folding the rolled-up scrolls in half lengthwise while they were fresh and flexible, causing an area of weakness in the center that would crumble or actually disintegrate as the scrolls grew old and brittle.

In view of the extreme fragility of old birch bark, as illustrated by the condition of the British Library manuscripts, the relatively excellent condition of the KDhP scroll is all the more remarkable. Although it is now divided in numerous fragments, it is certain that it was intact and in one piece when discovered in or around 1892 (Brough 1962: 15), after which it was apparently torn into smaller sections by its finder(s) with a view to selling them separately and thereby maximizing their gains. The manuscript seems also not to have suffered from the sort of cracking caused by compression that is so prominent among the new manuscripts, since the periodic cracks across its width were more likely caused by its being folded concertina-fashion after it was unearthed (see 5.3). Thus, the KDhP scroll, unlike the British Library manuscripts, must have been interred, probably by itself, in some secure and airtight container—perhaps the clay jar that was reported to have been found with it (3.1.1)—while it was still fairly new and in good condition, and then lain undisturbed until it was rediscovered a century ago. But exactly why and how this happened we unfortunately have no way to know, given the obscure circumstances of its discovery.

5.4. Scribal Materials and Techniques

5.4.1. Preparation and Usage of Birch Bark

The bark of the birch and certain other trees is naturally well suited for use as a writing material, being readily procured and prepared, easy and convenient to write on, and visually attractive. But it has, as we have seen, one serious disadvantage: its lack of durability. Birch bark has been employed for writing or drawing in many parts of the world (see, e.g., Janert 1955–6: 68 n. 49), though in few regions was it adopted as the primary material, and nowhere was it so widely used as in the northern and northwestern reaches of the Indian subcontinent, in some parts of which (especially Kashmir) it remained the standard writing material until modern times (Bühler 1877: 29 n. †; Kaye 1927: 4). The usual species used for writing was the silver birch (*Baetula utilis* or *Baetula bhojpattr*), which is found throughout the Himalayan regions and also in parts of Afghanistan (Janert 1955–6: 67 n. 45). The use of birch bark (Skt. *bhūrja, bhūrjatvac; bhojpatr* in modern Indian languages) as a writing material in premodern India is attested both by the many surviving manuscripts from all periods and by frequent literary references in works from or about India. Among Indian writers, Kālidāsa twice mentions writing on birch bark, in a description of the Himalayas, "where pieces of birch bark are inscribed with mineral ink" (Kumārasambhava I.7, *nyastākṣarā dhāturasena yatra bhūrjatvacaḥ*), and in a description of a love letter: "Here is a letter on birch bark" (Vikramorvaśīya II.11/12, *bhūrjapatragato 'yam akṣaravinyāsaḥ*). Among works by non-Indian authors, we find references to writing on bark in India in Q. Curtius Rufus (see Bühler 1904: 6 and 92, and Janert 1955–6: 68) and in al-Bīrūnī (Sachau 1888: 1.171).

It is now clear that in the earliest times from which any birch bark documents survive (i.e., from the early centuries of the Christian era), the scroll was the standard format. Later on, the standard Indian poṭhī format of long, unbound leaves was adopted for birch bark documents, as exhibited, for example, in the Bower manuscript (Hoernle 1914) from Kucha, which probably dates from about the fourth or fifth century A.D., and in the Gilgit manuscripts from a slightly later period. It is perhaps not insignificant that the shift to the standard Indian format coincides with the adoption of the Sanskrit language and Brāhmī script, representing the gradual dissolution of the distinctive features of the Gandhāran linguistic and literary tradition and their replacement by the mainstream traditions of classical India. At a later period, there developed in Kashmir, probably under the influence of Islamic culture, the distinctive local tradition of writing birch bark texts on pages taller than they are wide and bound together like modern books.

The traditional methods of preparation of birch bark for writing purposes are unfortunately not well known; according to Bühler, "the method of preparing it has been lost" (1877: 30) in Kashmir. The only clear testimony[13] is that of al-Bīrūnī, who reported in the eleventh century A.D.: "In Central and Northern India people use [for writing material] the bark of the *tûz* tree. . . . It is called *bhûrja*. They take a piece [of *bhūrja*] one yard long and as broad as the outstretched fingers of the hand, or somewhat less, and prepare it in various ways. They oil and polish it so as to make it hard and smooth, and then they write on it" (Sachau 1888: 1.171). Unfortunately, the delicate condition of the British Library manuscripts, which are now permanently encased in glass, does not allow for technical studies of their material and preparation. For the same reason, it has not been possible to study in detail the character of the individual fragments with regard to such matters as the varying quality of the bark and the number of component layers or laminations (Hoernle 1914: 18).

The new scrolls accord with Kaye's observation that "[i]n all birch-bark manuscripts the writing is parallel to the lenticels, which on the bole of the tree are horizontal" (1927: 8). The correct explanation for this is again presumably the one offered by Kaye, namely, that "the reason for this direction of the writing is that the bark tends to split in the same direction" (i.e., horizontally) (1927: 8, see also p. 5). Thus, the bark of the new scrolls, or rather on their component sections, is positioned as it originally was on the birch tree, and this explains why the scrolls were constructed as composites. Although it might seem simpler to use longer single

13. Hoernle refers to "the process (probably boiling in milk or water) by which the bark was prepared for the reception of writing" (1914: 18), but Janert rightly questions the authority of this statement, which he calls "pure conjecture" (1955–6: 72).

strips taken from around the circumference of the tree, this, given the convention of writing across the scroll, would have involved writing against the natural grain of the surface and caused splitting and other problems. Thus the composite scrolls were evidently prepared from a section of a convenient height which was peeled off from around the tree and then cut into parallel strips that were joined together vertically to form a scroll of the desired length and with the desired orientation, namely, with the lenticels and grain of the bark positioned horizontally, as on the original tree.

5.4.2. *Writing Implements and Scribal Techniques*

The scrolls were written in black ink with a split-reed pen. The effects of the split nib are visible in numerous places where the pen ran low on ink, as a result of which the center of the line becomes faint or even totally absent, resulting in a split line. Such an effect is visible, for example, in the syllables *rana* near the end of line 21 of fragment 16, r (the sixth line visible in the detail photograph in pl. 11). This phenomenon is typically seen in the last or last few syllables of a word, as in the present example, where a word division is indicated by the dot following the last letter (*na*). As a matter of fact, in some texts there is a regular pattern of darker letters at the beginning of words and lighter ones at the end. This is clear, for instance, on line 20 of the same fragment (fifth line in pl. 11), reading *samudanido˙ mahasamudro adirno˙ y. . .*,[14] where the first syllable of each of the words stands out as noticeably darker than the rest. This shows that the scribe was evidently in the habit of writing a single word with one load of ink and avoided refilling his pen before finishing a word, even if he was running low on ink. This habit sometimes provides a useful clue for the modern interpreter in showing where the word boundaries are. This is important because word or phrase division markers of the sort mentioned above are used only in some texts, and then sporadically and inconsistently (sometimes even incorrectly), while word boundaries are not otherwise marked (e.g., by spacing) in any of the texts.

On the same fragment 16, r, we can discern the effects of wear on the nib of the reed pen. In line 28 of this fragment, the letters begin to be distinctly thinner and slightly ragged in appearance, and in the following line, this impression becomes even more pronounced. But then in line 30, the letters have returned to normal thickness. Evidently the scribe stopped here to trim the point of his pen, or perhaps discarded it entirely for a new one.

The visual effect of writing with this type of pen varies considerably from hand to hand. Some scribes, such as the writer (hand no. 1) of the Anavataptagāthā (frag. 1; see pl. 4) and several other texts, held the pen in such a way as to

14. On this passage, see also section 6.7.3.

produce a consistently wide line throughout. Others, notably the scribe of the Rhinoceros Horn Sūtra (frag. 5B; hand no. 9), held their pens at an angle, producing a strong contrast between thick and thin lines. An outstanding use of this technique is displayed by the scribe of fragments 26 and 29 (hand no. 20), whose ornate hand is the only one among the new manuscripts that could be considered truly calligraphic.

Although no specimen of such an ancient reed pen seems to have survived from this region, we can get an idea of what they must have looked like from the two copper pens, 5.81 and 4.37 inches long, found in the excavations at Sirkap (Taxila), which according to Marshall are "shaped like reed pens with the point divided by a cut, as in the modern nib. This is a reproduction in metal of the reed pen" (Marshall 1951: 2.598; see also 1.190 and 3.pl. 173gg and hh). The Sirkap excavations also yielded several examples of copper ink pots (Marshall 1951: 2.597 and 3.pl. 176, nos. 328–35), including ornate types with a serpentine handle, a sunken lid with a hole for the pen, and a stopper for the hole, attached to the handle with a chain (e.g., no. 335; Marshall 1951: 3.pl. 35a, pl. 176, no. 335, and pl. 184n). It may be surmised that the scribes who wrote the British Library manuscripts used implements similar to these.

Chapter 6

Paleographic and Linguistic Features of the Gandhāran Scrolls

6.1. The Gāndhārī Language and the Kharoṣṭhī Script

The name "Gāndhārī" is a modern coinage for the language that prevailed in ancient times in and around the region of Gandhāra on the northwestern fringe of the Indian subcontinent (see 1.1). This name was initially proposed by H. W. Bailey (1943–6: 764) and has won general acceptance in scholarly circles. In earlier publications, and sometimes still in more recent ones, the language has been referred to as "Northwestern Prakrit." As this latter name indicates, Gāndhārī is one of the regional dialects of the Prakrit, or more precisely Middle Indo-Aryan (MIA), tongues, and broadly speaking it shows the same processes of phonetic change, morphological simplification, and syntactic reconfiguration of Sanskrit, or more accurately of the Old Indo-Aryan (OIA) parent language, as do the other MIA languages. However, Gāndhārī has certain peculiarities, mainly with respect to its phonetic structure, that set it off from all the other MIA dialects. Two features in particular are especially characteristic of Gāndhārī phonology. The first is the preservation, in most phonetic contexts, of the three sibilants (*ś*, *ṣ*, *s*) as they were in OIA, in contrast to all other MIA languages, where the three sibilants were reduced to one (*ś* or *s*, depending on the dialect). The other distinctive phonetic feature of Gāndhārī is the preservation of several of the OIA consonant clusters, particularly those involving stop consonants plus the semivowels *r* and *v*, which in the other dialects were simplified by gemination. Thus, for instance, Sanskrit *sarva,* which becomes *savva* or *sabba* in other MIA dialects, remains unchanged in Gāndhārī. Historical remnants of these and certain other distinctive phonetic features of Gāndhārī have been traced in the modern Dardic languages of northern Pakistan, proving that they were legitimate dialect features and not merely orthographic survivals or artificial Sanskritisms.

The other feature which sets Gāndhārī off from all the other MIA languages is the script in which it is written (see fig. 12). Whereas the other Prakrits were always written in the Brāhmī script and its various derivatives, ancient and modern, Gāndhārī invariably appears in the Kharoṣṭhī script, which evidently came into being as an adaptation for this Indian language of the Aramaic script that was widely used in the Achaemenian Empire of Iran.[1] Since Gandhāra was incorporated

1. For further information on the origin and development of Kharoṣṭhī see Salomon 1998: 42–56.

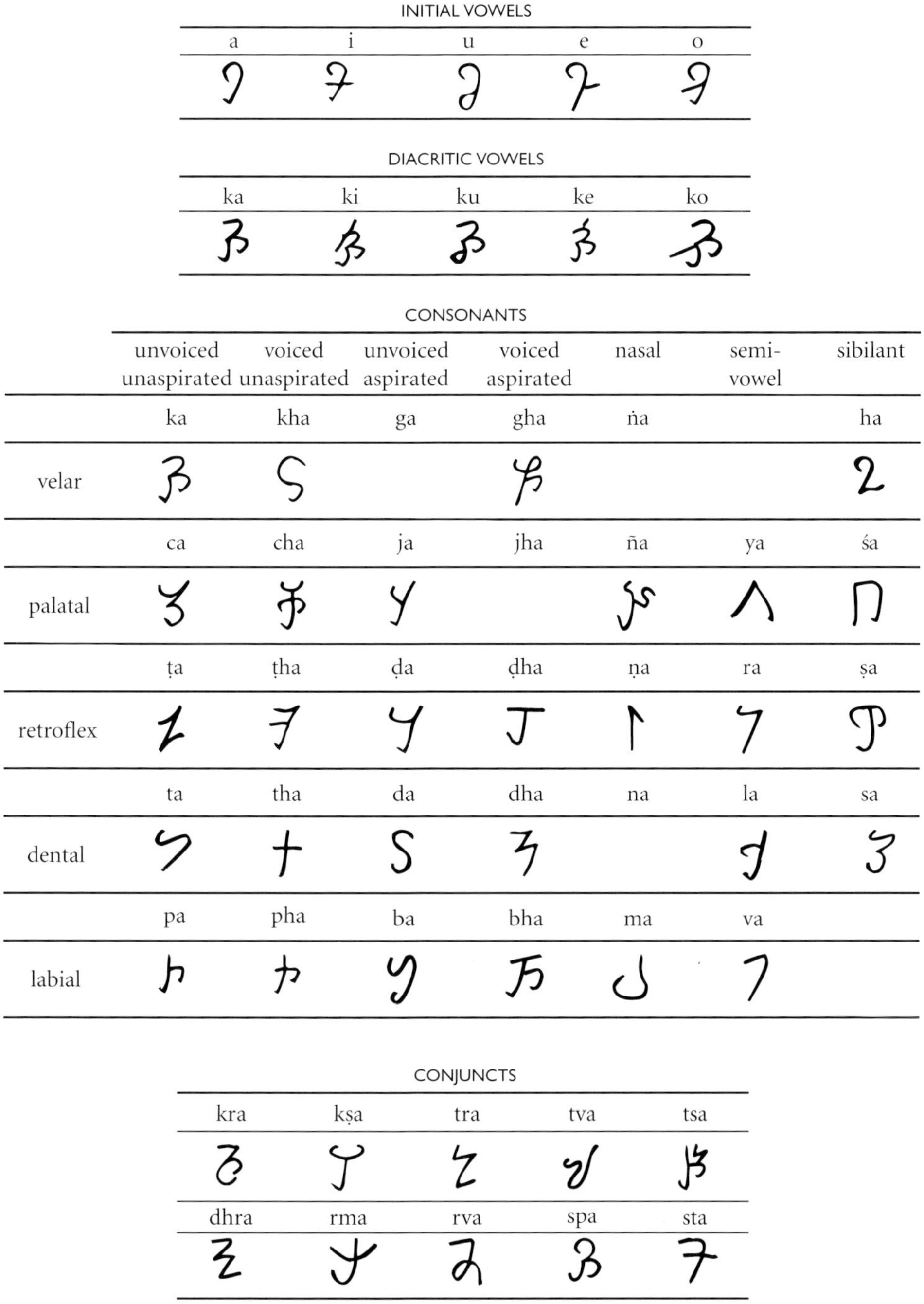
INITIAL VOWELS
a i u e o
DIACRITIC VOWELS
ka ki ku ke ko
CONSONANTS
unvoiced unaspirated
voiced unaspirated
unvoiced aspirated
voiced aspirated
nasal
semi-vowel
sibilant
ka kha ga gha ṅa ha
velar
ca cha ja jha ña ya śa
palatal
ṭa ṭha ḍa ḍha ṇa ra ṣa
retroflex
ta tha da dha na la sa
dental
pa pha ba bha ma va
labial
CONJUNCTS
kra kṣa tra tva tsa
dhra rma rva spa sta

Fig. 12. Chart of Kharoṣṭhī script, as written by the scribe of fragments 1, 12 + 14, and 16 + 25 (hand no. 1)

within that empire from the sixth to the fourth century B.C., it is easy to understand how such a script would have arisen and become entrenched there. Although Kharoṣṭhī shares with the Brāhmī script that prevailed in the rest of ancient India essentially the same system of graphic representation, namely, the characteristic diacritically modified consonant-syllabic structure, it differs considerably from Brāhmī in detail. The two most fundamental distinctions are, first, that whereas Brāhmī was written from left to right, Kharoṣṭhī goes from right to left and, second, that whereas Brāhmī distinguishes vowel quantity, Kharoṣṭhī does not, using the same symbol for each pair of short and long vowels.

Thus, although in theory Gāndhārī and Kharoṣṭhī are both part of the larger sphere of Indian languages and scripts, in practice they developed and maintained a separate identity and represented a distinct cultural area. Consequently, they have formed a separate area of focus in modern linguistic, epigraphical, and textual scholarship. This special position is due not only to their linguistic and graphic peculiarities and relative geographical isolation but also to their unique cultural role as the vehicle of Buddhism in the northwest.

Our understanding of the Kharoṣṭhī script and the Gāndhārī language, with which it is almost always linked, has been based, until now, on four classes of documents. The first group consists of inscriptions on stone, various types of metal, and earthenware materials, nearly all of which, except for the Kharoṣṭhī/Gāndhārī versions of the Aśokan rock edicts at Shāhbāzgaṛhī and Mānsehrā, record Buddhist donations or foundations. These inscriptions date from the time of Aśoka, that is, the middle of the third century B.C., until the third or possibly the early fourth century A.D., at which time the Kharoṣṭhī script seems to have fallen out of use in the Indian world and been replaced by local derivatives of Brāhmī script (Salomon 1998: 46–7). Kharoṣṭhī inscriptions are particularly abundant in the first two centuries of the Christian era, that is, from the time of the Scythian, Parthian, and Kuṣāṇa dynasties of the northwest. The fundamental collection of Kharoṣṭhī inscriptions is still Sten Konow's volume in the Corpus Inscriptionum Indicarum (vol. 2.1, published in 1929), which contains the approximately one hundred examples then known. Since that time, a great deal of new material has been discovered, so that we now have well over twice that number of Kharoṣṭhī inscriptions. References to Kharoṣṭhī inscriptions published since 1929 were collected and evaluated in Fussman 1989, but now even that is somewhat outdated, since several more inscriptions, including some of considerable importance, have appeared subsequently.

The continuing discovery of new inscriptions and other documents confirms the increasing sense among epigraphists and Buddhist scholars that the degree and range of influence of the Gāndhārī language in the Buddhist cultures of northwestern India and beyond, especially in the early centuries of the Christian era, were far greater than they had appeared in decades past, when our knowledge of the script and language was restricted to a relatively small number of inscriptions from the northwestern edge of the Indian subcontinent. Not only the number but also the geographical range of Kharoṣṭhī inscriptions have been vastly expanded by recent discoveries, including two inscriptions found in China (in Lo-yang and Chang-an), numerous inscriptions from Termez and neighboring areas of the southern part of modern Uzbekistan and Tajikistan, and dozens of graffiti on rocks in the valleys of the upper Indus and its tributaries in the Northern Areas of Pakistan (Salomon 1998: 143).

The second group of Kharoṣṭhī/Gāndhārī documents comprises the legends on the coins of the Indo-Greek, Indo-Scythian, Indo-Parthian, Kuṣāṇa, and other kings or states. These legends are often recorded bilingually, mostly with Greek and Brāhmī scripts but also with Chinese in central Asia. Although this vast body of material is of great value for historical studies, as well as for having provided the keys to the decipherment of Kharoṣṭhī script in modern times (Salomon 1998: 209–15), the coin legends are of limited use for linguistic and literary studies.

The third major body of Kharoṣṭhī/Gāndhārī texts consists of the documents, now numbering nearly one thousand (Lin forthcoming), that were found in the ruins of the oasis cities of the silk roads bordering the Tarim Basin in what is now the Xinjiang-Uighur Autonomous Region of China. Most of these documents were discovered by Aurel Stein at Niya and other sites along the southern silk route and published in Boyer, Rapson, and Senart 1920–9, which contains 764 documents. Several more documents of this type have been published subsequently (see Salomon 1998: 159 and n. 128), and many more, most of which remain to be published, have been discovered in the course of recent Chinese archeological expeditions in Xinjiang. Most of the central Asian Kharoṣṭhī documents are legal and administrative ephemera, written in ink on wooden tablets or pieces of leather. Their script and language are local variants of Indian Kharoṣṭhī and Gāndhārī, characterized by such distinctive features as the widespread adoption of loanwords from Greek, Iranian, and other local languages and the development of new consonantal characters and ligatures required to represent them. These documents show that in and around the third century A.D. Gāndhārī had become the administrative language of the oasis kingdoms of the southern silk route, presumably as a result of trade and political connections promoted by the vast Indo–central Asian empire of the Kuṣāṇas. On the northern silk route as well, some Kharoṣṭhī documents have been discovered, but these remain to be published and are not yet well understood (see Salomon 1998: 47).

The fourth class of Kharoṣṭhī/Gāndhārī documents consists of literary texts, taken in the broad sense of the term to include Buddhist texts in manuscript form. Until now, this class has essentially been represented only by a single document—the KDhP—although among the aforementioned central Asian Kharoṣṭhī documents there are also a few stray specimens of poetic texts (nos. 204, 510, and 511 in Boyer, Rapson, and Senart 1920–9). The new documents introduced in this volume will therefore provide us with a far more detailed and extensive understanding of this class of materials and will serve as a balance to the previously better documented classes of inscriptional, numismatic, and administrative texts in Kharoṣṭhī. Until now, our understanding of the Gāndhārī language has been severely limited by the special character of the majority of the specimens. The inscriptions, for the most part, are highly formulaic, repetitive, and largely shaped by pan-Buddhist ritual terminology (Fussman 1982: 37). The central Asian documents are equally constricted by administrative and legal formulae and the associated technical jargon. Thus we get from these two classes of material a rather limited and restricted picture of the language as a whole, particularly with respect to the spoken vernacular. This will no doubt prove to be the case, for the most part, with the new manuscripts as well, but their relatively large number and highly diverse contents will help to balance this limitation. Indeed, some of the new materials, particularly the avadāna and related texts, do reflect a more colloquial form of Gāndhārī, less influenced by the style and formulae of other Buddhist languages (see 6.7.3). These texts in particular may give us a much clearer picture than ever before of the Gāndhārī language in its original form.

In the rest of this chapter, some notable or unusual features of the script and language of the new documents will be discussed under the conventional headings of paleography, orthography, phonology, morphology, syntax, and lexicon. But it should be admitted at the outset that these distinctions are to some degree arbitrary. The informal, unstandardized, and inconsistent practices that prevailed in writing Gāndhārī, in these as in other documents, often make it difficult to clearly separate these categories; for example, what according to a superficial analysis may seem to be a difference in morphology may actually be only a matter of variant spellings of the same spoken form. Nonetheless, in order to present the data in a reasonably orderly fashion it is necessary to make such distinctions, albeit with these words of caution as to the limitations of their validity.

6.2. Paleographic Features

A preliminary paleographic analysis and comparison of the approximately twenty-one different hands represented in the British Library collection (see 2.5) reveals that they comprise a wide variety of different styles, forms, and orthographic practices. Thus the large, curving letters of the avadāna scribe (hand no. 2) contrast with the tiny, cramped hand of the scribe (no. 15) of fragment 15, while the unadorned, starkly functional forms of the latter in turn are strikingly different from the ornate, almost baroque appearance of fragments 26 and 29 (hand no. 20). And yet, these prominent differences are in a sense superficial, in that comparisons of the individual letter forms of the various hands reveal that all or nearly all of them reflect essentially the same stage of development of Kharoṣṭhī script. The contrasts among the various hands thus in all probability result not so much from chronological differences, or even, as far as can be determined, from geographical or sectarian styles, but rather reflect free stylistic variations within a script that had not become fully standardized by this time (and apparently never did). Indeed, this phenomenon of nonstandardization and apparently idiosyncratic variation is not restricted to writing styles but is equally characteristic of the orthographic practices and even of the morphology of the new documents, as we will see later in this chapter.

6.2.1. Paleographic Analysis of Test Letters

The general contemporaneity of the different writing styles among the new manuscripts can best be established by a comparison of those letters, such as the consonants *ka*, *ca*, *cha*, *ya*, and especially *sa*, that underwent the most extensive formal changes, mostly in the direction of cursivization and stroke reduction, during the five centuries or so during which the Kharoṣṭhī script was in use in India and that therefore serve as the most reliable and convenient "test letters" for the chronological evaluation and comparison of different specimens of the script.[2]

Sa is generally considered the most revealing and reliable test letter because it had three clearly distinct forms at different historical periods: the archaic, closed form (𐨯) seen in the Aśokan Kharoṣṭhī inscriptions and in some other early inscriptions; the semi-open form (𐨯), in which the vertical stem of the letter was still written as a separate stroke but was commenced below the upper line of the first stroke, leaving a gap between them, rather than touching it as in the old form; and the late, open form (𐨯), in which the character has been cursively reduced to a single stroke with a full opening at the left side. In general the intermediate, semi-open form is characteristic of inscriptions of the Indo-Scythian and Indo-Parthian period, that is, the late first century B.C. and early first century A.D., while the late, open form is most characteristic of—though not limited to—inscriptions from the time of Kaniṣka and his successors in the Kuṣāṇa dynasty, that is, from the late first or early to middle second century A.D. (depending on which of the possible dates for Kaniṣka one prefers) onward. The new manuscripts consistently have the late, open form of *sa*. However, it should be added that this type of *sa* can be further divided into two subtypes: an earlier subvariety that preserves a point[3] and sharp angle where the lower part of the letter turns from a leftward to a downward direction (𐨯) and a further-cursivized subvariety in which this point has been completely eliminated (𐨯) and, in Konow's words, "head and leg is only one wavy line" (1929: cxxiv). This latest form of *sa*, which is characteristic of inscriptions of the time of the

2. See also the comments on the special problems and limitations involved in the paleographic dating of Kharoṣṭhī in section 7.3.

3. This point is the remnant of the junction of the two separate strokes that originally constituted the letter.

post-Kaniṣka Kuṣāṇa kings,[4] is never found in the new documents, all of which have forms, with slight variations, of the open but pointed *sa*.

A similar but slightly more complex pattern emerges in connection with *ya*, which is generally the second most useful test letter, after *sa*, for the chronological comparison of Kharoṣṭhī documents. This letter has two distinct forms, an earlier one consisting of two diagonal lines meeting at a point at the top (𐨩) and a later one in which a separate top line or curve links two more or less upright strokes (𐨩). The later form is, broadly speaking, characteristic of the inscriptions of the time of Kaniṣka and later. However, the situation is complicated because the later variety has several subvarieties that do not appear to be consistently distributed. Moreover, unlike *sa*, whose form is quite consistent among the different manuscripts in the new corpus, *ya* appears in several different forms. Some hands, such as no. 1, the scribe of the first texts on fragments 1, 12 + 14, and 16 + 25, and no. 9, who wrote the Rhinoceros Horn Sūtra (frag. 5B), show the old angular form of *ya* (𐨩), while others, such as hand no. 2, the scribe of the avadāna texts, use the subvariety of the later type in which a short line sloping diagonally down toward the left connects the tops of the two uprights (𐨩). There are no cases, however, of the very late variety seen in some inscriptions (e.g., Wardak), where the connecting line at the top has become horizontal (𐨩), so that the *ya* becomes virtually indistinguishable from *śa*.

The test letter *ca* has two distinct forms: the old shape, consisting of two semicircular strokes arranged vertically and open at the top and bottom respectively, either touching each other or, more often, connected by a short vertical (𐨕); and a later, cursivized form, in which the letter has been reduced to a single stroke by the addition of a diagonal line connecting the right end of the old upper semicircle with the left tip of the lower one (𐨕). To judge from the inscriptional evidence, the shift from the earlier to the later type took place in and around the early first century A.D.; only the later variety occurs in the new manuscripts. The situation is similar with *cha*, which has an archaic variety, in which the lower horizontal stroke is a straight line (𐨖), and a later one, in which the lower stroke becomes a curve opening toward the bottom (𐨖). As in the case of *ca*, the transitional period is reflected in inscriptions of the early first century A.D., and all of the new manuscripts have the later form.

Finally, *ka* is essentially stable through the early and middle stages of the development of Kharoṣṭhī, though it shows minor variant forms. In some late varieties of the script, however, the two strokes of the letter are reconfigured, from a vertical stem with a horizontal line to the left at the top plus a hooked line added to the right side of the vertical (𐨐), to a longer, curved stroke at the top and right with the vertical stem inserted below the top stroke (𐨐). This new form is characteristic of the

4. It appears, for example, in the Ārā inscription of Kaniṣka [II], [Kaniṣka] year 41, and the Wardak inscription of the time of Huviṣka, [Kaniṣka] year 51 (Konow 1929: pls. XXXII.1 and XXXIII).

latest (i.e., post-Kaniṣka) variety of Kharoṣṭhī, though it sporadically appears earlier. Among the new manuscripts, the older type of *ka* strongly predominates, although the later variety is used regularly in at least one text (frag. 10).

Two significant points emerge from this preliminary and partial paleographic survey of the new documents. First, the letter forms are generally consistent among all of the fragments, the variations in form for a given character being for the most part at the level of what might be called "handwriting," that is to say, of individual style or preference rather than of different chronological or geographical origins. The divergent forms of *ya* do constitute a notable exception, but probably not one that is sufficient to overrule the overall pattern, since, as will be discussed in the following section, the coexistence of older and newer forms at a given point in time is the rule rather than the exception in Kharoṣṭhī paleography generally. Second, among the characters which take distinctly different forms at different stages of the history of Kharoṣṭhī, the new manuscripts regularly show the later varieties; but where the late forms can be subdivided into later and latest, as in the case of *sa* and *ya*, they consistently are the former rather than the latter. Here too, though, *ya* is a partial exception, in that some texts still retain the oldest form.

6.2.2. Evaluation and Implications for Dating

Taken at face value, the comparisons presented above might lead one to conclude that the new manuscripts should be dated, on paleographic grounds, to the middle Kuṣāṇa period, that is, to the time around Kaniṣka's reign in the late first or early to middle second century A.D. But to jump to such a conclusion without considering other relevant factors would be misguided. The first and most important of these additional factors is the universal rule that in all scripts monumental letter forms, that is, those used in inscriptions on hard surfaces such as stone or metal, tend to be more conservative than manuscript forms, which are written (typically) in pen and ink on a soft surface. This is especially true when, as is the case with the Kharoṣṭhī examples described in the preceding section and also with the paleographic development of most other scripts, the innovative forms are based on cursivized pen-and-ink developments.[5] That is to say, a change in the form of a

5. Note, for example, the comments of Fussman: "The engraving of the Kurram and Wardak reliquaries, like that of many metal objects, was done by a craftsman specialized in the use of a punch and small hammer. . . . Although the craftsman may often be skillful and reproduce the forms of the Kharoṣṭhī akṣaras with fairly high accuracy, the writing engraved in this way is inevitably less cursive than that of a manuscript written in ink. Like all monumental writing, it can be slightly archaizing" (1989: 437). ("La gravure des reliquaires de Kurram et de Wardak, comme celle de nombreux objets de métal, a été faite par un ouvrier spécialisé au moyen d'un poinçon et d'un petit marteau. . . . Bien que le graveur soit souvent habile et reproduise avec une assez grande fidélité le tracé des *akṣara* khar., l'écriture ainsi gravée est nécessairement moins cursive que celle d'un manuscrit écrite a l'encre. Comme toute écriture monumentale, elle peut être légèrement archaïsante.")

particular letter will normally begin to appear in inscriptions considerably later than in manuscript writing, and therefore, to compare the two without due allowance for this pattern is almost certain to lead to inaccurate results. The approximate dates for the appearance of the later forms of Kharoṣṭhī *sa, ya,* etc. cited in the preceding section are based entirely on data from inscriptions, so that it is a priori possible, and in fact likely, that the actual date of the manuscripts will be somewhat earlier than it would seem from a direct comparison of their letter forms with those of inscriptions.

This is confirmed by the fact that the innovative forms in question typically begin to appear sporadically in inscriptions at an earlier date than those referred to above, those being the dates by which the new forms had become more or less standard and regular in epigraphic style. For example, although the late, open form of *sa* is consistently used only from the time of Kaniṣka onward, it is occasionally seen in earlier inscriptions, for example, in the Takht-i-Bāhī inscription of A.D. 46 (Konow 1929: pl. XII.1), the Indravarman reliquary of A.D. 6 (see Fussman 1980: 7–8), and even in the Mathurā lion capital inscriptions, which probably date from the first century B.C.[6]

The coexistence at a particular point in time of earlier and later forms of a particular letter and the overlapping of the chronological ranges of their use are well attested for Kharoṣṭhī in general (as for other scripts), and in the case of *sa* in particular this phenomenon is clearly illustrated by a set of three reliquary inscriptions that were published together in Fussman 1980. Two of the three are dated, and the earlier of them, Indravarman's reliquary of the Azes year 63 (= A.D. 6), consistently has the *sa* of the intermediate, partly open type. But the later of the two dated inscriptions, Ramaka's reliquary of year 74 of the same era, regularly has the old type of closed *sa,* despite the fact that it is eleven years younger than the inscription that uses the more modern form of the letter. Moreover, the third inscription of the group, which is undated but which must be more or less contemporary with the second one because it also records a donation by Ramaka, has, in the portion of the inscription on the reliquary lid, two *sa*'s of the late, open type, while the *sa*'s on the base of the reliquary are more like those of the intermediate type, with a slight extension of the vertical stem above its juncture with the upper stroke.

This situation can only mean that all three forms of *sa* (early, middle, and late) were in use simultaneously and at a relatively early period, namely, the beginning of the first century A.D. The preference for one or the other form on the part of a particular scribe might have been determined by any number of factors, including but not limited to his age. But what is certain is that the occurrence of a

6. See Salomon 1996: 442. However, Dani has expressed suspicions about the unexpectedly advanced forms of some of the letters in this relatively early inscription and has suggested that it might be an ancient forgery which "was actually engraved in the time of the Kanishka group of the Kushāṇa rulers" (1960: 147).

particular form of a letter such as *sa* does not establish a precise date for a document containing it, but only a broad range of possible dates, and that the range of possible dates for earlier and later forms of a given character overlap, possibly by a considerable span of time.

With this in mind, and also taking into account the aforementioned overall principle that graphic innovations tend to appear first in handwritten documents and only gradually make their way into epigraphic use thereafter, the probable range of dates for the new manuscripts arrived at purely on paleographic grounds runs from the earlier part of the first century A.D., when late forms for letters such as *sa* first appear sporadically in inscriptions and hence were likely to have already been common in manuscript usage, to around the time of Kaniṣka, in the late first or early to middle second century, by which time these developed forms had become well established in epigraphic style. A later date than this is less likely on paleographic grounds because the latest forms of letters such as *sa* and *ya* are not found anywhere in the new documents. As will be discussed at length in chapter 7, historical information in and associated with the manuscripts points toward a similar range, and particularly toward its earlier part, that is, the first century A.D., as the most likely date for the manuscripts.

6.2.3. Comparisons with the Khotan Dharmapada

Although the paleography of the new manuscripts is broadly comparable to that of the Khotan manuscript of the Gāndhārī Dharmapada, it differs in several details. With regard to the date of the KDhP, Brough notes "a reasonable similarity to the styles of writing on the Kurram casket and the Wardak vase" but adds that this is "an impressionistic judgement which admittedly is provisional" (1962: 55). Fussman thinks that the KDhP could date from anywhere from the late first to the late third century A.D., "with a slight and subjective preference for the second century" (1989: 438). Although Fussman rules out the possibility of a date before the time of Kaniṣka (i.e., the late first century, according to his preferred chronology) on the grounds of the consistent use of the late, open *sa,* the examples cited above of earlier epigraphic specimens of this form raise doubts about this lower limit. In terms of chronologically distinctive letters like *sa, ya,* and *cha,* the KDhP is broadly in agreement with the new manuscripts in that it shows the later, but not the latest, most cursive forms. But the specific forms of many of these and other letters in the KDhP are notably different from those which prevail among the new manuscripts, though unfortunately not in a way that is chronologically distinctive. Characteristic peculiarities of the KDhP style, such as the hooked flourish at the lower right of *bha,* the curved vertical of *ba,* and the extra hook at the bottom of *dha,* have not been observed in the new documents, but it is not yet possible to determine whether these contrasts represent chronological changes, geographical and/or dialectal features, or merely idiosyncratic variants. As yet, our knowledge of the paleography of Kharoṣṭhī manuscripts is even more rudimentary than that of the epigraphic version of the script, though we can anticipate that when, in due course, the paleography of the new manuscripts has been studied in detail, their chronological and other relationships to the KDhP will become clearer.

One point that is already clear, however, is that the differences between the paleographic characteristics of the KDhP and the new texts are consistent with a broader pattern applying to other topics such as orthography and morphology, as discussed later in this chapter. In all of these categories we find a general similarity between the two but differences in detail that when taken singly seem minor, but when seen as a whole give the impression that they stem from separate, though closely related, cultural spheres. Although it is tempting to explain these differences on the grounds that the KDhP is, as some scholars have claimed, a central Asian manuscript in origin rather than an import from the Indian subcontinent, this explanation is subject to doubt on other grounds, as noted in sections 5.3.2 and 6.4.3. Detailed paleographic and linguistic studies of the new texts may eventually clarify this issue, but for the moment it must be left open.

6.3. Orthographic Features

Like their paleography, phonology, and morphology, the orthography of the new manuscripts exhibits numerous idiosyncratic variations which do not appear to be reducible to any simple or consistent pattern. The principal variables discussed below, such as the presence or absence of anusvāra and the use of the "special" sibilant ṣ̱, do not fall into coherent groupings with respect to the various manuscripts but rather seem to follow the personal preferences of the individual scribes, who apparently did not have any single authoritative standard on which to model their writing.

The variable notation in Kharoṣṭhī of nasalized vowels or nasals preceding consonants—that is to say, the usage or avoidance of the anusvāra—is already a well-known phenomenon in the inscriptions and other Gāndhārī documents. For instance, in the KDhP manuscript anusvāra is almost totally absent, while in the central Asian documents it is commonly and fairly consistently written. Among the inscriptions, we find many specimens with and many without anusvāra, as well as many examples of the troublesome category of "pseudo-anusvāra," discussed in the Appendix (sec. 3, pot C). This inconsistent treatment of anusvāra must reflect a weakening of nasalization in the spoken Gāndhārī language or at least a leveling of nasalization as a phonemic category, as has been discussed at length in Fussman 1989: 473–9. This presumably is the reason that among the new manuscripts we find some scribes who never use anusvāra, others who use it more or less regularly and in the usual fashion, and yet others who use it sporadically or in particular contexts only. On the whole, it appears, on the basis of a very preliminary survey, that the majority of scribes did employ anusvāra with reasonable regularity but that a sizable minority avoided it. This latter group, however, includes two scribes (hands nos. 1 and 2) who are represented by multiple fragments in the collection.

The distribution of the nasal consonants that are conventionally transcribed as dental *n* (𐨣) and retroflex *ṇ* (𐨞) also typically varies among different Kharoṣṭhī documents. Like the problem of anusvāra, this reflects or at least involves the phonemic leveling of the two sounds, particularly in the middle and later stages of development of the Gāndhārī language. Thus, we need not be surprised to find that among the new manuscripts, as in many previously known Kharoṣṭhī documents, most texts use one to the exclusion of the other, though there also seem to be a few examples in which, for example, a scribe who prefers *ṇ* will occasionally use *n*. In general, more scribes seem to prefer the retroflex *ṇ*, but a fair number write *n*. Among the two best-represented scribes, hand no. 2, the avadāna specialist, always uses *n*, while hand no. 1 writes only *ṇ*. It is typical of the aforementioned inconsistent grouping of orthographic practices among the various scribes and manuscripts that these two prominent scribes agree in avoiding anusvāra but disagree in their usage with regard to the nasal consonants.

The "special" sibilant *s̱* (𐨯𐨹) has a complex and, once again, highly variable history in the Kharoṣṭhī script as a whole. Some experts (e.g., Brough 1962: 69) believe that it originally arose as a cursivized reduction of a ligature for *sya*. This theory is based in part on the regular use of *s̱* in some documents to represent the genitive singular ending *-s(y)a*, apparently under the influence of a Sanskritized spelling. But whatever its origin may have been, *s̱* is also widely used in Kharoṣṭhī documents of various classes to represent the sounds corresponding to the original Sanskrit consonants *th* and *dh* in intervocalic position, indicating that this letter came to represent a voiced interdental fricative (/ð/) or similar sound which developed in the course of the phonetic history of Gāndhārī and for which the script had no original primary character. It is mainly in these situations, rather than as a genitive case inflection as in the central Asian documents and some of the Indian inscriptions, that we find *s̱* used in the majority of the new manuscripts—but once again, inconsistently. For example, here too our two best-represented scribes part company. Hand no. 2 uses *s̱* regularly for old intervocalic *th* and *dh:* for instance, writing *bos̱isatva-* for Sanskrit *bodhisattva-* (frag. 25, r, line 19) and *pranis̱i-* for *praṇidhi-* (v, line 7). Hand no. 1 never uses *s̱*, writing an ordinary *s* in such contexts, as in *prasaṇa-* = Pali *padhāna-* (frag. 12, r, line 39). We also find that some scribes occasionally use *s̱* where it is not etymologically justified, for example, in *uvas̱akramita* = Sanskrit *upasaṃkramya* (frag. 4, part 6, v, lines 6 and 11). In such cases *s̱* seems to have become more or less interchangeable with ordinary *s*, a state of affairs that also prevailed in the KDhP (see below).

The use of diacritic additions to various consonant signs, either to represent modified pronunciations or to mark abbreviated forms of consonantal clusters, is another prominent variable feature in Kharoṣṭhī orthography, and the new documents show many examples of such usages, usually in situations identical or similar to those observed in other types of Gāndhārī documents. Such diacritics often take the form of a horizontal line above the consonant, which, for instance, is used frequently with *ṣ* (𐨮𐨸, transcribed *ṣ̄a*) in various types of Kharoṣṭhī documents, almost always in positions corresponding to Sanskrit *ṣṇa*. Thus, in the new documents we find, very frequently, the word *taṣ̄a* = Sanskrit *tṛṣṇā*, "thirst," "craving." The horizontal diacritic is also applied, again as in previously known documents, to *j* (𐨗𐨸, transcribed *j̄a*) in phonetic situations corresponding to *jh* in Pali and other MIA languages, probably representing /z/ or a similar sound. This character appears frequently in the word *j̄aṇa-*, "meditative state" (= Pali *jhāna* < Skt. *dhyāna*). The same diacritic is also seen in a few cases with *c*, where it presumably represents an original cluster *śc*, as in other Kharoṣṭhī documents; thus, *pac̄avita* (frag. 4, part 6, v, line 18), apparently = **paścāpita*, "set behind," "rejected." Other well-attested types of diacritic marking, such as *g* or *t* with a small horizontal stroke at the right side of the base to indicate, apparently, a fricative pronunciation (e.g., 𐨒𐨹, *ǵ*), are also sporadically found in the new texts.

While the uses of diacritics present nothing startlingly new, some of the new manuscripts do show unusual treatments of certain consonantal conjuncts. Particularly interesting is the use in some of them of the subscript preconsonantal *r* in places where, contrary to normal Kharoṣṭhī usage, it seems not to be etymologically justified. Thus, in the Rhinoceros Horn Sūtra manuscript (frag. 5B), the word for "rhinoceros," which occurs in the refrain of each verse, is spelled consistently as *kharga* (𐨑𐨒𐨿𐨪). This is not the normal derivative of Sanskrit *khaḍga* in Gāndhārī, where we would expect to find, as in Pali and other MIA dialects, *khagga*. Several examples of what would seem to be the same or a related phenomenon appear among the avadāna texts, where we find, for example, forms such as *uparno* = Sanskrit *utpannaḥ* (frag. 4, part 6, r, lines 26, 30, etc.), *pradivarno* = *pratipannaḥ* (frag. 4, part 5, v, line 10), and *bhirno* = *bhinnam* (frag. 25, r, line 20). The common denominator among all examples of nonetymological *r* noted so far is that they occur in places where a simple geminate consonant would have been expected. It is therefore possible that preconsonantal *r* came to have a secondary function of marking geminates, which were otherwise not indicated in the Kharoṣṭhī script. If this is actually what happened, it curiously prefigures similar developments in later Brāhmī-derived scripts, where, for example, in manuscripts from Bengal and Nepal the superscript preconsonantal *r* is often written, without etymological justification, when the following consonant is a geminate.[7] This peculiar usage is rare but not

7. This development presumably represents the influence of vernacular pronunciations in which Sanskrit clusters of the form *r* + consonant (r-C) were pronounced as a geminate of the following consonant (/CC/). But such an explanation for what seems to be a parallel graphic development in Gāndhārī is less cogent, since *r* plus consonant groups were generally more stable in that language than in other MIA dialects. The phenomenon thus remains to be fully clarified.

totally unprecedented in Kharoṣṭhī, since in the KDhP we have the forms *sabarṇo* = Sanskrit *sampannaḥ* and *samavarṇo* = *samāpannaḥ*,[8] and it may be significant that here, as in many of the cases in the new texts, the nonetymological *r* appears in connection with derivatives of Sanskrit past participles in *-nna*, particularly in forms of *panna* (< √*pad*).

Some of the new manuscripts use vowel signs which are not normally seen in Kharoṣṭhī, although these "special" vowels, like most of the orthographic peculiarities of the new texts, have been observed occasionally in other documents. For example, in at least one case, the word *manasikṛta* (frag. 29, part 2, v, line 9), the Sanskrit syllabic *ṛ* is represented as such with a special diacritic vowel sign (𐨐𐨃 = *kṛ*). The notation in Gāndhārī of the syllabic vowel *ṛ*, which is lost in all other MIA languages, has previously only been observed in a few cases among the central Asian documents (Boyer, Rapson, and Senart 1920–9: 3.298) and coin legends (Das Gupta 1958: 404, table IV, no. 19-IV). The use of *ṛ* is presumably influenced by a tendency toward Sanskritized orthography that is characteristic of some Kharoṣṭhī documents, especially in the later period of the use of that script. It may be significant that the only one of the new manuscripts in which *ṛ* has so far been noted, the sūtra(?) text in fragments 26 + 29, is written in a calligraphic style and hence seems to embody a more formal style of writing than most of the others.

Some of the new manuscripts also sporadically note certain long vowels. Although Kharoṣṭhī normally does not distinguish vowel length, the occasional diacritic indication of long vowels has, once again, been previously observed in some varieties of Kharoṣṭhī, most frequently in the central Asian documents (Boyer, Rapson, and Senart 1920–9: 3.298–9). Among the new manuscripts, this usage seems to be limited to the full (nondiacritic) form of the vowel *ā*, which is sometimes represented by a normal *a* with the addition of a diagonal stroke running downward to the right from a point near the bottom of the stem of the letter (𐨀𐨌). Examples of long *ā* have to date only been noticed among the avadāna texts written by hand no. 2, and there only sporadically, for instance, in *āyiviga* (= *ājīvika-*; frag. 1, part 5, r, line 30).

In conclusion, all or nearly all of the distinctive or unusual orthographic features of the new manuscripts have parallels in at least one of the previously known classes of Kharoṣṭhī documents (i.e., the inscriptions, coins, central Asian documents, and the KDhP manuscript), although their significance had not in all cases been clear until now. But the distribution of the orthographic variants and peculiarities does not, at this point at least, seem to follow any regular pattern. Most, if not all, of the variable features seem to have been adopted merely according

8. See Brough 1962: 98. Brough's idea that the intrusive *r* in these forms marks the following nasal as retroflex does not accord with the evidence of the new documents and therefore can be discarded.

to the personal preference of the individual scribe, and there is no evidence of any sort of standardization of usage. Further study of these features and of the individual texts will undoubtedly clarify at least some of the details of the history, significance, and distributional patterns of these features, but it is unlikely to disprove the overall impression of a nonstandardized scribal tradition.

Finally, a comparison of these orthographic features with those of the KDhP scroll reveals more contrasts than similarities, even though one might have expected the KDhP to resemble the new texts, since in terms of its contents it is the most similar among the aforementioned classes of Kharoṣṭhī texts. For example, one of the distinctive orthographic characteristics of the KDhP is that, unlike most other Kharoṣṭhī documents, it not only uses the signs for both nasals *n* and *ṇ* but also maintains a consistent distinction between them, the former being regularly used at the beginning of words and the latter in internal position.[9] No trace of this pattern of distribution between *n* and *ṇ* has been found in the new documents, or elsewhere in Kharoṣṭhī. The distribution of *s* and *s̱* in the KDhP too is very different from what we find in the new documents. In the KDhP, the two are mere mechanical graphic variants, with the choice being determined by the vowel diacritic (if any) attached to the consonant: the syllables *s̱a, s̱i,* and *s̱e* are always written with "special" *s̱,* while *so, su,* and *saṃ* are written with the normal *s* (Brough 1962: 67). This is entirely different from the usage of the new documents, as well as from all other known varieties of Kharoṣṭhī. Thus, contrary to what might have been expected, we find that in terms of these two important variables, among other points, the orthography of the KDhP differs markedly from that of the new manuscripts, whose orthography, broadly speaking, has more in common with inscriptional and central Asian Kharoṣṭhī. This is another example of the pattern noted above (6.2.3) of a surprising degree of difference with regard to paleographic, linguistic, and material features between the KDhP and the new Kharoṣṭhī manuscripts.

6.4. Phonological Features

6.4.1. Treatment of Intervocalic Consonants

In Gāndhārī, as in the MIA languages generally, the clearest index of the stage of linguistic development of a given document is the treatment of intervocalic consonants, particularly the stops. The new documents generally reflect a stage in which most of the stops in intervocalic position have been voiced and/or fricativized, with some of the "weaker" consonants such as the gutturals and palatals being elided. In other words, the documents represent a middle stage of development, between that of the early MIA languages such as Pali, in which intervocalic stops are mostly preserved in their original form (i.e., as they appear in Sanskrit), and that of the late

9. The distribution pattern is actually a little more complicated than this, but the details need not concern us here; see Brough 1962: 97–8.

MIA dialects such as Māhārāṣṭrī Prakrit, in which most of them (except the retroflexes) have been elided. This middle stage of phonetic development is generally consistent with that of Kharoṣṭhī inscriptions up to the latter part of the first century A.D., as was shown by Fussman (1989) in his definitive study of the historical development of the Gāndhārī language. It is around this time that we begin to regularly find characteristics of the later stage of MIA, mainly the extensive elision of intervocalic consonants, particularly dentals; for example, in the Kalawān inscription of the Azes year 134 (= A.D. 77) we find forms such as *sarvastivaaṇa* instead of the previously usual *sarvastivadaṇa* for Sanskrit *sarvāstivādānām* (Fussman 1989: 457).

The following chart summarizes the results of a preliminary survey of the treatment of intervocalic consonants in a representative sampling of the new texts. The data are derived primarily from six texts that are relatively well preserved and have already been studied in some detail.[10] Some less common consonants for which no or very few examples were found are omitted from the chart, as are those (such as the semivowels other than *y*) that are generally preserved unchanged. Since the data were generally consistent among these six texts, it can reasonably be expected that further examination of the remaining texts will not drastically change the picture.

Original Consonant	Renditions in Intervocalic Position
k	*g*, *ǵ*, Ø
g	*g*, *y*, Ø
c	*y*, Ø
c(c)h	*ch*
j	*y*, Ø
ṭh	*ḍ*, *ḍh* (both rare)
ḍ	*ḍ* (rare)
t	*t*, *d*, Ø (two cases)
th	*s*, *s̱*[11]
d	*d*, *t* (sporadic, in two texts only), Ø (one case)
dh	*s*, *s̱*[12]
p	*v*, Ø
bh	*bh*, *h* (one case)
y	*g*, Ø

10. The texts are the Anavatapta-gāthā (frag. 1, first text); part of a verse commentary text (frags. 9 and 13); a sūtra text (frags. 12 + 14, first text); the Rhinoceros Horn Sūtra (frag. 5B); and two avadāna-type texts (frags. 1, second text, and 16 + 25, second text).

11. See section 6.3.

12. See section 6.3.

In general, the representation of intervocalic consonants in the new manuscripts closely parallels that of the majority of the previously known Kharoṣṭhī inscriptions, including the KDhP (Fussman 1989: 464). Unfortunately, data of this type are of very limited value for absolute or even relative dating, due mainly to the strongly conservative and (mostly in later documents) even intentionally archaizing orthographic tendencies, which have the effect of disguising or at least minimizing phonetic changes (Fussman 1989: 485). Therefore, while the appearance of later phonetic features in a given document may be taken as an indication of a later date, their absence does not prove that a document is early. Thus, although Fussman found that the stage of phonetic development reflected in the KDhP corresponded to that of the second half of the first century B.C., he felt that the actual date of the manuscript was likely to be at least a century later than that (1989: 465).

We do find in the new manuscripts a few sporadic cases of the elision of original intervocalic dental stops (*t* and *d*), which are diagnostic of the later stages of phonetic change in MIA. Thus, the Anavatapta-gāthā has *piu* = Sanskrit *pitur* (frag. 1, part 2, r, line 20) and *ṇaï[ti]ru* for *nadītiram* (part 4, r, line 1),[13] and the verse commentary text (frag. 9, part 3, r, line 11) has *paṃḍia,* apparently = *paṇḍitaḥ*.[14] But it is hard to be sure whether these relatively few examples among the fairly large number of data collected so far should be taken as indications of a later date for the texts as a whole. According to Fussman's principle enunciated above, this would, in theory, be the case. But on the other hand, it is by no means unusual to find what Fussman calls a "fore-runner" (avant-coureur) (1989: 464 n. 42), that is, an anomalous spelling in a relatively early text reflecting a phonetic change that is not regularly observed until later, the classic case being *sasumate* = Sanskrit *sādhumata-* in Aśoka's Shāhbāzgaṛhī rock edict I, which seems to anticipate the development of intervocalic *dh* to *s̱* (i.e., /ð/, written as *s̱*; see 6.3, p. 121) in later Gāndhārī.[15] As a matter of fact, examples of the elision of original intervocalic *-t-* are found in inscriptions as early as the beginning of the first century A.D., as in *maüleṇa* for Sanskrit *mātulena,* "with maternal uncle," and *maülaṇie* = *mātulānyā,* "with maternal uncle's wife," in the Indravarman reliquary inscription of A.D. 6.

In short, in view of the peculiarities of Kharoṣṭhī orthography, which exhibits on the one hand a strong tendency toward archaic spellings and on the other hand sporadic anticipations of incipient phonetic shifts, texts can be dated

13. But five lines later the same word is spelled *ṇaditiru,* with typical inconsistency.

14. Also, the Saṅgīti-sūtra commentary (frag. 15, part 3, r, line 41), which is not among the samples tabulated above, has *acaüṭha* = Skt. *acaturtham.* Note that a similar spelling for the related word *caüdiśami* (= *caturdiśe*) appears in the inscription on British Library pot D; see section 7.2.2.1.

15. Fussman himself doubts the linguistic significance of this particular example, but Caillat (1989a: 426 n. 70), referring to Fussman, does see it as "a fact of the actual language; an anticipation, perhaps, of an evolution well attested later on."

on the basis of their (apparent) phonetic features only in terms of broad estimates. With regard to the present collection, we find a general predominance of features that coincide with those of dated inscriptions of the first century A.D., but in the current state of our knowledge, it would be imprudent to claim any more certainty or precision than this.

6.4.2. Representation of Voiced Aspirates

It has often been noted that the aspirate consonants, and in particular the voiced aspirates, are represented inconsistently in some Kharoṣṭhī documents, and this has been taken, no doubt correctly, to indicate a dialectal weakening of the distinction between aspirates and nonaspirates (e.g., Brough 1962: 100). This feature is attested more vividly in some of the new manuscripts than in any previously known documents, especially in the texts written by hand no. 1 (fragments 1, 12 + 14, and 16 + 25), who invariably writes *gha* in place of *ga* and often also *dha* for original *da*. Thus, in the Anavatapta-gāthā (frag. 1, first text) we find, for example, *sughadiṣu* = Sanskrit *sugatiṣu* (part 1, r, line 4), *gharu* = *gṛham* (part 2, r, line 13), and *araghae* = *ārāgayeyam* (line 15). No exceptions to the substitution of *gha* for *ga* have been found in any of the texts written by this scribe; that is to say, the letter *ga* never occurs in his manuscripts. A sporadic tendency to write *gha* for *ga* has been noticed in other documents; for example, in *drugha* = Pali *duggā* in the KDhP (verse 132) and *bhaghava* = *bhagavat-* in an inscription of (probably) the Azes year 157 (= A.D. 100) (Salomon 1995b: 138). But nowhere else has such a complete and consistent leveling of *ga*/*gha*, or of any other nonaspirate/aspirate pair, been observed.

Scribe no. 1 often writes *dha* in place of expected *da*, but only in word-initial position, and even then not always. Thus, we find in the Anavatapta-gāthā fragment *dhrohikṣu* or *dhrohikṣe* = *durbhikṣe* (part 5, r, lines 3 and 5), *dhośehi* = *duṣyaiḥ* (part 2, r, line 14), *dhrispa* or *dhrispaṇa* = *dṛṣtvā* (part 2, r, lines 36 and 40), and *dhakṣiṇa* = *dakṣiṇā* (part 4, r, line 35), but also *dade* = Sanskrit *dade*, "I gave" (?) (part 2, r, line 14) and *deva* = *devaḥ* (part 2, r, line 17). A similar change of initial *d-* to *dh-* has been noted a few times in inscriptions (Fussman 1989: 482, *dhakṣiṇami*) and, in noninitial position, in several cases in the KDhP, for instance, in *kusidhu* = Pali *kusīto* (Skt. *kusīdaḥ;* verse 316; cf. Brough 1962: 95). But this change appears to be statistically much more frequent in the manuscripts written by scribe no. 1 than in previously known documents.

As for the other voiced aspirates, *ḍha* occurs very rarely in the new manuscripts. In most cases where it would have been expected etymologically, the corresponding nonaspirate appears, for instance, in *paḍidu* = *paṭhitum* (frag. 1, part 4, r, line 39). This is not surprising, as *ḍha* is generally seen in Kharoṣṭhī only in early inscriptions. As for *jha,* which is also rare overall in Kharoṣṭhī, it has been found only in the proper name *jhadamitra* or *jhadimitra,* the hero of two of the avadānas in the second text on fragment 1 (part 3, v, line 1, to part 2, v, line 28). The name seems to be of Iranian derivation, and *jh* is here apparently being used to represent /z/ (see also sec. 7.1.2, n. 6). *Bha,* on the other hand, is mostly stable in all positions in the new texts, as is generally the case in Kharoṣṭhī. In a few instances, however, in intervocalic position it is reduced to *h, v,* or *vh;* for example, in *dhrohikṣe/u* = *durbhikṣe* (frag. 1, part 5, r, lines 3 and 5), *avisameti* = *abhisameti* (frag. 4, part 4, r, line 39), and *avhilaṃbyi* = *abhilambī* (?) in the stotra text (frag. 5C, r, line 2). Such spellings are well attested in other Kharoṣṭhī documents (see, e.g., Brough 1962: 96–7).

Thus, with regard to the treatment of the five voiced aspirates in the new documents, two of them (*gha* and *dha*) are often written in place of the corresponding nonaspirates, two others (*jha* and *ḍha*) are largely absent, and one, *bh,* is preserved regularly. This seemingly inconsistent pattern confirms the theory of a general weakening of the aspirate/unaspirate contrast among voiced consonants (with the possible exception of *bh*) in Gāndhārī. The peculiar frequency of aspirate/unaspirate variations in the manuscripts of one particular scribe (hand no. 1) brings to mind the opinions of earlier authors who were inclined to attribute such alternations to writers who were native speakers, not of Gāndhārī, but of other, non-Indo-Aryan languages. Thus Konow attributed similar instances in Indian Kharoṣṭhī inscriptions to "the influence of the Iranian tendencies of some of the individuals who made use of the language" (1929: cii), while Burrow explained the incorrect notation of aspiration in the central Asian Kharoṣṭhī documents on the grounds that "the native language of Shan-Shan had no aspirates and consequently in pronouncing the Prakrit they neglected them" (1937: 9). The theory that the incorrect treatment of voiced aspirates reflects the linguistic habits of particular scribes who were not native speakers of Gāndhārī or other Indian languages might also be supported by a recently published brief dedicatory inscription on a stūpa model (Sadakata 1992: 2), in which *dh* and *bh* are regularly written in place of *d* and *b* respectively, for instance, in *dhanamukhe* = Sanskrit *dānamukham* and *bhudhaṇadhasa* = *buddhanandasya.* The concentration of this pattern in certain documents may indeed indicate that they were written by nonnative speakers, and it may be true that the influence of other languages to some extent affected the development of the aspirates in Gāndhārī, especially in central Asia. But a broad pattern of weakening of the voiced aspirate/unaspirate distinction is sufficiently well attested in Kharoṣṭhī documents in general, including the new manuscripts, to show that this phenomenon was essentially an internal development within Gāndhārī. Of course, it is not a coincidence that the weakness of the voiced aspirates in Gāndhārī echoes their absence in the Iranian languages which were its direct neighbors to the west, but the new information suggests that we should view this similarity as a common areal feature rather than as a contamination resulting from the adoption of Gāndhārī by nonnative speakers.

6.4.3. Treatment of Nasals + Homorganic Stops

One of the most distinctive phonological features of the KDhP is its peculiar treatments of nasals + homorganic stop combinations, which typically involves the voicing of unvoiced consonants (e.g., *śadi* < *śānti*) and elision of voiced consonants (e.g., *vinadi* < *vindati;* see Brough 1962: 98–100). This development is paralleled in the central Asian Kharoṣṭhī documents (Burrow 1937: 17) but is not usually observed in Indian Kharoṣṭhī inscriptions. In this regard, as in several others, the new manuscripts agree more with the usage of inscriptional Kharoṣṭhī than with that of the KDhP. The only apparent instance of a sound change of this type noticed so far is *paṃjamo* = *paṃcamaḥ* (frag. 9, part 3, r, line 7), but this seems in any case to be an anomalous spelling, since the word *paṃca* appears regularly in its standard spelling in the same text (lines 5, 15, and 21).

The absence of any significant evidence among the new documents for the special sound changes involving nasals + stops might seem to support the theory that this feature of the KDhP reflects a central Asian dialect of Gāndhārī, since it also appears in the Niya documents but not in the inscriptions or in the new manuscripts from the India subcontinent. However, Bloch (1912) demonstrated that similar sound changes occur in some later and modern dialects of western and northwestern India, for instance in Sindhi and Punjabi, and hence they may reflect, not a central Asian dialect feature, but rather an underlying dialectal and/or orthographic variation within Indian Gāndhārī. Moreover, there is at least one exception to the general absence of these sound changes in inscriptions from the subcontinent: the word *sabradu* = *samprāptaḥ,* "arrived," used in several of the Kharoṣṭhī graffiti from the Alam Bridge site in northern Pakistan (Humbach 1980: 102).

It is also important to note that two supplementary notes added onto the KDhP scroll itself lack this characteristic feature of the main text and treat the nasal + stop combination in the manner normal to Indian Kharoṣṭhī inscriptions and other documents. The first of these two passages is the introductory verse at the head of the scroll, identifying it as the property of one Buddhanandin, whose name is spelled *budhaṇadisa* in the manner of epigraphic Kharoṣṭhī rather than **budhananisa* as would have been expected in the orthography of the KDhP text itself (Brough 1962: 177). The second additional passage consists of two verses (nos. 343 and 344 in Brough's numbering) added in a different hand to the otherwise blank verso of fragment B. Here we find *vaditva* (343c) for (probably) *vanditvā,* written in normal Indian Kharoṣṭhī orthography, instead of **vanitva* as would be expected in the KDhP text (Brough 1962: 281).[16] These points cast further doubt on

16. There is another later addition to the KDhP scroll on the verso of fragment A (opposite line 161 of the recto), which does not appear in any of the published photographs and which has apparently not been noticed until now. It consists of eight or nine akṣaras, several of which are blurred so that it is difficult to give a coherent reading, and therefore no linguistic conclusions can be drawn from it.

the theory that the KDhP's peculiar treatment of stop + homorganic consonant is a distinctive feature of central Asian Gāndhārī and consequently further obscure the issue of whether that manuscript was composed in central Asia or imported from India. Nevertheless, the differences in this respect between the orthography of the KDhP and the new scrolls do confirm the pattern of minor but numerous contrasts between them and strengthen the suspicion that they were written in different parts of the Gāndhārī-speaking area. But whether these contrasts reflect different usages within south Asia, or beyond it, remains uncertain.

6.5. Morphology and Syntax

6.5.1. Nominal Forms

Varying forms of nominal inflections frequently pose complex problems of analysis in Gāndhārī texts of all types. For example, *-o, -e, -u, -a,* and occasionally other endings as well are all attested as terminations for the nominative singular of masculine and neuter stems in *-a.* Moreover, it is quite common to find two or more of these endings alternating according to no discernible pattern within the same document, or even within the same phrase; the inscriptional example cited by Fussman (1989: 460), *vaga stratego puyaide,* "Vaga, the commander, is honored," is by no means unusual. Not surprisingly in view of such a situation, efforts to establish conventional dialect isoglosses for such alternative forms have been largely unsuccessful. This became clear even at an early stage of the study of Gāndhārī on the basis of the Indian inscriptions: among Aśokan inscriptions the *-e* ending predominated in the eastern version at Mānsehrā and *-o* in Shāhbāzgaṛhī to the west, but in later inscriptions the pattern appeared to be reversed, with *-e* generally prevailing to the west of the Indus River and *-o* to the east (Konow 1929: cxii). This apparent contradiction led Brough to suspect that "the contrast between the two forms in Gāndhārī may have been less clear-cut than is suggested by the writing" (1962: 115). Subsequent discoveries and analyses have confirmed this impression, to the point that Fussman is surely correct in stating, with reference to Kharoṣṭhī inscriptions of the early first century A.D., that "the final vowels were no doubt pronounced very weakly, to the point that they were no longer differentiated" (1989: 460). Unsatisfying as this conclusion may seem, and inadequate as it may be for purposes of philological analysis, it is the only one that can explain the otherwise incomprehensible distribution of variant endings in the nominative singular masculine and neuter, as well as in several other morphological categories.[17]

17. This means that the alternate endings in such cases are not, strictly speaking, a matter of "morphology," but rather of orthography. Nevertheless, they are discussed here under the former heading, not only as a matter of convenience, but also because they are of some value, despite their inconsistency, in the philological analysis of the new texts. Although they are not morphological alternatives in the strict sense of the term, detailed study of their patterns of occurrence and alter-

As in other Gāndhārī documents, this bewildering variability of inflectional forms is best attested among the new documents in the nominative singular masculine and neuter endings, if only because of the statistical frequency of these forms. For the nominative singular, most of the new texts use two or more different endings with no consistent principle of distribution, but there are significant differences among the particular patterns observed in individual texts. Some of them, such as the Anavatapta-gāthā, use *-u*, *-o*, *-a*, and *-e* in declining order of frequency, with the first three approximately equally common and the last comparatively rare. Others, such as the avadāna and related texts, do not use *-u* at all but have a strong preference for *-o*, with an occasional *-e* and *-a* ending. In the Rhinoceros Horn Sūtra (frag. 5B), *-o* also predominates, along with some *-a* endings, but none in *-e* or *-u*.[18] Thus, in the new documents as a whole, *-o* is the most common ending for the nominative singular, but in any given document it alternates in varying patterns with one or more of the other possible endings.

Despite the complexity of the distribution of these endings, certain patterns indicate that they are not totally random. For example, in some texts the nominative in *-a* shows a strong tendency to be attached to adjectives or participial forms rather than to substantives; thus, three of the four nominatives in *-a* in the Rhinoceros Horn Sūtra are present participles in *-maṇa*. Significant patterns also emerge among the endings of the accusative singular. In general, these endings vary in ways similar to the nominative, but accusatives in *-e* are absent from all of the sample texts analyzed to date, including those that use *-e* in the nominative. Also, in the Rhinoceros Horn Sūtra the preponderance in the nominative of *-o* over *-a* (twenty-six to four) is reversed in the accusative, where thirteen examples end in *-a* versus only eight in *-o*. Brough's analysis (1962: 113) of the endings of the nominative and accusative singular masculine in the KDhP yielded broadly similar results, with a much greater frequency of *-a* in the accusative than in the nominative (107 vs. 19 cases), and thus we must agree with him that, despite the great flexibility in spelling that prevailed in all types of Gāndhārī, "the forms in *-o*, *-u*, *-a* are not distributed at random, as might have been expected if the scribe (or translator) had been unaware of any difference between masculine and neuter, and between nominative and accusative" (1962: 114).

nation can sometimes be helpful in interpreting the grammar and syntax of the texts, and hence they do in a sense function as quasi-morphological elements. Examples of this principle will be illustrated below.

18. The following chart summarizes the results of a rough preliminary count of nominative singular masculine endings in these three representative texts. The avadāna-type text cited is the best-preserved portion (r, line 14, to v, line 8) of fragments 16 + 25 (second text):

	o	*u*	*e*	*a*
Anavatapta-gāthā	20	26	6	19
Avadāna sample	26	0	3	4
Rhinoceros Horn	26	0	0	4

The phonetic leveling of vowels in word-final position described by Fussman is no doubt also the explanation for the occasional cases of locative singulars in *-o*, *-u*, and (possibly) *-a* instead of the normal *-e* (or *-ami*). Thus the Aṅguttara fragment (12, r, line 27) has *viharadi jedavaṇo aṇasapiḍiasa aramu*, "was staying in the Jetavana, in the grove of Anāthapiṇḍika," as an equivalent to the familiar Pali formula *viharati jetavane anāthapiṇḍikassa ārāme*. Similarly, in the Anavatapta-gāthā (frag. 1, part 5, r, line 3) we read *dhrohikṣu batamaṇae*, "while a famine was going on," where the corresponding Sanskrit version (in the Gilgit manuscript; Bechert 1961: 137) has *durbhikṣe vartamāne ca*. Similar phenomena, especially a locative in *-a*, have been occasionally observed in Kharoṣṭhī inscriptions, where they have been again explained by Fussman on the grounds of "weakening of final vowels" (1989: 456; see also 458 and 471–2).

Some other morphological peculiarities of the new documents that have not been previously observed in Gāndhārī texts can also be attributed to the phonetic neutralization of final vowels. Thus, in the numerous avadāna texts, nearly all of which were written by the same scribe, the instrumental singular ending (masculine or neuter) is consistently *-eno* rather than the expected *-ena*, and the genitive plural ending is equally regularly *-ano* instead of *-ana* (< Skt. *-ānām*). Examples are *teno kalen(o*) tano*[19] *samageno*, "at that time, at that juncture" (frag. 16, r, lines 16–17) = Sanskrit/Pali *tena kālena tena samayena;* and *pacano indrigano* (frag. 2, r, line 11) = Sanskrit *pañcānām indriyāṇām*.

In the Rhinoceros Horn Sūtra, the ending of the locative plural is regularly *-eṣo* instead of the usual *-eṣu*, as in *putreṣo dareṣo* (frag. 5B, subfragment 2a, line 2) = Pali *puttesu dāresu*. This accords with a previously attested tendency toward alternations between *o* and *u* in final and other unstressed positions (Brough 1962: 80), which is also manifested among the new manuscripts in spellings like *aṇorakṣaṇa-* (frag. 14, r, line 10) = Pali *anurakkhana-*.

6.5.2. Verbal Forms and Syntax

Verb morphology, usage, and syntax differ considerably among the various texts and genres of the new documents. Particularly striking is the contrast between texts with pan-Buddhist parallels such as the Anavatapata-gāthā and the Aṅguttara fragments on the one hand and the apparently locally composed texts of the avadāna class on the other.[20] In the former group, we find a rich variety of finite (especially preterite) and nonfinite verb forms that are mostly parallel to those of other MIA languages, especially Pali, and that appear to reflect the influence of

19. Here *tano* = *tena*, as also in the passage cited in section 6.7.3; cf. *ñaṇaṇa* = *jñāneṇa* in the passage quoted in 2.2.2, and n. 18 there, and *taṣa* = *teṣām* in the KDhP (Brough 1961: 82).

20. The commentatorial and scholastic texts generally have relatively few verb forms, and these mostly in the present tense, so that they provide less material for analysis in this regard.

the underlying language or languages from which these texts were evidently translated into Gāndhārī. The avadānas, in contrast, have a minimal verbal system whose repertoire of finite verb forms is limited mainly to the present and future tenses, with the preterite being almost always expressed periphrastically with the past participle.

In the Anavatapta-gāthā, for example, besides numerous present tense forms and occasional specimens of the future, optative, and imperative, we find a large number of finite preterites of what may broadly be called the "aorist" type, such as *viaghaṣe,* "he expounded" (= Pali *vyākāsi,* Skt. *vyākārṣīt;* frag. 1, part 4, r, line 12), and *abhiṇirkhami,* "I went forth" (= Pali *abhinikkhamiṃ;* part 3, r, line 5). Frequently, the preterite augment is preserved, as in *adhrakṣema,* "we saw" (Pali *adassāma,* Skt. *adrākṣma;* part 2, r, line 33), and *aghami,* "I went" (Pali *agamaṃ,* Skt. *agamam;* line 38). A wide variety of gerund forms is also attested in the Anavatapta, including ones that resemble Pali and Buddhist Sanskrit types such as the doublet *dhrispa* and *dhrispaṇa,* "having seen" (cf. Pali *disvā/disvāna;* part 2, r, lines 36 and 40), and more characteristically Gāndhārī types like *sastarita,* "having spread out" (Skt. *saṃstīrya;* part 2, r, line 14), and *pariarita,* "having gone about" (Skt. *paricarya;* line 46).

In the avadāna texts, in contrast, the narration of past events is expressed by a mixture of present tense forms with narrative past value such as *hovati,* "was," and *matredi,* "said," and past participle forms such as *hodo,* "was," "became," *gado,* "went," and *atarahido,* "disappeared." To date, no specimens of active preterite forms or of gerunds have been noticed in these texts. Imperative expressions are generally formed with the passive gerundive construction, for example, *iśa pradighetavo,* "this is to be taken," that is, "take this" (frag. 16, r, line 32). In general, the avadāna texts display a much simpler and more colloquial style of Gāndhārī than the other texts, a style which in some respects resembles the phrasing of inscriptional usage but which also probably represents something much closer to the contemporary colloquial form of Gāndhārī than anything that is seen in the technical or translated texts (see also 6.7.3).

6.6. Lexicon

In the past it has been difficult to discern distinctive elements of the local lexicon in Gāndhārī texts, mainly because of the strong predominance in the available documents of Buddhist terms common to all Indo-Aryan languages as used by Buddhists. Nonetheless, in at least one well-documented case it has been possible to show that a word occurring in a Gāndhārī inscription reflects local vocabulary as attested by its derivatives in the modern Dardic and neighboring Indo-Aryan languages of the northwest, which are, broadly speaking, the descendants of Gāndhārī. This is the word *spasana/spasuna,* "of [my] sisters," appearing in both Kharoṣṭhī versions (Shāhbāzgaṛhī and Mānsehrā) of Aśoka's rock edict V and contrasting with *bhaginīnaṃ* and the like in the other (Brāhmī) versions. As was shown by Morgenstierne (1950), the same contrast is reflected in the geographic distribution of words for "sister" in the New Indo-Aryan (NIA) languages, among which derivatives of OIA *svasṛ-* are represented only in the Dardic languages (Shina *sa(s)*, Tirahi *spas*, etc.), while all the rest of the NIA languages have derivatives of *bhaginī* (Hindi *bahin*, Marathi *bhain(i)*, etc.).

While pan-Buddhist vocabulary is of course as prominent in the new documents as it is in the previously known Gāndhārī texts, the sheer volume of the new texts, as well as the more colloquial character of some of them, makes it possible to identify several other instances of what seem to be regional words. One is especially inclined to suspect such cases when a word in a Gāndhārī text contrasts with a different but synonymous one in a corresponding text in another Indo-Aryan language, as occurred in the case of the Aśokan words for "sister" noted above. For example, in the Anavatapta-gāthā, *baṭa* occurs three times (frag. 1, part 3, r, lines 18–20) where it contrasts with *upalā[ḥ]* and *pāṣāṇā[ḥ]*, "stones," in the Sanskrit version of this text (Bechert 1961: 132). Gāndhārī *baṭa* is evidently a derivative of **varta*, "round stone" (Turner 1966: 1.661, §11348), whose derivatives are widely attested in Dardic (e.g., Torwali *bāṭ*, Tirahi *baṭ*), Nuristani (Ashkun and Waigalī *wāṭ*), and northwestern Indo-Aryan languages (Punjabi *vaṭṭā*, etc.).[21] It is true that this word is also attested in Oriya (*bāṭi*) and Bihari (*baṭṭā*, "stone roller for spices"), but the absence of derivatives in any of the central NIA languages is more significant, since a similar pattern of geographic distribution, reflecting "inner" and "outer" strata of Indo-Aryan vocabulary, is observed in connection with several other words of this class, as will be discussed below.

A particularly interesting case of this is *vadi* in the phrase *so gado kaśavasa vadi*, "he went to Kāśyapa," in an avadāna text (frag. 4, part 7, r, line 5). This is certainly the same word, derived from Sanskrit *upānte*, that appears frequently as a postposition in the central Asian Kharoṣṭhī documents in the form *vaṃti*, "with," "to," "in the presence of," etc. (Burrow 1937: 42–3 and 118), but that has not previously been found in Kharoṣṭhī/Gāndhārī documents from the Indian subcontinent. Modern Indo-Aryan derivatives of this term are attested only in Nuristani (e.g., Waigalī *Wā̃t*, name of a village), Dardic (e.g., Pašaī *ōda*, *udē*, "near"), Punjabi (*vā̃dā*, "separate"), and Sinhala (*vata*, "edge," and *veta*, "vicinity"; Turner 1966: 1.108, §2303). A similar pattern appears with regard to the use, with great frequency and regularity, especially in the avadāna texts, of *matredi* in the neutral sense of "say" (as also in the central Asian documents). Once again, the modern derivatives of Sanskrit *mantrayate* in the general sense of "say," "speak," are, according to Turner (1966: 1.565, §9837), restricted to Dardic (Kalasha [Rumbūr dialect] *mātrem*, "I speak"), Nuristani (e.g., Waigalī *matrām*, "I ask, say"), and Assamese (*matibā*, "to speak, recite").

21. For further details see Fussman 1972: 2.274–6.

From this handful of examples, we begin to discern a pattern of what appears to be local vocabulary mixed in among the more standard Indo-Aryan and Buddhist lexicon of the new texts. The later and modern derivatives of such words are concentrated at, but not limited to, the northwestern borders of the Indo-Aryan language area (i.e., the Dardic and Nuristani languages, and Punjabi and neighboring dialects), for they also pop up at the eastern (Assamese, Oriya, Bihari) and southern (Sinhala) edges. This is no doubt a manifestation of the well-known pattern of distribution of various linguistic phenomena among the Indo-Aryan languages into "inner" and "outer" circles. As noted by Morgenstierne, this pattern reflects the principle that "innovations in India, as elsewhere, have often radiated from the centre, leaving a disconnected margin with more archaic forms" (1950: 31). Thus, it may be that, at a deeper historical level, the "distinctive" Gāndhārī/Dardic vocabulary which is beginning to emerge among the new documents actually reflects the retention of archaic, originally far more widespread words. Such a situation would hardly be surprising, in view of the general historical principle of the relative resistance to change among the less central members of a language family, and in particular of the conservative character of the Dardic and Nuristani languages.

All of this is, of course, based on a preliminary and very incomplete survey of the materials, and further study should clarify the situation and provide more and better examples of this pattern. But in any case, it is already clear that these new documents do provide a distinct, if limited, indication of the local character of the vocabulary of colloquial Gāndhārī.

Another example of interesting lexical data from the new manuscripts is *chado*, "sound" (accusative) in the Aṅguttara fragment (frag. 16, r, line 44), corresponding to Pali *saddaṃ* (Skt. *śabdam*). The same word appears in the form *chada* in verse 37 of the KDhP, but since the word was at that point a hapax legomenon, Brough was uncertain whether it was "a *sandhi*-alternate . . . due to the specific context of the verse in question, or whether . . . it had become the normal form of the word within the dialect" (1962: 101). But Buddruss, noting that Nuristani words for "sound," etc. suggested a derivation from *chada*, proposed that this was indeed the normal form of the word in Gāndhārī (1975: 39), and the appearance of this form in a new Gāndhārī text now confirms this.

6.7. General Remarks and Conclusions

6.7.1. The Overall Unity of the Language of the Documents

The preliminary and partial survey whose results have been presented above shows that the new Gāndhārī documents are all in essentially the same script and language, despite what seem to be considerable differences in paleography and morphology. The majority of these contrasts are essentially minor variations and superficial distinctions reflecting, on the one hand, the nonstandardized character of the Gāndhārī language and, on the other, the differences in style and content among the various texts. Thus, with regard to the apparently different "grammar" of the various texts, for example, in noun morphology, it has been shown that in most cases the variant inflections are actually only different ways of writing what, in the spoken language, were probably more or less the same endings, the quality of whose vocalic element had been neutralized and which therefore could be represented by different vowels, evidently at the whim of the scribe. With respect to the widely differing usage of verb forms and syntax, however, the contrasts seem to be determined mostly by the nature of the texts. Those that were translated from prototypes in other MIA languages are full of verbal forms and syntactic structures such as aorist-type preterites and gerunds in *-tva* or *-tvaṇa* that were probably not part of the living colloquial Gāndhārī of the time but rather reflect a general Buddhist jargon. In short, we are probably dealing in all of these texts with essentially the same language, whose underlying unity is masked by its nonstandardized character and by the different stylistic features and linguistic backgrounds of the texts composed in or rendered into it. This preliminary conclusion will of course have to be tested and refined by detailed studies of the individual texts, but it can be expected that, on the whole, these will tend to confirm the underlying unity of the Gāndhārī language represented in the new manuscripts.

6.7.2. The Problem of Nonstandardization of Gāndhārī

Despite the seeming chaos of Kharoṣṭhī/Gāndhārī orthography, a measure, or at least an approximation, of consistency within the individual texts in the British Library collection can still be discerned. For example, although a particular scribe may alternate, apparently at random, among two, three, or even more endings for the nominative singular (see 6.5.1), each scribe does have distinct preferences for certain endings over others. Similar patterns emerge with regard to other points of orthographic variation, such as the use (or not) of the variant form of the sibilant s̱, which is usually employed with some regularity and consistency within the works of a particular scribe, though the patterns of use vary widely from scribe to scribe.

A priori, one would expect such patterns to reflect independent orthographic traditions, whether based on chronological, geographical, sectarian, or perhaps other distinctions. Since it can be assumed that our scribes learned to write through some formal training process,[22] the preferences they show for particular orthographical alternatives presumably reflect those of their teachers. Thus, there must have been, in some form or other, different traditions of ways to write Gāndhārī. The material that we have, however, does not (at least not yet) permit us to determine what the basis or distribution of such varying orthographies may have

22. The story told in the Lalitavistara of the future Buddha's first day in school (*lipiśālā-saṃdarśana*) illustrates the methods of elementary instruction in reading and writing used in ancient times, and it has been shown that this story is based on a Gandhāran original in which the script being taught was Kharoṣṭhī in the Arapacana order; see Brough 1977 and Salomon 1990b.

been. The wide variety of orthographic preferences exhibited by the fairly large selection of new texts from, in all likelihood, the same monastery library gives the impression that these habits coexisted side by side with no coherent pattern of distribution, that is, that the different modes of writing Kharoṣṭhī were governed merely by the habits or personal whims of each scribe. Nevertheless, common sense suggests that there must be more to it than this. It remains to be seen whether further study will reveal any meaningful patterns.

However this may be, the fact remains that the Gāndhārī language at the time of these new documents and, as far as we can tell, throughout the period of its use as a literary medium was never subjected to any single authoritative orthographic and grammatical standard. The question is why this should be the case. We now know, much more clearly than before, that the Kharoṣṭhī/Gāndhārī textual tradition was not, as it might once have appeared, an isolated and ephemeral provincial phenomenon but rather was well entrenched, widely used, and highly influential over a vast area of south and central Asia. The textual and epigraphic materials now known are impressive in their number and geographical extent, and the indications (discussed in chapter 3) that the newly discovered manuscripts constitute a tiny fraction of a very large number of such texts that must have existed in ancient times confirm what many scholars have already suspected—namely, that Gāndhārī was a major Buddhist language and cultural vehicle in the early centuries of the Christian era. Given this situation, one might have expected that an impulse would have arisen to standardize the language, as had occurred at an earlier date with Sanskrit and would occur later on with Pali. And yet, despite the abundant materials now available to us, there is no evidence at all that this ever happened.

The best explanation may simply be that such a process of linguistic standardization would indeed have happened had Gāndhārī continued to play the important role in Buddhist culture that it did, albeit relatively briefly, in the time of the Scythian, Parthian, and Kuṣāṇa dynastics. But in fact, the Gāndhārī language and Kharoṣṭhī script gradually fell out of use in India in or not much later than the third century A.D. Although the reasons for this decline remain to be definitively ascertained, it is surely no coincidence that it accompanied the collapse of the dynasties that are so closely linked with the florescence of Gandhāran Buddhism. The failure of Gāndhārī to undergo the process of "linguistic canonization" (Salomon 1989: 279, 281, 289) that was applied to some other Indo-Aryan languages and dialects used for the transmission of Buddhist texts was essentially a historical accident caused by its premature death. Had historical circumstances been different and had Gāndhārī continued to be the canonical language of a flourishing regional Buddhist tradition in the northwest, an authoritatively standardized and defined form of canonical Gāndhārī would surely have developed, complete with grammatical treatises, probably similar in form and concept to those composed for Sanskrit, Pali, and other MIA languages. But as things actually happened, there was apparently not enough time for such a process of scholastic standardization to develop—or at least so it appears from the documents that have been discovered to date.

6.7.3. Stylistic Varieties of Gāndhārī: Scholastic and Colloquial Language

Despite their underlying linguistic unity, the new documents present us with an unprecedentedly wide view of styles and registers of the Gāndhārī language, ranging from formulaic scholastic compositions to specimens that seem to approach the genuine colloquial form of the spoken language. The latter, moreover, include narrative texts that appear to have been originally composed in Gāndhārī rather than translated from or at least based on models in other Indo-Aryan languages, as had been the case with most other previously known specimens of the language. In terms of style, then, the new texts can be conveniently divided into those that seem to represent something close to "real," colloquial Gāndhārī and those that are largely patterned after styles and formulae common to Indian Buddhist textual traditions in the Indo-Aryan languages generally.

The latter type can be further divided into two subcategories: the scholastic or commentatorial style, and the narrative or poetic style. Specimens of the scholastic style are widely represented among the new texts, and not surprisingly there is little in them that is distinctively Gāndhārī other than the use of the Kharoṣṭhī script and the phonology of the words; with regard to their vocabulary, phrasing, and contents they differ little from similar texts in Pali and other Buddhist languages. Therefore, it is not easy to determine whether such scholastic texts were originally composed in Gāndhārī or translated from another MIA dialect. A representative example of the scholastic style is provided by the following extract from the Saṅgīti-sūtra commentary (frag. 15, part 3, r, line 41):[23]

> *trae kasavastue atitaṃ ba arabha kasevi anakataṃ ba etarahi va pracupaṃna˙ acaüṭha apaṃcama kasavastu bhavate˙*
>
> There are three topics of discussion (*kasavastu* = Pali *kathāvatthu*/Skt. *kathāvastu*): one may speak either of [something] that began in past time or that is yet to come or that has presently come into being. There is no fourth [or] fifth topic of discussion.

The narrative/poetic style of texts such as the Anavatapta-gāthā and the Rhinoceros Horn Sūtra has a distinct "translationese" flavor, betraying their origins as translations from other Indo-Aryan languages at every turn. In reading them,

23. Compare the corresponding passage in the Pali Saṅgīti-suttanta (Dīgha-nikāya 3.220): *tīṇi kathā-vatthūni. Atītaṃ vā addhānaṃ ārabbha kathaṃ katheyya. . . . Anāgataṃ vā addhānaṃ ārabbha kathaṃ katheyya. . . . Etarahi vā paccuppannaṃ addhānaṃ ārabbha kathaṃ katheyya.*

one gets the same impression that Brough got from the KDhP, namely, that such texts "might be described more appropriately as word-for-word transpositions of their original rather than as translations in the usual sense. . . . the translation involved . . . is scarcely more than a mechanical transposition between the sound-systems of the dialects" (1962: 113).[24] As noted above (6.5.2), this Gāndhārī translationese contains numerous grammatical formations and syntactic constructions that are unlikely to have been natural in colloquial Gāndhārī. A characteristic verse from the Anavatapta-gāthā (frag. 1, part 4, r, lines 16–8) reads:[25]

pharuṣa bhaṣiṣu baya baṭa bhujaï bhuyaṇo
teṇa karmavivagheṇa ṇiraghehi kṣeviṣu ciru˙

I spoke harsh words [to my mother]: "Eat stones for your food!"
By the ripening of the karma [from this act], I passed a long time
in the hells (*ṇiraghehi* = Skt. *nirayeṣu*).

Although such specimens may not teach us much about "real" Gāndhārī, they are potentially of considerable philological importance for their reflection of the underlying dialect from which they were translated and for the elucidation of the process of their later Sanskritization.

A very different matter is the material, mostly consisting of avadāna and similar texts, that does show us something like colloquial Gāndhārī language and style. These texts show few of the sort of forms and stylistic turns that result from the translation from an original in another language, and in these texts we are apparently dealing with material that was originally composed in Gāndhārī with a minimum of interference from other languages. The impression is reinforced by the content of these avadānas, for which few parallels have been located in other Buddhist traditions (see 2.2.4) and which therefore can be presumed to be local Gandhāran lore. Of course, these are not the only extant texts that were originally composed in Gāndhārī. The many Kharoṣṭhī inscriptions were composed in Gāndhārī, but their value as specimens of the colloquial language is limited by their stereotyped character, which often consists of little more than a patchwork of standardized ritual phrases (see 6.1 and Fussman 1989: 485–6). The central Asian documents too were originally composed in Gāndhārī, but this is a provincial Gāndhārī

24. See also the remarks in a similar vein in Bechert 1980: 12 and on related questions of "translation" and "transposition" in Norman 1993: 95–8.

25. The corresponding Sanskrit verse in the Gilgit manuscript of the Mūlasarvāstivāda-vinaya (Bechert 1961: 132) reads:

+ + + + + *vāṃ vāca upalāṃ bhuṃkṣva bhojanam*
tena karmavipākena narake kṣepitaṃ bahu

spoken in a region far distant from the homeland of the language and is heavily overlain with stereotyped legal and bureaucratic jargon. Thus, it is in the new avadāna texts that we now find the clearest approximation to colloquial Gāndhārī as it might have actually been spoken in its original territory, although they too of course also partake of common Buddhist words and turns of phrase. A characteristic specimen is the following passage (frags. 16 + 25, r, lines 19–21), describing the previous birth (*provayoge*) of the Bodhisattva:

> *boṣisatva vaniage ho[va](di*) . . . [sa]mudravanige tano*[26] *paño samudanido˙ mahasamudro adirno˙ y(anapatro*) bhirno˙ vaniaga talavilayam avarnage˙*

This can be tentatively translated as

> The Bodhisattva was a merchant . . . , an oceangoing merchant. He assembled his wares. He went down[27] to the great ocean. [His boat] broke. The merchant lost his support(?).[28]

As noted in 6.5.2, these texts are characterized by short, simple sentences using the historical present tense and past participial verb forms, giving the impression of a direct written rendition of an informal oral narrative style.[29] The prevalence of the passive participle construction for the past tense of transitive verbs, for example, is characteristic of the vernacular style of MIA generally (as well as of later Sanskrit and the modern Indo-Aryan languages). All in all, these texts provide us with something much closer to the "spoken norm" (norme parlée) (Fussman 1989: 485) of the Gāndhārī language than anything we have seen hitherto.

---

26. *tano* = Skt. *tena* (see 2.2.2, n. 18, and 6.5.1, n. 19).

27. Given the context, *adirno* would be expected to correspond to Pali *otiṇṇo*/Skt. *avatīrṇaḥ*, "descended"; cf., e.g., Divyāvadāna (ed. Cowell and Neil), p. 376, *mahāsamudram avatīrṇaḥ*. Perhaps it is a scribal error for *odirno*.

28. That is, he was cast adrift. The word *avarnage* probably = Skt. *āpannaḥ* (see 6.3). The phrase *tala-vilayam* seems to mean something like "loss of support" (literally, "dissolution of basis").

29. It should be noted that this Gāndhārī avadāna style has much in common with the simpler narrative style of the Sanskrit prose avadānas, as seen, for example, in some sections of the Divyāvadāna. But this does not necessarily argue against the idea that the new avadānas are specimens of colloquial Gāndhārī. In fact, the truth could be the opposite, that is, that the Sanskrit texts were influenced by, or even translated, directly or indirectly, from originals in Gāndhārī or some similar MIA dialect.

Chapter 7

The Date of the Manuscripts

7.1. Internal Evidence for Dating

Despite its importance, a complete discussion of the problem of the date of the manuscripts has been deferred to this point, mainly because the complexity of the issue requires that it be addressed only after certain other issues have been discussed in detail. The paleographic and linguistic indications of their date have already been discussed in the previous chapter, but here the question is reexamined comprehensively from all relevant points of view.

The most important and reliable clues for attributing a date to the new manuscripts, or at least to their prototypes, are the references in them to two historical figures who were previously known from other sources, namely, coins and inscriptions. The persons in question are Jihonika, who is mentioned once in fragment 2 as a mahākṣatrapa, or great satrap, and Aśpavarman, whose name appears four times in the avadāna text on the verso of fragment 1, part 2, the first time with, possibly, the title stratega (Greek στρατηγός), or commander.

7.1.1. The Jihonika Fragment

The reference to Jihonika comes, unfortunately, in a small and very fragmentary text (frag. 2, r, line 2; pl. 15). This fragment is the right side of the bottom of a scroll, whose original dimensions cannot be determined. It is evidently written in the same hand (no. 2) as most of the avadāna-type texts (including the one mentioning Aśpavarman discussed in the following section) and also resembles them in that it apparently consists of separate, numbered textual units; the one in which Jihonika's name is mentioned is probably the fifth. Although the contents are not explicitly labeled as avadānas in the surviving portion of the original text, the interlinear notation partially preserved between lines 8 and 9 on the recto, the legible portion of which reads *sarva ime avada[na]* . . . , apparently refers to them as such (although there is a slight problem about its reading; see 4.2). Like many of the avadāna texts in the British Library collection, the text preserved in fragment 2 does not consist of the sort of previous-life stories or karmic histories that are typical of the genre as it is generally known from later Buddhist literature. Rather, it seems to represent a broader class of legends, including ones with historical content, in the modern sense of the term (see 2.2.4).

Only the right-hand portions of, apparently, the last six lines of the story that contains Jihonika's name are preserved, for the seventh line of the fragment begins with a circular punctuation mark followed by the numerical figure 5, apparently marking the end of the fifth story in the compilation. It is, however, also possible that the Jihonika story was actually the fourth story, whose end and number were somewhere in the lost left-hand portions of lines 3–6.

The text reads as follows:

1. *paśido praṣa[do] ya[vi] ///*
2. *ra jihonige mahakṣatra ///*
3. *riadi˙ manuśa pradi ?*[1] *///*
4. *āva [di]rila˙ ku[.e] ///*
5. *gadharami o ? ///*
6. *ve[stra]ge na bahadi kri[ś.] ///*
7. ○ 4 1

From these fragmentary remains, I am not able to discern the subject of the narration or Jihonika's part in it or offer a coherent translation. My comments are therefore limited to the following notes:

Line 1: *paśido* would seem to be a form of the root *paś,* "see." The ending suggests a past participle, but the past participle of the verb "to see" in Gāndhārī, as in the other MIA languages, is usually formed from the root *dṛś* (*driṭha-*). The form therefore remains uncertain. *Praṣa[do]* could correspond to Sanskrit *prasāda-,* "favor," or *prāsāda-,* "palace." The use here of the "special" *s̱* instead of *s* (see 6.3) is untypical of the avadāna scribe, who generally writes *s̱* only in positions corresponding to original intervocalic *th* or *dh,* rather than as an alternative spelling for an original sibilant, as seems to be the case here. The word *yavi* is used very frequently in the avadāna texts at the beginning of sentences, apparently as a conjunction meaning, perhaps, "then." The etymology is unclear, though a connection with Sanskrit *yāvat* is possible, especially since *yāvat* is often similarly used as a narrative conjunction at the beginning of sentences in Buddhist Sanskrit (e.g., in the Divyāvadāna).

Line 2: *ra* must be the last syllable of a word continued from the missing end of line 1. *Jihonige* is presumably the same proper name as *jihoṇika* in the Taxila silver vase inscription (Konow 1929: 81–2) and ΖΕΙΩΝΙΣΗΣ/*jihunia* of the bilingual (Greek and Gāndhārī) coin legends; the variation of *k/g/Ø* is normal in Gāndhārī (see 6.4.1). The *-e* ending is presumably nominative singular; the avadāna texts generally prefer the nominative in *-o,* but *-e* is an occasional variant (6.5.1 and n. 18). *Mahakṣatra ///* is certainly to be reconstructed as *mahakṣatrape,* or perhaps *-po,* that is, "the Great Satrap Jihonika."

1. Only a small trace of this last syllable is visible, most of it being covered by a loose chip of bark.

Line 3: *riadi* appears to be the end of a verb in the third-person passive present, of the type *kariadi,* "is done" (= Skt. *kriyate*); but the context is too fragmentary to propose a reconstruction. In the phrase *manuśa pradi ? ///, manuśa,* "man," could be either nominative or, perhaps more likely, accusative.[2] It is therefore probably either the agent or object of a following verb beginning with the prefix *pradi-* (Skt. *prati-*).

Line 4: *āva [di]rila* is completely obscure, and the word division given here is no more than a guess. The syllables *ku[.e]* could perhaps represent *kule,* "line," "clan," or *kupe,* "well."

Line 5: *gadharami* must mean "in Gandhāra." Although partly obscured in the photograph, the reading of the third syllable as *ra* is clear on the original fragment.

Line 6: *ve[stra]ge* is obscure. A possible alternative reading is *ve[kra]ge.* The words *na bahadi* could correspond to Sanskrit *na vahati,* "does not ride/bear."

For lack of any parallel or similar text, or any other sort of external assistance, it does not seem possible at this point to make much of the narration in which Jihonika's name appears. Neither does the rest of the fragment offer any direct help. The Jihonika story, apparently the fifth in the collection, is followed by the very brief sixth story, which starts at the beginning of line 7 and ends in the next line. Nothing can be made of this story except that it is set in Taxila (line 7, *takṣaïla*). The next episode begins in line 8 with the enigmatic word *maṣrugaha.* Line 11 begins with a large circular punctuation mark, but here, unlike the ones in lines 7 and 8, it is not followed by a number, so that it is not clear whether the text continues the "*maṣrugaha* story" or is the beginning of a new one. In any case, the text from here until approximately line 11 of the verso seems to be a continuous narrative concerning five *idrigas* (Skt. *indriya*), apparently here meaning "leaders," who seem to be occupied in dealing with thieves (e.g., r, line 13, *corasamagule siyadi* = Skt. *corasamākulaḥ syāt,* "may be infested with thieves"). Finally, the last two lines of the verso seem to introduce a new episode, whose contents cannot be ascertained from its very meager remains.

None of this helps us much with understanding what Jihonika's role in this fragmentary text may have been, but at least it is certain that he is referred to by the title mahākṣatrapa, "great satrap." Jihonika was previously known from the Taxila inscription and coins as a kṣatrapa, or satrap, but in view of the numerous instances in Indo-Scythian history of the promotion of a satrap to great satrap, we can easily assume that Jihonika at some point in his career was awarded the superior title. Moreover, there appears to be numismatic confirmation of this. Mitchiner (1976: 596, type 886) ascribes a coin to Jihunia (Jihonika) as mahākṣatrapa, but the

2. There seems to be an overall tendency for the ending *-a* to be used more frequently in the accusative than in the nominative; see section 6.5.1.

legend in the specimen illustrated by him is not clearly legible. However, I have been informed by Robert Senior that better specimens of coins of Jihonika as mahākṣatrapa have been found and will be published shortly.

In short, despite the minor differences in titles, there is little reason to doubt that all the references are to the same Jihonika, especially since this is an unusual and otherwise unattested name. With regard to Jihonika's date, the only specific evidence[3] is the date of the Taxila vase inscription, which Konow reads and interprets as *ka* 1 100 20 20 20 20 10 1 *maharaja[bhra][ta Ma*][ṇi][gula*]sa putrasa Jihoṇikasa Chukhsasa kṣatrapasa,* "Year 191 (during the reign) of Jihoṇika, the kṣatrapa of Chukhsa, the son of Maṇigula, the brother of the Great King." But the interpretation of the date is controversial due to its peculiar notation, which involves two problems. First, *ka* is nowhere else attested as an abbreviation for "year,"[4] and second, even if it does mean "year," it is not clear to which of the several eras that were in use in the Indo-Scythian period it refers. As to the first problem, Konow (1929: 82) thought that *ka* might be an abbreviation for *kale,* "at the time," though the use of this word instead of the usual *saṃvatsare,* etc. is not attested in any contemporary documents. Perhaps because he was unsatisfied with this interpretation, Konow later (1931–2: 255) offered the revised reading *saka,* taken to refer to "an era designated as a Saka institution," which he proposed to identify with the era of Azes.[5] Since the Azes era is now firmly established as commencing in 58–57 B.C. (i.e., it is the same era as the modern "Vikrama" era), this would give a date for Jihonika around A.D. 134. Others, however, notably Marshall (1951: 1.61), have assigned Jihonika's year 191 to the "Old Saka" or "Indo-Bactrian" era, which probably commenced around 155 B.C., which would put Jihonika's date at about A.D. 35.

This latter date is clearly preferable on archeological grounds, since,

3. A recently published inscription on gold leaf (Sadakata 1996b: 305–8, 1996c), said to be from Haḍḍa, is dated in the Azes year 39 (= 19 B.C.) and contains the name Jihoṇia twice (lines 7 and 14). Sadakata (1996b: 308) thinks that this is probably not the same Jihonika known from the Taxila inscription, because of the early date of the new inscription. But he also notes (p. 307) some peculiarities about the formulation of this date, and this is one of several reasons, including the untypical phrasing and formulation, unusual format, and peculiar handwriting, that I strongly suspect that this inscription is a modern forgery. It will therefore not be taken into further consideration here.

4. It is not out of the question that the figure 191 does not represent a date at all but rather the weight of the silver vase. Recent discoveries have confirmed that it was common practice in the Indo-Scythian period to mark the weight of silver objects with Kharoṣṭhī inscriptions (see Salomon 1996a: 431). However, the weight units most commonly used in such inscriptions are staters (abbreviated *sa*) and drachmas (*dra*), and no unit abbreviated *ka* has been seen elsewhere. If this is in fact a weight inscription, *ka* could perhaps stand for an otherwise unattested *kārṣāpaṇa* or some other measure. But such an interpretation could only be confirmed by reference to the actual weight of the object, and this does not seem to have been recorded in any publication.

5. As pointed out by Lohuizen-de Leeuw (1949: 377 n. 197), "Konow changed his mind with regard to this (*Sa*)*ka* several times," returning in a later article published in 1948 to his original reading *ka.*

according to Marshall, the form of the vase is "typical of the first century B.C. to first century A.D. work" (1951: 2.611), and on numismatic grounds, as has been shown in persuasive detail by MacDowall (1973). MacDowall demonstrated that Jihonika's silver coinage fits neatly in a metrological and typological sequence between the late and posthumous (imitation) base-silver issues of Azes II and the billon tetradrachms of the stratega Aśpavarman (see the following section). Since the dates of both of these rulers are now well established in the first half of the first century A.D., the attribution of Jihonika's inscriptional date to the "Old Saka" era is virtually confirmed, as is his reign in or around the first quarter of the first century. Moreover, MacDowall adduces strong evidence from archeology and classical literature to corroborate a date for Jihonika's coins in or near the third decade of the first century.

7.1.2. The Aśpavarman Fragment

The name Aśpavarman occurs four times (with several probably inconsequential variant spellings) in the eighth avadāna (frag. 1, part 2, v, lines 9–28; pl. 21) of the avadāna collection that is the second text on fragment 1, beginning at the very bottom of the recto and continuing throughout the verso. The main character in this avadāna is one Jhādamitra or, as the name is occasionally also written, Jhādimitra. This unusual name, which contains the only instance so far discovered in any of the new manuscripts of the consonant *jha* (6.4.2), is probably of Iranian origin,[6] which is not surprising in view of the strong Scythian presence in northwestern India at the time with which we are concerned.[7] It is unfortunately not clear, however, who this Jhādamitra might have been. The name, as far as I have been able to determine, is otherwise unattested in Buddhist tradition and thus must have been part of the local Buddhist lore that is reflected in several of the new texts but that evidently did not make its way into the mainstream of Buddhist tradition.

Jhādamitra is also the "hero" (i.e., the title character) of the avadāna in this same collection (no. 7; frag. 1, part 3, v, line 1 to part 2, v, line 7) that precedes the

---

6. The element Jhāda- presumably represents the Iranian *zāda* (= Skt. *jāta*), "born [of]," a common element in Iranian names, including several attested in Kharoṣṭhī texts, where it is spelled *jada, jhada,* etc.; for example, Avakhajada in the Chārsada reliquary inscription (Konow 1940: 307). It is unusual, however, to find it as the initial, rather than the final, element of such names. But in later Iranian names at least, *zād-* does appear as an initial element, where, according to Justi (1895: 377), it is a contraction of *āzād*, "well-born," "noble," "free"; in fact, in Justi 1895: 378 we find the name Zādmihr, attested in the eighth century A.D., which would seem to correspond to our Jhādamitra. But Jhādamitra could also be an "Umkehr-Name" of the type observed in similarly constructed Old Iranian names such as *Dāta-miθra = Miθra-dāta (Mayrhofer 1973: 280); that is to say, it is to be understood as Zāda-miθra = *Miθra-zāda.

7. The Indo-Scythian cultural background of the British Library manuscripts, and particularly of the avadānas, is further corroborated by the appearance in one of them of an (unnamed) Saka (*sago*) as a main character (see 2.2.4).

one in which Aśpavarman appears. To judge from the fragmentary remains of that story, it seems that in it Jhādamitra encounters a Buddhist monk (*ṣamana* = Skt. *śramaṇa*) and makes a vow to attain individual enlightenment (part 2, lines 5–6, *yadi sadhama atarahide hakṣa[di] aha pra[ca]geboṣ(i*) praüiśa*, "If the true dharma will disappear, I will attain individual enlightenment").[8] At a guess, we might imagine that Jhādamitra was a member of the dominant class of Saka nobles who became a Buddhist and, to judge by the contents of the second avadāna concerning him, used his influence with Aśpavarman, whom we know from other sources to have been an important Saka ruler, to the benefit of the saṅgha (monastic community). In any case, the fact that not one but two avadānas concern Jhādamitra suggests that he was a prominent figure in the Buddhist lore of his time.

Though still quite fragmentary, the surviving portions of the text concerning Aśpavarman are much more extensive than those of the Jihonika fragment, so that it is possible to get at least a general sense of the contents of the story. In general, the right-hand margin of the scroll is intact, while varying amounts of the left side have been lost, though a few lines are preserved completely. The portions of the lines that do survive are for the most part legible.

The following is a preliminary reading of the story:

9. *○ 4 1 1 1 jhadamitrasa cevo˙ bidige avada[na]*
10. *evo ṣ[u]yadi jhadimitro karya [tva] ? ? ///*
11. *ṣavaṣo˙ uvagado˙ aśpavarmano sa [stra] ? + + + ///*
12. *sarva suhasaneno nimatrido˙ yada sapuruṣasa*
13. *vado ghi*[sic]*nido˙ vacad[i]˙ [te]na + + + + +*
14. *naro avadhaḍitri na[gha]ha˙ nami˙ [va] ? ? ? ?*
15. *? vido˙ ya(vi*) ? [ha]ḍo˙ so bhato jha(damitro*) ///*
16. *+ + + (u*)*[9]*vaṭhayaǵasa matr[e]d(i*) ///*
17. *hi [hi]do sapuruṣasa yavada[th.] ? a[ha-]*[10]
18. *ro yavi dito jhadamidro matre[di]*[11] +
19. *ta sapuruṣasa ma + + + mi[da] ///*
20. *deś[o] vaṣu piśaṣi yav[i] [gado] + + ///*
21. *tatro pradeśami˙ vistar[e] [y.ṣ.](yupamano si-*

8. The Sanskrit equivalent of this sentence would be *yadi saddharmo 'ntarhito bhaviṣyati, aham pratyekabodhiṃ prāpsyāmi.*

9. Cf. Pali *upaṭṭhāka*/Buddhist Skt. *upasthāyaka-*, "servant," "attendant" (Edgerton 1953: 144).

10. The last two syllables of this line are on a section of bark that adhered to the upper left corner of the lower section of this fragment when the joint between its component sections separated; see plate 21.

11. Here again the last two syllables of the line adhered to the separated lower section, except that a small portion of the two lines at the upper right corner of the syllable *tre* remains in its original place at the end of line 18.

22. *ya**[12])*di˙ yavi āśpava[r]ma*[13] + + + + ///
23. + *di ? ki(ci)* + + + + ///
24. *abhayo me dahi yavi* + + ///
25. *[a]śpavarmo vacadi* + ///
26. *śano so co bhadato vaṣagro kara[man.]* ///
27. *? ? [a]śpavarmo sap(u*)ru[ṣ]o [a] ? [.o]* ///
28. *[sa]r[va] [vi]stare yaṣayupamano siya(di*) ? [4] ?*[14] ///

Although it is not yet possible to offer a coherent translation of the entire episode, some of the better-preserved portions are fairly comprehensible. The first five lines, for example, can be rendered as follows:

> . . . 7.[15] Also (*cevo* = *caiva*) of Jhādamitra, a second avadāna.[16] Thus it is heard: "Jhādamitra [etc.]" is to be recited.[17] . . . The time of the retreat for the rainy season[18] came. By (?) the commander (?) Aśpavarman [they] all were invited to sit comfortably. When the word (*vado* = Skt. *vādaḥ*) of a good man is accepted,[19] he says . . .

The story as a whole evidently involves some interaction between Aśpavarman and Jhādamitra with regard to the provision of a place for the monks to stay during the rainy season, and apparently also to the construction of a shelter there. This latter theme is indicated by such phrases as *tatro pradeśami* (21), "in that place," and *vaṣagro kara[man.]* (26), "building a residence for the rainy season."[20]

12. The end of line 21 and beginning of 22 can be reconstructed by comparison with the phrase *vistare yaṣayupamano siyadi* and similar expressions which appear frequently in the avadāna texts, for instance, in line 28 below. For a possible interpretation of this phrase, see section 2.2.4, n. 46.

13. Here, anomalously, the first syllable of Aśpavarman's name is spelled with the diacritically modified form of *a* which normally represents the long vowel *ā* (see 6.3).

14. The expected reading here would be ○ 4 4, but the text is too badly damaged to confirm this.

15. This is the number at the end of the previous avadāna, whose main character was also Jhādamitra.

16. That is, "the second avadāna of Jhādamitra." Gāndhārī *bidige* = Skt. *dvitīyam*.

17. Here, *karya* is probably a shortened form of one of the abbreviation formulae such as *vistare sarvo karya*, "The whole is to be done [i.e., recited]," indicating that some formulaic elements at the beginning of the story, perhaps the description of the location, are to be supplied by the reader/reciter from the preceding avadāna(s) and/or from memory.

18. We can confidently restore *va* at the missing end of line 10, hence (*va**)*ṣavaṣo* = Skt. *varṣāvāsaḥ*.

19. In the central Asian Kharoṣṭhī documents, *ghinido* = Skt. *gṛhītaḥ*; cf. *gi(ṃ)nita-*, *ginitaǵa-*, etc. Note also the Dardic and other derivatives, such as Phalura *ghin*, "seize," listed in Turner 1966: 1.227, s.v. *gṛbhāyati* (§4236, para. 2).

20. *Vaṣagro* probably means "shelter from the rains" or the like; cf. Buddhist Skt. *varṣaka* (Edgerton 1953: 472) and Pali *vassika*, *vassagga*. Cf. similar phrases such as *bhikṣuṇī-varṣakaḥ kāritaḥ* (Avadāna-śataka [Speyer's ed.] 1.269) and *rāja . . . tayo pāsade kārāpesi, ekaḥ vassikaḥ* (Dīgha-nikāya 2.21).

Thus, Aśpavarman seems to be appearing in the role of a patron of the Buddhist saṅgha. The term *sapuruṣa,* presumably = Sanskrit *satpuruṣa-*, "good man," recurs four times (lines 12, 17, 19, and 27).[21] The first occurrence is apparently a reference to the benefits (?) of "accepting the word of a good man," and in the last occurrence, at the end of the story, the term is apparently directly applied to Aśpavarman. The point of the whole story may be that, in granting residences to the saṅgha, Aśpavarman proved himself to be a "good man."

Unfortunately, it is not clear whether or not Aśpavarman is actually accorded the title of stratega (commander) in line 11, as the end of the line is badly damaged. After the letter which is fairly clearly *stra,* there is a trace of a practically illegible syllable, for which *d(e**) would be at least a possible reading. After this the surface is so damaged by peeling and tearing that the rest of the line is completely illegible. Thus it is possible, though far from certain, that some form of the word *stratega-* originally was written at the end of this line. Its position, following Aśpavarman's name, would be parallel to that of Jihonika's title (*jihonige mahakṣatra*(*pe**)) in fragment 2. The comparative rarity of the conjunct *stra,* and also the well-attested association of the title stratega with Aśpavarman in coins and an inscription (cited below), increase the temptation to reconstruct this word here. But it must also be conceded that the reading of the syllable *stra* is not certain, and moreover that the syllable *sa* following *aśpavarmano* is problematic. Were it not for this syllable, the text could have been reconstructed as *aśpavarmano stra[de][geno*],* "by the commander Aśpavarman,"[22] which fits the context perfectly, but the *sa,* which is fairly clear, remains to be explained.

Although the reading of his title, if that is what it is, is quite uncertain, the name of Aśpavarman is well known as that of the son of Indravarman, a scion of the line of the Apraca kings, who ruled, apparently, in Bajaur and adjoining areas of the modern frontier region between Pakistan and Afghanistan,[23] and there is little reason to doubt that the Aśpavarman mentioned in this fragment is the same person. Aśpavarman is known from the inscription on a silver saucer found at Taxila (Sirkap), reading *aśpavarmasa strategasa sa 10 1 dra 2 dha 2,* "[Property] of Commander Aśpavarman; [weight,] 11 staters, 2 drachmas, 2 *dhanes*."[24] He is also known from numerous coins issued jointly with either Azes (II) or Gondophares, with the Kharoṣṭhī legend *indravarmaputrasa aśpavarmasa strategasa,* "[Coin] of Commander Aśpavarman, son of Indravarman." Aśpavarman's date can be approximately but

21. It may be relevant that the equivalent term *sapurisa-* is regularly applied as an honorific to the names of the venerables inscribed on the relic caskets found at Sanchi stūpa no. 2. In Marshall and Foucher 1940: 1.289, it is rendered as "saint."

22. For instrumentals in *-ano* for *-eno* (= Skt. *-ena*), see section 6.5.1, n. 19.

23. On the history of the Apraca dynasty, see below, 7.2.2.2, and Salomon 1996a: 443–50 and further references provided there.

24. For the reading and interpretation, see Marshall 1951: 2.613, and corrections suggested in Salomon 1990a: 154 n. 7.

securely fixed at around the second and third decades of the first century A.D, first by reference to the date of his father, Indravarman, who dedicated a reliquary in A.D. 6 (Salomon and Schopen 1984), and second by reference to the dates of his overlords Azes II and Gondophares, the latter of whom overthrew the former in about A.D. 19 according to the evidence of the Takht-i-Bāhī inscription (Konow 1929: 57–62). These dates indicate that the two Indo-Scythian rulers Jihonika and Aśpavarman mentioned in the new manuscripts were contemporaries, or very nearly so, and this impression is confirmed by the other sources. The coins demonstrate a close relationship between Jihonika and Aśpavarman, with the former, according to MacDowall's analysis (1973), being slightly earlier than the latter. Moreover, silver vessels bearing inscriptions mentioning both of them were found at the same site, Sirkap, at Taxila. All in all, there can hardly be any doubt that these two princes were contemporaries in the Indo-Scythian world of northwestern India in the early first century A.D., and that the occurrence of their names in separate but related texts within the new corpus of Kharoṣṭhī manuscripts is not at all a matter of coincidence.

7.1.3. A Reference to Another Kṣatrapa

The second story in the avadāna collection that is the second text on fragments 12 + 14 refers, in an uncertain context, to a kṣatrapa, or satrap, whose name is either illegible or not mentioned. The avadāna (frag. 14, v, lines 1–9) seems to concern some crime, *(apa*)radha* (line 4), and a penalty, *daḍo* (= Skt. *daṇḍaḥ*, line 5), imposed by a king. Line 7 reads *maharayasa pade paido na usa ? ? kṣatrapo [spi]*, which seems to mean "He fell at the foot of the Great King, [saying?] 'I am not . . . satrap.'" Unfortunately, the illegible part of the line prevents us from knowing what satrap is being referred to, but in any case this additional reference to a satrap, along with the one to (Great) Satrap Jihonika in fragment 2, confirms that these texts stem from the Indo-Scythian period, in which this Iranian-derived title was in wide use.

7.1.4. Context and Significance of the References to Indo-Scythian Rulers

Jihonika's role in fragment 2 cannot be determined due to the poor condition of the text, but it is likely to have been similar to that played by Aśpavarman in fragment 1, that is, a patron of Buddhism, and this association would not be surprising for either of them. Although we have no other direct evidence of Aśpavarman's patronage of the saṅgha, his parents, Indravarman and Uttarā (see fig. 13), have been revealed by several recent epigraphic discoveries to have been active supporters of Buddhism (Salomon 1996: 443–4). As for Jihonika, the inscription on the Taxila silver vase bearing his name may have been intended to mark it as his donation to the saṅgha rather than as his personal possession, since it was found as part of a large hoard in a house immediately adjacent to a Buddhist apsidal temple (Marshall 1951: 1.156).

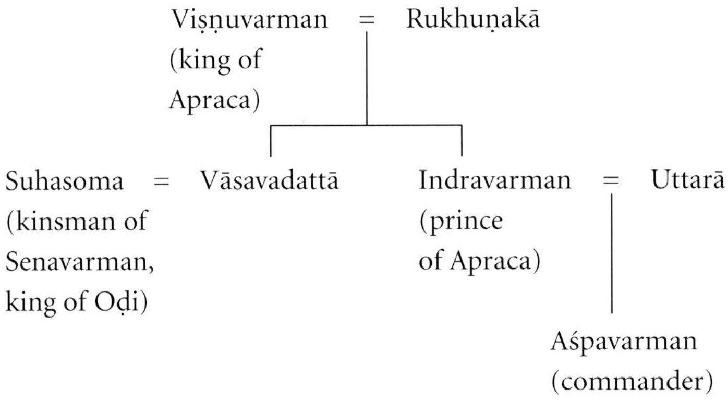

Fig. 13. Genealogical chart of Aśpavarman and his immediate relatives in the line of the kings of Apraca

Though unexpected, the references to these two rulers in the texts, and possibly to another contemporary satrap in fragment 14, are not inconsistent with attested patterns in Buddhist literature. The references to Jihonika and Aśpavarman are presumably no different in principle from the glorification of better-known royal patrons like Aśoka and Kaniṣka in north Indian Buddhist literature, and it is perhaps only an accident of history that their names were forgotten in Buddhist tradition and have only now been retrieved.

As to the date of the manuscripts themselves, these references to datable historical figures strictly speaking give us only a terminus post quem, and this, not for the manuscripts themselves, but only for the texts contained in them. Thus, all that we know for sure, to this point, is that the texts concerned, namely the avadāna collections in fragments 1, 2, and 14, and by association, presumably, the other texts in the collection, could not have been written before about the second decade of the first century A.D., this being the earliest likely date for the reigns of Jihonika and Aśpavarman. But there is no way to know for sure whether the texts referring to these rulers were composed during their lifetimes, or whether the references to them were posthumous. I consider the former alternative to be a priori more likely, since such stories seem to be designed primarily to celebrate their patronage and presumably also thereby to stimulate and perpetuate it, although one could also argue that such propaganda was aimed at their descendants or successors, by way of setting an example to be emulated.

Moreover, the actual manuscripts of these texts could, in theory, have been written any time after the original composition of the texts, during or after the lifetimes of Jihonika and Aśpavarman, although their upper chronological limit is established, albeit in a much less precise manner, by their linguistic and paleographic features, at around the time of Kaniṣka, that is, the late first century or first half of the second century A.D. Unfortunately, it is not possible to definitively determine their date within this range, but some possible indications are discussed in the following sections.

7.2. Dating of the Pots and Their Inscriptions

7.2.1. Dating on Stylistic and Technical Grounds

A thermoluminescence test performed on British Library pot C at the British Museum in September 1996 indicated a possible range of dates of 1200 to 2000 years B.P., or between about the first to eighth centuries A.D. In his study of the pots and potsherds associated with the scrolls (Appendix, sec. 1), Raymond Allchin concludes on stylistic and technical grounds that they most closely resemble ceramics datable to the early and middle Kuṣāṇa period, mainly on the basis of comparisons with ceramics from Shaikhān Ḍherī and other sites. The combined weight of these two examinations thus points to a likely range of dates for the pots and potsherds in or around the first to second century A.D.; a range which, as will be shown below, is consistent with the paleographic, linguistic, and historical features of the pots themselves and of the associated manuscripts.

7.2.2. Dating of the Pot Inscriptions

7.2.2.1. The Inscription on Pot D. Unfortunately, of the five inscribed pots in the British Library collection, pot D, which probably originally contained the scrolls, is the one with the briefest inscription and therefore offers the least help for dating. The inscription on it reads simply *saghami caüdiśami dhamaüteaṇa [p]arig[r]ahami*, "[Given] to the universal community, in the possession of the Dharmaguptakas."[25] This is the briefest possible version of the donative formula used on clay pots and other objects presented to the congregation, specifying only the name of the recipients, namely, the Buddhist community in general (*saghami caüdiśami* = Skt. *saṅghe caturdiśe*) and the Dharmaguptakas in particular. But neither the name of the particular Dharmaguptaka monastery nor even, surprisingly, the name of the donor is mentioned,[26] so that we do not have any historical or geographical clues of the sort that are sometimes provided by such donative records, including those on some of the other pots in this collection. To date such an inscription we can only turn to paleographic and linguistic features; but these, as usual, offer only a broad range of possible dates.

The first character of the inscription is *sa,* which is generally the most reliable test letter for the paleographic dating of a Kharoṣṭhī text (see 6.2.1). It has an archaic or transitional subvariety of the later cursive (one-stroke) form, in which the scribe extends the point of juncture between the head portion and the vertical stem

25. For a detailed discussion of the pot and inscription, see the Appendix, pp. 214–7.
26. See the Appendix, section 5.1, for discussion of this point.

upward, nearly closing the "mouth" of the letter (𐨯). This style of *sa* is characteristic of the late first century B.C. and the early first century A.D. and is rarely seen thereafter. Thus, the most reliable paleographic index suggests a relatively early date for this pot. Also worthy of note is the somewhat unusual shape of *dha,* formed with straight, rather than curved, lines and ending in a straight vertical downstroke rather than curving toward the left as in the usual form of this letter. This peculiarity does not, however, seem to be attributable to Kharoṣṭhī of any particular period. Similar forms of *dha* are given in Dani's paleographic chart for inscriptions of the first century B.C. and early first century A.D. (1963: pl. XXIIIa, lines 5–7), but the published reproductions of the inscriptions in question do not clearly confirm that this form regularly appears in them.

Although the paleography of the inscription on pot D points to an earlier date, it also has a phonological feature—the elision of the original intervocalic *t* in *caüdiśami* = Sanskrit *caturdiśe*—that might be taken to suggest a later date. (The other pot inscriptions in the British Library collection that contain this phrase—those on pots B, C, and E—have *cadurdiśami, caturdiśe,* and *catudiśe* respectively.) However, it has already been pointed out (see 6.4.1) that instances of the elision of *-t-* are found sporadically as early as the very beginning of the first century A.D. (in the Indravarman reliquary inscription of A.D. 6), so this feature is no definite proof of a later date.

In short, it is not possible to date the inscription on the pot in which the manuscripts were probably found with any more precision than sometime in or around the first century A.D.; a conclusion that, not coincidentally, accords with the one arrived at regarding the manuscripts themselves on similar grounds of paleographic and linguistic analysis. In any case, it should be remembered that, even if one could come up with a more precise date for the dedication of the pot, this date would not necessarily apply directly to the manuscripts that were placed in it at some later time. According to my understanding of the relationship between the pot and the manuscripts (see chapter 4 and the Appendix, sec. 5), the relationship is only a secondary one, in that the worn-out scrolls were at some point placed in the pot, which was probably also already old. We don't know whether the pot is older than the manuscripts or vice versa, but given their general similarities in script and language, it is not likely that the difference in age is very great.

7.2.2.2. The Other Pot Inscriptions. The dedicatory inscriptions on the other pots in the British Library collection, particularly the one on pot A, are more susceptible to precise dating on historical grounds, though unfortunately there is no way to be sure of their archeological, and hence chronological, relationship with the crucial pot D. The inscription on pot A (see Appendix, sec. 3) records that it was donated by one Vāsavadattā, wife of Suhasoma. Among documents of the Indo-Scythian period, the name Vāsavadattā is attested as that of one of the sisters of the Apraca prince Indravarman in his reliquary inscription of A.D. 6. Suhasoma is the name of a royal kinsman (*aṇakaa*) and officer (*aṣmaṇakara*) of Senavarman, king of Oḍi, mentioned in line 9a of the latter's Kharoṣṭhī reliquary inscription on a gold leaf (Salomon 1986). Senavarman's inscription is dated in his fourteenth regnal year, for which the absolute equivalent is unknown, but the reference in it to a member of the Kuṣāṇa royal family named Sadaṣkaṇa, the son of Kujula Kadphises (line 8g, *kuyula-kataphsa-putro sadaṣkaṇo*), indicates a date around the early to middle first century A.D. Thus, if the Vāsavadattā and Suhasoma of British Library pot A can be identified with the persons of the same names in these two Kharoṣṭhī inscriptions, the pot would be firmly dated to the first half of the first century A.D. This cannot be proven absolutely, but I consider it a priori very likely because no other historical personage named Vāsavadattā is known from this general period, and, moreover, the unusual name Suhasoma is completely unknown except in the inscription on pot A and in Senavarman's inscription. In short, it is probable, though not absolutely certain, that British Library pot A dates from the first half of the first century.[27]

Unfortunately, for lack of reliable information as to their provenance and original situation, there is no way to prove that the datable pot A was archeologically associated with pot D, which evidently contained the manuscripts. These, as well as the other pots in the British Library group and also some others that have been recently discovered (see, e.g., Salomon 1996b: 238–42), all appear to belong to the general class of inscribed clay jars that was particularly common at Haḍḍa and other nearby stūpa and monastery complexes in the Jalalabad Plain. However, they presumably did not all come from the same site, since the ones which contain inscriptions mentioning the location of the donees refer to different places: Purnagarañа (British Library pot B), Rayagaha (British Library pot C), and Masenarana (Salomon 1996b: 238–42). The critical question for the dating problem, however, is the relationship between pot D, which contained the manuscripts, and pot A, which contains the name of known historical figures, and neither of the inscriptions on these pots contains a toponym.

Nevertheless, a connection between pots A and D can be hypothesized, though not proven, on historical grounds. If the Vāsavadattā who donated pot A was in fact the sister of the Apraca prince Indravarman, as I think is very likely to be true, she was also the aunt of Aśpavarman, Indravarman's son, who is mentioned prominently in the avadāna text discussed in section 7.1.2 (see fig. 13). This connection between the manuscripts and pot inscription A is unlikely to be a coincidence but rather must reflect the direct involvement of the Apraca kings and their families in the patronage of the Buddhist establishments of the Nagarāhāra region (see 8.3.3). The appearance of the names of close blood relatives in the manuscripts and in one

27. If this is correct, it would also establish that there was a marital alliance between the Saka houses of Apraca and Oḍi, a fact not previously known but entirely plausible on historical and geographical grounds.

of the pot inscriptions increases the likelihood, though it does not conclusively prove, that pot A did come from the same monastery and was interred at about the same time as the pot that contained the scrolls (pot D). If this is correct, it would mean that the references to Aśpavarman and Jihonika in the manuscripts were in fact contemporary references, and that the manuscripts date from their time, that is, from the early decades of the first century A.D.

7.3. Conclusions

As has been discussed in chapter 6, the paleographic and linguistic features of the new manuscripts are broadly attributable to a period ranging from about the early first century A.D. to the middle of the second century A.D., but it is impossible, at least in the current state of our understanding of the Kharoṣṭhī script and the Gāndhārī language, to authoritatively fix them more precisely within this span. This difficulty arises from two problems. The first is the nonstandardization of orthography and morphology, such that variations and changes cannot be fixed to a particular date but rather tend to appear sporadically over long periods. The second problem is that, until now, we have had only one significant specimen, of uncertain date, of a Kharoṣṭhī manuscript of the type that we are concerned with here, namely, the KDhP scroll, and nothing to compare it to. Even with the addition now of a large new corpus, we still lack fixed points from which to begin constructing a framework for the chronological development of the manuscript forms of Kharoṣṭhī script. The detailed study of the new documents may eventually provide us with the means to refine our understanding, but this will take time.

The dating of the pots possibly associated with the manuscripts, including the one (pot D) in which they were almost certainly originally found, is similarly ambiguous, and according to the expert opinion of Allchin, the most likely range of dates is approximately the same as that determined on linguistic and paleographic grounds. So, at least for the present, the only way to pin down the date of the documents with more precision is through their historical associations. Here, as we have seen, the references to well-known historical figures in the manuscripts themselves give a firm terminus post quem at about the second decade of the first century A.D. The evidence of an inscription on a possibly related artifact, pot A, suggests that the manuscripts are indeed likely to be more or less contemporary with the Indo-Scythian rulers whose names appear in them, but due to the irreparable loss of their archeological context this cannot be established with certainty. Nevertheless, the suggestive pattern of linkages of persons associated with the Apraca lineage and their contemporaries such as Jihonika and the kings of Oḍi, and through them with Kujula Kadphises, the first Kuṣāṇa king of India, makes an early-first-century date, and in particular a date between about A.D. 10 and 30, the most likely one for the composition of the scrolls. Although their paleographic features could be conservatively interpreted as indicating a somewhat later date, perhaps in the late first or early second century, I am inclined to place more weight on the historical data, which, though by no means free of uncertainties, are much more likely to be accurate.

In any case, the references in the manuscripts to Jihonika, Aśpavarman, and possibly other contemporary historical figures prove that the cultural tradition of the texts, if not the scrolls themselves, stems from the Indo-Scythian Buddhist world of the early first century A.D. This point is ultimately more important than the date of the actual manuscripts and is likely to have wide-ranging ramifications for the history of Gandhāran Buddhism, as will be discussed further in section 8.3.3.

Chapter 8

Preliminary Evaluation of the New Corpus

8.1. Observations on the Contents of the New Corpus

8.1.1. The Gāndhārī Canon Issue Revisited

It has already been stated (sec. 1.2) that the manuscripts described here confirm the old hypothesis of the existence of a Gāndhārī canon, at least in a loose sense of the term "canon," referring to a substantial and at least partly systematic and organized body of texts. But we must now address the question of exactly what sort of "canon" the British Library Kharoṣṭhī manuscripts might constitute. Although it is not practically possible to address here in any detail the complex questions of the conceptions and manifestations of canons in Buddhist tradition in general, let alone in other religions, it should be pointed out that most Buddhist traditions seem to have developed, at some point in their history, at least a "notional" canon that was conceived as comprising the totality of the "scriptures," that is to say, the words of the Buddha (*buddha-vacana*), however conceived.[1] Such comprehensive canons are actually manifested, for example, in the Pali Tipiṭaka and the Tibetan Kanjur. If we accept as historical the accounts of the communal recitations (*saṅgīti*) of the Buddha's words at the earliest Buddhist councils, this sense of a need to collect the Buddha's teachings in a complete and standardized corpus would go back to the very roots of the tradition, and hence be fundamental to it. But it must also be kept in mind that the historicity of these traditions is not beyond doubt, and the concept of a comprehensive collection of the teachings is not conclusively proven to be original to Buddhism.

Indeed, observation of Buddhist practice in many different periods and places suggests that the complete canon, if present at all, tends to be more an abstract entity, or at best a set of books that sit, mostly unread, on a shelf, rather than a central focus of the monks' and lay followers' daily study and worship. In practice, the number of texts actually read, chanted, and studied in a given tradition is generally quite limited; according to Collins (1990: 103), "[t]he evidence suggests that both in so-called 'popular' practice and in the monastic world, even among virtuosos, only parts of the Canonical collection have ever been in wide currency." Indeed, some

1. On the various understandings of the concept of *buddha-vacana*, see McDermott 1984.

highly successful Buddhist sects focus on a single text—for example, the Lotus Sūtra—virtually to the exclusion of all others, conceiving of that text as the essence and totality of all the *buddha-vacana*.

We have, then, evidence of various types of "canons" embodied in the scriptures of various Buddhist traditions. At one extreme is the comprehensive, voluminous, and even (at least in the Theravāda case; see Collins 1990: 91 ff.) exclusive canon; and at the other, the "canon" is reduced in effect to a single text that is endlessly chanted, copied, and explicated to the effective exclusion of the others. Between these extremes, there is a wide range of intermediate "canons," including, perhaps most importantly, what Collins calls the "ritual canon," which "contains the texts, canonical or otherwise, which are in actual use in ritual life in the area concerned" (p. 104). It seems reasonable to assume that the British Library manuscript fragments, which probably represent a random sampling from a larger, perhaps much larger, corpus of written texts (4.4), are part of such a written "canon" falling somewhere between the two extremes outlined above in terms of its extent and comprehensiveness. On the one hand, even this relatively small group of fragmentary texts displays a considerable range and diversity of genres and individual texts. On the other hand, we should not assume that it represents the surviving portion of a comprehensive written canon of the sort with which we are all familiar in the Pali canon of the Theravāda sect. As shown by Collins (1990), this type of definitive, exclusive, written canon is prone to develop only under certain historical conditions, and there is no evidence that such circumstances had arisen in Gandhāra at the time in question. Indeed, there is not much reason to suppose that such a comprehensive canon, in the strict sense of the term, was ever developed in Gandhāran Buddhism.[2]

In this chapter, an attempt will be made to determine what can be deduced about the character, contents, arrangement, and affiliations of the "Gāndhārī canon" as represented in the British Library fragments and, furthermore (in sec. 8.3), what this may tell us about Buddhism in Gandhāra generally, which up to now has been known mostly from abundant but inherently limited archeological and epigraphical sources. The understanding of the Gāndhārī canon that can be derived from the new manuscripts is enhanced by the fact that, although they represent a random collection, they are sufficiently numerous and diverse to be of more than incidental value. Moreover, the texts contained in them do seem to fall into significant patterns that provide at least some hints as to the contents and arrangement of the larger corpus of texts of which they presumably constitute a fraction. Needless to say, the conclusions, or rather hypotheses, presented here are provisional at best, as they are based for the most part on preliminary surveys, readings and, where

2. Although the germ, at least, of such a development might seem to be implied by the account of Kaniṣka's council of Kashmir as recorded by Hsüan-tsang (Beal 1884: 151–6), the significance and historicity of this event are subject to considerable doubt.

possible, identifications of the individual texts, and the detailed studies of them that are to be pursued in years to come will undoubtedly clarify and correct whatever is offered here. Indeed, most of the material in this chapter is presented more by way of guidelines for future investigations than of hard facts or final conclusions.

8.1.2. Parallels and Relationships with Other Text Collections

8.1.2.1. A List of Novice Texts in the Mahāsāṅghika-vinaya. In a groundbreaking article in which he assembled from vinayas of the Buddhist sects references to recitations of particular groups of texts or textual genres, Sylvain Lévi (1915) referred to a passage from the Chinese translation of the Mahāsāṅghika-vinaya (T. 22 [no. 1425], 337a) where the Buddha cites a set of sūtras that "serve for the instruction of novices" (pp. 422–3). Lévi rendered the list as follows: "the sacred text of the Eight Groups (= Aṣṭa-varga sūtra), the sacred text of the *Po-lo-ye-na* (Pārāyaṇa), the sacred text of the difficulties of discussion, the sacred text of Lake *A-neou-ta,* the sacred text of the Pratyekabuddhas, and all sorts of texts of this type" (p. 423). As to the identification of these texts, other than the first two, Lévi says: "The other texts cited are obscure. It seems, however, that we still have to do with collections. The Anavataptahrada sūtra is probably the first teaching of Abhidharma expounded by the Buddha. . . . The Loun-nan recalls by its title the Tsa nan 'Various difficulties (or questions)' which the Vinaya of the Dharmaguptas . . . classes in the Kṣudraka" (p. 424).[3]

Although Lévi identifies "the sacred text of Lake *A-neou-ta,*" or "Anavataptahrada sūtra," with the first discourse on abhidharma, I think it far more likely that it refers to the now well known Anavatapta-gāthā, of which a large fragment survives among the new British Library fragments. Lévi's failure to identify it as such is probably to be attributed to the fact that the Anavatapta-gāthā was not known at that time as an independent text. Since then, however, numerous fragments of the Sanskrit text of the Anavatapta-gāthā have been discovered, both as incorporated into the Bhaiṣajyavastu of the Mūlasarvāstivāda-vinaya in the Gilgit manuscripts and as an independent text among the fragments from Kyzil in Xinjiang (Bechert 1961). These discoveries, combined now with that of the Gāndhārī recension of the same text, show that the Anavatapta-gāthā was a popular and widespread text in the northern Buddhist tradition, and hence almost certainly the one referred to in the Mahāsāṅghika-vinaya's list of novice texts. This identification is corroborated by the fact that one of the central Asian texts of the Anavatapta (ms. 466; Bechert 1961: 49)

3. ". . . le texte sacré des Huit classes . . . (= Asta-varga sūtra), le texte sacré du *Po-lo-ye-na* . . . (Pārāyaṇa), le texte sacré des difficultés de discussion . . . , le texte sacré du lac *A-neou-ta* . . . , le texte sacré des Pratyekabuddha . . . et toutes sortes de textes de ce genre . . ." (p. 423).

"Les autres textes mentionnés sont obscurs. Il semble pourtant qu'il s'agit encore de collections. L'Anavataptahrada sūtra est probablement le premier enseignement d'Abhidharma prononcé par le Bouddha. . . . Le Loun-nan rappelle par son titre le Tsa nan 'Difficultés (ou Questions) diverses' que le Vinaya des Dharmagupta . . . classe dans le Kṣudraka . . ." (p. 424).

was found as part of a manuscript that also contained the Sanskrit version of the Pārāyaṇa, while another Anavatapta manuscript (ms. 1072; Bechert 1961: 50) also contained the Arthavargīya-sūtra (otherwise known as Aṣṭavarga-sūtra, etc.; Lévi 1915: 412–4). It is surely no coincidence that both of these texts which were written together with the Anavatapta-gāthā in central Asian manuscripts are also included along with it in the Mahāsāṅghika list of novice texts.

Lévi offers no comments regarding the identification of the "sacred text of the Pratyekabuddhas" in the same list, but I think it is very likely that this refers to the Rhinoceros Horn Sūtra, which again is found in a Gāndhārī version among the British Library fragments. Although the word *pratyekabuddha* (solitary enlightened one) does not appear in this version or in the previously known Pali or Sanskrit versions of the Rhinoceros Horn Sūtra, it is unanimously agreed by the commentatorial and interpretive traditions that each verse of this poem represents the inspired utterance of a particular pratyekabuddha, and the association of this poem with the pratyekabuddhas is so widespread and consistent that one can easily imagine that it could have come to be known as "The Sūtra of the Pratyekabuddhas."

8.1.2.2. Connections with the Sutta-nipāta and Khuddaka-nikāya. Thus we find that at least two of the five texts cited in the Mahāsāṅghika list of novice texts can be identified, with reasonable certainty, with texts found among the British Library fragments. This in itself would be interesting, but hardly conclusive. However, it is possible to establish further connections, albeit less direct than the ones presented above, between two other texts in the Mahāsāṅghika-vinaya list—namely, the "Aṣṭa-varga sūtra" and the Pārāyaṇa—and the new collection. The Pali equivalents of these texts—the Aṭṭhaka-vagga and the Pārāyaṇa-vagga—are incorporated in the Theravāda canon as the fourth and fifth (and final) sections of the Sutta-nipāta, itself the fifth of the fifteen parts of the Khuddaka-nikāya. Now, in general there is a decided concentration among the British Library fragments of texts whose Pali correspondents are found in the Khuddaka-nikāya generally and the Sutta-nipāta in particular. Among Khuddaka texts, we find the Dharmapada fragment, which constitutes part of a compilation that is the approximate counterpart of the Pali Dhammapada, the second text in the Khuddaka-nikāya. As it happens, most of the small part of the Dharmapada that is preserved in the new collection (frags. 16 + 25, first text) contains a set of parallel verses using as a refrain the metaphor of the snake shedding its skin (*so bhikhu jahadi oraparo uragha jinam iva tvaya purano,* "That monk discards this shore and yonder shore, as a snake discards his old, worn-out skin"). In the Gāndhārī tradition this sequence of verses was incorporated into the Bhikhu-varga of its Dharmapada (as shown by the more complete version of that text preserved in the Khotan scroll), but in Pali it was separately preserved as the first sutta, called "The Snake Sutta" (Uraga-sutta), of the first section of the Sutta-nipāta (which is named Uraga-vagga after it). It is presumably just a coincidence that this particular passage happens to be the one that survived from what was evidently a complete, multivolume text of the Dharmapada (see 5.1.1), but this coincidence nonetheless illustrates the close connections and flexible relationships that obtained among the texts of this genre as a whole.

Among texts in the new collection that correspond more directly with those in the Pali Sutta-nipāta, the most striking case is the Rhinoceros Horn Sūtra, which in the Pali canon is the third sutta of the aforementioned Uraga-vagga, the first of five sections of the Sutta-nipāta. It is worthy of note that two of the new Gāndhārī texts correspond, directly in this case, indirectly in the case of the Uraga-sutta, with suttas placed in very prominent positions—the first and third suttas out of seventy overall—in the Sutta-nipāta. This suggests that these were texts of particular popularity and importance, perhaps precisely because of their suitability for the general instruction of lay followers and novice monks, and this impression is confirmed by the fact that both texts are repeated elsewhere in the various canons. For example, the Rhinoceros Horn Sūtra appears three times in the Pali canon (see 2.2.3), while another version of the Uraga-sutta is found as a separate section at the end of the Patna Dharmapada (Cone 1989: 209–15).

Another text in the new collection that exhibits a connection with the Pali Khuddaka-nikāya in general, with the Sutta-nipāta in particular, and with the Pārāyaṇa- and Aṭṭhaka-vaggas of the Sutta-nipāta even more specifically is fragment 9 (described in 2.2.2), which is the best-preserved specimen of the several texts consisting of citations of verses and commentaries thereon. The following table enumerates the parallels in the Pali canon, as far as they can be identified, to the verses cited in fragment 9:[4]

Pali Text Containing Corresponding Verse	Number of Citations in Fragment 9
Sutta-nipāta, total	11 (including 1 doubtful case)
Aṭṭhaka-vagga	5
Pārāyaṇa-vagga	4
Mahā-vagga	1
Uraga-vagga	(1 doubtful)
Cūla-vagga	0
Theragāthā	2
Itivuttaka	1
Dhammapada	1
Udāna	1
[Unidentified or illegible]	4

4. Including the text on both the recto, which was summarized in section 2.2.2, and the verso, which was not cited there.

Thus, all of the verses cited in this fragment for which Pali parallels have been identified (sixteen out of twenty in all) correspond more or less directly with verses found in various texts included in the Pali Khuddaka-nikāya; of these sixteen Khuddaka verses, eleven are in the Sutta-nipāta; and of these eleven, nine are in the Aṭṭhaka-vagga or Pārāyaṇa-vagga. Thus, although the exact nature of the verse collection on which this commentatorial text is based remains uncertain, it is evident that it comprises material similar to that of the Pali Khuddaka, and especially of the Aṭṭhaka-vagga and Pārāyaṇa-vagga sections of the Sutta-nipāta.

These two compilations of short suttas, which in the Pali canon (but not in the other extant canons) were lumped together with three other collections to form the larger unit of the Sutta-nipāta, are known from other sources to have circulated as independent units in many parts of the Buddhist world. These sources include the Chinese traditions cited in Lévi 1915, the central Asian manuscript remains (Bechert 1961: 11), and indications within the Pali canon itself (Norman 1983: 63). It is not yet certain whether this was also the case in the Gandhāran tradition, since the Aṭṭhaka and Pārāyaṇa citations cited here are embedded in a text which also contains citations corresponding to other parts of the Sutta-nipāta as well as to other Khuddaka-nikāya texts. This may become clearer as these commentary texts are studied in detail, and it would be interesting to learn whether the Gandhāran tradition had any kind of larger grouping corresponding to the Sutta-nipāta of the Pali Tipiṭaka, since this compilation, which contains some of the most important and apparently oldest texts in the Tipiṭaka, has no correspondent in any of the other Buddhist canons, although many of its component texts and subtexts—once again, most notably, the Aṭṭhaka-vagga and Pārāyaṇa-vagga—are widely attested.

In any case, it is clear that—not surprisingly—the Gandhāran tradition represented in the British Library fragments did include materials similar to those found in other recensions of the Pali Khuddaka-nikāya, the Sanskrit Kṣudrakāgama, and the Chinese translations thereof. This implies, though it does not prove, that the Gandhāran tradition represented by these texts had some sort of Kṣudrakāgama collection or approximate equivalent thereof, though its arrangement and contents are not yet known. The list of the contents of the Kṣudrakāgama of the Dharmaguptakas given in the Chinese translation of the vinaya of that school (Lévi and Chavannes 1916: 33–4) does show some similarity with the contents of the British Library Gāndhārī fragments, which are almost certainly associated with the Dharmaguptaka school. Among the twelve works listed are the equivalents of the Aṭṭhaka-vagga, the Pārāyaṇa-vagga, Dharmapada, Avadāna, and Sthaviragāthā, the last of which is a text associated, and in some traditions possibly identified or confused, with the Anavatapta-gāthā (Bechert 1961: 11–12, esp. 12 n. 1).

But to return to our main subject, namely, the correspondence of the contents of the British Library fragments with groupings of texts attested in other Buddhist canons, we can now summarize the results of the comparison with the list of five novice texts in the Mahāsāṅghika-vinaya discussed in the previous section:

Two of them, "the sacred text of Lake *A-neou-ta*" and "the sacred text of the Pratyekabuddhas," can be directly identified with the Anavatapta-gāthā and Rhinoceros Horn Sūtra texts in the new collection.

Two others, "the sacred text of the Eight Groups" (Aṣṭa-varga sūtra) and "the sacred text of the *Po-lo-ye-na* (Pārāyaṇa)," are represented, not as separate texts within the new collection, but indirectly as the most prominent sources of the verses cited in the commentary text on fragment 9.

The fifth text, "the sacred text of the difficulties of discussion," remains unidentified, though it is still possible that further study of the new manuscripts may eventually establish some relationship.

Though neither perfect nor complete, the correspondences between the Mahāsāṅghika-vinaya list of novice texts and the contents of the British Library fragments are far too close to be dismissed as coincidence. This parallel could be taken to mean that the manuscripts in question are specimens of the kinds of texts that were particularly favored for the instruction of novices and lay followers in the monastery from whose collection they came, though they may well have also been used for other purposes, such as communal recitations. In any case, it is clear that texts of this class have some special status and popularity. Thus, it is not surprising that they should be relatively well represented in this apparently random sample of the monastery's entire corpus of written texts, since it could be expected that such texts would have been in frequent use and hence prone to be worn out, copied, and discarded. If this interpretation is correct, moreover, it would establish that the random fragments in the British Library collection, meager as they probably are in comparison to the complete collection of texts in the hypothetical source library, are nonetheless numerous enough to have some statistical significance and to represent at least some of the major genres and types of texts in the entire collection and hence to give us some conception of that "canon's" contents.

It need not trouble us that the correspondence between the Mahāsāṅghika-vinaya list of novice texts and the ones found in the British Library fragments is not exact. For one thing, the list is an open one, concluding with "and all sorts of texts of this type," so that one could imagine that other texts found among the new collection, such as the Dharmapada and possibly also the avadānas, could also have been part of such a novice curriculum or set of general texts. Neither should too much be made of the fact that the list in question belongs to the Mahāsāṅghika sect, while the Gāndhārī fragments come, in all probability, from a Dharmaguptaka institution (see 8.2). Although it might be argued that the Mahāsāṅghika list is therefore irrelevant here, it is actually likely that such groups of basic texts were more or less similar across sectarian lines, and hence it is of no particular significance that the list happens to be preserved in the Mahāsāṅghika tradition. Here the observation of Paul Mus that "the *primary* cycle of instruction in Buddhism was common to all the sects" (1939: 191), though made with reference to a different period and class of literature, is in principle applicable.

In support of this position it may be noted that the sort of texts in question do indeed tend to be found, albeit in different languages, arrangements, and locations, in different sectarian canons. The Anavatapta-gāthā, for example, is known in Sarvāstivādin, Mūlasarvāstivādin, and now, probably, Dharmaguptaka recensions, as well as in the form of a closely related text included in the Apadāna of the Theravādins (Bechert 1961: 29). The claim that other schools would be likely to have had groupings of texts similar to those found in the Mahāsāṅghika list is moreover directly confirmed by the co-occurrence, noted above, of the Anavatapta-gāthā with both the Pārāyaṇa and the Arthavargīya-sūtra (= Aṣṭa-varga sūtra) in central Asian manuscripts of the Sarvāstivādins.

8.1.3. Comments on the Distribution of the Texts of Other Genres

If it can be accepted that the distribution of the British Library fragments belonging to the class of basic texts and associated commentaries is significant for reconstructing a broader picture of the "canon" of which they are a small part, we may proceed to an examination along similar lines of the texts of other genres. Here, however, the results will inevitably be less clear-cut, since we are dealing with a much larger and more diverse corpus. Indeed, it may be more useful to note what is absent from the corpus as a whole than to try to categorize what is there, for there is one striking lacuna: the total absence (or at least so it seems on the basis of the still preliminary survey of the contents of the collection) of vinaya texts of any kind. This absence could, of course, be simply an accident of chance, or it could be determined by some other, as yet unknown factor. One could, for example, hypothesize that vinaya manuscripts were in some way treated differently, perhaps interred or otherwise disposed of separately from those of other classes. But, given the otherwise wide diversity of texts and genres that were disposed of together in a single pot, I do not consider this likely. There is no evidence, direct or indirect, of any process of selection or separation among these fragments, and hence no reason to hypothesize that vinaya texts, or any other particular class of manuscripts for that matter, were treated specially.

I therefore think that we should consider the possibility that the reason there are no vinaya texts among the British Library fragments is that there were few or no vinaya texts in the hypothetical source library as a whole. In other words, it may be that, at this relatively early stage of the written preservation and transmission of Buddhist texts, not all texts or genres of texts had yet been set down in writing. For reasons that will be discussed further in 8.1.4.2, it appears that at this point in the development of the written tradition of Buddhist texts, writing was viewed primarily as a practical matter; texts were set down in written form only when this seemed necessary or useful, as for instance when, for one reason or another, a text was not firmly set in memory or was perceived to be in danger of being forgotten. If this was the case, certain classes of texts, particularly the basic vinaya texts, namely the prātimokṣas, would have been the least likely to be written down, since their frequent communal recitation would preclude any danger of their being forgotten or corrupted.[5]

This would be merely a matter of speculation were it not for the fact that a strikingly similar pattern has been noted by Lore Sander among the earliest strata of central Asian Sanskrit Buddhist manuscripts, those from before the fifth century A.D., among which she finds a "total absence" (1991: 142) of vinaya texts, which she attributes to the continued vitality of the bhāṇaka recitation traditions in this period, as attested by Fa-hsien (p. 141). This absence of vinaya manuscripts among the early Sanskrit texts, moreover, is in striking contrast to the situation in later centuries, when they become very common in central Asia. So the complete absence of vinaya texts from both the British Library Kharoṣṭhī fragments and from the early group of central Asian Buddhist texts can hardly be a coincidence, and thus it corroborates the theory that vinaya texts were not yet set in writing at this relatively early period.

With regard to other genres, especially sūtra texts, however, the situation is less clear-cut. Among the early central Asian texts, Sander found sūtra texts, like vinaya texts, to be totally absent, but this does not correspond to the situation in the Gāndhārī fragments, wherein we find at least one manuscript of a sūtra text without commentary (the Aṅguttara-like text on frags. 12 + 14), one other probable example (the dhyāna [?] text in frags. 26 + 29), and one specimen of a sūtra with commentary, the Saṅgīti-sūtra (frag. 15). Nevertheless, sūtra texts are relatively sparsely represented in the collection as a whole—at most, apparently, three out of a total of about two dozen or so distinct texts. If this is not a mere statistical accident, it may reflect an early or transitional phase in which writing was being used as a secondary or supplemental technique for the preservation of sūtras, which were presumably still being transmitted primarily by oral recitation.

In contrast to the wholly absent vinaya texts and the relatively few sūtra texts, the classes of texts which are best represented overall among the British Library fragments are the commentaries on unidentified verse collections and the avadānas. If we can judge from the lack of success to date in finding parallels for these texts in other traditions, they would seem to be local compositions. It remains to be seen whether the statistical predominance of texts of this type is significant, for instance in indicating that such texts were more frequently rendered in written form than the

5. As for the expanded vinaya texts of the vibhaṅgas and skandhakas, their absence would have to be accounted for on other grounds, which cannot be fully explained at this point. One possibility, however, that has been proposed recently by Schopen (1994a: 552–3) is that such texts had not been composed yet, or at least were only in their formative stages, during the period at which the British Library fragments are most likely to have been written (i.e., the early first century A.D).

sūtra and vinaya texts, or whether this is merely a coincidence. More detailed studies of these texts and, should they occur, future discoveries of similar materials might eventually clarify this question, but for the moment it must be left open.

8.1.4. Conclusions regarding the Character of the Gandhāran Canon

8.1.4.1. Local versus Translated Material. As was observed in reference to the linguistic characteristics of the new texts, some of them are obviously translated or, rather, more or less mechanically "transposed" into Gāndhārī from preexisting versions in some other, not precisely identifiable MIA language(s), whereas others—most notably the several avadāna collections—show few characteristics of "translationese" and hence are likely to have been composed originally in Gāndhārī. Still other texts, more technical and scholastic in nature, are more difficult to pin down as to their linguistic origins, but at least some of them are likely to be commentaries written directly in Gāndhārī on texts whose archetypes were in other MIA dialects. Thus, the materials that are most likely to have been directly composed in Gāndhārī are precisely those for which no parallels have been located in other Buddhist traditions, and this is presumably not a coincidence. These texts evidently reflect local exegetical and didactic traditions, distinct from but based on the common core of Buddhist canonical texts, of the sort that can be presumed to have developed separately in most, if not all, regional centers of Buddhism, in south Asia and beyond. In the commentatorial texts, for example, we may well have something analogous to the lost Sinhala prototype of the Pali commentaries, and had Buddhism continued to flourish in the northwest as it did in Sri Lanka and Southeast Asia, texts such as these would probably have survived—though perhaps in a Sanskritized garb—through the ages. When fully analyzed, they should provide us with an unprecedented insight into the formative stages of such a tradition of local vernacular commentaries and didactic texts.

8.1.4.2. Written and Oral Components of the Gandhāran Textual Corpus. As explained above, there is reason to think that the textual corpus of Gandhāran Buddhism in or around the first century A.D. was only partly transmitted in written form, and that at least some texts and textual genres, notably vinaya materials, were still preserved exclusively or primarily in oral form. Such a mixed system is directly attested, moreover, by the avadānas, whose abridged, sometimes extremely terse texts with numerous formulae of abbreviation seem to fall somewhere between written and oral tradition. Like the corresponding texts in the considerably later and geographically remote Bairam Ali manuscript (see 2.2.4), the Gāndhārī avadānas seem to be more in the nature of notes or memory aids than of formal written texts. In other words, they fall somewhere between the strict division of written versus oral texts, serving, evidently, as written supplements to oral deliveries.

It is difficult, however, to know what criteria determined whether a given text would be transmitted in oral or written form, or both. The absence of written vinaya texts in the new collection, as in the early central Asian manuscripts, seems to imply that those texts which were best known and most widely memorized would be the least likely to be written down, and, conversely, the presence of relatively large numbers of commentary texts could be taken to make the same point. But the presence of written versions, in somewhat smaller but still not insignificant numbers, of sūtra texts and of well-known verse texts such as the Anavatapta-gāthā warns us that the matter may be more complex than that, and that other factors, as yet undetermined, may be at work. Although further studies may at least partially clarify the question, the amount of material in the British Library collection may not be sufficient to provide a definitive answer.

In any case, the new manuscripts indicate that the writing down of texts served as a supplement to, and not a substitute for, the traditional method of oral/aural transmission. This is hardly surprising, as it is entirely in keeping with overall trends in Buddhism (and, for that matter, in traditional Indian culture generally), where oral and written forms of texts have typically functioned side by side, with complex patterns of interaction. Parallels from other parts of the Buddhist world show that writing, once introduced, does not necessarily supersede oral transmission; thus, according to Bechert, "to a certain extent oral transmission exists along with the written . . . among the Buddhists (especially in Burma) even to the present day" (1980: 28). Similarly, Collins, with reference to the Pali tradition as a whole, remarks that "despite the existence of written texts, the Buddhist tradition remained in various ways also an oral/aural one" (1992: 121). What is particularly interesting about the new materials, however, is that we now have, for the first time, substantial specimens of written text from a period at which, in all likelihood, the use of writing for the preservation of texts was still in a formative or at least a relatively early stage of development. The comprehensive study of these documents can therefore be expected eventually to clarify this critical transition from a purely or primarily oral to a largely written mode of textual transmission and preservation.

8.2. Sectarian Considerations: The Dharmaguptaka Connection

The early photographs showing the scrolls inside pot D, which bears a dedication to the Dharmaguptakas, can be taken as an indication, though not absolute proof, that the manuscripts were the product of, or at least were kept in, a monastery of that school. Although it is theoretically possible that the manuscripts had been removed from an original container, presumably one of the other inscribed pots in the British Library collection, and placed inside pot D by some unknown person, it is hard to imagine why this would have been done, and there is no external indication of it. Nonetheless, it would still be desirable to be able to confirm on internal grounds that the manuscripts, or rather the texts that they contain, can be associated with the Dharmaguptakas, and fortunately there is evidence that points strongly in this direction. Before proceeding to a detailed discussion of this point, however, it may be useful to summarize current theories about the Dharmaguptaka school and its Gandhāran connections.

8.2.1. Hypotheses on the Dharmaguptakas and Gandhāra

8.2.1.1. The Dharmaguptakas in India, Central Asia, and China.

The Dharmaguptakas figure prominently among the so-called Hīnayāna or Nikāya schools mentioned in the various accounts of the formations of the Buddhist sects. In these accounts, the Dharmaguptaka school is generally presented as one of the subsects derived from the Sarvāstivādins, and in some sources, for instance, in Vasumitra's Samayabhedoparacanacakra and in the Pali Theravāda tradition (Bareau 1955: 16–19, 29–30, 34; Lamotte 1988: 529–32), it is identified more specifically as an outgrowth of the Mahīśāsaka sect, itself a Sarvāstivādin subsect. Although the history of the Dharmaguptaka school in India[6] has, until now, been very obscure, its prominent role in early Buddhism in central Asia and especially in China is well attested. Lamotte, for example, comments:

> In the list of the five schools drawn up in China, it was the Dharmaguptakas who most frequently occupied the place of honour. There is nothing surprising in this considering the rôle played by that school in the diffusion of the Vinaya in China. The first formularies (*karmavācanā*) . . . pertained to that school. According to I ching, China followed mainly the Dharmaguptaka Vinaya and . . . the *Prātimokṣa* of that school was considered to be the paramount code of Hīnayānist Buddhism until the final years of the Empire. (1988: 538; see also Bareau 1955: 39)

This early primacy of the Dharmaguptakas in China is one of the reasons that certain scholars, most notably Bernhard, have postulated that "an early wave of Buddhist mission in Central Asia" (1970: 59) was sponsored by this sect, using Gāndhārī as its language medium. Probably the strongest single piece of evidence cited by Bernhard (p. 59) is the fact that, according to him, one of the central Asian Kharoṣṭhī documents from Niya (no. 510) contains six verses which correspond to the concluding verses of the Prātimokṣa-sūtra in the Dharmaguptaka version, implying that its writer belonged to this sect. At the least, this would show that Dharmaguptaka monks were present in the Buddhist communities of the Shan-shan Kingdom in and around the third century A.D., and since there is no direct

6. Here and elsewhere in this section, "India" is used in its wider, traditional sense, referring to the Indian subcontinent as a whole, including the borderlands of the northwest, rather than to the modern national boundaries of India.

evidence there for the presence of any other particular sect at this relatively early period, it is reasonable to hypothesize that the Dharmaguptakas were the dominant school there.

Even from the later phase of central Asian Buddhism, when the Sarvāstivāda and, to a lesser extent, the Mūlasarvāstivāda schools had become predominant, there are a few textual remnants of the Dharmaguptakas in the form of Sanskrit manuscript fragments that can be attributed to this sect on the basis of parallels with Chinese translations of their texts. The most secure of these is a fragment, probably from Kyzil, of a Prātimokṣa text which is attributed to the Dharmaguptakas on the basis of the exact correspondence in the order of its rules with the Chinese translation of the Dharmaguptaka-vinaya (Waldschmidt 1965: 297–8, no. 656; see esp. p. 298 n. 2).[7] Another important example is a fragment of the Mahāparinirvāṇa-sūtra from Murtuq (Waldschmidt 1968: 3–16), whose contents and ordering diverge widely from the corresponding sūtra of the Sarvāstivādins/Mūlasarvāstivādins but agree closely with the version of that sūtra included in the Chinese translation of the Dīrghāgama, which is believed to represent the Dharmaguptaka version of the collection (see 8.2.2.2).[8] These two fragments indicate that the Dharmaguptaka school continued to have a presence in Chinese central Asia even after it had lost its dominant position there.

In India itself, however, the textual and archeological remains of the Dharmaguptakas have until now been very scanty. From Hsüan-tsang's memoirs we learn that some Mahāyāna monks in Uḍḍīyāna (i.e., Swat) still followed the vinaya of the Dharmaguptakas, as well as of several other "Hīnayāna" schools, in the early seventh century A.D. (Beal 1884: 121), while I-ching confirms that, later in the same century, the Dharmaguptaka school survived in India only in Uḍḍīyāna (Takakusu 1896: 20). This concentration in the Swat Valley in the seventh century does not in and of itself prove anything about the geographical origins of the school in earlier times, but a long-standing connection with northwestern India and adjoining regions to the west is supported by the fact that several of the early translators of Dharmaguptaka texts into Chinese were natives of Sogdia, Parthia, and Chi-pin, which toponym, according to Enomoto (1994: 361), refers broadly to northwestern India, probably including both Gandhāra and Nagarāhāra. According to Przyluski, this "is proof that the Dharmaguptaka school had already taken root in Iranian territory by the third century of our era" (1926: 326).

In general, the most direct and reliable evidence for the localization of Indian Buddhist sects comes from inscriptions, and although it is not correct that

7. Note that, according to von Hinüber, "[t]he ordering of the rules . . . is always a very strong argument with regard to sectarian affiliation" (1985: 67).

8. On the linguistic features of these two texts, see Waldschmidt 1980: 162–9 (part II, "The Language of the Ch'ang-a-han-ching and Dharmaguptaka Texts").

"[n]o inscription mentions them as a sect" (Lamotte 1988: 527; at least two Dharmaguptaka inscriptions were already known when Lamotte published the original French edition of his monumental work on the early history of Indian Buddhism in 1958), it is true that, until recently, inscriptions mentioning them were rare. Until now, only two Kharoṣṭhī inscriptions referring to the Dharmaguptakas have been known. The first is the Jamālgaṛhī stone inscription, Lüders's corrected reading of which (1940: 17–20; see Appendix, sec. 3, pot D) revealed that it recorded a donation to the Dharmaguptakas (*dhamaütea(na*) parigrahe*). This, as noted by Lüders, provided the first clear evidence that "in the first centuries A.D. the Dharmaguptakas had a place in northwestern India too, whereas until now they had been epigraphically attested only in Mathurā" (p. 20). The other Kharoṣṭhī inscription referring to the Dharmaguptakas was the so-called Qunduz vase (Fussman 1974: 58–61), whose exact findspot is not known but which is reported (p. 59) to have come from somewhere in northern Afghanistan, that is, in ancient Bactria. The inscription on this copper vase records, in the usual phraseology, that it was presented to the Dharmaguptaka teachers (*acariyanaṃ dhaṃmagutakana parigrahe*).

These two Kharoṣṭhī inscriptions support the conclusion drawn from the Chinese sources that the Dharmaguptakas were prominent in the northwestern fringe of greater India and in the adjoining regions to the west. But, as noted by Lüders, this school is also epigraphically attested in Mathurā, in the heartland of northern India. Lüders refers to a Brāhmī inscription on the base of a bodhisattva statue (Lüders 1961: 187, no. 150), whose findspot is unknown but which presumably came from Mathurā or its environs. The inscription records, in hybrid Sanskrit, the statue's donation to the Dharmaguptaka teachers (*acāryana dharmagutakāna pratigrahe*). Another Brāhmī/hybrid Sanskrit pedestal inscription from the Mathurā region (Girdharpur), recording a dedication to the Dharmaguptakas (*dharmaguptikanaṃ parigrahe*) in the year 29 of Mahārāja Huviṣka, has been noted by Rosenfield (1967: 229–30 and fig. 32; see also Shizutani 1979: 131), though as far as I have been able to determine, it has never been definitively edited.

Thus, the previously published inscriptional records of the Dharmaguptakas place them precisely and exclusively within the territories associated most closely with the Indo-Scythian and Kuṣāṇa kings of the northwest: Bactria in the far west, Gandhāra in the heartland of their empires, and Mathurā in India proper. The Dharmaguptakas are notably absent from the epigraphic records of other parts of north India as well as of the Deccan and the south, and moreover the numerous new discoveries of Dharmaguptaka inscriptions, described below in section 8.2.3.1, confirm their concentration in the greater Gandhāra region.

8.2.1.2. The Dharmaguptakas and the Gāndhārī Language. Since it is now well established that the Dharmaguptakas were prominent in northwestern India and the neighboring regions of the Iranian world in the early centuries of the Christian era, it would be only reasonable to suppose that their preferred language was Gāndhārī; and indeed, there is already ample evidence of this. For instance, there is the case of Kharoṣṭhī document no. 510 from Niya, discussed in the previous section, containing the concluding verses of the Dharmaguptaka Prātimokṣa-sūtra in Gāndhārī. Another indication of an association between the Dharmaguptakas and Gāndhārī is the evidence, on phonetic grounds, that the Chinese Dīrghāgama, which is evidently a Dharmaguptaka text (see 8.2.2.2), was translated from a Gāndhārī prototype rather than from an original in some other Prakrit dialect or in Sanskrit (Brough 1962: 50–4; 1965: 608). Also, there is the testimony from the Dharmaguptaka-vinaya that members of that sect used the Arapacana formula, whose origin is closely connected with Gandhāra and Gāndhārī (Salomon 1990b, esp. 255), in their recitation formulae (Lévi 1915: 439–40; Lamotte 1988: 497).

Finally, and most important, there is the much-discussed question of the sectarian affiliation of the KDhP scroll. Although the matter is far from settled, there is something approaching a consensus among experts that this text is most likely a Dharmaguptaka document. Brough was characteristically cautious in his conclusions, declaring that the Dharmaguptakas or Kāśyapīyas were the most probable candidates, although "other possibilities cannot be ruled out" (1962: 45). He arrived at this conclusion primarily by deduction, beginning with a list of sects epigraphically attested in the northwest and eliminating those (the Sarvāstivādins and the Mahāsāṅghikas) for whom other versions or equivalents of the Dharmapada (the Udāna-varga and the extracts from a Dharmapada-type text incorporated in the Mahāvastu respectively) were already attested (p. 41). Brough did not make any clear choice between his two remaining candidates, the Dharmaguptakas and Kāśyapīyas, but several scholars since him have been inclined toward the former alternative, and some have even unreservedly ascribed the KDhP to them. For example, von Simson includes it without hesitation among "the little that is left to us of the Dharmaguptakas in an Indian language" (1985: 84; similarly, von Hinüber 1989: 354 and Fussman 1994: 21). More cautious opinions are expressed, for example, by Bernhard, who suggests such an association but warns that "there are no internal textual arguments which make it possible to identify the Gāndhārī Dharmapada dogmatically" (1970: 60), while de Jong states, more emphatically, "It is not possible to determine to which school the Gāndhārī Dharmapada belonged" (1987: 63).

The discovery among the new fragments, found in a pot that belonged to the Dharmaguptakas, of a small portion of what was evidently a manuscript of the Dharmapada (or rather one scroll from a multivolume manuscript; see 5.1.1) in a version very similar to that of the Khotan text constitutes something approaching definite proof of a Dharmaguptaka affiliation for the latter. This in turn confirms what already seemed highly likely on the basis of previously known materials: the language used by the Dharmaguptaka sect for its texts in the period in question, both in India and in central Asia, was Gāndhārī. A note of caution must, however, be added, to the effect that this does not mean that any Buddhist text written in

Gāndhārī can automatically be assumed to be a Dharmaguptaka text, since inscriptional evidence shows that other sects, such as the Sarvāstivādins and Mahāsāṅghikas, could have also had texts in Gāndhārī (Brough 1962: 42; see also von Hinüber 1983: 33). Bernhard warns that "scholars over and over again speak of *the* Sanskrit canon and of *one* canon in northwestern Prakrit, as though there could be only one canon in the same language. In Sanskrit, canonical works of at least four and perhaps even of five sects have come down to us and there is no reason for assuming that the use of the Gāndhārī dialect was limited exclusively to one single sect" (1970: 61; see also von Hinüber 1985: 75 and 1989: 353–4). In other words, the use of Gāndhārī by at least three sects (Dharmaguptaka, Sarvāstivāda, and Mahāsāṅghika) was simply conditioned by their activity in the Gandhāra region, in keeping with the long-established tradition of adopting the local language for the transmission of the dharma.

These words of caution notwithstanding, it does appear that most, perhaps all, of the Gāndhārī manuscript texts that we have belong to the Dharmaguptakas. It remains to be seen whether this is simply a matter of chance, that is to say, that Gāndhārī manuscripts of, for example, the Sarvāstivādins simply happen not to have come to light; or whether it reflects some more significant factor, such as a predominant role, previously unclear but now becoming more apparent (see 8.2.3), on the part of the Dharmaguptakas in the formative period of Gandhāran Buddhism, as well as in the transmission of Buddhist religion and texts into central Asia. In this regard, it will be most interesting to learn more about the small fragment of the Mahāparinirvāṇa-sūtra in Gāndhārī that has reportedly come to light in St. Petersburg (see 3.1.2). Since at least one fragment of a later Sanskrit version of the Dharmaguptaka recension of this text has been found in central Asia (8.2.1.1), there is reason to expect that this older Gāndhārī text will also prove to belong to this school, and if so, this will further confirm the central role that the Dharmaguptakas played in the early transmission of Buddhism beyond its Indian homeland.

8.2.2. Internal Textual Evidence for the Sectarian Affiliation of the British Library Fragments

8.2.2.1. The Saṅgīti-sūtra Commentary. The survival among the British Library fragments, in one of the longest and relatively best preserved texts (frag. 15), of the Saṅgīti-sūtra with a commentary (see 2.2.1) is a lucky circumstance in that it provides ideal textual material for the examination of sectarian affiliation. The Saṅgīti-sūtra is extant in several versions belonging to different schools: a Theravāda version in Pali (sūtra no. 33 of the Dīgha-nikāya), a Sarvāstivāda/Mūlasarvāstivāda recension (see Tripāṭhī 1985) preserved in Sanskrit fragments from Afghanistan (Bamiyan; Lévi 1932: 9–11) and central Asia (Stache-Rosen 1968) as well as in Chinese translation (T. 1 [no. 12], pp. 226c ff.), and finally what is probably the Dharmaguptaka recension (as explained in the following section) preserved in Chinese translation in the Dīrghāgama (T. 1 [no. 1], pp. 49b ff.). Since the Saṅgīti-sūtra consists of lists of numerically grouped topics, it is easy to compare the numbers and orderings of topics in the various recensions to clarify the relationships and contrasts among them. The following chart, based in part on Stache-Rosen's concordance ("Konkordanz zu Saṅgītisūtra, Saṅgītisuttanta, Saṅgītiparyāya" in 1968: 213–7), compares the list of topics discussed in the best-preserved part of the new Gāndhārī text of the Saṅgīti, comprising the end of the topics grouped in threes and the beginning of the fours, with the numbers of the corresponding topics in the other recensions.

Comparison of British Library Fragment 15 with Other Recensions of the Saṅgīti-sūtra

Part and Line in Frag. 15	Name of Group in Gāndhārī version of Saṅgīti-sūtra	Number of Corresponding Group in Chinese Dīrghāgama Version of Saṅgīti-sūtra	Number in Sanskrit Saṅgīti-sūtra	Number and Name in Pali Saṅgīti-sutta
3, r, 40	trae cot'aṇa	III.32	III.29	III.39 tīṇi codanā-vatthūni
3, r, 41	trae kasavastue	III.33	III.22	III.57 tīṇi kathā-vatthūni
3, r, 43	trae raśie	III.34	III.28	III.28 tayo rāsi
3, r, 45	. . . [soyeo]	III.35	III.46	III.52 tīṇi soceyyāni
3, r, 46	[sara](?) thero	III.36	III.27	III.37 tayo therā
3, r, 47	trae cakhu	III.37	III.39	III.46 tīṇi cakkhūni
3, r, 50	catvari va(ya-ducarita*)	IV.1	IV.45	IV.41 cattāro anariya-vohārā
3, r, 54	catuhi arie voharehi	IV.4	IV.46	IV.42 cattāro ariya-vohārā
3, r, 54	catvarime ahara	IV.5	IV.22	IV.17 cattāro āhārā
4, r, 7	catvari dhaṃma-samataṇa	IV.6	IV.35	IV.24 cattāri dhamma-samādānāni
4, r, 14	catvari uvadaṇa	IV.7	IV.39	IV.35 cattāri upādānāni
4, r, 18	catvari kaagratha	IV.8	IV.40	IV.34 cattāro ganthā
4, r, 22	catvari śa[la]	IV.9 (*tz'u*, "thorn")	—	—
4, r, 23	catvari yoṇi	IV.10	IV.29	IV.36 catasso yoniyo
4, r, 27	catvari [satuvaṭhaṇa]	IV.11	IV.1	IV.1 cattāro satipaṭṭhānā
4, r, 21	catvari i[dh]ivada	IV.13	IV.3	IV.3 cattāro iddhipādā
4, r, 25	catvari apravaṃña	IV.15	IV.7	IV.6 catasso appamaññāyo

The conclusion to be drawn from this representative sampling is obvious: the number and sequence of the topics in the newly discovered Gāndhārī version of the Saṅgīti-sūtra agree almost perfectly with the corresponding sūtra in the Chinese Dīrghāgama but differ widely from both the Sanskrit and the Pali versions of the same text. The slight discrepancies between the Gāndhārī and Chinese texts are probably insignificant, in that the topics that seem to be missing in the Gāndhārī (nos. IV.2–3, 12, 14) probably were present in the original manuscript but were lost or have become illegible due to fragmentation. Moreover, it is likely in the case of the "threes," and presumably of the other numerical groupings as well, that not only the ordering but also the total number of groups were the same, since the last triad in the Gāndhārī text, *trae cakhu,* is also the last triad (III.37) in the Chinese. In short, the arrangement of the Gāndhārī and Chinese Dīrghāgama texts of the Saṅgīti-sūtra is very similar, indeed nearly identical, and this must mean that they represent the texts of one and the same school, especially since the ordering of topics in this important list, like the ordering of rules in the Prātimokṣa (see n. 7), is the type of feature that is most likely to be distinctive in different sectarian traditions.

8.2.2.2. The Sectarian Affiliation of the Chinese Dīrghāgama. It being established that the Gāndhārī Saṅgīti-sūtra is virtually identical with the corresponding version in the Chinese Dīrghāgama, the next step is to determine the sectarian affiliation of the latter. According to Waldschmidt, "widespread agreement has been reached . . . in attributing the Dīrghāgama (Ch'ang-a-han-ching) to the school of the Dharmaguptakas" (1980: 136), and Mayeda confirms that this view is "widely accepted . . . by almost all scholars in Japan" (1985: 97). The main grounds for this claim are, first, that the monk Buddhayaśas of Chi-pin (i.e., of northwestern India; see 8.2.1.1), who along with Chu Fo-nien translated the Dīrghāgama in A.D. 412–3, was also the translator of the Dharmaguptaka-vinaya, which he was said to be able to recite by heart (Shih 1968: 89), and, second, that the preface to this Dīrghāgama translation describes a vinaya whose structure (in four parts and ten recitations) agrees with the vinaya of the Dharmaguptakas (Przyluski 1926: 355). Moreover, Bareau has presented what he describes as "the definitive proof of the Dharmaguptaka origin of the Dīrghāgama translated into Chinese by Buddhayaśas and Chu Fo-nien" (1966: 49), mainly on the grounds that the donative rites described in connection with the gift of the mango forest in the Mahāparinirvāṇa-sūtra in the Chinese Dīrghāgama agree closely with those mentioned in connection with the account of the gift of the bamboo forest in the Dharmagupta-vinaya but differ from the parallel accounts in the other vinayas (Theravādin and Mahīśāsaka); these differences reflect the conflicting doctrinal positions of these sects regarding the relative value of gifts to the Buddha and to the saṅgha.

In addition to the textual evidence, it has also been argued, initially by Waldschmidt (1932: 231) and later by others (see, e.g., 8.2.1.2), that the transcription of proper names in the Chinese Dīrghāgama, particularly in the Mahāsamāja-sūtra, reflects an original text in Gāndhārī rather than in some other MIA language or in Sanskrit. Although the details of the argument are complex and not entirely beyond question, this theory has been accepted by the majority of experts. Brough, for example, concluded that "it is difficult to see how the general picture can be explained except on the hypothesis that the original of these *Dīrghāgama* transcriptions was fundamentally the same language as that of the [Gāndhārī] Dharmapada" (1962: 54).

Although the Dharmaguptakas were probably not the only Buddhist school using Gāndhārī in the early centuries of the Christian era (8.2.1.2), we do now know that this language was characteristic of them, and thus the linguistic argument, combined with the textual evidence, makes the theory of a Dharmaguptaka origin for the Chinese Dīrghāgama very strong. This, taken together with the close textual linkage of the new Gāndhārī text of the Saṅgīti-sūtra with the Chinese Dīrghāgama—that is, the Dharmaguptaka—version and the fact that it was found in a pot that had been dedicated to the Dharmaguptakas make it virtually certain that we are indeed dealing with the textual tradition of that sect.

8.2.2.3. Confirmation and Ramifications of the Dharmaguptaka Connection. Although a Dharmaguptaka identity is now firmly established for the Saṅgīti-sūtra fragment, this does not automatically prove that all the texts found with it are also Dharmaguptaka texts, though this is certainly suggested by the fact that they were all interred together in a vessel belonging to members of that school. Unfortunately, it will be more difficult to confirm the sectarian affiliation of the other texts on internal, textual grounds than it was for the Saṅgīti, where we happen to have another Dharmaguptaka version of the text as a basis for comparison. But at least one other case points distinctly in the same direction: the striking parallels between the descriptions of the previous lives of Ājñātakauṇḍinya and Ānanda in fragments 16 + 25 and the corresponding tales in the Fo pên hsing chi ching, which is probably a Dharmaguptaka biography of the Buddha (see 2.2.4). Although the details and ramifications of these parallels remain to be worked out, this example (and perhaps others remain to be discovered among the avadāna texts) is the strongest confirmation yet found of the theory that the collection as a whole represents Dharmaguptaka literature.

In some other cases, it may be possible to establish that certain of the Gāndhārī texts represent a different recension, presumably reflecting a different sectarian origin, from other known versions, though this would not necessarily prove directly that they are Dharmaguptaka texts. This is the situation, for example, in the case of the Anavatapta-gāthā, wherein we find a version that differs significantly in language, wording, and arrangement from the previously available sectarian recensions of the same text (the Sarvāstivādin, known from central Asian fragments, and the Mūlasarvāstivādin, known from the Gilgit manuscripts and from Chinese and Tibetan translations). Here it is evident that the Gāndhārī recension belongs to a separate tradition, and circumstantial evidence points toward the Dharmaguptakas, but the text itself does not seem to provide any direct proof of this.

In other cases, it may eventually become possible to establish sectarian connections for some of the sūtra and abhidharma texts on internal grounds, for example, by reference to their doctrinal positions. But this will have to await detailed studies of individual texts, and in any case this approach is more likely to provide isolated clues than clear and conclusive proof.

It should not always be assumed—though it often is—that different versions (in terms of language, contents, and arrangement) of a given text necessarily correspond to sectarian divisions or that, conversely, a particular sect will necessarily have a single and distinct version of a given text. Especially in the case of nontechnical texts of the type used in the instruction of novices and lay followers, texts which were common to most or all schools and regions of Buddhism, it is entirely possible that different sectarian recensions were not always clearly distinguished and standardized, especially at the relatively early period with which we are concerned here. Therefore, simplistic identifications of particular recensions with particular schools may produce misleading results. Nevertheless, it is clear that more technical and formally standardized texts, such as the Saṅgīti-sūtra, did at this period have distinct sectarian versions, and it is on these that we will probably have to depend most heavily for the study of sectarian affiliation. The apparently complete absence of vinaya texts is unfortunate in this respect, since these would naturally have provided the most direct, reliable, and definitive markers of sectarian identity.

Despite these cautions, there remains little doubt that the British Library fragments represent, in part at least and quite possibly as a whole, a selection of the textual corpus of a Dharmaguptaka monastery. This in turn reinforces the theory, proposed by several scholars in the past but not until now clearly supported by archeological evidence, that the Dharmaguptaka school flourished in Gandhāra. Fortunately, a sizable body of new epigraphic data has now become available to further corroborate this hypothesis.

8.2.3. A Revised Picture of the Buddhist Schools in and around Gandhāra

8.2.3.1. New Epigraphic Evidence for Dharmaguptaka Institutions. Pot D, which contained the manuscripts, is the only one of the five complete inscribed pots in the British Library collection that was dedicated to the Dharmaguptakas. Of the other four pots, two (B and C) were given to the Sarvāstivādins, while the inscriptions on the remaining two do not specify any sect. However, the British Library collection also includes twenty-six inscribed potsherds (see Appendix, sec. 4) of uncertain provenance but possibly from the same site as the pots or from a neighboring site, of which at least three (nos. 8, 11, and 17) and possibly a fourth (no. 26) recorded donations to the Dharmaguptakas; the names of no other sects were discernible on any of these sherds. The Dharmaguptakas are similarly prominent among other recent finds of pots and potsherds with Kharoṣṭhī inscriptions that probably also came from eastern Afghanistan, although once again their exact provenance unfortunately cannot be determined. For instance, a pot I saw recently in a private collection has a complete Kharoṣṭhī inscription, in duplicate, recording the pot's donation to the Dharmaguptaka teachers at Sreṭharaña; the inscription begins *saghe cadudiśe s[re]ṭharañe acaryana dharmaütakana para*[sic]*grahami.*[9] The same collection also includes a small sherd with the letters *takaṇa,* which can be confidently restored as part of the same or a similar phrase, that is, *acaryaṇa dharmaütakaṇa parigrahami* or the like. Among the twenty-two inscribed pots and potsherds (seventeen with Kharoṣṭhī inscriptions, five with Brāhmī) in this private collection, besides these two references to the Dharmaguptakas there is only one other reference to a particular Buddhist sect, the Mahīśāsakas (*aryaṇa* [sic] *mahiśasakana ///*), which occurs in a Kharoṣṭhī inscription on a large potsherd.

Sadakata (1996b: ins. d, 1996c) has also published a pair of sherds, which are evidently parts of the same original pot, with the inscription */// cadudiśami sreṭhara[ñami] /// /// maütaka ///*. This is obviously part of the same formula as that of the pot inscription cited above, which therefore must have come from the same place, the Sreṭharaña monastery. Another large sherd, also illustrated by Sakadata in figure d (1996b), but not transcribed by him, contains yet another reference to the same place (*/// [gha]mi cadudi[śa]mi sreṭhara[ñami] . . .*). The text that follows this is not legible in Sadakata's photograph, but presumably it would have also contained some variant or part of the phrase *acaryana dharmaütakana parigrahami* or the like. I have seen a photograph of another inscribed potsherd, apparently from the same group though not illustrated by Sadakata, which reads *[ma]üta*; this once again can be confidently restored to something like *acaryaṇa dharmaütakaṇa parigrahami.*

Finally, in 1996 I saw another privately owned pot, similar in form to British Library pot E, with a complete Kharoṣṭhī inscription. The pot itself, whose present whereabouts are not known to me, was in excellent condition, but the inscription was worn and damaged, making it very difficult to read. However, the phrase *acaryana dharmaütaana parigrahe* could be made out fairly clearly. Before this was a word ending in *-rañe,* no doubt the name of the monastery, but the full name was illegible.

8.2.3.2. The New Picture of the Dharmaguptakas and Related Sects. Thus, we have among recently discovered materials at least nine definite cases, and possibly two more, of pot or potsherd inscriptions in Kharoṣṭhī recording dedications to the teachers of the Dharmaguptaka sect. Among the other inscriptions in the collections concerned, only two other sects are mentioned, the Sarvāstivādins twice (in

9. This inscription is partially edited (. . . *acaryana dharmautakana parigrahe* . . .) in Sadakata 1996b (ins. c) and 1996c.

the British Library pots) and the Mahīśāsakas once. This new material drastically shifts the balance of the representation of Buddhist sects in Kharoṣṭhī inscriptions in general, including reliquary and other types of dedicatory inscriptions as well as inscriptions on pots. Previously the Sarvāstivādins, and to a lesser extent the Kāśyapīyas, had predominated, especially in Gandhāra proper, while the Dharmaguptakas were represented by only two Kharoṣṭhī inscriptions, one from Gandhāra proper (Jamālgaṛhī) and one from Bactria. But among the new materials, nine of twelve definite references to particular sects are to the Dharmaguptakas. Unfortunately, the provenance of none of these objects is reliably reported, but their overall similarity makes it likely that they came from the same general area, and all indications are that the area in question is the Jalalabad Plain, that is, the ancient Nagarāhāra.

Thus, it begins to appear that Nagarāhāra was a stronghold, quite possibly even the principal center, of the Dharmaguptaka sect in the early centuries of the Christian era. The new inscriptional and textual discoveries confirm the indications from Chinese sources that pointed to a northwestern origin and/or concentration for this school, showing the Dharmaguptakas centered in the northwest, and particularly, it would seem, in eastern Afghanistan, where they evidently flourished under the patronage of the Indo-Scythian kingdoms affiliated with the House of Azes. Yet, even during the period of their apparent dominance and in the region in question, the Dharmaguptakas were no doubt coexisting with other sects, especially the Sarvāstivādins (see Sadakata 1996b: 312). Thus, it appears that the Dharmaguptakas and Sarvāstivādins were probably the dominant sects in Nagarāhāra in the first and second centuries A.D.

As to their specific location, all that we know for sure is that the Sarvāstivādins were present at Haḍḍa, as shown by the jar inscription from the Chakhil-i Ghundi site published by Fussman (1969) bearing a dedication to that sect and by another jar with a Sarvāstivādin inscription reported to have been found at the Tapa Shutur excavations at Haḍḍa (Tarzi 1976: 409) but not yet published.[10] Whether the Dharmaguptakas also had monasteries at these or other sites at Haḍḍa itself, or whether they were located at some of the many other sites in the neighboring area, unfortunately cannot be determined now, but it is quite possible that the members of both schools coexisted at Haḍḍa, since the cohabitation of followers of different sects is well attested, at least for a somewhat later period, by the reports of the Chinese pilgrims in India (Lamotte 1988: 519). Probably still other sects were present in the area as well; for example, the Mahīśāsakas, who in most of the traditional genealogies of the Buddhist sects are closely connected with the Dharmaguptakas, are attested in one of the new potsherd inscriptions, as well as in another recently discovered Kharoṣṭhī inscription (Fussman 1985b) of unknown provenance, dating

10. See Fussman's comment in Sadakata 1996b: 311 n. 34.

from about the same period (Azes year 126 = A.D. 69).[11] Further archeological investigations could probably clarify these and related issues, but given the conditions currently prevailing in Afghanistan it is unlikely that any such can be carried out in the foreseeable future.

8.3. Conclusions: A New View of Buddhism in Gandhāra

8.3.1. Doctrinal Orientation of the New Manuscripts

Although it would be premature at this point to draw detailed conclusions about the doctrinal positions of the tradition represented by the British Library fragments, it is worth mentioning that the preliminary studies carried out to date reveal no clear traces of Mahāyāna ideas or tendencies. The only possible exceptions noted so far are phrases such as *śuñatae praña* (= Skt. *śūnyatāyāḥ prajñā*), observed in an uncertain context in an unidentified text (frag. 10, v, line 9), apparently a commentary of some sort; but such terminology, though characteristic of the Mahāyāna, is by no means exclusive to it. In general, the fragments seem to concern issues and subjects that are typical of "mainstream" (i.e., pre- or non-Mahāyāna) Indian Buddhism.[12] Of course, closer analyses of individual texts, including the one just cited, might bring to light material that would require modification of this statement, but on the whole it appears that the manuscripts come from a time and place in which Mahāyāna ideas had not come into play at all, or at least were not being reflected in scholastic texts. This issue is of particular interest because these texts come from a period and region—first-century A.D. Gandhāra—which, according to some views at least, played a central role in the origins of Mahāyāna. It remains to be seen in what way, if any, the new manuscripts may contribute to this issue, but it now seems most likely that any such contribution will be a negative, or at best an indirect, one. Of course, further analysis and possible future discoveries could well change the picture, but as matters stand at this point, the British Library scrolls do not offer any support for the hypothesis of a relatively early origin for Mahāyāna Buddhism.

8.3.2. Gandhāra as a Center of Buddhist Intellectual Activity

Even before the discovery of the new Kharoṣṭhī manuscripts, there was no doubt that Gandhāra had been an important center of Buddhist scholarship at various periods. Hsüan-tsang, for example, reports, "From old times until now this border-land of India has produced many authors of *śastras*" (Beal 1884: 98; see also Zwalf 1996: 1.30 and 33 n. 12), and the abhidharma tradition preserved in Chinese translation also testifies to the extensive intellectual activity there. Nevertheless, direct evidence of original Gandhāran texts has until now been lacking, and this has

11. For the revised interpretation of this date, which Fussman tentatively read as the Azes year 26, see Salomon 1995b: 130.

12. On these terms, see section 2.2.2, n. 21.

led to skepticism on the part of some scholars about the intellectual originality and regional distinctiveness of Gandhāran Buddhism in the early centuries of the Christian era. Fussman, for instance, remarks: "The list of sects active in Gandhāra and the epigraphical attestations . . . assure us, in any case, of the nonexistence in Gandhāra of texts truly specific to that region. The same texts were studied there as elsewhere in north India. . . . On the level of ideology, the Buddhism of Gandhāra is not distinguished at all from Gangetic Buddhism" (1994: 43).[13] Such skepticism may have been justified on the basis of the previously known textual evidence, mainly inscriptions, whose "doctrinal content . . . contains nothing but the most banal" (Fussman 1994: 22). But the new discoveries reveal—not surprisingly, in hindsight—that the inscriptions gave us a very incomplete and therefore misleading picture. They reflect, for the most part, ritual activities concerned with the relic cult and pious donations to monasteries, and as such there is no reason to expect them to contain much more than stereotyped formulae, or to be surprised that such "textual" passages as they do contain are no more than "a collection of cliches" or "an anthology of more or less accurate citations, not extracted from any particular text" (Fussman 1982: 37). But we now know that the absence of regionally distinctive textual materials in the inscriptions did not mean that they did not exist, merely that they were not expressed therein. With the benefit of hindsight, it seems only natural that Gandhāran Buddhism of the first and second centuries A.D. should have developed an extensive and distinctive textual and intellectual tradition to match its tremendous achievements in the material expression of its beliefs in the form of sculpture, architecture, etc. Indeed, it would have been surprising if this period of Gandhāran Buddhism had *not* had a rich intellectual tradition of its own—though this too is easier to say in hindsight.

Of course, it still remains to be determined exactly how much of the new textual material is in fact original to Gandhāra. As mentioned above, the scholastic texts, which are the most important in this respect, happen also to be the type of material whose origins are most difficult to pin down on linguistic and stylistic criteria. If it can be provisionally assumed that those texts for which no parallels have been found in other Buddhist traditions are of Gandhāran origin, the amount of such distinctive material is quite large in proportion to the total extent of the fragments. But this is a dangerous assumption, since it is quite possible that parallels for at least some of these texts will eventually be identified, and moreover, even if they are not, this may mean only that they happen not to have survived in those other traditions, not that they were never known to them.

13. "La liste des sectes actives au Gandhāra et les témoignages épigraphiques . . . nous assurent en tout cas de l'inexistence au Gandhāra de textes véritablement spécifiques à ce pays. On y étudiait les mêmes textes qu'ailleurs en Inde du Nord. . . . sur le plan idéologique, le bouddhisme du Gandhāra ne se distingue en rien du bouddhisme gangétique."

There is at least one important class of textual materials, however, for which a local Gandhāran origin is nearly certain: this is the avadāna texts, whose local character is indicated by references to historical figures of the region and by their marked contrasts with the avadāna traditions attested in Buddhist schools of other regions. This in itself is enough to compel a modification of the view, quoted above, that "the same texts were studied there as elsewhere in north India." To what degree the new manuscripts will prove to represent a distinct intellectual tradition will become clear only gradually as they are studied in detail, but there is every reason to expect that they will confirm that the material richness of Gandhāran Buddhism was matched by its scholastic achievements.

8.3.3. The Geographic and Chronological Context of the British Library Scrolls

The references in the avadāna texts to the rulers Jihonika and Aśpavarman indicate that the textual tradition represented in these manuscripts, though not necessarily the manuscripts themselves, goes back at least to the time of the later Indo-Scythian kingdoms of the early first century A.D. This shows that the great flowering of Gandhāran Buddhism was not exclusively or even primarily a phenomenon of the Kuṣāṇa period, particularly of the time of Kaniṣka, as it may have appeared in the past. Later Buddhist tradition itself, among other influences, has given us this impression through its enthusiastic celebration of Kaniṣka's patronage, and his generosity seems to have outshone that of his Indo-Scythian predecessors and in effect expunged them from Buddhist historical tradition. But other factors may be at work as well. The textual and epigraphic material presented here makes it possible to conceive a situation wherein the Dharmaguptaka school was the predominant one, at least in parts of the northwestern region, in the earlier part of the first century A.D., while it enjoyed the patronage of the Indo-Scythian kings. Under their successors, the Kuṣāṇas, however, the Sarvāstivādins seem to have gained the upper hand, and it is surely no accident that Kaniṣka is portrayed as the great patron, a latter-day Aśoka as it were, in the Sarvāstivādin tradition. Such a shift in sectarian fortunes would be consistent with parallel developments that have been posited for early central Asian Buddhism, where the Dharmaguptakas seem to have prevailed at an early period before they were eclipsed by the Sarvāstivādins. It would also contribute to an explanation of the apparent disappearance of much of the tradition represented in the new manuscripts. Kaniṣka's role as the patron par excellence of the Sarvāstivādins might have led to the suppression, or perhaps just the displacement, of references to earlier Dharmaguptaka patrons such as Jihonika and Aśpavarman, so that their names were entirely forgotten in subsequent Buddhist traditions.

The new evidence of scholastic activity in Gandhāran Buddhist institutions in the Indo-Scythian period accords with numerous recent discoveries of relic inscriptions dedicated by the Apraca kings and other Indo-Scythian rulers of the late first century B.C. and early first century A.D. (see Salomon 1996a: 443, 450). Thus, Fussman's assertion, based mainly on the epigraphic evidence, that "the Indo-Scythian period *and* the Kushana period are the golden age of Gandharan Buddhism" (1994: 32; emphasis mine) is confirmed by the new material. The geographical connections involved, however, are less clear, not only because the exact provenances of the manuscripts and many of the other relevant artifacts are not known, but also because of our sketchy knowledge of the territories of the Indo-Scythian rulers associated with them. Among the Indo-Scythian rulers mentioned in the new manuscripts, Jihonika is entitled in his Taxila inscription (cited in 7.1.1) "Satrap of Cukhsa," a toponym generally believed to correspond to the modern Chach, representing approximately the area around Taxila (Konow 1929: lxix; Marshall 1951: 1.48, 2.773–4). The territories of Aśpavarman are more difficult to pin down, but they presumably were at least partly equivalent to those of his forefathers, the kings of Apraca, who seem to have ruled in Bajaur and perhaps in the adjoining regions to the east bordering on the lower Swat Valley (Salomon 1995a: 30). Although there is no direct evidence during the period in question of the political status of the Nagarāhāra region, where the manuscripts were evidently stored and copied and presumably also originally written, the region was probably within the Indo-Scythian Empire, so that even if it was not part of the personal territories of Jihonika or Aśpavarman, it is not surprising to find that they were active there as patrons.[14] One can easily imagine, for example, that they undertook tours of pilgrimage in this area, in the course of which they bestowed their largess on the many Buddhist institutions there. This hypothesis is supported by the inscription on British Library pot A (see 7.2.2 and Appendix, pp. 198–9), which records its dedication by one Vāsavadattā, who is probably the sister of the Apraca prince Indravarman and hence the aunt of Aśpavarman.

In conclusion, the preliminary survey and analysis of the British Library scrolls presented here indicate that they represent a random but reasonably representative fraction of what was probably a much larger set of texts preserved in the library of a monastery of the Dharmaguptaka sect in Nagarāhāra. At least some of the unanswered questions about these texts and their origins, significance, and influence on later Buddhist traditions will gradually be answered as the texts are studied and edited in years to come, though it is probably also wise to assume that they will raise at least as many new questions as they will answer old ones—this being the na-

14. Although the Buddhist sites at Haḍḍa and neighboring places are generally dated to the late and post-Kuṣāṇa period, this is probably only a result of the incomplete archeological investigations that have been carried out there. It is not at all unlikely that some of these sites, if not the surviving structures, go back to the first century A.D. or possibly even earlier (see Mustamandi 1974: 111). For example, the evidence of coin hoards from reliquary deposits in stūpas at Haḍḍa and adjoining sites assembled in MacDowall 1990 (esp. pp. 732–3) shows that several of these deposits go back to the time of Gondophares and Wima Kadphises, that is, to the early first century A.D.

ture of such discoveries. No doubt these future studies will also necessitate extensive revisions, and quite possibly also retractions, of what has been presented here, so I hasten to repeat what was said at the outset, namely, that most of the statements in this book are more or less provisional and that it is presented more in the spirit of an agenda for future discussion than of a definitive treatise. It is much too soon to try to predict what effect this discovery will ultimately have on our understanding of the early history and development of Buddhism, but it is probably safe to say that it will provoke the rethinking of issues such as the regional character of early Indian Buddhist traditions, the process of the formation of standardized written canons, and the transmission of Buddhism into central and east Asia.

Appendix

Inscribed Pots and Potsherds in the British Library Collection

1. Technical Description and Evaluation of the Pots and Potsherds (*by Raymond Allchin*)

1.1. Character and Comparative Status of the Ceramic Craft Exemplified in the Collection

Miller (1985) has shown that globular vessels of one kind or another are still regularly manufactured in villages throughout India and Pakistan. Such vessels are generally known by specific type-names, which vary from region to region and with the language or dialect spoken (*matka, ghara, kundi, goli, maman,* etc.). In his study of the pottery of a central Indian village, Miller found that each of the several type-names of the globular pots was in theory associated with a specific function, but that in practice the vessels might be used for a variety of functions apart from water carrying and storage. These included the storage of numerous varieties of grain and other foodstuffs. We have also seen instances of such globular pots being used for burying ashes collected from cremations. That they should serve as repositories for worn-out manuscripts or other relics in a religious context is entirely credible. We shall see below that waterpots of this kind are frequently found in Buddhist monasteries in northwest Pakistan, and that examples inscribed with Buddhist donative or dedicatory phrases are a regular occurrence in this region. Callieri's (1997) summary of data relating to discoveries of pottery in Buddhist monasteries in Swat confirms this statement.[1] These prefatory remarks are intended to indicate the difference between the theory of a potter making a pot of a particular form which is known by a particular name and which ideally should be used for a particular function, and actual practice, in which any of several differently named pots may be used for any of several functions.

1.2. The Inscribed Pots

Of the five inscribed pots in the British Library collection, four are complete (pots B, C, D, and E), and one (pot A) has lost its neck and rim. All five belong to the class of globular or near-globular jars used for the carrying and

1. [This publication is not yet available to me, and hence has not been consulted—RS.]

storage of water and for domestic storage of a wide range of commodities.

In spite of minor differences in the rims, the four complete pots are essentially all of one type. They are all made from a finely sorted alluvial clay, which gives the impression that it was derived from a single, probably local source. The clay of pot B is slightly less well sorted than that of the other three, and the body clay includes numerous small particles, apparently of mica. The pots are manufactured by a well-known technique which involves the initial throwing of a small, thick-bodied vessel on the wheel. This vessel is subsequently expanded by beating out the body with the aid of a wooden paddle and an anvil. In many parts of south Asia anvils are often found in archeological assemblages. They are occasionally made of stone, but more commonly of terra-cotta. The beating of the globular body is applied by the paddle from outside while the anvil is held in the other hand inside the pot. A good description of the technique as it is practiced today in northwestern Pakistan can be found in Rye and Evans 1976: 50–3; the method is used, with regional minor variations, throughout the Indian subcontinent and has been described many times in the past century or more. The rim and neck of the pot are thrown on the wheel as a separate unit, and once the expanded body and the neck are leather-hard the two are luted together to make the finished form. One can confidently infer the use of these processes from the telltale traces they occasionally leave. In the interior of the globular body, some visible traces are almost always left by the anvil in the form of slight concavities; similarly, at the junction of the neck and body of the pot, the interior often retains the finger marks made during the luting process.

The surface of the British Library vessels has been smoothed or lightly burnished, possibly with a string of beads, and a light wash or slip, of cream or buff color, has been added, apparently before firing. Pots A, B, and C have been further decorated with stamped impressions of lotus rosettes (numbering three, three, and four respectively). The pots have been well fired, the clay has burnt to a pink-to-red oxidized color, and the surface wash is generally of a lighter pink to creamy buff color. The ink inscriptions and the occasional red ocher lines appear in all cases to have been added to the pots after firing.

1.3. The Inscribed Potsherds

The inscribed potsherds display several decorative features that are not in evidence on the complete pots, although in terms of their original forms one may hazard a guess that almost all are fragments of similar waterpots. The principal exception is a shallow bowl, or "beaker," having a distinctive profile, in which the upper half of the wall is concave, with a rounded rim, while the lower half is markedly convex (no. 14; fig. 55). The type doubtless has its origins in the imitations of metallic forms found at Shaikhān Ḍherī and elsewhere in the Indo-Greek period, and continuing in modified form through all subsequent periods down to the late Kuṣāṇa. Following Marshall (1951), we may reasonably infer that the missing base for such a beaker was a standard foot. The closest parallels for the British Library example come from the middle Kuṣāṇa period at Shaikhān Ḍherī (Husain 1980: type 11.2, pl. 25, nos. 1–4; see below).

As far as can be seen, the clay of the sherds is very similar to that of the pots. As a rule the sherds have burned to a good pink-red color. The surface is in most instances covered with a cream-buff wash, part of which has sometimes flaked off, revealing the redder body clay beneath. A new feature of surface treatment is supplied by the use of a wooden paddle scored with parallel grooves. This produces a distinctive surface decoration, applied as a diagonal band in the case of no. 24 and as two diagonally opposed lines producing a herringbone effect in no. 3. Several sherds have one or more bands of wavy lines incised in the wet clay (nos. 1, 13, 20, and 25). No. 9 has been incised with what appears to be a roulette (fig. 52). Nos. 20 and 22 are decorated with appliqué bands, incised diagonally to make what look like cables in the case of the latter and a chain in the former (figs. 57–8). Stamped decorations can be seen on several sherds. Nos. 6 (fig. 50), 10, and 18 have lotus rosettes, and no. 25 shows the edge of a rather different form of rosette, surrounded by an outer ring of dots. No. 3 has a characteristic wheat-ear motif stamped upon its upper section. No. 7 has a unique stamped oblong motif measuring approximately 3 by 4 cm (fig. 51). Its subject is not clear. It may represent a *lajjā gaurī*, a headless nude female with knees raised and thighs spread wide to reveal the genitalia. But it is more probably intended to represent the head of a lion or other beast with forepaws crossed, emerging from a cave in the manner seen in the Gandhāran icon of the visit of Indra to the Buddha in his mountain retreat (see Marshall 1960: pl. 83).

1.4. Possible Provenance of the Pots and Potsherds

The information derived from this short view of the potter's craft in the two groups leads to certain tentative conclusions. First, the whole collection appears to be coherent and evidently represents the production of a single potter's yard, or at least a single group of potter's yards. The probability is that the wares were produced locally and sold to the users, who added their own inscriptions and employed the pots for their own purposes. To know more of these purposes, the nature of the inscriptions must also be taken into account. Unfortunately, no information is available regarding the site from which the finds were derived. There are, however, certain pointers toward the general area in which it may have been. The context suggests that the site was a Buddhist monastery, and judging by other finds of comparable pottery, we may infer that the collection comes either from somewhere in the North-West Frontier Province of Pakistan or from adjacent parts of Afghanistan.

A number of good comparative examples come from the former region. Marshall and Vogel (1902–3) discovered four large "*chattis*,"[2] three bearing inscrip-

2. The term *chatti* is Anglo-Indian, deriving from the Tamil name for a waterpot.

tions, during excavations in the Buddhist monastic complex of Pālāṭū Ḍherī (see 4.3), a short distance from Chārsada. Their description of these vessels and their manufacture suggests that they were more or less identical to the British Library pots and provides a good early account of the beating technique. The Kharoṣṭhī inscriptions were republished by Konow (1929: 120–2), who also described potsherds bearing related inscriptions from Takht-i-Bāhī and Sahrī Bahlol (pp. 63 and 112–2). In all these cases the inscriptions reinforce the clear archeological indications that they were discovered in Buddhist monastic sites.

A further body of data, in the form of twenty-four inscribed sherds, was brought to the representative of the Archaeological Survey of India in Peshawar shortly before partition. They were studied and published by B. C. Chhabra (1949–50), the government epigraphist at that time. The exact whereabouts of the discovery was not known and could not be ascertained, but Chhabra inferred that they had probably been discovered in a Buddhist monastic institution in the vicinity of Peshawar itself.

Inscribed pottery, including a "water jar," is reported in the Italian excavations in Swat (Callieri 1989: 227; 1997). From farther east in Pakistan, Taxila offers a well-excavated series of sites for comparison with the craft aspects of the British Library collection. Certainly, Taxila provides evidence of the early occurrence of globular jars from ca. 200 B.C. and their continuation until at least ca. A.D. 100, and probably thereafter. A late find of this sort came from stūpa deposits at Bhamāla (stūpas A5 and A15), datable to the fifth century (Marshall 1951: 1.394). But inscribed pots do not appear to have been found at any of the excavated monastic sites at Taxila. It is also noteworthy that the local clay in that region is recognizably not as finely sorted as that of the Vale of Peshawar or the alluvial plains of the Indus or its main tributaries.

Although there were undoubtedly many Buddhist monasteries in the area of Nagarāhāra around Jalalabad in eastern Afghanistan, and although there are references to discoveries of pottery and in some instances even of inscribed pottery there, the publication of this material is scarcely adequate to allow critical comparison to be made with the British Library materials (see Callieri 1997: 424–5). My recollection of the pottery of that region and my knowledge of the terrain indicate that equally finely sorted alluvial clays are also common there. I must therefore enter a caveat against drawing any inference either positive or negative from an argumentum ex silentio in this context, but we may conclude that this area must be regarded as one of the possible sources for the British Library collection.

1.5. Probable Dates of the Pots and Potsherds

The ceramic evidence offers a surprisingly clear indication of the date of manufacture of the British Library collection. This is largely thanks to a detailed study of the pottery obtained from the well-stratified excavations at Shaikhān Ḍherī

(Dani 1965–6). Regrettably, the study in question is as yet unpublished, but it is available in the form of the Ph.D. thesis of Dr. Javed Husain (1980). Further evidence is available from the well-published accounts of pottery finds throughout the excavated sites at Taxila (Marshall 1951). Another excavation that will undoubtedly be helpful when it is published is that of Barikot in Swat. The broader perspective on the history of the globular jars or waterpots can be augmented by reference to sites in the Ganges Valley. At Hastināpura and Atranjikherā these vessels make their first regular appearance in the period of the northern black polished ware and thus neatly coincide with the evidence from Taxila mentioned above.

At Shaikhān Ḍherī, Husain classifies waterpots as his type 31 and globular jars as his type 32.1. Although both these types deserve our attention, it is particularly the former which we may compare with the British Library pots. The globular body does not convey much information, but the neck and rim forms do. They suggest that our pots are equally close to the early Kuṣāṇa and the middle Kuṣāṇa examples from Shaikhān Ḍherī. The British Library beaker (no. 26) is closely similar to a type that occurs at both Taxila and Shaikhān Ḍherī; at the latter site it is represented by Husain's type 11.2, which is found in every period in the excavation (i.e., Indo-Greek; Scytho-Parthian; and early, middle, and late Kuṣāṇa). Here too, the closest resemblances are to examples from the early and middle Kuṣāṇa periods. At Taxila, Marshall refers to a type of open-mouthed pots with standard bases which occur during the late Saka-Parthian period at Sirkap. This type is probably earlier than our example, but it seems probable that the Shaikhān Ḍherī type 11.2 was also originally mounted upon a standard base, as Husain suggests. One other possible cross-dating point is available for the tanga-like motif painted on sherd no. 12 (fig. 53). This closely resembles an example illustrated by Härtel (1993: fig. 115) from Sonkh and there assigned to the Kuṣāṇa period.

To sum up: my reading of this evidence points toward the early and middle Kuṣāṇa periods at Shaikhān Ḍherī as the time of closest resemblance between the British Library and the Shaikhān Ḍherī ceramics. There is, however, no question that many elements of the pottery at Shaikhān Ḍherī and similar sites originated several centuries earlier than this date, and related examples occur not only in the Indo-Greek and Saka-Parthian periods but in some instances also in the late Kuṣāṇa period. However, the closest parallels for our British Library inscribed pottery are to be found in the intermediate early and middle Kuṣāṇa periods.

2. Kharoṣṭhī Pot and Potsherd Inscriptions

Inscribed pots or, more often, fragments of pots made of clay, or occasionally of metal, have been found at many sites in the area of ancient Bactria and Gandhāra and adjoining regions of modern Pakistan and Afghanistan and Uzbekistan (see map 3). Like the British Library pots and potsherds, they typically have

Kharoṣṭhī or sometimes Brāhmī[3] inscriptions recording their donation to Buddhist monasteries. Konow's corpus of Kharoṣṭhī inscriptions (1929) included specimens from Takht-i-Bāhī (no. XXII), Pālāṭū Ḍherī (LV), Sahrī Bahlol (LVI), and Tor Ḍherai (XCII). Since the publication of Konow's volume, many more examples of such inscriptions have been discovered.[4] Particularly important specimens have been found from Peshawar (Chhabra 1949–50), Qunduz (Fussman 1974: 58-61), and Kara Tepe and Faiz Tepe near Termez, Uzbekistan (Vorob′eva-Desjatovskaja 1983: 24–42; Vertogradova 1995). Other examples include those from Bāsawal (Mizuno 1971: 1.23, 2.39–41, 108–9), Butkara (Petech 1966), Tepe Zargarān (Balkh; Schlumberger 1949: 183–4),[5] Gul Dara (Fussman and Le Berre 1976: 92–3, pl. li), Saidu Sharīf (Fussman in Callieri 1989: 225–30), Mekhāsaṇḍā (Mizuno 1969: 58, 93–4), Rāṇigāṭ (*Gandhāra 2* 1988: 59–62, 127–30), and Shaikhān Ḍherī (Dani 1965–6: 109–13), as well as examples of unknown provenance (Sadakata 1996b: part 4, 1996c; Salomon 1996b: 238–42). Of particular interest in the present context are the several inscriptions of this type found at Haḍḍa. Only two of them have been published (no. 1: Konow 1929: no. LXXXII and Konow 1935–6; no. 2: Fussman 1969), while a third, found at the Tapa Shutur site and apparently recording a dedication to the Sarvāstivādins, was briefly mentioned by Tarzi (1976: 409).

There are also probably many other inscriptions of this type in various museums and private collections which have not been properly reported or published. For example, "a considerable number" of potsherds with Kharoṣṭhī inscriptions, containing as many as eighteen akṣaras, were found by D. B. Spooner and Aurel Stein during the excavations at Sahrī Bahlol (Konow 1929: 122 and references given there in nn. 3 and 4), but these have apparently never been published or illustrated. Also, a private collection (see 8.2.3.1) contains seventeen pots and potsherds with Kharoṣṭhī inscriptions, which I hope to publish in the near future. It is likely that many other inscriptions of this type have been found in the course of excavations, officially sanctioned or otherwise, but not properly reported or even saved.

At some of the sites noted above, large numbers of specimens of fragmentary inscriptions of this type have been found. These include Gul Dara (eight), Saidu Sharīf (eleven), Shaikhān Ḍherī (twenty-three), Peshawar (twenty-

3. Inscriptions of this type in Brāhmī script have been found in good numbers in the northwest; see, e.g., the several examples from Termez and other sites in Vorob′eva-Desjatovskaja 1983: 42–9 and Vertogradova 1995: 89–113. The periods of use of the two scripts must have been at least partly overlapping, since there are several examples of biscripts (Vertogradova 1995: 106–13), but in general the Brāhmī inscriptions can be presumed to be later than those in Kharoṣṭhī.

4. See the list and bibliography in Fussman and Le Berre 1976: 92, though this too is now out of date.

5. The reading by R. Curiel cited by Schlumberger (1949: 184) and Vorob′eva-Desjatovskaja (1983: 29), *khurośaṃmi* (*rva?*), is incorrect. The first four akṣaras are clearly *dudiśami,* obviously part of the standard formula *saghecadudiśami.* The following letter is apparently *ko,* after which there are traces of one or two more characters which cannot be read. This piece is also illustrated and briefly mentioned, without a reading, in Gardin 1957: 41, pl. XVI.5.

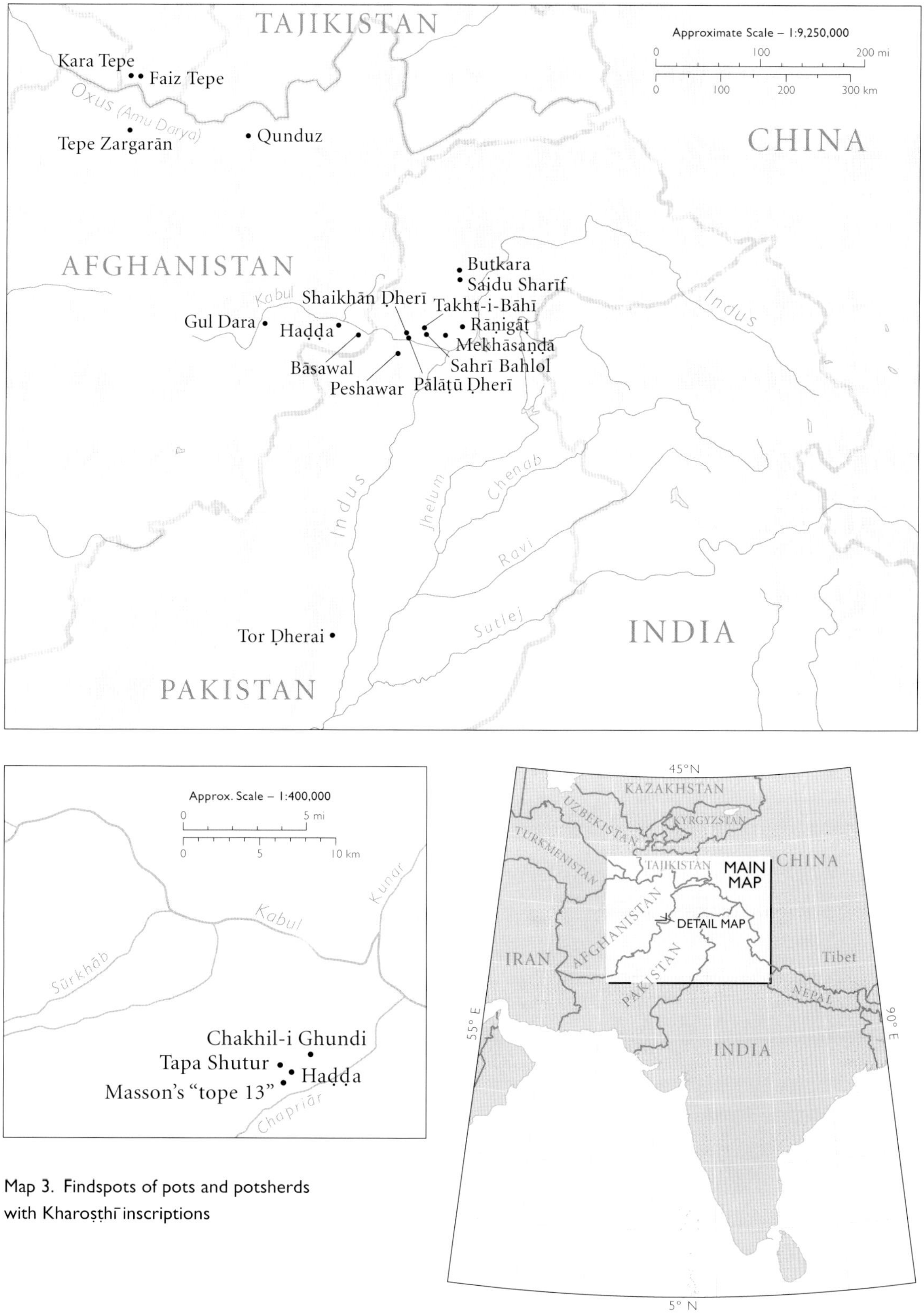

Map 3. Findspots of pots and potsherds with Kharoṣṭhī inscriptions

four), and especially Termez (at least ninety-four). In most cases, only sherds bearing small fragments of the original inscriptions have survived. Complete or nearly complete inscriptions such as the five being published here are relatively rare; the only previously known ones are the specimens from Qunduz and Haḍḍa (no. 1) and from an undetermined provenance (Salomon 1996b: 238–42).[6] Konow was able to piece together from the Tor Ḍherai fragments, which came from several different pots with identical or similar inscriptions, an almost complete text,[7] so that, from a textual point of view, they constitute in effect a full inscription.

The inscriptions on the clay vessels were typically written with black ink after the jars had been fired (Fussman and Le Berre 1976: 92), as is the case with the new specimens presented here. The inscription is usually placed on the shoulder of the pot, often just below a decorative line, either incised or inked. The quality of the writing varies widely, from highly calligraphic (as in British Library pot C) to semiliterate. Inscriptions of the latter class often present serious difficulties for their editors, but the interpretation of such records generally, and the reconstruction of the fragmentary ones, are facilitated by their formulaic character. Dedicatory inscriptions on the pots, like other types of Buddhist donative records, followed fairly standard patterns. The following would be a typical donative formula in the longer pot inscriptions (of which the reconstructed Tor Ḍherai inscription, quoted in n. 7, is a good specimen):

> This (water)pot [(*paṇiya-*)*ghaḍa* or -*kuḍika*] is the pious gift [*deyadharma* or *daṇamukha*] of so-and-so in the possession [*parigrahe* or *pratigrahe*] of the teachers [*acaryaṇaṃ*] of such-and-such a sect in the universal community [*caturdiśe saghe*] at such-and-such a place. May it be for a primary share [of the merit of the donation; *agre*- or *saṃme-pratyaṃśa*] on the part of [the donor's] parents, relatives, and all beings.

Within this general pattern, the texts vary considerably, particularly in the concluding blessing, which may also contain other wishes such as "for the benefit of [the donor's] own health" (*atmaṇasa arogadakṣiṇae*). Many examples (such as in the one edited in Salomon 1996b) use a much briefer donative formula, omitting, for

6. There are also two complete pot inscriptions in the private collection mentioned above.

7. *ṣahi-yola-miras(y)a viharasvamis(y)a deyadharmo yaṃ prapa svakiya* [or *[a *]taniya]-yola-mira-ṣahi-vihare saṃghe caturdiśe acaryanaṃ sarvastivadinaṃ parigrahe. ito ca s(r)amaparityagato agre [*ma]tapitrinaṃ [pratiyaṃ*]śo sarvasatvanaṃ agre pratiyaṃśo dharmapatis(y)a ca dirghayu[ta bhavatu*].* Konow (1929: 176) translates: "Of the Shāhi Yola Mīra, the master of the vihāra, this water hall (is) the religious gift, in his own Yola-Mīra-shāhi-Vihāra, to the order of the four quarters, in the acceptance of the Sarvāstivādin teachers. And from this right donation may there be in future a share for (his) mother and father, in future a share for all beings and long life for the master of the law."

example, the label "This (water)pot," the blessing, and other portions of the full formula such as the sect of the recipients. In some cases, as in pot D described below, even the donor's name is omitted, surprising as this may seem.[8]

The Buddhist sects mentioned as recipients in inscriptions of this class are the Sarvāstivādins, in the Haḍḍa (no. 2) and Tor Ḍherai inscriptions, as well as in British Library pots B and C described here; the Dharmaguptakas, in Qunduz, British Library pot D and potsherds 8, 11, 17, as well as in several other pots and potsherds, mostly still unpublished; the Mahīśāsakas (one unpublished piece; see 8.2.3.1); the Kāśyapīyas and(?) the Bahuśrutikas, in the Pālāṭū Ḍherī potsherd, and possibly also the Kāśyapīyas in Takht-i-Bāhī;[9] and the Mahāsāṅghikas, in as many as twelve inscriptions from Termez.[10]

3. The Inscribed Pots in the British Library Collection

Pot A

Pot A (pls. 22–3 and fig. 14) is a large wheel-made vessel of coarse red clay with gritty inclusions, globular in form with a round bottom. The neck is lost, and the jar has been reconstructed from the surviving fragments, which compose most, though not all, of its body. One of the missing pieces contained part of one of the inscriptions (no. 2), of which about 9.5 cm has therefore been lost, but the missing text can be reconstructed from formulaic parallels. The pot, in its present condition (i.e., without the neck), is 37.6 cm high, with a maximum diameter of 40.5 cm. It is decorated, just below the neck, with five parallel incised horizontal grooves, below which is a single wavy line. Lower down on the shoulder, about 11 cm from the lower edge of the (lost) neck, is a thick blurry line of red pigment, which runs through three circular stamped designs, spread more or less evenly around the circumference of the pot, consisting of six-petaled lotuses inside a circle. There was probably also a fourth such stamp in the missing portion of the vessel. These symbols are stamped into the jar at the level of the main inscription (no. 2), which is written just below the red line. With reference to the inscription, the stamped designs fall at the beginning (before *aya*), between *susomabharyae* and *atmanasa,* and between *suhasomasa* and *saṃmepratyaśae.*

8. See below, section 5.1 for further discussion of this point.

9. Only the first syllable, *ka,* is preserved. This could stand for *kaśaviyaṇa,* "of the Kāśyapīyas" (Konow 1929: 63).

10. Kara Tepe nos. 2, 6, 36, 63 (Vertogradova 1995); Faiz Tepe nos. 11, 14, 23, 25, 30, 32, 36b, 37 (Vorob′eva-Desjatovskaja 1983). In most of these examples the word *mahasaṃghigaṇa,* "of the Mahāsāṅghikas," or the like is incompletely preserved but can be confidently restored from the context and the parallels provided by the sherds which do have the complete word (Kara Tepe no. 63 and Faiz Tepe no. 37).

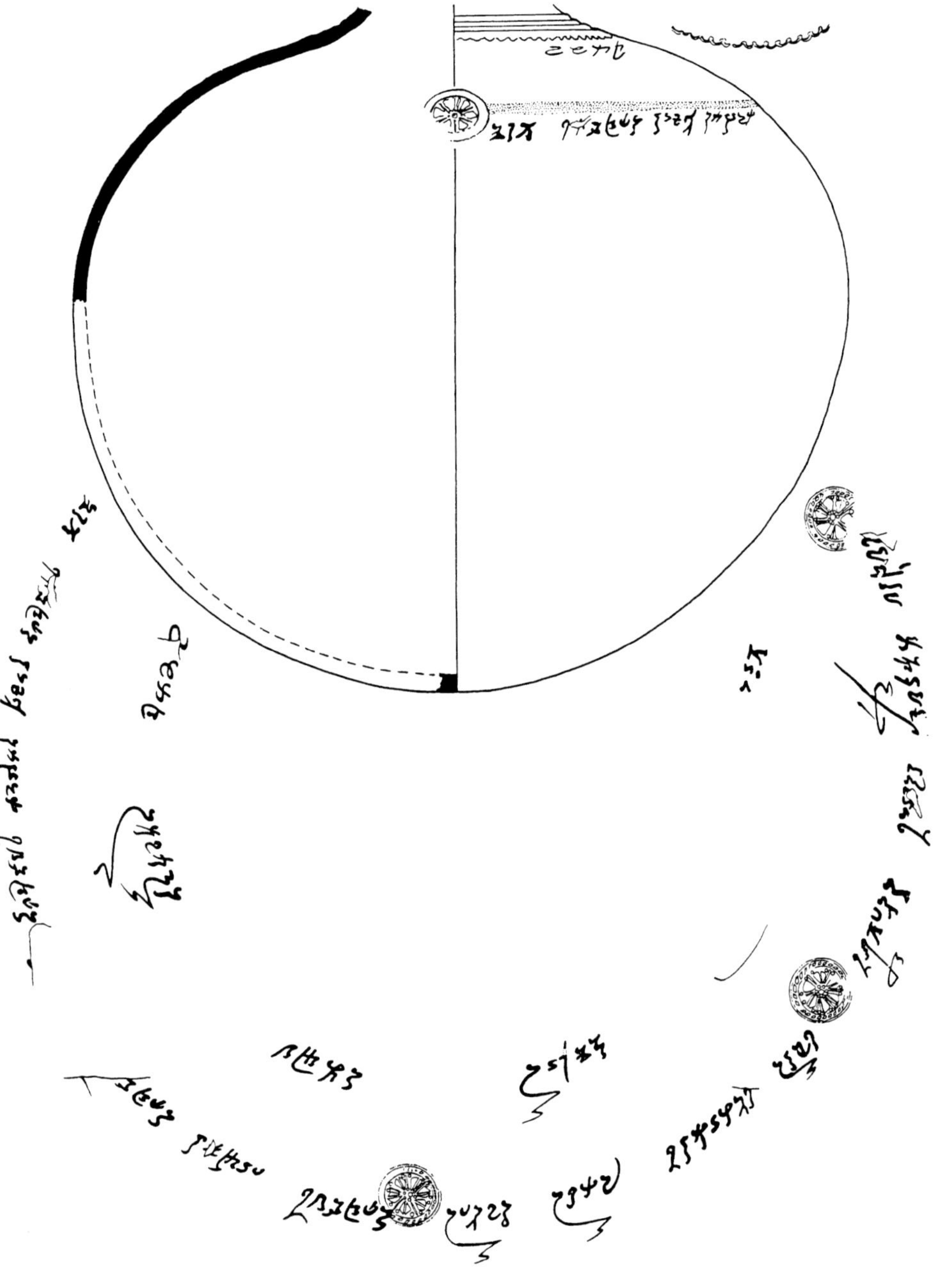

Fig. 14. Cross section of pot A,
with inscriptions 1 and 2

Fig. 15. Detail of inscriptions 1 and 2 on pot A

This jar bears two inscriptions. The briefer inscription (no. 1, pl. 23 and figs. 14–15, 19–22) is written near the top, about 5 cm below the neck and slightly below the decorative incised lines. The five words of this inscription are spaced evenly around the circumference, covering a total space of 60 cm. The letters are similar in size to those of the main inscription (no. 2)—that is, about 0.8–1.2 cm in height on average—and are in the same hand. Except for the second word, the inscription is clear:

bhadaṃta [ca]t[ula]sa saghapriya sadhaṃviharisa pratigraha

The possession of the Reverend Catula(?), pupil of Saṃghapriya.

The formulation here is unusual in that it records a dedication to an individual monk; most dedicatory inscriptions of this sort are addressed to the universal community (*saghe caturdiśe*), often also specifying the teachers (*acarya*) of a particular sect or at a particular monastery (see below, sec. 5.2). The use of the apparently endingless *pratigraha* instead of the usual locative form (*pratigrahe* or *pratigrahami*) is paralleled in the Wardak vase inscription (line 4, *eṣa vihara acaryaṇa*

Fig. 16. Detail of inscription 2 on pot A

mahasaṃghigaṇa parigraha),[11] which Konow (1929: 170) takes as a nominative ("This vihāra is the acceptance of the Mahāsāṅghika teachers"), but which Fussman (1989: 472) considers to be an example of the locative in *-a* (cf. above, 6.5.1). This latter interpretation is possible, in which case the translation would be "[Given] in the possession of . . . ," but in light of the parallels from other inscriptions that serve to label the pots they are written on as the property of an individual monk (see below, sec. 5.2), I have followed Konow's interpretation and taken *pratigraha* as a nominative in *-a*.[12]

Unfortunately, the second word of the inscription, which gives the name of the donee of the pot, is badly damaged, so that the reading is uncertain. If the proposed reading, Catula, is correct, this name is not one that occurs elsewhere in Kharoṣṭhī inscriptions or other relevant documents. The name of the donee's preceptor,[13] Saṃghapriya, however, is familiar, since it also occurs as that of the donor in potsherd inscriptions nos. 2 (partially reconstructed) and 4 (in the variant form *saghapriha-*). These three inscriptions could refer to the same person, but in view

11. The terms *pratigraha-* and *parigraha-* seem to be used more or less interchangeably in these formulae.

12. With regard to the translation of this word as "possession," note that Edgerton (1953: 321) gives "property" as a gloss for the synonymous (see n. 11) *parigraha,* citing Saddharmapuṇḍarīka 85.4 (*gṛhaṃ . . . puruṣasya ekasya parigrahaṃ bhavet*).

13. The term *sadhaṃvihari-* (= Skt. *sārdhaṃvihārin-*) designates a monk's (here Catula's) relationship to his *upādhyāya,* or preceptor (here Saṃghapriya). On the problems involved in the translation of this term, see the comments by Brough (1962: xx and 177).

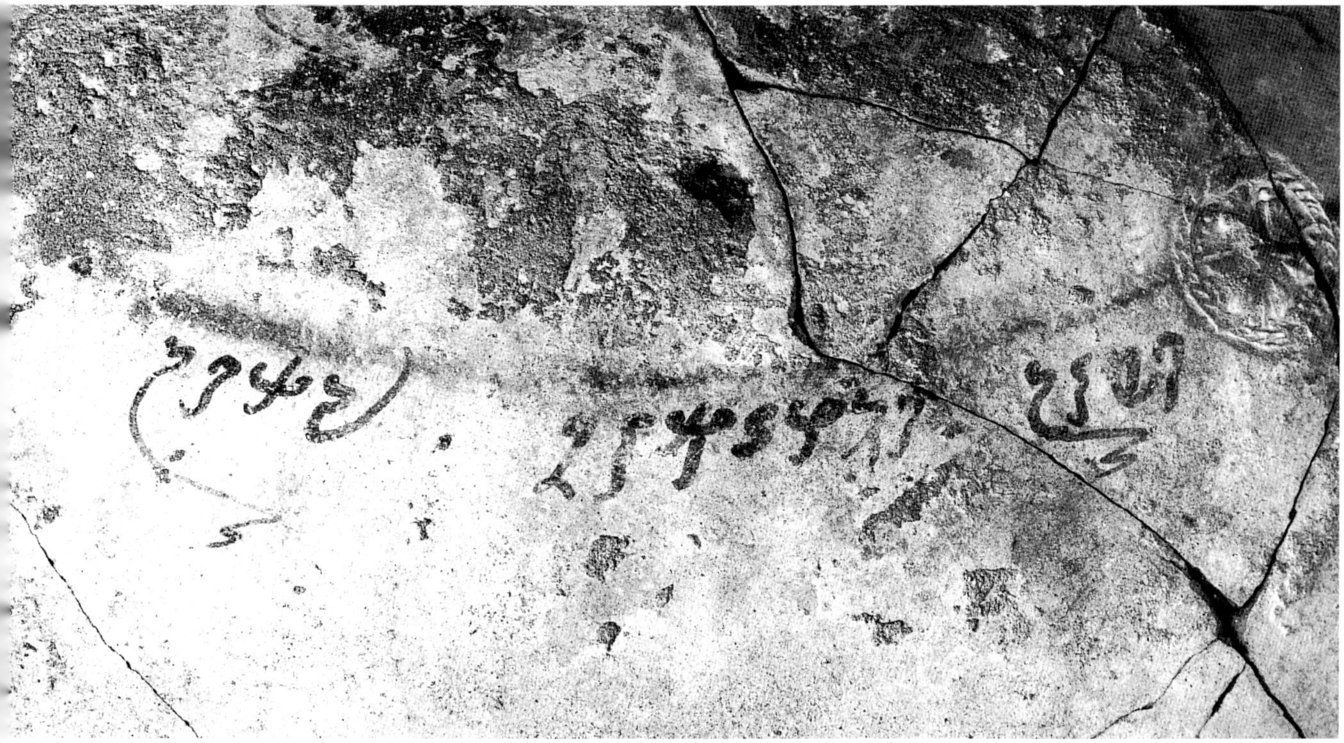

Fig. 17. Detail of inscription 2 on pot A

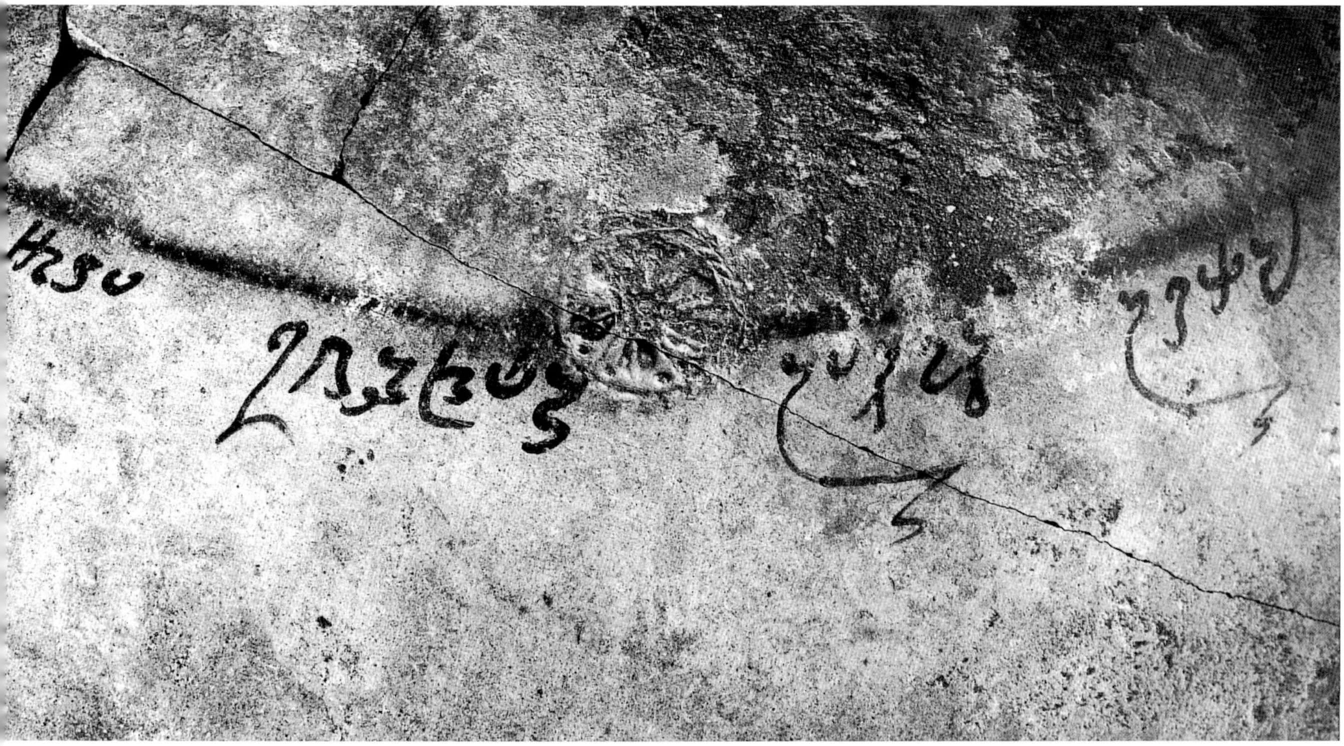

Fig. 18. Detail of inscription 2 on pot A

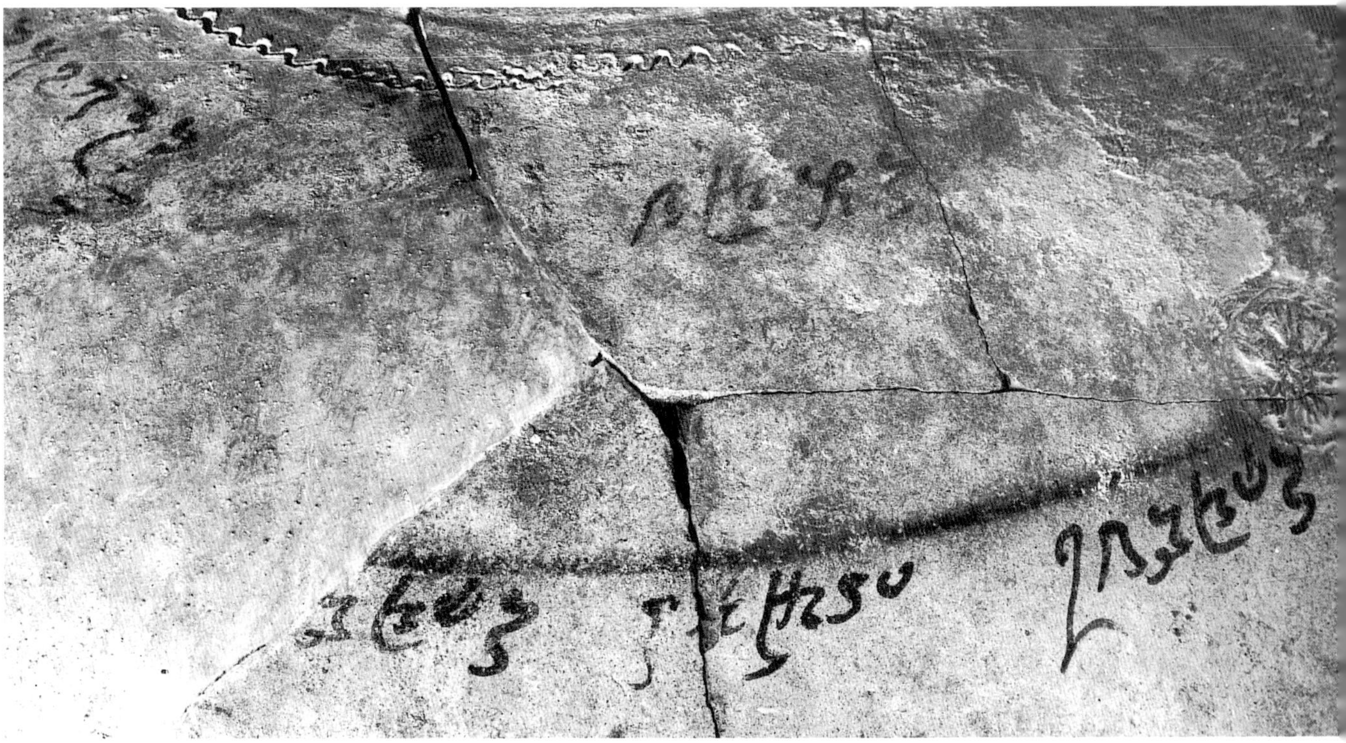

Fig. 19. Detail of inscriptions 1 and 2 on pot A

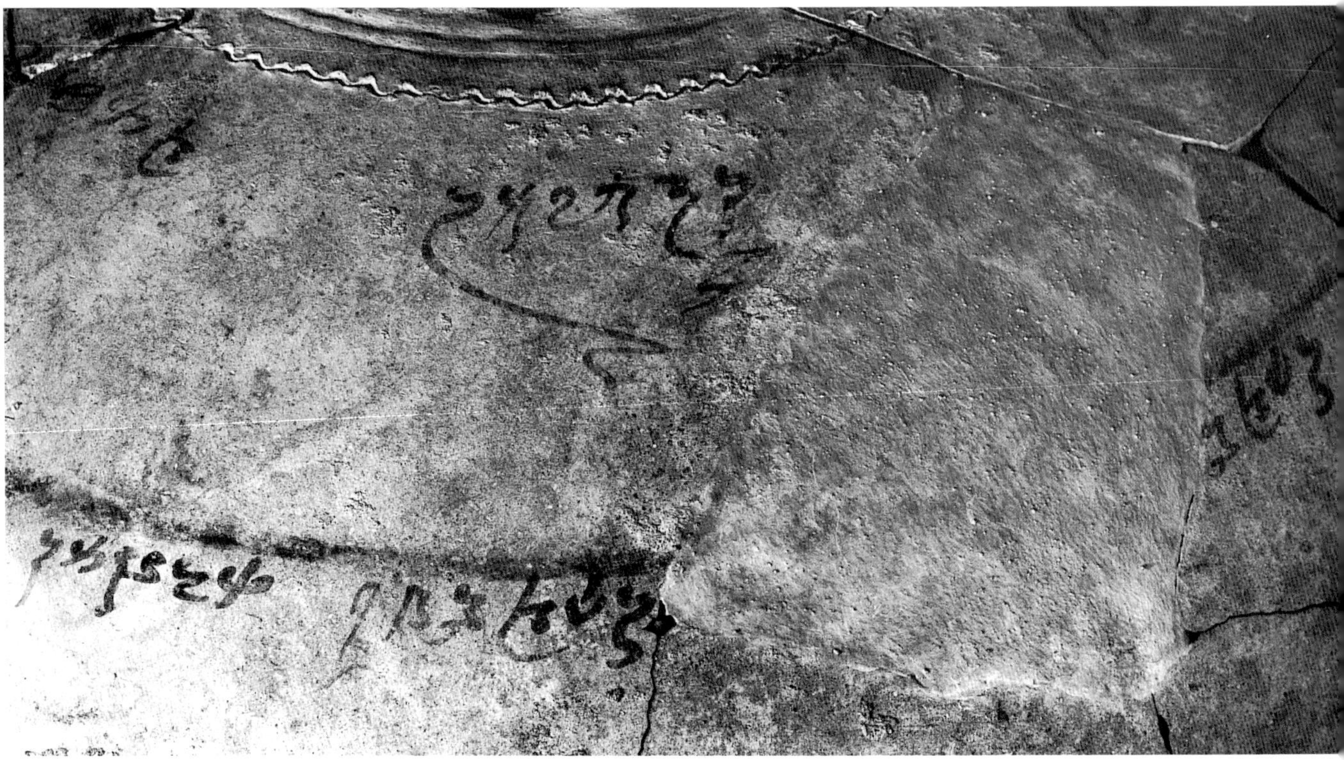

Fig. 20. Detail of inscriptions 1 and 2 on pot A

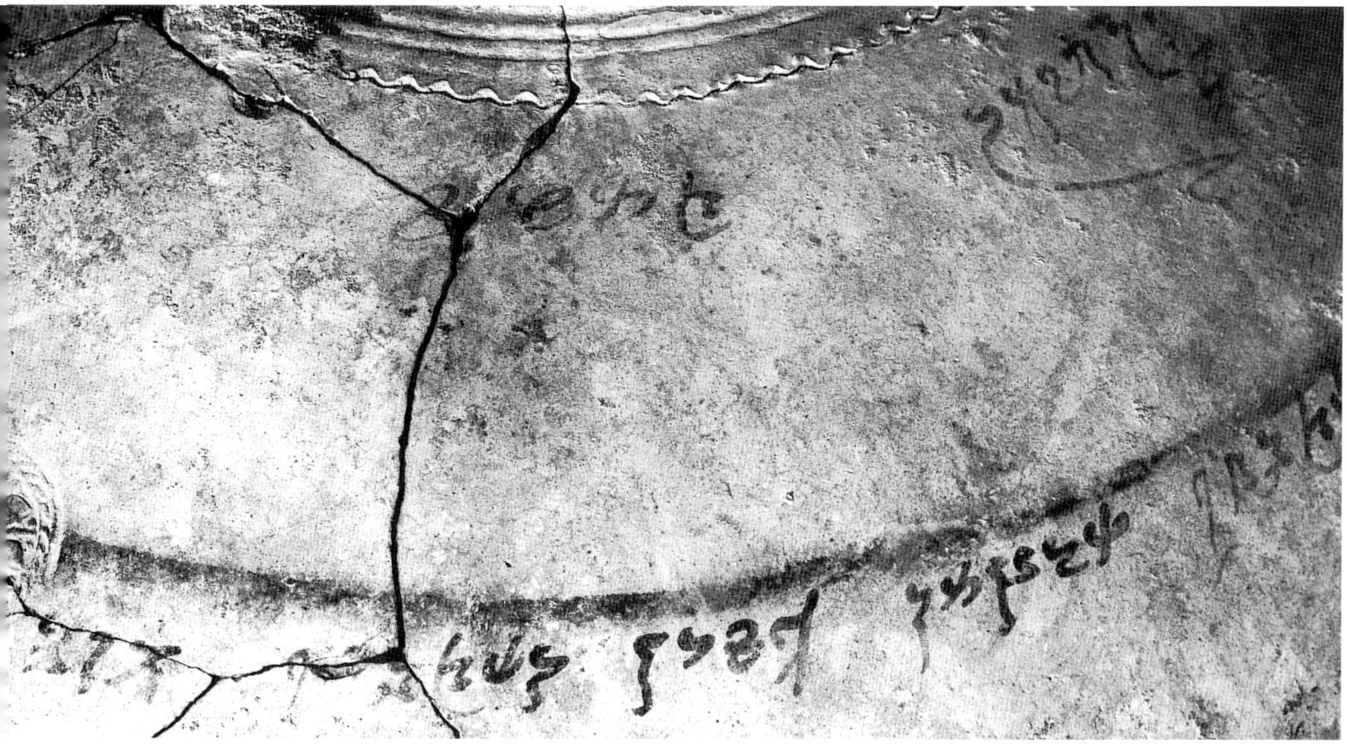

Fig. 21. Detail of inscriptions 1 and 2 on pot A

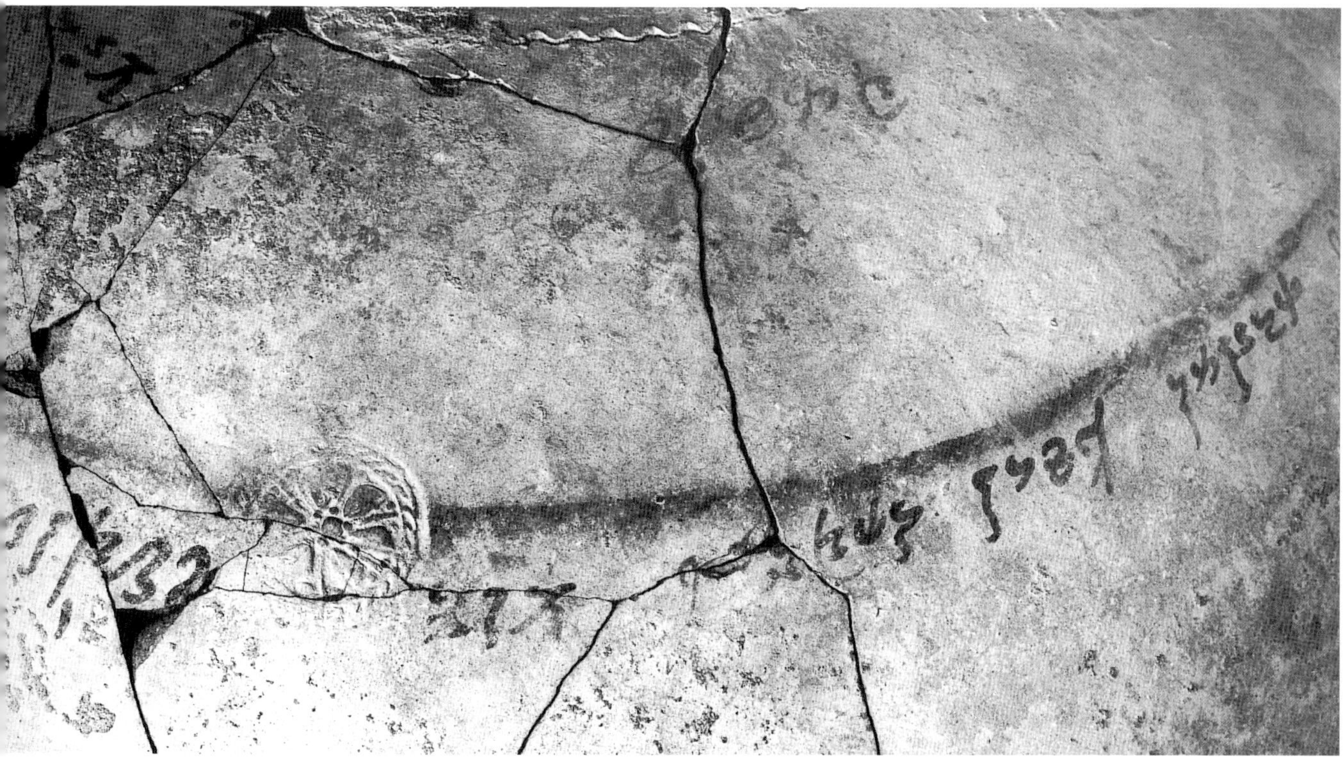

Fig. 22. Detail of inscriptions 1 and 2 on pot A

of the generic Buddhist character of the name Saṃghapriya and of the uncertainty as to whether the potsherds came from the same site as this pot, it is impossible to be sure of this.

Inscription 2 (pl. 23 and figs. 14–22) is written around the shoulder of the jar, about 11 cm below the neck. The maximum height of the letters is 3.5 cm (*rme*) and the minimum 0.5 (*ma, ta*), while the average height is about 0.8–1.2 cm. The total length of the inscription, which covers the whole circumference of the pot, is 128 cm. As in inscription 1, the words are arranged neatly around the circumference, with a space of 1.5–3.5 cm between words, and the text is placed so that the stamped decorations fall in the spaces between words. In two cases, however—*ayaṃ pānaya* and *ghaḍe deyaṃdharme*—short phrases are grouped together without spaces between their component words. In the phrase *mitrañatisa lohitana* [sic], the scribe has incorrectly divided the compound *mitra-ñati-salohitana* (= Skt. *mitra-jñāti-sālohitānām*), presumably because he mistook the *sa-* at the beginning of *salohitana* for a genitive singular ending on the preceding word.

> *[a]yaṃpānaya ghaḍedeyaṃdharme va[sa]vadatae susomabharyae atmanasa arogadakṣinae svamiasa suhasomasa saṃmepratyaśae madapi[t]rina saṃmepratya + + + + + + +*[14] *saṃmepratyaśae mitrañatisa lohitana saṃmepratya[śa]e bhava[tu]*

> This waterpot is the pious gift of Vasavadata [Vāsavadattā], wife of Susoma,[15] for the benefit of her own health. May it be for a proper share on the part of (her) husband Suhasoma, for a proper share on the part of (her) mother and father, for a proper share on the part of [all beings], for a proper share on the part of her friends, kinsmen, and blood relatives.

Paleographically, the two inscriptions on pot A are noteworthy for their calligraphic qualities. Several letters have elaborate decorative extensions, particularly the final *sa* of *sadhaṃviharisa* in no. 1 and of *atmanasa, svamiasa,* and *suhasomasa* in no. 2, in which the bottom of the letter is extended in a long curve to the right ending in a double hook below. It is clear that this is not intended to represent a Sanskritic spelling *sya* for the genitive ending, since in *saṃmepratyaśae* we have (four times) the normal form of the subscript *y,* with a loop leading into a curved line pointing to the left. The extension of the final *sa* is thus evidently a mere flourish without phonetic significance, such as is found occasionally added to certain letters in other Kharoṣṭhī texts, particularly in word-final position.

The *sa* of *vasavadatae* also has an anomalous bend at the bottom of the

14. A comparison with similar donative formulae in other inscriptions such as Tor Ḍherai (see n. 7) indicates that the missing letters here were probably *-śae sarvasatvaṇa* or the like.

15. On the identity of Vāsavadattā and Su(ha)soma, see section 7.2.2.2.

letter upward and to the right. This resembles the normal form for a subscript *r*, but since the context makes this reading unlikely, I prefer to dismiss it as another phonetically insignificant flourish.

Other decorative features include the treatment of the subscript preconsonantal *r* in *susomabharyae*, whose loop ends in a double-hook shape at the right.[16] The superscript preconsonantal *r* in *deyaṃdharme* is also treated calligraphically, with a radical extension of the straight vertical and curved horizontal portions at the top of this ligature. Such a treatment of *rma* has not been noted elsewhere in inscriptions, but a similar form with the extended vertical is occasionally seen in the KDhP manuscript, for instance, in line 57d. This, like the form of the subscript *r*, is evidently a pen-and-ink style of calligraphic ornamentation.

In the syllable *tu* in the second word of inscription 1 and at the very end of inscription 2, there is an extra horizontal stroke to the left above the diacritic *u* at the bottom of the character (). A similar treatment of diacritic *u* appears in the inscriptions on pot C (in *hetuvatiṇaṃ*) and potsherd 20 (*.u*).

In *pānaya-*, the long vowel is indicated by means of a short, slanting, almost vertical line near, but not touching, the foot of the consonant *p*. The diacritic notation of long vowels, usually *ā*, is very sporadic in Kharoṣṭhī inscriptions, but it also occurs in a variant form of the same word (*ayaṃ pāniya-kuṃḍika*) in one of the similar water jug inscriptions from Kara Tepe (Vertogradova 1995: 49 and fig. 2). Another fragment of the same inscription contains a second example of this diacritic in *mahādharmakathi[ka*-]*, confirming that it is in fact a long-vowel indicator.[17] The sporadic notation of long *ā* is also observed in some of the new manuscripts; see above, 6.3.

Pot B

Pot B (pls. 24–5 and fig. 23) is a globular, round-bottomed vessel, similar in overall form and material to pot A but slightly smaller (33.3 cm in height, 35.5 cm in diameter) and much better preserved. The neck is 3.5 cm high, with an everted lip at the top, whose outer diameter is 12.5 cm. The exterior has a buff slip, but a dark red slip is visible on the inside of the neck, and there are also a few red spots on the shoulder. The vessel is decorated with one pair of incised parallel lines at the base of the neck and another on the shoulder, just above the inscription. Additional decoration consists of three stamped designs of four-petaled lotuses inside a circle, spaced around the circumference just below the inscription.

The inscription (pl. 25 and figs. 23–7) is written on the shoulder of the jar, 4.5 cm below the bottom of the neck. Unlike the inscriptions on pots A and C,

16. Similar calligraphic elaborations of subscript *r* are seen among the manuscripts only in fragment 10. For a similar form in an inscription, see Fussman 1985c: 149.

17. *Contra* Fussman 1989: 474 n. 53; cf. Vertogradova 1995: 20.

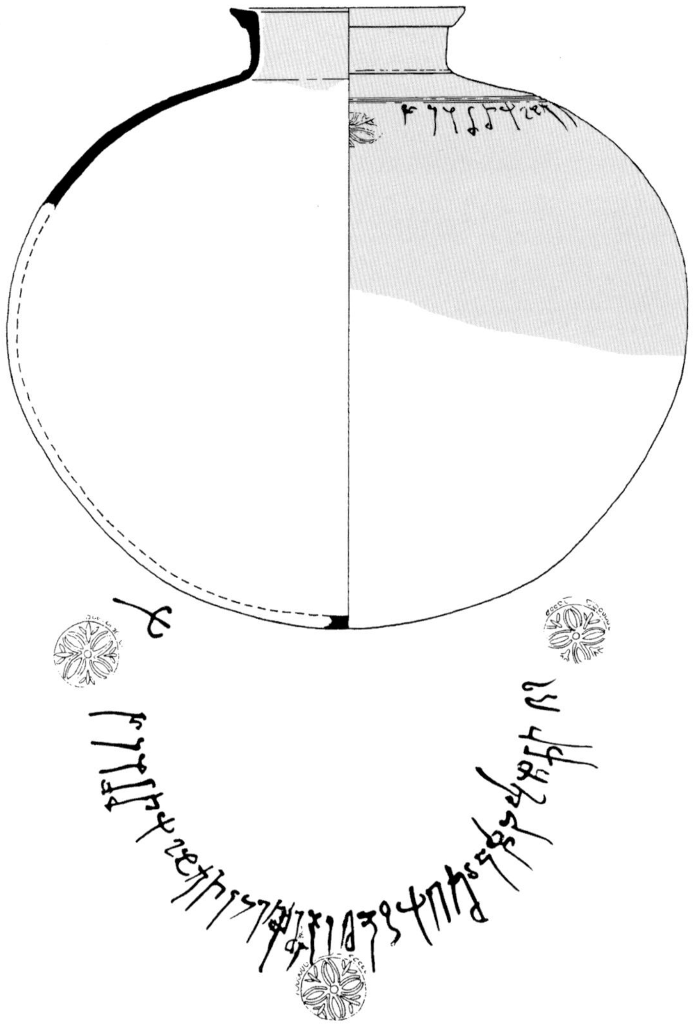

Fig. 23. Cross section of pot B, with inscription

it does not cover the full circumference of the vessel but ends about two-thirds of the way around, covering a total space of 44 cm. Between the last two syllables, the scribe has left a blank space 4 cm long to avoid writing over the upper edge of the stamped design. The letters are on average about 2.5 cm high, with a maximum of 4 cm (*ḍe, sti*) and a minimum of 1 cm (*ta, du*).

> *aya panighaḍe saghe cadurdiśami acaryana sarvastivatana parigrahami pu[r]nagarañami*[18]

> This waterpot [is a gift] to the universal community, in the possession of the Sarvāstivādin teachers in the Purnaga grove.

18. This inscription was read in part by Sadakata (1996b: 312, ins. a; 1996c: 22, ins. a) as "... *saghe cadurviśami* [Read *cadurdiśami*] *acaryana sarvastivatana parigrahami*. . . ."

Fig. 24. Detail of inscription on pot B

Fig. 25. Detail of inscription on pot B

Fig. 26. Detail of inscription on pot B

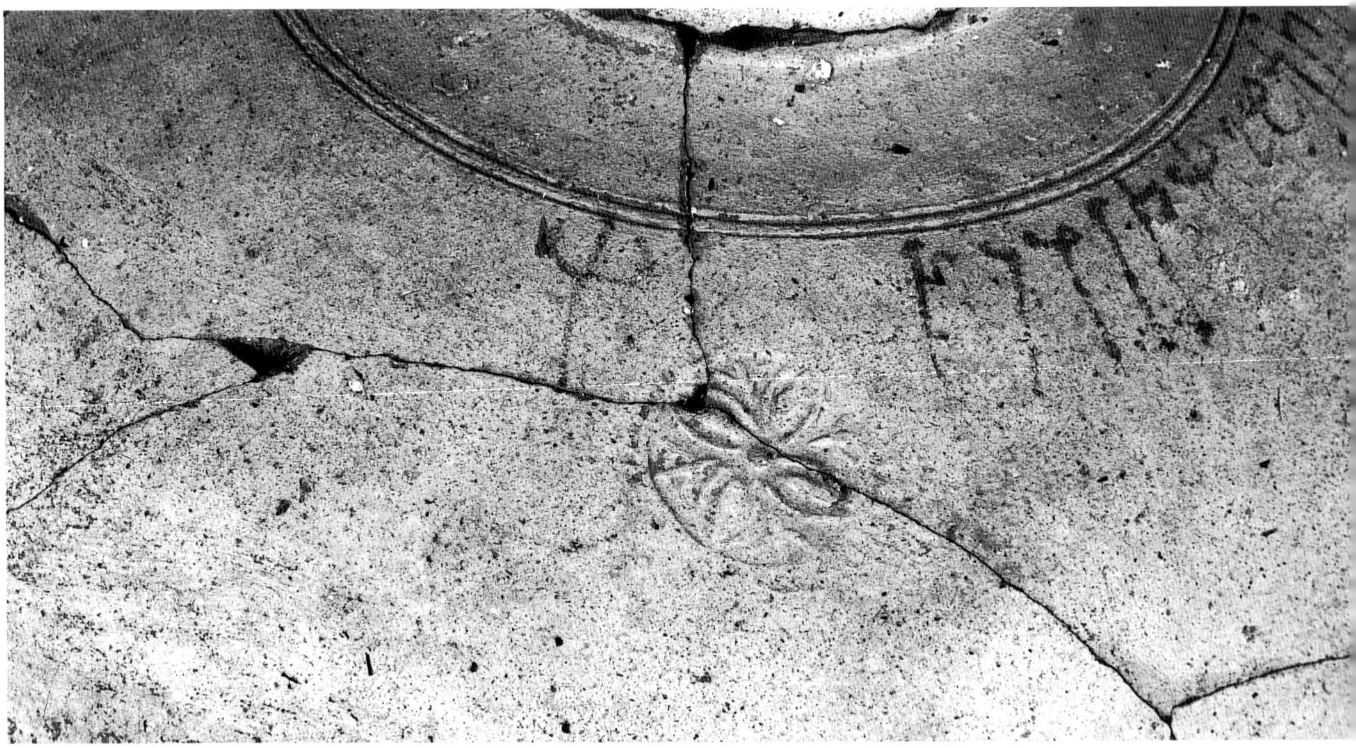

Fig. 27. Detail of inscription on pot B

The inscription follows the short form of the donative formula, which probably was used in some of the previously known fragmentary specimens but is attested here in full for the first time. On the omission of the donor's name (as also in pot D), see below, section 5.1.

Paleographically, this inscription is less noteworthy than those on pots A and C. The hand is upright and unadorned, without the cursive and calligraphic features of A and C. This would seem to be in keeping with the humbler, "generic" character of the inscription. There are no spaces between words and phrases.

The final word, *pu[r]nagarañami,* provides the name of the "grove" (Skt. *araṇya*), that is, the monastery, that was the residence of the Sarvāstivādin teachers who were the recipients of the donation. For similar uses of the term *(a)raña-* in this sense, see Konow 1929: nos. XLV and LXXX (line 1) and Konow 1935–6: 42;[19] Salomon 1995b: 138 and Salomon 1996b: 242; and below, section 5.2. *Pu[r]naga-* presumably corresponds to Sanskrit *pūrṇaka-*, which is not to my knowledge attested elsewhere in inscriptions as the name of a monastic establishment.

Pot C

Pot C (pls. 26–7 and fig. 28) is another globular, round-bottomed, wheel-made vessel of coarse red clay with gritty inclusions, with a buff slip on the exterior. It measures 38 cm in height and 37.2 cm in diameter. Its condition is good, except for some chipping of the lip of the spout and peeling of the lower surface. The neck, 6 cm high, has a thick everted lip 2 cm high with a diameter of 12.7 cm. It is decorated with two pairs of incised grooves around the lip, another pair at the middle of the neck, three more pairs just below the neck, and, below them, a single line of incised spiraling. On the shoulder, just above the level of the inscription, are four stamped designs consisting of five-petaled lotuses within a circle, spaced around the circumference.

The inscription (pl. 27 and figs. 28–35) is written on the shoulder, just below a faded line of red ink, about 10–11 cm from the bottom of the neck. The full length of the inscription was 95.5 cm, but a section of the pot has been lost which contained about 16 cm of the inscription, though the tops of three of the missing letters and the bottom of one are preserved. Probably about eleven akṣaras are lost in the missing portion. The letters are on average 1–2 cm high, with a maximum of 4.8[20] (*ṇa* in *acaryaṇaṃ*) and a minimum of 0.8 (*ta* in *viratatae*). Short spaces, 1–1.5 cm long, are left between words, though in two cases (*aya panighaḍa* and *saṃghe caturdiśe*) phrases are written together without a space between their component

19. The term here (line 1) is *ramaraṃñami,* "in the Rāma grove"; this is a correction of Konow's previous reading (1929: 158), *rajaraṃñaṃmi.*

20. The letter *rma* whose distinctive upper part is preserved above the missing part of the inscription must have originally been considerably larger than this.

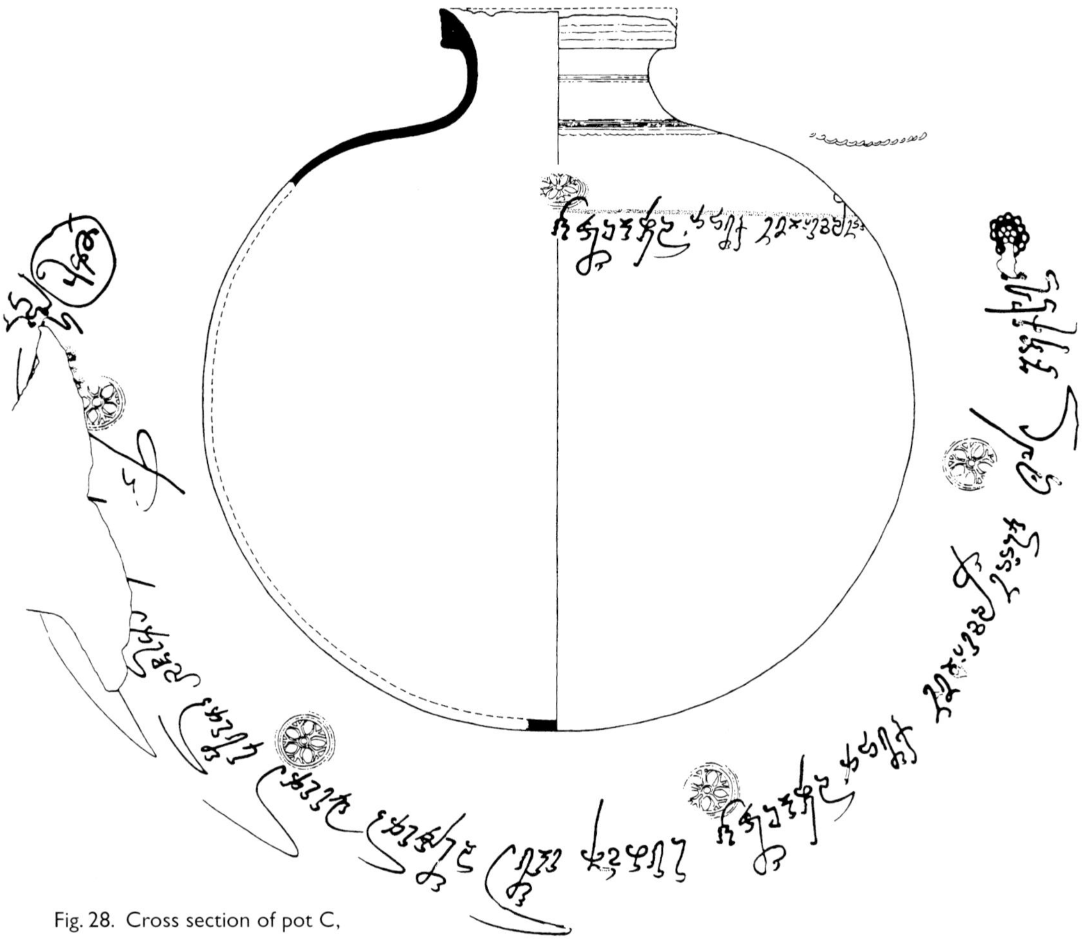

Fig. 28. Cross section of pot C, with inscription

Fig. 29. Detail of inscription on pot C

words. The inscription covers almost the entire circumference of the pot but for a space of 4 cm between the beginning and end, where the remains of a badly blurred inked design, apparently a floral motif, are visible.

> *[a]yapanighaḍa [da]ṇaṃmukh[o] viratatae*[21] *[srva]hiama-bharyae niryateti saṃghecaturdiśe rayagahami acaryaṇaṃ sarvastivatinaṃ k[r]iavatiṇaṃ viryavatinaṃ hetuvatiṇaṃ [.i]*[22] *+ + + + + + [rm.] + + [ṇaṃ]*[23]*[b..?] pra[ti]gra*
>
> This waterpot [is] the pious gift of Viratata, wife of Srvahiama; [she] presents [it] to the universal community at Rayagaha (Skt. Rājagṛha), in the possession of the Sarvāstivādin teachers, who teach actions, who teach energy, who teach causation . . . , (who teach karma), . . .

This inscription is distinguished by several unusual paleographic features. The characters are highly ornate, and many are furnished with elaborate calligraphic extensions. For example, the true anusvāra sign (as opposed to the "pseudo-anusvāra," discussed below) attached to *na* and *ṇa* is regularly extended into a large hook, open to the left and coming to a point with an acute angle at the right, as in *acaryaṇaṃ sarvastivatinaṃ k[r]iavatiṇaṃ viryavatinaṃ hetuvatiṇaṃ*[24] and in *[da]ṇaṃmukh[o]*.[25] Also regularly subject to calligraphic treatment is the subscript preconsonantal *r*, which, as in the inscription on pot A, has an extra decorative bend in the right side of the loop, clearly seen, for example, in *acaryaṇaṃ sarvastivatinaṃ*.

In several places, diacritic vowel signs are accorded anomalous treatments, presumably with calligraphic intent. For example, in *rayagahami* the *i* vowel

21. The second syllable in this word could also be read as *sa*, but *ra* is more likely. The fourth syllable superficially looks like *tra* or *dra* (fig. 30), but close examination shows that this is an illusion caused by the nearly complete fading of a portion of the horizontal line at the middle of the *ta*.

22. The top of what is probably the vowel diacritic *i* (or possibly *e*) that was attached to the first missing syllable in the lost portion of the inscription is preserved on the intact surface above the broken piece.

23. Only a very faint trace of the top of this letter and a part of the distinctive curve of the anusvāra below are preserved. Given the pattern of the preceding intact portion of the inscription (*k[r]iavatiṇaṃ viryavatinaṃ hetuvatiṇaṃ*), it seems likely that this last word too ended in *ṇaṃ* or *naṃ* (i.e., it was in the genitive plural). Since the distinctive top part of the ligature *rm* is also preserved a few letters before this, we can tentatively reconstruct the last missing word as *(ka*)[rm](avati*)[ṇaṃ]* (see p. 213).

24. Part of the last letter is lost with the damaged portion of the jar, but the top and the right side of the calligraphic extension below are preserved.

25. The spelling of this word with anusvāra is paralleled in *danaṃmuhe* in the Begram bas-relief inscription, where Konow (1933: 14) attributes it to "the well-known tendency to nasalize a vowel before a nasal."

Fig. 30. Detail of inscription on pot C

Fig. 31. Detail of inscription on pot C

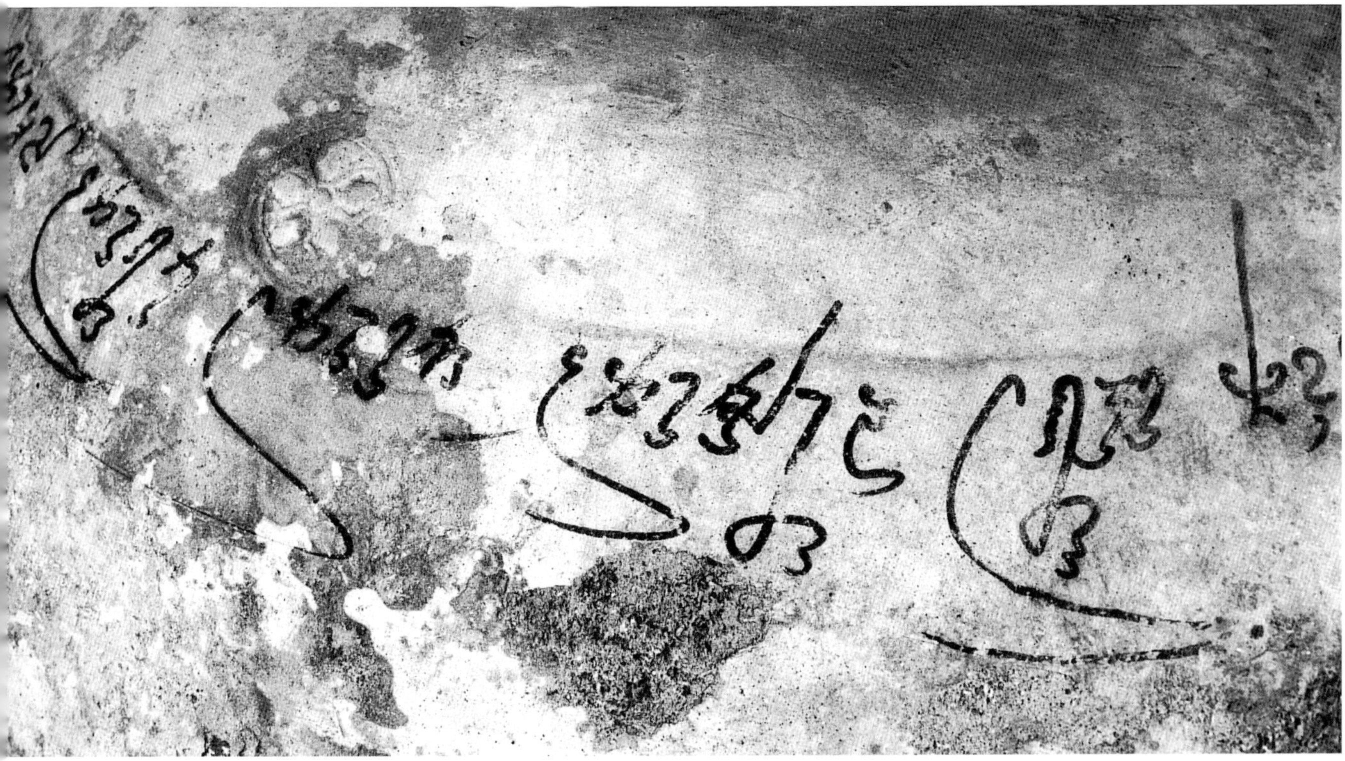

Fig. 32. Detail of inscription on pot C

Fig. 33. Detail of inscription on pot C

Fig. 34. Detail of inscription on pot C

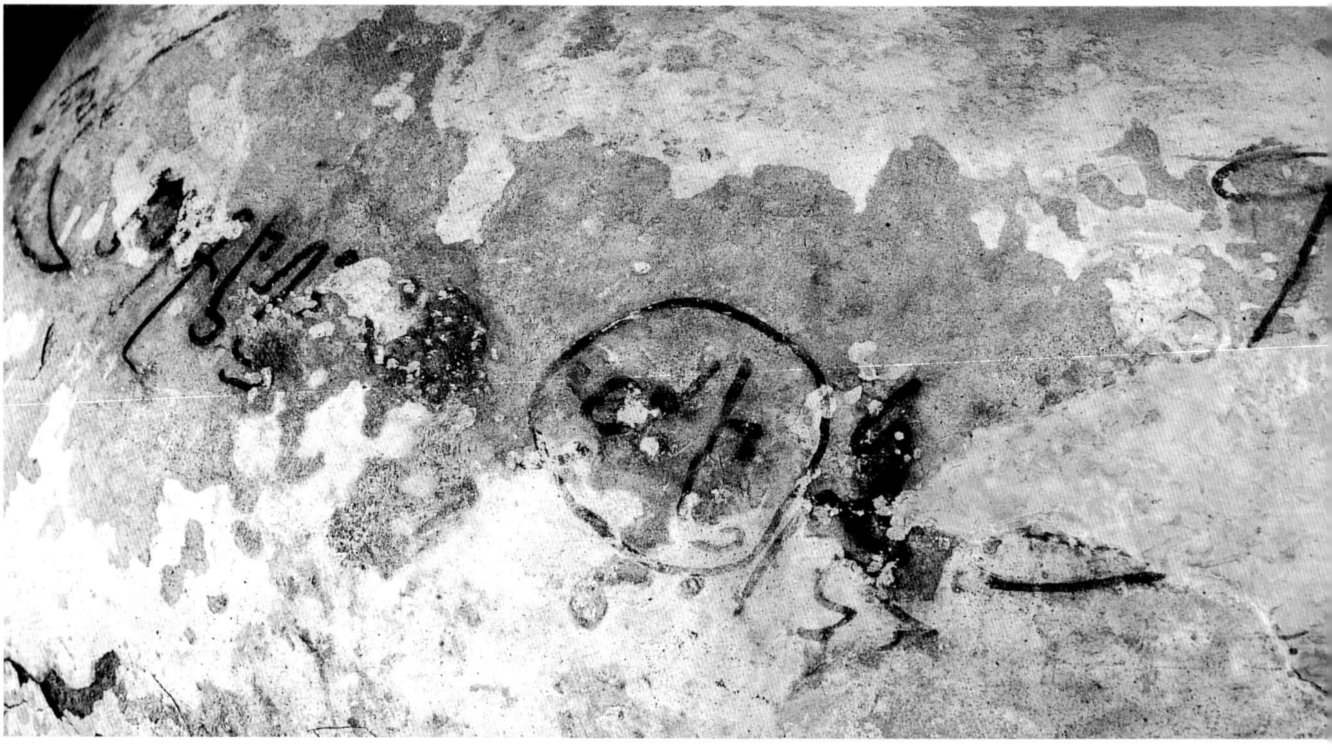

Fig. 35. Detail of inscription on pot C

diacritic of the final syllable is extended upward in a long straight line. Elsewhere, diacritic *i* is treated normally, and its special treatment here is probably attributable to the tendency of Kharoṣṭhī to apply extra calligraphic flourishes to the last syllable of a word. Another example of the calligraphic elaboration of diacritics is the *e* in the first syllable of *hetuvatiṇaṃ* (), whose right end is extended through a right-angle bend upward leading into a semicircular curve to the right and then downward.[26] The *u* diacritics in *caturdiśe* and *hetuvatiṇaṃ* have a triangular, rather than the usual round, form. Also unusual is the treatment of the ligature *rdi* () in *caturdiśe,* where the *i* diacritic, which diagonally crosses the upper left of the consonantal element *d,* is extended by an acute angle to the right, horizontally crossing the center of the *d,* then turning downward with a right-angle bend into a vertical line to which is attached the subscript (preconsonantal) *r* sign. This contrasts with the normal form of the ligature *rdi* (), commonly seen in inscriptions of this type in the same word, *caturdiśe,* where the loop representing preconsonantal *r* is attached normally to the bottom of the consonant *d* itself rather than linked to the vowel diacritic as here. This treatment, to my knowledge, is unique.

The form of the ligature *mu* in *[da]ṇaṃmukh[o]* is interesting; instead of the usual diagonal line with a curved hook attached at the lower left (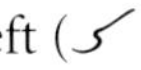), this akṣara consists of a long vertical line joined at a right angle at the bottom to a short leftward horizontal line which turns upward into a loop open to the left (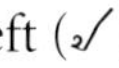). This variant, evidently a calligraphic elaboration, of the ligature *mu* occurs in a few other Kharoṣṭhī inscriptions, mostly late in date. It is used two or three times in the Kurram casket inscription, for example, in *śakyamunisa* at the end of line 1 ().[27] Konow (1929: 153) refers to this as "the peculiar *mu,*" without further comment. A similar variety of *mu,* which Konow here calls the "square, standing, form" (p. 93), appears in Jauliāṅ inscriptions nos. 2 (*danamukhe/o* [*sic*]; Konow 1929: pl. XVIII.2) and 12 (*śakamu(ṇi*)*; pl. XVIII.12). This ligature also occurs in a recently discovered Kharoṣṭhī jar inscription (Salomon 1996b: 241).

Besides these unusual but readily understandable formations, the inscription also contains a few anomalous characters that do present problems of interpretation. One of these is the initial akṣara () of the word tentatively read as *[srva]hiama-*, in which the bottom stroke of a normal *sa* is extended in a line curving upward and to the right (i.e., behind) the letter, ending far above it. This upward extension is provided with a loop, curving off from it to the left, then curving up and back across the stem and terminating in a downward, double-hooked flourish. This

26. The syllable *he* is usually formed with the vowel diacritic added to the top of the consonant, but occasionally it is attached, as here, to the right side of the middle. Such an example is seen, for instance, in *parigrahe* in the Haḍḍa jar inscription (Fussman 1969), though without the extra calligraphic extension noted here.

27. The other occurrences are in line 4 (D), *praticasaṃmupate,* and, apparently, in 3 (D), *saṃmudae,* though the reading is not clear here.

anomalous additional element is virtually identical to the one representing preconsonantal *r,* either in subscript position in normal combinations like *rya* and *rdi* or in superscript position in the incomplete *[rm.]* in the broken portion of the inscription. But we can hardly think of reading the syllable as *rsa,* first because of the phonetic implausibility of such a combination at the beginning of a word (even allowing for the fact that it is an unfamiliar and presumably non-Indic name), and second because, even if this were the intended reading, the scribe would have presumably used the normal (i.e., subscript) form of preconsonantal *r.* Disregarding this additional element, the line extending upward from the bottom of the *s* to its right looks more or less like the normal Kharoṣṭhī sign for a postconsonantal *v,* so that it seems as if the scribe were trying to represent some combination of the three consonants *s, v,* and *r.* His use of the preconsonantal form of *r* might imply that he was trying to represent something like *srva,* which I can only explain as an attempt to render some unfamiliar foreign (Saka or other Iranian?) phoneme, and for lack of a better explanation I have so rendered this very peculiar ligature.

Another, even more problematic ligature appears immediately after the damaged portion of the inscription. The upper part looks more or less like a normal *b,* below which there appear to be traces of several other lines, including, at the right, an element terminating in what looks like a small anusvāra sign, and to the left, a straight vertical. This whole area, however, is badly blurred and damaged, and I am unable to provide any plausible explanation for the peculiar letter. Moreover, this ligature seems to be out of context, as it follows a series of words in the genitive plural which, according to the standard pattern of such donative inscriptions, are governed by the word *pratigra* [*sic*] that follows the ligature under discussion. Therefore, one would have expected here another adjective in the genitive plural to follow the sequence *k[r]iavatiṇaṃ viryavatinaṃ hetuvatiṇaṃ,* etc., and it is possible that the scribe here tried in some way to squeeze in an abbreviated form of the last (probably the sixth) in this series of epithets describing the Sarvāstivādin teachers when he realized that he was running out of space on the circumference of the jar. We might guess, for example, that the intended reading was *b(oṣivatinaṃ*)* (= Skt. *bodhivādinām*) or the like.

The last word, *pra[ti]gra,* was obviously intended for the standard *pratigrahe* or *pratigrahami,* "in the possession (of)," but is peculiar in two respects. First, it is missing its last syllable, which one might be inclined to attribute once again to lack of space; but in fact there is enough room between the syllable *gra* and the floral design marking the beginning of the text for at least one more syllable. Second, the circle drawn around the word is unparalleled, to my knowledge, in Kharoṣṭhī inscriptions. One might speculate that this circle functions somewhat like a cartouche, intended to emphasize the word, but actually there does not seem to be any reason that a scribe would want to call attention to this ordinary word; if he were to stress anything in this way, it would presumably be the names of the donor and/or the recipients. Thus, the only thing that is clear is that the end of the inscription was somehow botched or disturbed, perhaps because of lack of space. Given the poor condition of this portion of the inscription and the loss of the part that immediately precedes it, it is not possible to completely explain the end of the text, though the intended sense is at least generally clear.

Another orthographic peculiarity of this inscription is the addition of small semicircular marks, open to the left, at the foot of many of the characters. This sign is virtually indistinguishable from the diacritic that, in standard forms of Kharoṣṭhī script, designates the anusvāra. This sign is seen, for instance, on each akṣara of the word transcribed above as *rayagahami,* but we cannot consider reading the word as *raṃyaṃgaṃhaṃmiṃ* or, for similar reasons, *aṃcaṃryaṇaṃ* instead of *acaryaṇam.* In other words, we are dealing with the phenomenon, well attested in Kharoṣṭhī, of the nonetymological "pseudo-anusvāra" (Fussman 1985a: 37, 1989: 474). In this inscription, there is in general a contrast between the smaller anusvāra-like signs that seem to represent the otiose pseudo-anusvāra and the larger diacritics which I take to be "true" anusvāra, especially since they appear in cases where a nasalization is etymologically expected (see n. 25).[28] I have therefore chosen to ignore the smaller, pseudo-anusvāra marks also in less etymologically clear contexts, such as in the phrase *viratatae [srva]hiama-bharyae,* which would otherwise have to be read as *viraṃtaṃtae [srva]hiaṃmaṃ-bharyae.* Although in his edition of the reliquary inscription of Traṣaka, Fussman (1985a) transliterated the pseudo-anusvāra by a superscript *ṃ* (e.g., *saṃva*^{m}*tsaraye* and *a*^{m}*pratiṭhavita-pruve*), this procedure seems inadvisable for the present inscription in view of its profligate use of this sign, which is applied, with only a few exceptions, to almost all of the characters that are not otherwise marked by a vowel or other diacritic sign. This circumstance makes it clear that pseudo-anusvāra is, in effect, nothing more than a semicalligraphic finishing flourish added by the scribe at the end of simple consonantal characters.[29]

Unlike many Kharoṣṭhī documents, this inscription retains separate signs for the retroflex and dental nasals, but their pattern of distribution, especially in the sequence *acaryaṇaṃ sarvastivatinaṃ k[r]iavatiṇaṃ viryavatinaṃ hetuvatiṇaṃ,* shows that they were interchangeable. Indeed, the regular alternation of *ṇa* and *na* in the endings of these five words suggests that the scribe was consciously playing with this alternative; similar examples of what seem to be whimsical scribal manipu-

28. This distinction, however, is not always absolutely clear. There are some cases where the hook sign under the letter is of a size somewhere between the large "true" anusvāra and the small "pseudo-anusvāra," and in such cases my transcription has been guided by etymology; thus, *saṃghe* but *hetuvatiṇaṃ* rather than *hetuvaṃtiṇaṃ.* Due to the inconsistent, even random placement of pseudo-anusvāra in this and other inscriptions, it is impossible to establish an absolutely consistent system of transcription for them.

29. See Fussman 1989: 474, where the pseudo-anusvāra phenomenon is discussed in terms of, on the one hand, a partial phonetic neutralization of nasalization in Gāndhārī and, on the other, a natural scribal tendency to add an anusvāra-like flourish to the bottom of the letter.

lations of the flexible Kharoṣṭhī orthography (see 6.7.2) were noted by Brough, who suspected that the scribe of the Dharmapada manuscript "took especial pleasure in using alternative possible spellings. . . . particularly when the two spellings can be balanced one against the other" (1962: 65).

Besides its several paleographic peculiarities, this inscription also exhibits some linguistic curiosities. The syntax of the phrase *[da]ṇaṃmukh[o] viratatae [srva]hiama-bharyae niryateti saṃghe caturdiśe,* "the pious gift of Viratata, wife of Srvahiama; [she] presents [it] to the universal community," is peculiar in its apparent mixing of the nominal construction commonly used in donation records of this type ("gift of . . . in the possession of . . . ") and the less common active construction ("gives . . . in the possession of . . . "). The active construction is more usual among Kharoṣṭhī inscriptions recording relic dedications, which are typically worded along the lines of " . . . establishes this relic . . . ," with the verb *pratiṭhaveti* or the like, whereas donative records in general and those on clay pots in particular are usually constructed without any verb at all, as in inscription 2 on pot A (*ayaṃ pānayaghaḍe deyaṃdharme vasavadatae*). The active verb *niryateti* is less usual in an inscription of this type, although various forms of the verb *ni*(*r*)*yat-* in the sense "give," "present," are common in other Kharoṣṭhī inscriptions and in Buddhist usage generally.[30] For example, British Library potsherd 5 reads (*pan**)*ighaḍe niryadide,* "(This water)pot was given." This and similar constructions with the past participle, such as *daṇamuhe ṇiyadide,* "pious gift was given," in the inscription on the Bimaran reliquary (Konow 1929: 52), suggest that the present active verb form *niryateti,* "presents," in the new inscription could have been written in error, the scribe having reversed the last two syllables of what should have been the passive participle *niryatite,* "was presented." With this emendation, the anomalous syntax of the inscription would become normal and would agree with that of the Bimaran inscription, though this is probably not sufficient grounds to emend the text, especially since such cases of mixed active/passive constructions are not uncommon in inscriptions generally (Salomon 1998: 97).

The series of honorific epithets, *k[r]iavatiṇaṃ viryavatinaṃ hetuvatiṇaṃ,* describing the Sarvāstivādin teachers is not, to my knowledge, paralleled elsewhere in Kharoṣṭhī inscriptions, where the recipients are usually characterized only by their sectarian affiliation and sometimes also their monastic location.[31] But similar sets of epithets do occur in various Pali texts, where they are applied to the Buddha(s) and other teachers, often in a polemic context. For example, in Aṅguttara-nikāya

30. See Edgerton 1953: 304, s.v. *niryātayati,* "[v]ery common in most texts."

31. There may be a partial parallel in the Mathurā lion capital inscriptions, where (lines N.1–3) a teacher is characterized, in Konow's translation (1929: 49), as "a khalula (dialectician?) to teach the foremost Mahāsāṃghikas the truth"; but the reading and interpretation of this passage are highly uncertain. Another possible parallel appears in the Shelārwāḍī cave inscription (Das Gupta 1949–50: 77), where the recipients are characterized (line 4) as *ācari[ye]hi bhata-vireyehi,* although the meaning of the latter word is, in the editor's estimation, "not clear" (p. 77 n. 5).

1.287, the Buddhas (*arahanto sammāsambuddhā*) are characterized as *kammavādā c'eva . . . kiriyavādā ca viriyavādā ca,* in contrast to the Ājīvika Makkhali who denied karma, action, and energy (1.286, *natthi kammaṃ, n'atthi kiriyaṃ, n'atthi viriyan ti*). In the inscription, the epithets *k[r]iavatiṇaṃ viryavatinaṃ* clearly correspond to Pali *kiriyavādā ca viriyavādā ca.* A parallel to the third epithet in the inscription, *hetuvatiṇaṃ,* "who teach causation," occurs in the Sanskrit Mahāparinirvāṇa-sūtra (40.57; Waldschmidt 1950–51: 384), where the *āgneya-jaṭila* ascetics are praised as *karmavādino . . . kriyāvādino hetuvādino vīryavādinaḥ.* This also suggests (see n. 23) that we should reconstruct the fifth epithet in the inscription as *karmavatiṇaṃ,* "who teach karma," though it could also be *dharmavatiṇaṃ,* "who teach the dharma." The latter possibility brings to mind similar sets of epithets of the Buddha such as *dhammavādī vinayavādī* in Dīgha-nikāya 1.4 and 3.135. This pair of epithets in turn suggests that the fourth epithet in the inscription, of which only the top of the diacritic vowel sign, probably *i,* of the first syllable remains, might have been *vinayavatinaṃ,* "who teach the discipline."

Thus, the inscription almost certainly lists five epithets, probably to be reconstructed as *k[r]iavatiṇaṃ viryavatinaṃ hetuvatiṇaṃ (v*)i(nayavatinaṃ ka*)[rm](avati*)[ṇaṃ],* and possibly also an abbreviated sixth epithet as well (perhaps indicated by the problematic character *[b..],* as discussed above) that were applied to the Sarvāstivādin teachers to whom the jar was presented. In the Pali texts, these epithets are generally applied to the Buddha(s), usually with a view to expressing the superiority of their doctrines to those of the other, heterodox teachers, so it is not too surprising to find them applied to the Sarvāstivādin teachers, though this has not been seen before in inscriptions. Perhaps the application of such epithets ending in *-vatinaṃ* (= Skt. *-vādinām*) was promoted by their similarity in formation to the sect name *sarvastivatinaṃ* (Skt. *sarvāstivādinām*).

Finally, the term *rayagahami* (= Skt. *rājagṛhe,* literally "at the king's palace"), given as the location of the Sarvāstivādin teachers who were the recipients of the pot, calls to mind various monastic institutions given names like *rājakārāma* and *rājavihāra* in honor of their royal founders, which are well attested in Buddhist tradition.[32] But the second element *gaha-* (= Skt. *gṛha-*) is unusual, such establishments being normally called *vihāra, ārāma,* or *araṇya.* Therefore, it is more likely that *rayagaha-* referred to a place of that name, presumably named after the original Rājagṛha in Magadha, renowned in Buddhist tradition.[33] It is much less likely that the name *rayagaha-* refers to a Buddhist establishment at or adjoining a royal palace, in view of the warnings in the vinayas (e.g., in the Pali vinaya, IV.159–60) of the dangers that monks are liable to upon entering a royal court (*rājantepurappavesane*).

32. See Vertogradova 1982: 153 for examples. But the apparently similar term *rajaraṃñaṃmi* read by Konow (1929: 158) on the Haḍḍa jar proved to be a misreading; see n. 19.

33. Note that Hsüan-tsang reports that Balkh was commonly referred to as "little Rājagṛha" (Beal 1884: 44 and n. 149).

Pot D

This pot (pls. 28–9 and fig. 36), which was evidently the one that contained the scrolls, is generally similar in form and material to the others but is somewhat smaller, with a height of 34.8 cm and diameter of 31.1 cm. The exterior surface and the interior of the neck have a buff slip. The neck, 5 cm high with a diameter of 12.8 cm, has a thick everted lip, 1.9 cm in height. Decoration is limited to two pairs of parallel incised lines just below the bottom of the neck, and below them, a roughly incised row of wedges.

The inscription (pl. 29 and figs. 36–9), written on the shoulder about 3.5 cm below the bottom of the neck, runs roughly two-thirds of the way around the vessel, covering a space of 34.5 cm. There are no spaces between words. The letters are between 2.2 and 2.7 cm high on average, with a maximum height of 4.0 (*mi*) and a minimum of 1.6 (*di*).

saghami caüdiśami dhamaüteaṇa [p]arig[r]ahami[34]

[Given] to the universal community, in the possession of the Dharmaguptakas.

The inscription is written in a plain, unadorned hand, lacking any of the decorative flourishes like those seen on pots A and C. In this respect, it resembles pot B, with which it also shares the peculiarity of omitting the name of the donor. The text embodies the briefest possible form of the standard donative formula, omitting not only the donor's name, as in B, but also the label "This waterpot" (*aya panighaḍe*), the word "teachers" (*acaryaṇa*), and the location of the recipients, all of which are included in the less drastically abridged wording on pot B.[35]

The identification of the recipients of the gift, the *dhamaüteaṇa,* with the Dharmaguptaka sect presents no problem. The same word in line 2 of the Jamālgaṛhī stone inscription was initially read wrongly by Konow (1929: 113) as *dhamaüte [oke]* and translated "an asylum connected with religion." But as shown by Lüders (1940: 17–20) and endorsed by Brough (1962: 44 n. 3), the correct reading is *dhamaüte[a](na*) parigrahe,* "in the possession of the Dharmaguptakas." Thus, the name of the sect is spelled in the Jamālgaṛhī inscription exactly (except for the inconsequential difference of dental versus retroflex nasal) as in the new inscription. This shows that Lüders's suspicion that in the Jamālgaṛhī inscription "it is much more likely that the vowel sign is an *-i* stroke that was not properly extended downwards and that *Dhamaütiana* is what was intended" (p. 19) is not justified, and that the reading is correct as it stands. His alternative suggestion, that the word be read

34. Sadakata (1996b: 312, ins. b; 1996c: 22, ins. b) read this inscription as *saghami caudiśami dhamauteana parigahami.*

35. See the further comments on these points below in section 5.1.

Fig. 36. Cross section of pot D, with inscription

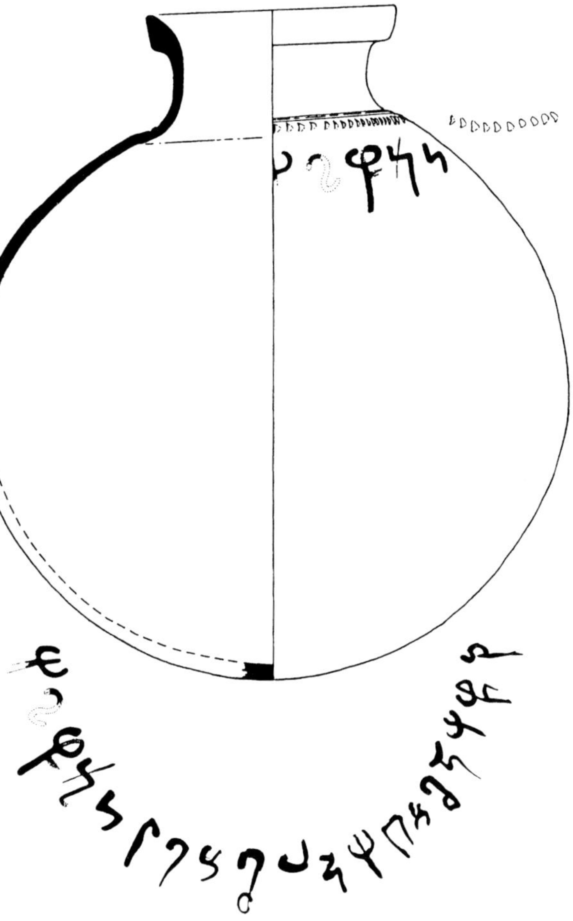

Fig. 37. Detail of inscription on pot D

Fig. 38. Detail of inscription on pot D

Fig. 39. Detail of inscription on pot D

as it is and taken to correspond to a Sanskrit **Dharmagupteyānāṃ,* is preferable, unless we want to posit an underlying **Dharmaguptikānāṃ* on the grounds of the Gāndhārī tendency toward alternation of *i* and *e* (Brough 1962: 80). In any case, this variant spelling is further confirmed by British Library potsherd 17, presented below.

Pot E

Pot E (pls. 30–1 and fig. 40) resembles the others in the group in material and form, particularly pot B with its squat profile and lip with a pronounced diagonal profile (although the lip of pot E slopes inward toward the top, and that of B slopes outward). The pot measures 35.5 cm in height and 37.0 cm in diameter, and the neck is 4.5 cm high with a maximum diameter (at the lip) of 13.0 cm. The everted lip is 1.5 cm high. The vessel is decorated with a pair of incised lines around the neck and, at the bottom of the neck, a single line, another pair of lines below that, and finally a scalloped line.

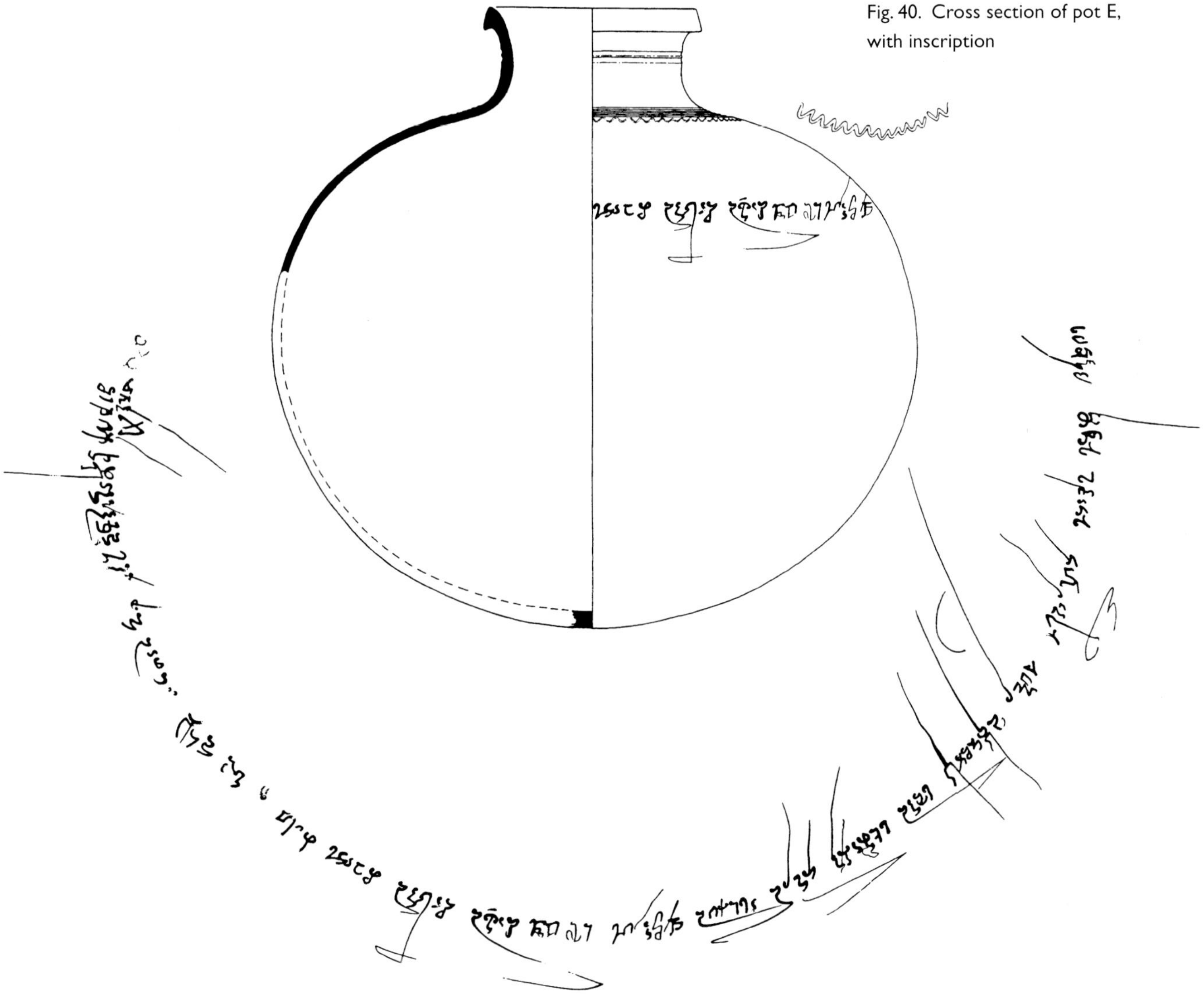

Fig. 40. Cross section of pot E, with inscription

The inscription (pl. 31 and figs. 40–8), written on the shoulder 12 cm below the bottom of the neck, runs almost completely around the pot except for a blank space of 3.5 cm between its beginning and end. Its length is 102 cm, and the average height of the characters is 0.8–1.2 cm, with a minimum of 0.5 (*da*). The largest letters are *rśa,* 4.5 cm high, and the calligraphically lengthened *śe* and *rma,* which are 13 and 16 cm long, measured diagonally. As in pots A and C, small spaces, 1.0–1.5 cm long, are left between words or phrases, but the phrase *saghecatudiśe* is grouped together as in pot C, and *ayapa[ni]ya ghaḍae* is incorrectly divided, as in pot A (ins. 2). The inscription is less well preserved than those on the other four pots, and in several places, especially in the latter part, the letters are so worn as to be difficult or impossible to read. Unlike the other inscriptions, this one is very carelessly written, with numerous misspellings and other apparent errors, which combine with its worn condition to make its interpretation difficult. Only with the aid of comparisons to similar formulaic inscriptions, and with some hypothetical suggestions for emendations of botched words, can any sense be made of it.

> *ayapa[ni]ya ghaḍae hastadatae teyavarmabharyae deyadharma saghecatudiśe atmanasa arogadakṣine tevarmasa aramiyasa bhikhuniyae ra[kṣva]?[ṇi]e sudaṣasa sudarśanasa gu[ha]datae ga?[śa]? [pri]? ? saṃ?[sa] ?taga[na]sa sakṣe ? ? [va]e sastaṣatvana da[gha]pacheya bhavatu yine bhra[do puya]*[36]

> This waterpot is the pious gift of Hastadata [Hastadattā], wife of Teyavarman, to the universal community, for the benefit of her own health. May it be for the principal share (?) of the monastery attendant (?) Tevarman, of the nun ?, of Sudaṣṇa, of Sudarśana, of Guhadata (Guhadattā), of ?, of ?, of ?, of ?; in short (?), of all beings (?); and in honor of [her] brother.

The hand of the inscription resembles that of pot A, with a similar tendency to place ornamental flourishes at the bottoms of the letters, especially at the ends of words. Many letters have the nonetymological pseudo-anusvāra (e.g., *hasta(ṃ)datae*), which is here ignored in the transcription for the reasons explained above in connection with pot C. Diagonal lines at the tops of letters, such as diacritic *e* or the stem of the ligature *rma,* are calligraphically extended far above the line. Many letters have peculiar and anomalous forms, which are not easy to interpret without contextual clues. For instance, the *ni* in *pa[ni]ya* is curiously malformed, with a shape somewhat like a *śe,* and but for the context it would have been impossible to read it correctly. The *gh* in *saghe* has, instead of the usual hook to the right of the vertical stem, a peculiar shape, somewhat resembling a *śa,* below the normally

36. The last six syllables are written above the main line of the inscription, beginning above the *ya* in *-pacheya.*

formed top of the letter; but here again the word is formulaic, so the reading is beyond doubt. In the syllable *ni* in *bhikhuniyae,* the diacritic vowel *i,* instead of touching the consonant, is placed above and to the left of it. The reading of the second syllable of the proper name *guhadatae* is little more than a guess based on context, since the form of the akṣara is unlike any in normal Kharoṣṭhī, though it somewhat resembles a badly malformed *ha.* All in all, one gets the impression that the scribe who wrote this inscription was careless, poorly trained, or both—a situation unfortunately none too rare in Kharoṣṭhī inscriptions.

In its contents and formulation too, this inscription resembles the one on pot A, though the two differ in details. Both begin with the phrase "This water-pot" (also used in pot C), and both include lists of sharers in the merits of the donation, beginning with the donor herself and her husband. In A, however, the other cobeneficiaries are mentioned only in general relational terms ("mother and father . . . friends, kinsmen, and blood relatives"), whereas inscription E provides the names of specific individuals, but in most cases without designation of their familial or other relationship with the donor.

In view of the many problems in the reading and interpretation of this inscription, a detailed phrase-by-phrase discussion is necessary. The opening phrase, *ayapa[ni]ya ghaḍae,* is normal except for the peculiar inflection of the final word. This may reflect an extended stem form (cf. Skt. *ghaṭikā-*), or it may result from contamination with the following word, *hastadatae,* in the genitive feminine. The formation of this donor's name, corresponding to Sanskrit Hastadattā, reminds us of that of the donor of pot A, Vāsavadattā. This, together with the other broad similarities between pots A and E, suggests that these two women might have been related to each other or at least may have come from the same region or cultural milieu. The names Hastadattā and Vāsavadattā were presumably nakṣtra-names,[37] which, according to Hilka (1910: 34), were particularly common among Buddhists; compare, for example, *muladataye* (= Skt. *mūladattayā*), attested in a Sanchi inscription (Hilka 1910: 37; Bühler 1894: 373, no. 153).

The following phrases, *teyavarmabharyae deyadharma saghecatudiśe atmanasa arogadakṣine,* follow the usual pattern and present no problems. This is the end of the first sentence of the text. The remainder of the inscription consists mainly of a long series of names and titles in the genitive case, all governed by the problematic *da[gha]pacheya* (to be discussed below) near the end. The name of the first of these beneficiaries of the donation is given as *tevarmasa aramiyasa.* This must be the donor Hastadattā's husband, who was previously introduced as *teyavarma.* The contracted form of his name is reminiscent of the two different spellings of the name of the donor's husband in the inscription on pot A, *susoma-*

37. Pāṇini (Aṣṭādhyāyī 4.3.34) gives Hasta among the personal names that can be derived from a birth-star.

Fig. 41. Detail of inscription on pot E

Fig. 42. Detail of inscription on pot E

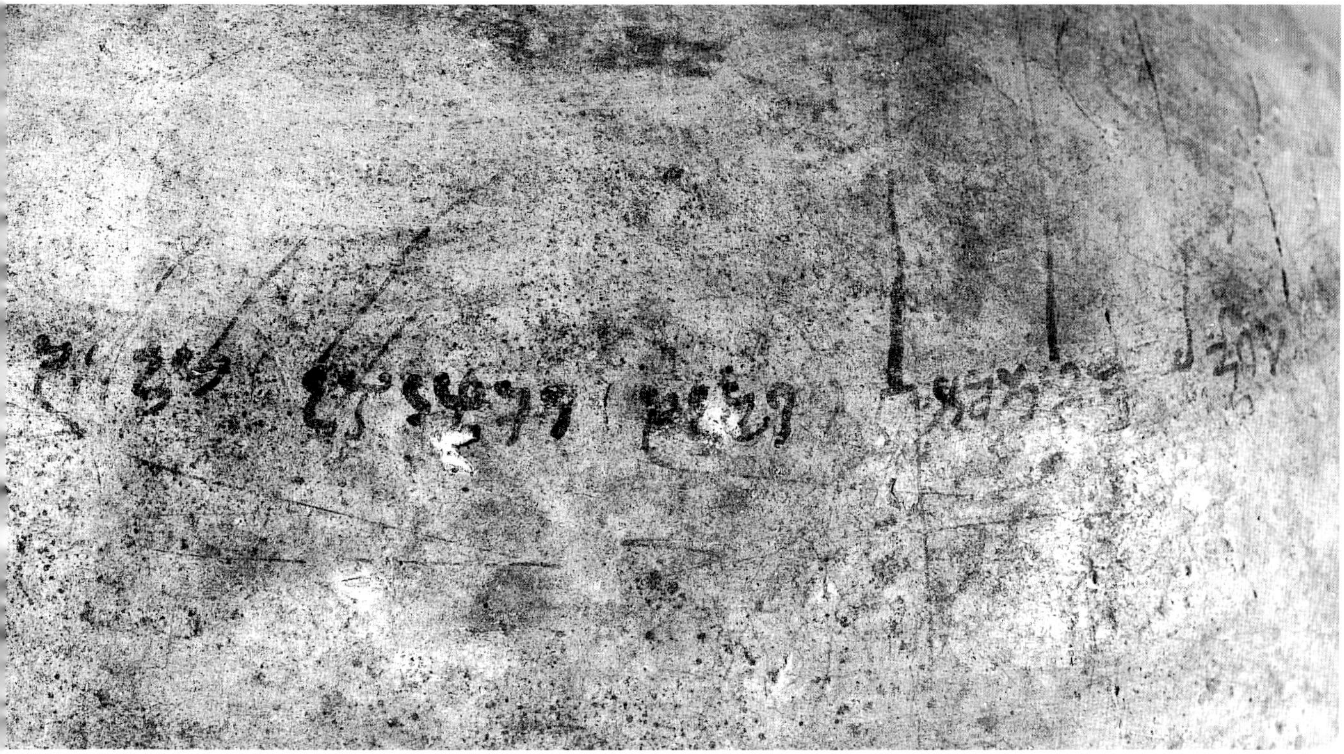

Fig. 43. Detail of inscription on pot E

Fig. 44. Detail of inscription on pot E

Fig. 45. Detail of inscription on pot E

Fig. 46. Detail of inscription on pot E

Fig. 47. Detail of inscription on pot E

Fig. 48. Detail of inscription on pot E

and *suhasoma-*. The name Te(ya)varma- is unfamiliar and is perhaps, like many Indo-Scythian names, a non-Indic name in semi-Indian guise. Also problematic is his title or epithet *aramiyasa*. This might seem to correspond to the Sanskrit/Pali *ārāmika*, "monastery attendant," but according to the usual formula we expect the word *svamiasa*, "husband" (cf. pot A, ins. 2, *atmanasa arogadakṣiṇae svamiasa suhasomasa*), and I strongly suspect that this was the intended reading. The incompetent scribe of this inscription might well have misinterpreted the ligature *sva* (𐨯𐨿𐨬) in an archetype that he was copying from as two separate syllables, *ara* (𐨀𐨪).

The rest of the list of beneficiaries is largely illegible, though we can make some reasonable guesses as to their identities. The first is a nun (*bhikhuniyae*) whose name is uncertain, but which appears to begin with *rakṣa-*. There follows a pair of masculine names, *sudaṣ̄asa*[38] and *sudarśanasa*, which, to judge from their similarity, might have been the names of brothers, presumably the brothers of the donor. The next name is the feminine *gu[ha]datae*, perhaps that of the donor's sister. This is followed by four more names, apparently masculine, which are mostly illegible and of which nothing can be made.

The phrase *sakṣe ? ? [va]e sastaṣatvana* means nothing as it stands, but the intended reading was probably something like *saṃkṣepe sarvasatvana*, "in short, of all beings." The restoration of the second word, at least, is quite secure (see n. 14); the scribe evidently misread the ligature *rva* (𐨪𐨿𐨬) in his archetype as *sta* (𐨯𐨿𐨟).

The next word, which seems to be *da[gha]pacheya*, is hopeless as it stands, and I can only guess at some sort of connection with the word *pratyaṃśa*, "share (of merit)," or similar terms that commonly occur in such contexts; compare, for example, *saṃmepratyaśae* (= Skt. *saṃyak-pratyaṃśāya*) in pot A (ins. 2) and phrases like *agre pratiyaṃśo* in the Tor Ḍherai potsherds (Konow 1929: 176) or *agri pracaya* in the first Haḍḍa jar inscription (Konow 1935–6: 42). *Da[gha]* could conceivably be a miswriting for the contextually anticipated *agra-*, and *pacheya* perhaps a garbled attempt at rendering something like the *pracaya* of the Haḍḍa inscription. Thus, for lack of anything better, I have provisionally translated the phrase *da[gha]pacheya bhavatu* as "May it be for the principal share of. . . ."

Finally, at the end of the inscription, the additional phrase *yine bhra[do puya]* is written in above the line (see n. 36), apparently as an insertion of a passage that was inadvertently omitted, or perhaps rather added on as an afterthought. The sense of the first word (?) *yine* eludes me entirely, but the remaining *bhra[do puya]* evidently means that the donor's brother is to partake of the merit of the gift; compare many other Kharoṣṭhī inscriptions where the names of the sharers of the merit are linked to the words *puyae*, "in honor of," or *puyaïta*, "is honored."

38. The name *sudaṣ̄a* (i.e., *sudaṣṇa*) also occurs in one of the new manuscripts (frag. 16, r, line 23), evidently as an alternative name of the legendary figure who is known in Pali as Vessantara; see section 2.2.4.

4. The Inscribed Potsherds in the British Library Collection

Besides the five complete pots, the British Library collection also contains twenty-six potsherds (pls. 32–4) with fragmentary inscriptions in Kharoṣṭhī and, in one case (no. 9), in Brāhmī. The provenance of the potsherds and their relationship, if any, with the complete pots are unknown, but they evidently belong to the same general class of artifacts and could well have come from the same site as the complete pots or from a neighboring one. Unfortunately, there is no way to confirm this.

All the pieces are fragments of red clay ware with buff slip. The dimensions of the potsherds are given in centimeters, indicating the maximum width and height, followed by the thickness. The height of the letters is given as a range where there is considerable variation in size, otherwise as a single average figure.

Potsherd 1 (pl. 32)

Dimensions:	13.5 × 7.8; 0.5–0.8
Decoration:	Four parallel incised lines and below them, a scalloped line above the inscription.
Height of letters:	1.5–2.5
Reading:	*/// mi kepeami taṣahoḍi[p.][g.][.e] ///*
Translation:	?

The text is unusual and problematic, not following the typical patterns of texts of this kind, so no translation can be offered. The first part seems to contain a phrase, presumably a toponym, in the locative case. The sense of the second half eludes me entirely, and the reading is not quite clear; the syllable read as *ta* could also be a *sa,* and the following one, read as *ṣa,* could be *na.* The syllables *hoḍi-* call to mind the (apparent) proper name *hoḍreaṇa* in a Taxila inscription (Dharmarājikā no. 2; Konow 1929: 90–1). At the left edge, there are small traces of the tops of two or three more characters, which can only be tentatively read.

Potsherd 2 (pl. 32)

Dimensions:	14.9 × 10.7; 0.4–0.7
Decoration:	None
Height of letters:	2.3–5.0
Reading:	*teryadharma saṃghap(r.*)i[y.] ///*
Translation:	Pious gift [of] Saṃghapriya.

The text is written in a thick, cursive hand. The phrasing and the small blank space at the right indicate that this is the beginning of the inscription. The first word, *teryadharma,* seems to be a hyper-Sanskritized variant of the usual *deyadharma,* "pious gift." The second word can be confidently restored as *saṃghap(r*)iy(asa*).* The *gha* has an unusual calligraphic extension in the form of a loop added to the bottom of its right-hand member. The name Saṃghapriya, possibly referring to the same individual, occurs on pot A (ins. 1) and potsherd 4.

Potsherd 3 (pl. 32)

Dimensions:	15.0 × 12.8; 0.6–1.4
Decoration:	Two rows of parallel diagonal lines on the lower part; at the right, after *vihare,* a stamped design shaped like a long thinleaf, and part of another such sign at the left edge.
Height of letters:	1.0–2.6
Reading:	*ayaṃ yarughaḍike [.e] /// ? + vihare*
Translation:	This water (?) pot . . . in the . . . monastery.

The sherd contains the beginning (*ayaṃ*) and end of the full inscription, which must have extended all the way around the pot. After *ayaṃ yarughaḍike,* we can reconstruct (*d**)*e*(*yadharma**), after which were probably given the names of the donor and the recipients and finally the name of the monastery. The term *yarugha-ḍike* is problematic. The many other inscriptions with terms like *panighaḍa* (pot C) suggest that *yaru* might be another word for "water" or perhaps for some other liquid substance, but I cannot explain it etymologically.

Potsherd 4 (pl. 32)

Dimensions:	7.9 × 8.8; 0.5
Decoration:	None
Height of letters:	2.6–3.2
Reading:	*/// saghapriha[sa] ///*
Translation:	. . . of Saghapriha . . .

The name *saghapriha* is presumably a graphic variant of the common Saṃghapriya. The writing of *h* in place of *y* in intervocalic position is attested elsewhere in Kharoṣṭhī texts, for example, in *ṣeho* = Skt. *śreyas-* in the KDhP (Brough 1962: 92). This Saṃghapriya may be the same person as the donor of potsherd 2 and/or the individual of the same name mentioned in inscription no. 1 on pot A.

Potsherd 5 (pl. 32 and fig. 49)

Dimensions:	8.6 × 9.4; 0.4–0.5
Decoration:	Above the inscription, a thick, blurry line of red ink; above this line, at the top center, the bottom of a chevron-shaped design in black ink.
Height of letters:	2.0 on average. The surviving portion of *rya* with its ornamentally extended subscript, broken off at the bottom, is 5.6 cm high.
Reading:	*/// [.i]ghaḍe niryadide ///*
Translation:	. . . [water]pot was given . . .

The letters are written in a thin, delicate hand. Ornamental extensions are applied to the bottom of *ḍe,* the *i* diacritic in *di,* and the subscript *r* in *rya.* At the right edge, nearly touching the middle of the *gha,* is the very end of a line which could be the *i* diacritic written horizontally across the stem of an *n.* The missing beginning of the text can therefore be reconstructed as (*aya pan**)*[i]*- (i.e., "This water[pot]").

For the use of *niryadida-*, etc. in donative formulae, see the comments above on *niryateti* on pot C.

This sherd may have come from the same pot as the following one, as discussed below.

Potsherd 6 (pl. 32 and fig. 50)

Dimensions:	12.0 × 8.4; 0.4–0.5
Decoration:	Above the inscription, a thick, blurry line of red ink. At the left-hand corner is preserved most of a stamped design consisting of a flower with six petals enclosed within a circle.
Height of letters:	0.8–2.0 on average. The remaining portion of the incomplete ligature *rva* is 6.7 cm high.
Reading:	*/// [da]rana na[vas]eana sarvasya ñativagras. ///*
Translation:	. . . of mother and father (?), of the Navaseas (?), of the entire group of kinsmen . . .

Fig. 49. Potsherd 5

Fig. 50. Potsherd 6

The inscription is written in a thin, delicate hand with ornate characters with long flourishes. The ornamental characters are similar to those seen on pot C, for example, the long hooked flourish below *ña*. The context (*ñati-* = Skt. *jñāti-*) shows that this is a decorative flourish or pseudo-anusvāra rather than a true anusvāra.

The slip is largely peeled off, causing some damage to the inscription, especially at the left side. The surviving portion of the inscription seems to be from the list of beneficiaries, given in the genitive case, which was presumably governed by a following word such as *saṃmepratyaśae* as in pot A, inscription 2. The sense of the last phrase, *sarvasya ñativagras.*, is clear enough although its formulation is slightly different from the usual general citations of relatives, such as *mitrañati-salohitana* on pot A. *Vagra-* is presumably a metathesized form of Skt. *varga* used as a collective suffix, like *saṃgha* in the Pālāṭū Ḍherī jar inscription C, *ñadiga-saṃghe* (Konow 1929: 122; the reading, however, is not certain).

The word partially preserved at the beginning of the potsherd may have been *madapidarana* or the like, that is, "of [the donor's] mother and father." The trace of a letter at the very edge of the sherd, before *rana*, could well be a *da*. The reading of the word following this is problematic due to the peeling of the surface, which has damaged several of the letters, and the sense of the apparent reading, *na[vas]eana*, is not clear. Most likely, it is a proper name, perhaps a family or clan name, such as appear, not infrequently, in the plural in Kharoṣṭhī inscriptions; compare, for example, *hodreaṇa* (Dharmarājikā ins. 2; Konow 1929: 91) and *iṃtavhriaputraṇa* (Taxila silver scroll; Konow 1929: 77, line 2).

This sherd quite possibly, though not definitely, came from the same vessel as potsherd 5. The ornate handwriting is very similar, as is the overall fabric of the sherd.

Potsherd 7 (pl. 32 and fig. 51)

Dimensions:	13.1 × 9.8; 0.6
Decoration:	At the upper left, a square stamped design with what appears to be a monstrous face (*kīrtimukha* or lion?).[39] At the right side, some inked lines resembling a face in profile.
Height of letters:	No complete letters.
Reading:	?
Translation:	?

Only the bottoms of two or three letters are preserved at the right side of the upper edge. No reading can be proposed.

39. See also Allchin's comments above (p. 185).

Fig. 51. Potsherd 7

Potsherd 8 (pl. 32)

Dimensions:	10.6 × 6.6; 0.5–0.7
Decoration:	At the upper left corner, a row of five incised dots, presumably the remnants of a decorative row that went all the way around the shoulder of the pot, above the inscription. Above the dotted line, a very small remaining section of a single continuous incised line.
Height of letters:	2.4+ (height of surviving portions); the only complete letter, *rma*, is 3.7 cm high.
Reading:	*/// [ca](r*)yaṇa dharma[ü] ///*
Translation:	. . . of the Dharmagu[ptaka*] teachers . . .

The letters, written in a thick, even hand, are all incomplete at the bottom, except for *rma*. Part of the inscription can be confidently reconstructed as *(a*)[ca](r*)yaṇa dharma[ü](teaṇa parigrahe*)* or the like. The surviving portion of the last letter is the upper part of the "alif," or vowel carrier sign, but it is virtually certain that it originally had a *u* diacritic at the bottom, on the basis of the parallels in pot D, potsherds 11 and 17, and other examples cited in section 8.2.3.1. The missing beginning of the inscription, following the usual pattern, must have been something like *aya panighaḍe deyadharme saghe caturdiśe;* compare, for example, the inscription on pot B.

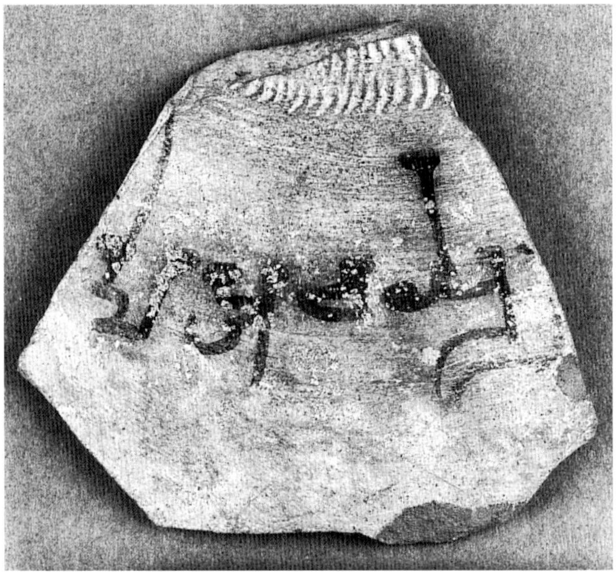

Fig. 52. Potsherd 9

Potsherd 9 (pl. 32 and fig. 52)

Dimensions:	10.9 × 10.2; 0.4–0.9
Decoration:	At the top, remnants of two lines of vertical hatching.
Height of letters:	1.2 (*ca*) to 4.8 (*ryya*)
Reading:	/// *mi acaryya* ///
Translation:	. . . [of] the teachers . . .

This inscription is the only one in this collection written in Brāhmī script, although groups of potsherds with inscriptions in both Kharoṣṭhī and Brāhmī are not unusual (see n. 3). The form of the script (particularly the letters *a* and *m*) appears to be rather late, so that the inscription could date from as late as the fourth or fifth century A.D. It is striking that the scribe has neglected to note the long vowels in *ācāryyā*(*ṇāṃ**). This seems to reflect the work of a scribe who was more accustomed to writing Kharoṣṭhī and thus prone to be careless about the marking of long vowels.

The *mi* at the beginning of the sherd is probably the end of the phrase *saṃghami caturdiśami.* The next word can be readily reconstructed as *acaryya*(*ṇaṃ**) [sic], which would have been followed by the name of the sect and then by *parigrahami,* "in the possession of." The locative ending in *-mi* in the first word indicates that the Brāhmī text was written in hybrid Sanskrit, or perhaps rather in Sanskritized Gāndhārī.

Potsherd 10 (pl. 33)

Dimensions:	8.6 × 7.4; 0.4–0.5
Decoration:	A thick, blurry red line at the level of the top of the inscription; at the upper left corner, part of a stamped circular design.
Height of letters:	1.5+ (*ya*) to 4.4+ (*ṇa*); average about 3.0.
Reading:	*/// [ya]ṇaraña[m.] ///*
Translation:	. . . [in] the . . . grove . . .

The letters are written in a thick, even hand, somewhat similar to that of potsherd 8. The surviving portion of the inscription evidently contains part of the name of the monastic institution where the recipients of the gift resided; for other names of monasteries ending in -(*a*)*raña*- (Skt. *araṇya*-), see pot B and comments thereon. The first character, read tentatively as *ya,* could also be *śa;* neither reading suggests a previously known institution. At the end, just before the broken left edge, is the small remnant of a letter which could be the right side of an *m,* in which case we can reconstruct the expected locative ending -*mi.* This potsherd almost certainly comes from the same vessel as no. 11.

Potsherd 11 (pl. 33)

Dimensions:	8.3 × 6.6; 0.4–0.5
Decoration:	Blurry red line at the level of the top of the inscription.
Height of letters:	2.0 (*ta*) to 3.4+ (*pa*)
Reading:	*/// [ma]ütaana pa ///*
Translation:	. . . [in the possession] of the [Dhar*]maguptaka . . . [teachers*] . . .

The letters are in a thick, even hand, evidently the same as that of potsherd 10. The inscription can be confidently restored in part to (*acaryana dhar**)*maütaana pa*(*rigrahe**) or the like, according to the usual donative formula.

The sherd almost certainly belongs to the same vessel as no. 10, since the form and material are identical, the hand is the same, and the texts are consistent. It is not possible to be sure what their relative order was, however, because in some cases the location of the recipient monastery (i.e., the text partly preserved in potsherd 10) comes before the name of the sect (e.g., in the inscription on pot C), and sometimes after it (as in pot B).

Fig. 53. Potsherd 12

Potsherd 12 (pl. 33 and fig. 53)

Dimensions:	8.0 × 14.4; 0.4–0.9
Decoration:	At the right side, a śrīvatsa (auspicious symbol) in ink.
Height of letters:	3.3 (*sa,* only complete letter)
Reading:	*sa[gh.] /// [m.]*
Translation:	. . . community . . . at(?) . . .

The fragment contains the beginning of the inscription, which can be reconstructed as *sagha(mi caturdiśami*)* or the like, according to the short form of the standard dedicatory formula (see pot D). At the upper right edge, there is a tiny trace of what must have been the last letter of the inscription. (The śrīvatsa thus separates the beginning and end of the inscription, which ran all around the pot, as in pot C.) This letter could be an *m,* in which case we can tentatively reconstruct (*-mi**) as the locative ending either of the word (*parigraha**)*mi* or of a toponym (see potsherd 10).

Potsherd 13 (pl. 33)

Dimensions:	9.1 × 6.4; 0.6–0.7
Decoration:	At top, five incised parallel lines plus one wavy line below them.
Height of letters:	1.1 (*du*) to 3.2 (*mi*)
Reading:	*/// [sa]ghami cadudiśa[mi] ///*
Translation:	. . . to the universal community . . .

Written in a small, neat hand.

Potsherd 14 (pl. 33 and figs. 54–5)

Dimensions:	7.0 × 8.8; 0.7–1.1
Decoration:	Three incised lines around the upper rim. Below the inscription, three more incised lines.
Height of letters:	1.5–3.0
Reading:	*/// mi· ghośyana [s.] ///*
Translation:	. . . at . . . of the Ghośyas(?) . . .

The sherd belongs to a different kind of vessel than the globular, narrow-necked jug of the other pots and potsherds. The inscription is written on a narrow depressed band 3 cm high. Above this band is the top rim of the vessel, 1.8 cm high. It seems to have been a shallow pot with a wide opening at the top, perhaps resembling a piece found at Taxila (Sirkap; Marshall 1951: 2.411, 3. pl. 122, no. 42) (see also sec. 1.3).

The inscription is in a moderately ornate style, with the familiar pseudo-anusvāra flourishes at the bottom of some characters (*mi, gho*). The sense is not clear. At the upper left of the first syllable, *mi,* there is a small dot of ink which could be meant to represent a word divider, as seen in several of the manuscripts. If so, the *mi* would be the locative ending of the preceding word. The following word, *ghośyana,* is presumably in the genitive plural and seems to be a proper name; compare the comments on *na[vas]eana* on potsherd 6.

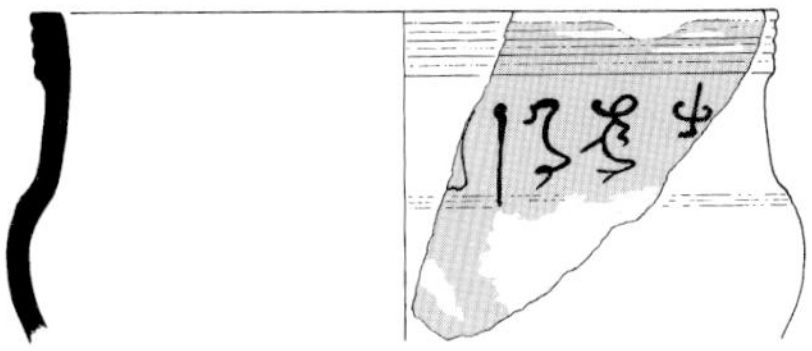

Figs. 54 and 55. Potsherd 14

Potsherd 15 (pl. 33)

Dimensions:	8.3 × 7.2; 0.5–0.8
Decoration:	None
Height of letters:	2.2–2.8
Reading:	*/// [tra]nadena*
Translation:	. . . by [Mi]trana[n]da.

This appears to be the end of the inscription; although the upper left corner of the sherd is broken away, the space remaining after the last letter (*na*) is slightly more than the normal space between letters. The surviving portion seems to be a proper name in the instrumental case, most likely (*mi**)*tranadena* (= Skt. *mitranandena*). The instrumental might have been governed by a participial verb such as *niryadide* (as in potsherd 5), that is, "given by."

Potsherd 16 (pl. 33)

Dimensions:	12.2 × 8.9; 0.5–0.8
Decoration:	None
Height of letters:	1.5–2.3
Reading:	*sra[tsasa]ti*
Translation:	?

The inscription, which is rather badly faded, appears to be complete, as there is a sizable blank space to the right, while on the left, near the edge, there is a spiral design that does not correspond to any Kharoṣṭhī letter and hence seems to be a punctuation mark or auspicious sign such as are often used to mark the end of an inscription. The reading and interpretation are uncertain. The first letter seems to be *sra* but could possibly be *bra*. The second is apparently the conjunct *tsa* (or possibly *spa*), and the third is probably *sa*. The word might represent the name of the owner, or rather the recipient of the vessel, but if so I cannot explain it etymologically.

Potsherd 17 (pl. 33 and fig. 56)

Dimensions:	9.8 × 5.0; 0.5–0.6
Decoration:	None
Height of letters:	2.0 on average; maximum 4.5+ (*rma*)
Reading:	*/// ca(r)ya dharmaüte pari ///*
Translation:	. . . in the possession of the Dharmagupta teacher[s] . . .

Fig. 56. Potsherd 17

The inscription is a cursively written and inaccurate rendition of the standard donative formula, in which the scribe has omitted the normal genitive plural endings. The intended reading is presumably to be restored as (a*)carya<na*> dharmaute<ana*> pari(grahami*). The syllable *te* (cf. the similar spelling of *dharmauteaṇa* in pot D) is rendered by a *t* with two parallel lines like a diacritic *e* above and to the right, but not connected with the consonant. Apparently the scribe first wrote the one at the right and, dissatisfied with its distance from the *t*, wrote it again slightly to the left, closer, though still not connected, to the consonant. The cursive character of this hand is also manifested by the rough and simplified forms of *ca*, *rya*, and *dha*.

Potsherd 18 (pl. 33)

Dimensions:	11 × 10.5; 0.7–1.0
Decoration:	At the lower left corner, most of a stamped circular six-petaled lotus design, similar to the ones on pot A and potsherds 6 and 10.
Height of letters:	About 1.2–1.5+ (more complete letters); all are incomplete at bottom.
Reading:	/// [t.]ñatisal.h. ///
Translation:	. . . [of friends,] kinsmen, and blood relatives . . .

The text can be restored to the familiar formula (mi*)t(ra*)-ñati-sal(o*)h(itana*); see the comments on potsherd 6. The letters l(o*) and h(i*) are separated by a space of about 2 cm where the scribe has avoided writing over the lotus design.

Potsherd 19 (pl. 34)

Dimensions:	10.2 × 8; 0.5–0.6
Decoration:	None
Height of letters:	1.5–4.0
Reading:	*/// [na] puyae ṣa[n]i ///*
Translation:	. . . in honor of . . .

The first letter, if *na* is the correct reading, is probably a genitive plural depending on *puyae,* "in honor of," which is part of a common formula for sharing the merit in reliquary inscriptions, though less usual in dedicatory records on pottery. The last letter is probably *ni* but could also be *tha.* I can offer no reconstruction for the last word, which is perhaps a proper name.

Potsherd 20 (pl. 34 and fig. 57)

Dimensions:	14 × 13.6; 0.6–0.7
Decoration:	Incised lines, described from the top down: above the inscription, three parallel lines; at the level of the bottom of the inscription, three parallel wavy lines; below the inscription, three parallel lines; another triple wavy line; a raised line, diagonally hatched; and another raised line, diagonally hatched in the opposite direction.
Height of letters:	Average 1.3–2.5; maximum 4.4 (*sya*)
Reading:	*[a] /// .u[dha]śavapu[tra]sya*
Translation:	[This] . . . of the son of [B]uddhaśava.

The inscription is written in a thick, upright hand. At the left edge, divided by a sizable blank space from the rest of the text, there is a portion of the bottom of a letter, which must have been the first syllable of the inscription that ran around the vessel. It could be *a,* in which case the text might have begun with *a*(*ya panighaḍa**) or a similar phrase. The end of the inscription is preserved at the right side of the sherd, and the genitive ending of the final word probably marks it as the gift or possession (see below, sec. 5.2) of the person whose patronymic it contained. Presumably this name is to be reconstructed as (*b**)*udhaśavaputrasya* (= Skt. *buddhaśravaputrasya*). The form of *tra* is peculiar, but this is probably due to the interference of the incised wavy lines with the scriber's pen. On the peculiar form of the *u* diacritic in the first syllable, see the discussion of pot A. The previous word probably would have been the personal name of the donor or owner.

Fig. 57. Potsherd 20

Potsherd 21 (pl. 34)

Dimensions:	9.5 × 9.7; 0.5–0.7
Decoration:	None
Height of letters:	All incomplete; probably originally about 2.0–2.5.
Reading:	*/// ? bh.r.. ///*
Translation:	. . . wife(?) . . .

Only the second syllable is more or less completely preserved. Of the first syllable, only a small trace remains at the left edge, and of the third, only the bottom. This latter has a looped flourish that is evidently a cursive rendition of a subscript (preconsonantal) *r,* although the loop is smaller than usual, making it resemble a form of the diacritic *e* that can be added to the bottom of certain letters, such as the *a* ("alif"). In view of the *bh.* that precedes it, the most likely reconstruction of the word is *bh(a*)r(ya*)-*, that is, Sanskrit *bhāryā,* "wife" (probably originally in the genitive or instrumental case, *bharyae*), which commonly occurs in donative inscriptions; compare, for example, *susomabharyae* in pot A, inscription 2.

Fig. 58. Potsherd 22

Potsherd 22 (pl. 34 and fig. 58)

Dimensions:	9.1 × 9.0; 0.8–1.2
Decoration:	At top, a series of horizontal incised lines above a thicker scalloped line.
Height of letters:	2.0–3.1
Reading:	/// *likhide bha[.r.]* ///
Translation:	. . . written . . .

The word *likhide,* "written," presumably marks a scribal signature, and the following word would have been the scribe's name, which probably began with *bha(d*)r(a*)-*, in the instrumental case. Such scribal signatures are sometimes found in reliquary and other types of inscriptions, for instance, in the Kurram casket (Konow 1929: 155, line 4, *aya ca praticasaṃmupate likhida mahiphatiena*). But this apparent instance on a pot inscription is, to my knowledge, unique. It is not entirely surprising, however, in view of the calligraphic efforts that some scribes dedicated to inscriptions of this type, such as the one on pot C.

Potsherd 23 (pl. 34)

Dimensions:	9.8 × 8.0; 0.4–0.5
Decoration:	None
Height of letters:	2.0
Reading:	*/// śara[ñasu] ///*
Translation:	?

The ink is badly faded, especially at the left side of the sherd, so that the reading is uncertain. The text may contain the name of a monastic establishment (*[a]raña-;* see the comments on pot B and potsherd 10), although the usual locative ending is absent.

Potsherd 24 (pl. 34)

Dimensions:	9.0 × 7.0; 0.6–0.8
Decoration:	Below the inscription, the sherd is covered with diagonal hatching composed of deeply incised lines.
Height of letters:	1.0
Reading:	*/// [s.]koḍa [a] ///*
Translation:	?

The fragment is too small to permit any interpretation. The writing seems to be cursive in style, with the *k* written in the variant in which the top horizontal is written in one stroke together with the right-hand member () instead of being joined to the vertical stem as in the more standard form (; see 6.2.1).

Potsherd 25 (pl. 34)

Dimensions:	8.5 × 8.3; 0.8–1.1
Decoration:	At the top, three pairs of parallel incised lines above a wavy line; at the bottom, the top edge of a circular design.
Height of letters:	0.7–2.2
Reading:	*/// [ṇaka]ṇa ja[khe]yapuṇa? ///*
Translation:	?

The inscription is cursively written and badly faded, so that no sense can be made of it. The letter read tentatively as *ka* appears to be of the cursive variety noted in potsherd 24, but it could also be some other consonant, perhaps *ṇ,* with the vowel sign *o.* The lower part of the syllable that is tentatively read as *khe* looks like the ligature *mu,* but this reading is rejected because it is placed lower down than *mu,* which is usually set above the line, and the trace of the vertical line above it would not be oriented in the way that is usual for the upper stem of that ligature. I have therefore preferred to take it, with considerable doubt, as a diacritic *e* on top of a partially obliterated *kha.*

Fig. 59. Potsherd 26

Potsherd 26 (pl. 34 and fig. 59)

Dimensions:	6.7 × 5.1; 0.5–0.6
Decoration:	None
Height of letter:	3.5
Reading:	*/// dha[r..] ///*
Translation:	?

The small fragment preserves only one complete letter, but there is also a trace of a horizontal ink stroke at the upper left, which might have been the upper part of the ligature *rma.* If so, this was probably part of the word *dhar(magupteana*)* or the like.

5. Conclusions: The Functions of the Inscribed Pots

5.1. Waterpots as a Form of Pious Donation

In four of the five complete dedicatory pot inscriptions presented here (pots A, B, C, and E), the object is labeled with the term *aya pani-ghaḍa,* "this water-pot," or some variant form thereof. Among the potsherds edited above, one (no. 5) has the word *ghaḍe,* which can probably be restored to *(aya pani*)-ghaḍe,* and another (no. 3) bears the similar but problematic designation *yaru-ghaḍike.* Other Kharoṣṭhī (and Brāhmī) inscriptions with similar labels are well attested among the inscriptions on pots and potsherds from Kara Tepe and Faiz Tepe in Termez, where we find such phrases as *iyo pāni-ghaḍa* (Kara Tepe no. 36, Vertogradova 1995: 69; reading revised according to Salomon 1997b: 408). On the whole, though, the synonymous word *kuṇḍika* and its variants are much more common among the Termez pot inscriptions than *ghaḍa;* for example, in Kharoṣṭhī, *ayaṃ pāniya-kuṃḍika* (Kara

Tepe no. 1, Vertogradova 1995: 49), and in Brāhmī, *ayaṃ pānika-kuṇḍika* (Kara Tepe no. 11, Vertogradova 1995: 97).[40]

In the corresponding context in the reconstructed text of the Tor Ḍherai potsherds we find the expression *yaṃ prapa,* which Konow translated, without comment, as "this water hall" (1929: 176). But since we now have numerous attestations of other words meaning "waterpot" in this context, we should consider whether *prapa* could not also have had this sense in the Tor Ḍherai inscriptions. In defense of Konow's interpretation, however, it may be significant that the inscription in question was "repeated on several jars" (Konow 1929: 174), so that they could have been intended as labels, not of individual jars, but of the "water hall" that contained them.[41] It is also true that Sanskrit *prapā* and Pali *papā* normally denote a watering place or a well rather than a jar as such. Nevertheless, given the parallels of the other inscriptions, which are otherwise very similar in wording and content, I am inclined to suspect that *prapā* did in fact have the extended sense of "jar" in the Tor Ḍherai inscriptions.

The majority of the pots (and potsherds, as far as their contents can be discerned) with donative inscriptions in Kharoṣṭhī do not have any such explicit labels. In these inscriptions, the donated object is usually referred to by general terms such as *deyadharma* or *danamukha,* "pious gift." This briefer formula is found in most of the inscriptions of similar type from the other sites listed in section 2 of this Appendix; for example, *saghe cadurdiśe masenarane danamukhe budhaghoṣasa* ("Pious gift of Buddhaghoṣa to the universal community at Masenarana") in an inscription of unknown provenance (Salomon 1996b: 239). Since explicit labels of the type *aya panighaḍa* are usually combined with one of these general terms (e.g., in British Library pot C, *aya panighaḍa daṇaṃmukho* . . . , "This water pot [is] the pious gift . . . "), the use of *deyadharma* or *danamukha* alone could be understood as an abridged equivalent of the longer formulae with an explicit label of the donated object. In some cases, such as British Library pot D (*saghami caüdiśami dhamaüteaṇa parigrahami*), an even more abridged formula is used, in which the inscription contains no label at all, specific or generic.

The overall consistency of the donative text in its longer and shorter forms, as well as the similarity of the objects on which they were written, suggests that most, if not all, of the inscribed vessels were originally intended for the same purpose: as containers for drinking water for the residents of the monasteries to which they were donated. Such pots were a common and widespread form of dona-

40. A similar donative Kharoṣṭhī inscription from Faiz Tepe (Vorob'eva-Desjatovskaja 1974: 117–22) labels the stone bowl on which it is written as *suyi-kuḍa,* which evidently corresponds to Sanskrit *śuci-kuṇḍa,* perhaps referring to a vessel used for ritual cleansing.

41. Such a "water hall" could conceivably be what is referred to in the Tibetan translation of the Kṣudrakavastu of the Mūlasarvāstivāda-vinaya as a "water house" (*chu'i khaṅ pa;* Derge Kanjur, Tha 109b.7).

tion on the part of worshipers and pilgrims at Gandhāran Buddhist monasteries, evidently by way of a minor gift. This is indicated, first of all, by the very large number of records of this kind, though mostly fragmentary, that have been found (but by no means always published) in the course of formal excavations or as casual finds at Gandhāran sites. Second, there is the small cash value of such vessels, which no doubt in antiquity as now were sold for a trivial price. Third, and most revealing, is the casual character of many, though by no means all, of the donative inscriptions on them.

It is true that in some cases, such as British Library pots A and C, dedicatory pot inscriptions are fairly elaborate in terms of their form, being written in calligraphic style, and their content, listing many beneficiaries, for example. Nonetheless, the briefer formula and casual style of writing are more common, and moreover such inscriptions occur on vessels of the same type and form (e.g., British Library pots B and D) as the more elaborately inscribed ones. This suggests that the length and degree of formality of the inscription were matters of personal choice on the part of the donor rather than an indication of any inherent difference in the nature of the gift itself.

The absence, however, in some of the short-formula inscriptions, including British Library pots B and D, of the donor's name is very striking, since this is normally understood to be the most important part of a donative record, that is, the part that ensured that the karmic merit generated by the gift would accrue to the donor (see Fussman 1969: 7–8). Such an omission would be virtually unthinkable in other types of Buddhist donative records, for instance, in those recording the foundation of a stūpa or a relic dedication, in which the sponsor's name, as well as those of his or her relatives, associates, and/or superiors, is almost invariably mentioned in a prominent position. So the surprising absence of the donor's name in some pot inscriptions is perhaps best explained on the grounds that these pots represented casual or minor gifts for which it was not felt absolutely necessary to record the donative formula, including even the donor's name, in full.

It is also significant that none of the many waterpot inscriptions is dated.[42] This feature too sets them off from more formal donative records, which were often, though by no means always, dated. This contrast reinforces the impression that, whereas donations of relics and reliquaries were events of some note which were probably accompanied by solemn ceremonies,[43] the presentation of a water jar

42. The first Haḍḍa jar inscription (now lost) seems to be an exception, since it is dated in the year 28, probably of Kaniṣka. But the inscription itself (*pratisthapita śarira ramaraṃñami thubami* . . .) shows that the vessel was presented as a reliquary and hence is not actually comparable, in terms of function, to the ones under discussion here, though it was apparently similar to them in physical form. One of the Kara Tepe potsherds (Vorob'eva-Desjatovskaja 1983: 32, no. 3) was read as containing the word *dive[se]*, "on the day . . . ," implying a dated inscription, but this reading has been shown by Vertogradova (1995: 52) to be incorrect.

43. Such a ceremony (in Khotan) was described by Hsüan-tsang (Beal 1884: 317–8).

was more on the level of a minor or symbolic gesture of piety and was not considered worthy of being inscriptionally recorded in the same detail as a relic donation.

5.2. Relationships between Inscribed Pots and Funerary Vessels

In numerous cases, which have been summarized in chapter 4, clay pots similar in form and type to the inscribed ones discussed here were found to contain human remains or the debris of birch bark manuscripts. Unfortunately there is as yet no clear, well-attested example of human remains found in an inscribed pot, but there is some reason to think that there may have been such cases. The strongest indication of this is the report concerning the second inscribed jar from Haḍḍa, kept in the Kabul Museum, which, according to Fussman (1969: 5), was accompanied by a note in Persian to the effect that the inscription "comes from Haḍḍa, found in a large jar with earth and bones." Fussman (1969: 9; quoted above in 4.3) deduced, apparently correctly, that this probably meant that the inscribed jar itself contained the bones. This, among other factors, led Fussman to suspect that the jar was intended as a funerary vessel from the very beginning, and that the inscription on it contained the name of the monk whose remains it was destined to contain. He also noted that the inscriptions on other clay pots were added to the pots after they were fired, which he took to indicate that they were not originally intended for the storage of liquids (presumably since liquids and moisture would tend to obliterate the unfired ink) but rather that some of them were designed to be funereal jars (Fussman and Le Berre 1976: 92).

Fussman did, however, concede that there are some problems with this interpretation (1969: 8), and subsequent discoveries of many more inscriptions of this type show that his reservations were justified. Although Fussman interpreted the phrase *samaṃtapaśe mahapriyasaṃñe* (as read by him) on the Haḍḍa jar as the name of the monk whose remains the jar contained (" . . . pious gift . . . to Samaṃtapaśa Mahapriyasaṃña"; p. 9),[44] inscriptions such as those on British Library pots B and C and the other examples mentioned above in connection with them show that the longer dedicatory formula on inscribed jars often included in the corresponding position the name of the monastic establishment to which the jars were presented; for instance, in pot C, *saṃghe caturdiśe rayagahami acaryaṇaṃ sarvastivatinaṃ.* Moreover, the names of such establishments very often contained the final element *(a)raña-*, "grove" (Skt. *araṇya-*), as in pot B, . . . *purnagarañami.* I would therefore propose that we should read, instead of *samaṃtapaśe mahapriyasaṃñe* on the Haḍḍa jar, *samaṃtapaśe mahapriyaraṃñe,* "at Samantapaśa in the Mahāpriya grove." The crucial penultimate syllable of this phrase does indeed appear in the photograph

44. The full text of the inscription, according to Fussman's reading, is *Sihaṣudaya atmaṇaṣa arogada[kṣ]i[ṇa- . . .] saṃghe caturdiśe Samaṃtapaśe Mahapriyasaṃñe acaryeṇaṃ sarvastivadiṇaṃ parigrahe deyadharme.*

(Fussman 1969: pl. III) to be *raṃ* rather than *saṃ* and in view of the parallels cited should, I think, be read as such and reinterpreted accordingly.

A similar revision may be proposed with regard to Fussman's (1974) interpretation of the inscription on the Qunduz copper vase, which, although written on a different material, follows the same formula. Here again Fussman takes the phrase *staraya baliyaphaïṃkavihare*[45] to indicate that "like the Haḍḍa jar, the Qunduz vase was intended for the ashes of the monk Stara" (p. 61). He reaches this conclusion, among other reasons, on the grounds that "*Starayabaliyaphaïṃka* would be a very long toponym. That is why we are resigned to dividing *Staraya Baliyaphaïṃkavihare*, 'for Stara, in the monastery of Baliyaphaïṃka'" (p. 60). But here too a comparison with the numerous parallels now available from other inscriptions indicates that *starayabaliyaphaïṃka* probably was indeed the name of the monastery to whose teachers the vase was donated, and that there is no reference to an individual monk for whose ashes it was destined. Such monastic institutions (*vihara* or (*a*)*raña*) seem to have been named, in some cases at least, after their patrons or "owners,"[46] as may be the case, for example, with the *purnagaraña-* of pot B and the *ramaraña-* of Haḍḍa pot no. 1 (Konow 1935–6). A long name such as *starayabaliyaphaïṃkavihare* might reflect more than just the simple name of its founder. For example, it could contain the names of two (or more?) joint founders or perhaps the founder's personal name plus an ethnonym or patronymic. For the latter possibility, we might compare the long (and incomplete) monastery name . . . *vhara-gulavhara-jhada-viha*(*rami**), "in the Vihāra of . . . vhara, son of Gulavhara" (Kara Tepe no. 58; Vertogradova 1995: 45 and 84).

Thus, in light of comparisons with the more recently discovered inscriptions of similar type, there is no longer any compelling reason to believe that the Haḍḍa and Qunduz jars were originally intended as funereal vessels. The pattern and formulation of their dedicatory inscriptions agree well with those of the many others now known, including those several examples which tell us explicitly that the inscribed vessel was intended as a water jar. Fussman's argument that the addition of the inscriptions to the jars after firing indicates that they were not intended to be used to contain water but rather were meant to be funerary vessels from the very beginning is hardly compelling in light of the new inscriptional evidence to the contrary. Rather, I would be inclined to explain this casual treatment of the inscriptions as reflecting the objects' status as minor and informal gifts, whose inscriptions, unlike those in or on reliquaries, were not expected to last as permanent records.

This is not to deny that, on the one hand, some of these vessels were donated to individual monks for their personal use (though not for the disposal of

45. The full text is . . . *budhaputrasa Ana. . . . pasa deyadhaṃma saghe catudiśe Staraya Baliyaphaïṃkavihare acariyanaṃ dhaṃmagutakana parigrahe savasatvanaṃ h*(*i*)*tasukhaya.*

46. On these and related terms and their ramifications, see Schopen 1996: esp. 84–6.

their bodily remains) and, on the other hand, that some of them were reused, at a later date, as funereal vessels or for analogous purposes. As a matter of fact, both of these seem to have been the case. As for donations of pots to individual monks, we have among the new specimens one example, pot A, which, in addition to the standard donative formula in the longer inscription (no. 2), also has a separate, shorter inscription that explicitly marks it as a donation (*pratigraha*) to a particular monk, apparently named Catula. So there can be no doubt that pot A was in fact specifically donated to a particular monk within the larger community. Moreover, it is equally definite that it was not meant to contain his ashes: inscription 2, which is in the same hand and hence can be presumed to have been written at the same time as 1, tells us that the object of the donation (*deyadharme*) was "this waterpot" (*[a]yaṃ pānayaghaḍe*).

Despite the concerns expressed by Fussman (1969: 8–9) and Vertogradova (1995: 46) that such donations seem to violate the vinaya rules concerning the personal possessions that can be given to an individual monk, the evidence of the inscriptions shows beyond a doubt that the pot was in fact presented to an individual. In fact, the Pali vinaya contains specific stipulations for the designation of gifts to particular monks (Dutt 1924: 185). Moreover, we now have evidence from inscriptions from other Buddhist sites that clay jars were frequently marked as the personal possession of individual monks. At Kara Tepe, for example, numerous water jars were explicitly labeled by inscriptions as the "personal possession" (*pugaliga/pudgalīya*, etc.) of individual monks; for instance, *ayo kuḍiya bhikṣusya budhaśirasya pugaligasya* [sic], "This jar is the personal property of the monk Buddhaśiras" (Vertogradova 1995: 109). Similar examples were noted by von Hinüber (1991) among vessels with Brāhmī inscriptions from the Buddhist site of Salihundam in Andhra Pradesh, showing that this practice was widespread in the Indian Buddhist world.

As to the possibility that some of the donated inscribed waterpots were secondarily used as funerary vessels or for related purposes, there are strong indications that in some cases this was actually done, although unfortunately the archeological documentation is not sufficiently detailed and reliable to establish this with certainty. One indication is the note that was attached to the Haḍḍa pot, cited above, suggesting that it was found with bones, or rather (as explained by Fussman) contained bones. Another example could be one of the "funereal jars" from Haḍḍa on which, according to Masson (in Wilson 1841: 113; see sec. 4.3 and n. 9), "an inscription was scratched." Since no further information on this item is available, and since the inscription is not legible in Wilson's plate IX, it is impossible to draw any definite conclusion about the nature of this object, but I think it likely that, like the other inscribed Haḍḍa pot, it was originally a waterpot that was later reused as a funereal vessel.

If, as seems very likely, some of the inscribed waterpots were later reused as funereal jars of the type that are well attested in Gandhāran Buddhist sites (see

4.3), this was a secondary and incidental function. Presumably, such vessels were available in large numbers in Gandhāran monasteries, and they might have been chosen, perhaps more or less at random and without regard for the original donative inscription (or lack thereof), when the need arose for a burial.

The use of such clay pots as funereal vessels may have been conditioned, on the one hand, by established practice going back to prehistoric times in this region (similar vessels were used in burials of the Gandhāran grave culture, whose sites often coincide with stūpa sites of the historical period) and, on the other hand, by certain requirements of Buddhist monastic practice. As demonstrated by Schopen (1996: 112–9) on the basis of the Mūlasarvāstivāda-vinaya, monks were obligated to put any property or objects that were donated to them to continuous use for as long as possible, in order to produce the maximum merit (*paribhogānvayaṃ puṇyam,* "merit arising from use") for their donors. Moreover, according to a passage cited by Schopen (pp. 114–5) from the Kṣudrakavastu, this rule even applied to minor gifts such as "dishes" (Tibetan *sder spyad* = Skt. *bhājana*). And even when a donated object had become so worn out as to be useless, it could not simply be thrown away but was to be recycled in such a way as to enable it to continue to generate merit for its donor, as prescribed in another Kṣudrakavastu passage: "Even when it is completely useless the cloth should not be thrown away. You should mix it with dung or mud and use it as a filler for cracks in the pillars or holes in the wall. The merit of the donor will then be multiplied over a long period of time" (Schopen 1996: 117). The secondary use of surplus water jars as funereal vessels, as indicated by the archeological and epigraphic record, may have been a function of this law. Using a discarded jar as the receptacle for the remains of a dead monk would, like incorporating the scraps of a donated cloth into the structure of the monastery, enable it to continue producing merit for its donor indefinitely.

The use of old waterpots for the ritual burial of "dead" manuscripts, as proposed in section 4.4, would have been an analogous practice, for which clay jars, inscribed or otherwise, might have been taken more or less at random as the need arose. Here too documentation is sparse, but in the new materials we have clear evidence of old scrolls being placed in pots bearing donative Kharoṣṭhī inscriptions that have no connection with this secondary function. To sum up, the epigraphic and archeological evidence indicates that the clay jars bearing Kharoṣṭhī inscriptions were originally intended as water storage jars donated to Buddhist monasteries by their patrons by way of a minor gift, and this appears to be the sole import of the dedicatory inscriptions, whether or not they explicitly label the vessels as "waterpots." In some cases, however, these waterpots were subsequently put to use as funerary vessels, whether in the conventional sense, that is, for the burial of the bodily remains of dead monks, or in the extended sense of containing the "bodily" remains of "dead" books.

5.3. A Possible Exception to the Rule

At least one Gandhāran clay pot may indicate that what was said above about the original and secondary functions of such objects is not the whole story. This is the inscribed and decorated[47] pot (see 4.3 and pls. 17–20) now in the Ashmolean Museum, Oxford, that may have come from the same site as the British Library pots or from a neighboring site. It was clearly used as a funereal vessel since it contained charred bones, presumably human (pl. 20). But the drawings on it of human figures, including that of an aged monk, give the impression that it might well have been made as a funereal vessel from the very beginning, rather than being an ordinary jar that was used in a secondary function, as in the other cases discussed above.

The inscription, written to the left of one of the bowing figures, is of critical importance to the interpretation of this unusual object, but unfortunately it is only barely visible in the earliest available photograph (pl. 19) and has subsequently completely disappeared, apparently as a result of incompetent cleaning. It consists, apparently, of seven syllables, most of which are out of focus in the photograph and hence only very tentatively legible. A possible reading is *[dhamavaja]ṇ[e] ṣama[ṇa]*. The reading is too uncertain to justify an extended discussion, but it seems that the inscription contains the name of a monk (*ṣamaṇa*) and hence could be a label for the contents of the pot, the bodily remains of that monk. This inscription seems to have little in common with the formulaic donative inscriptions seen on all other clay pots with Kharoṣṭhī inscriptions, and the pot itself is evidently in a different class from them. It appears to be a funereal vessel in the strict sense, that is, one that was originally intended and designed as such, unlike the other known specimens, which were used for funereal purposes only secondarily. If this is correct, we would hardly expect it to be unique, and other such items must have existed, though none have apparently come to light yet. This does not, however, invalidate the conclusions drawn above concerning the nature of the more usual type of inscribed pots, since these evidently belong to a different class.

47. For another decorated but not inscribed Gandhāran clay pot, generally similar in form to the ones under consideration here, see Eskenazi 1995: 12–3.

Glossary

The terms are given in their Sanskrit (Skt.) form, unless specified as Pali (P.); where appropriate, the equivalent in the other language is added in parentheses. Terms printed in italics in the definitions are defined separately.

abhidharma (P. abhidhamma): The exegesis of Buddhist doctrine, as presented in a genre of texts that systematically elaborate and analyze the doctrines expounded in the discourses (*sutta*). These abhidharma texts constitute one of the three "baskets" of the Buddhist canon (*Tipiṭaka*).

Ājīvika: A fatalist sect, whose members were among the rivals with whom the Buddha debated.

akṣara: The basic syllabic unit of Kharoṣṭhī script (and of other Indian scripts), consisting of a single vowel (e.g., *a*) or, more frequently, a consonant or a ligature of two or more consonants plus a following vowel (e.g., *te* or *rya*).

Aṅguttara-nikāya (P.; the equivalent text in Skt. is called Ekottarāgama or Ekottarikāgama): "The collection increasing by units," one of the five nikāyas (collections) that make up the *Sutta-piṭaka* of the Pali Buddhist canon. It consists of short discourses (*sutta*) grouped according to numerical principles, from one to eleven.

anusvāra: A diacritic mark added to the foot of a Kharoṣṭhī character to indicate nasalization.

Aśoka: Mauryan dynasty emperor (ca. 269–232 B.C.), renowned in Buddhist tradition as its greatest royal patron.

avadāna: A story illustrating Buddhist principles, particularly the operations of the law of karma, often by reference to events in a past life of a particular individual, such as one of the disciples of the Buddha. Compare *jātaka.*

bhāṇaka: "Reciter," a monk who specializes in the recitation of a particular portion of the Buddhist canon.

bodhisattva: "Enlightenment-being," in traditional usage, the designation of the Buddha before his enlightenment; in Mahāyāna usage, a person who voluntarily defers his own liberation in order to assist other beings toward enlightenment.

Dardic: The subgroup of *New Indo-Aryan* languages spoken on the northwestern fringe of the Indo-Aryan linguistic area, in approximately the same areas where Gāndhārī was spoken in ancient times.

dhāraṇī: A magical formula believed to protect its reciter or writer.

dharma (P. dhamma): "The way" or "the truth," a collective term for Buddhist doctrines and principles. (The term also has several other more specific and technical meanings.)

Dharmapada (P. Dhammapada): An extremely popular collection of verses on general moral principles. Included as one of the texts of the *Khuddaka-nikāya* in the Pali canon. Other versions or equivalent texts are also extant in Sanskrit (the Udāna-varga), Gāndhārī, and other Buddhist languages.

Dīgha-nikāya (P.; Skt. Dīrghāgama): "The long collection," one of the five nikāyas (collections) that make up the *Sutta-piṭaka* in the Pali canon, containing the longer discourses (*sutta*).

Ekottarāgama/Ekottarikāgama: See *Aṅguttara-nikāya.*

gāthā: A verse, particularly an inspired or uplifting one. Compare *udāna.*

hīnayāna: "The inferior vehicle," a polemic term used by adherents of the *mahāyāna* to refer to traditional or conservative Buddhism, which is also known as "mainstream Buddhism," "Nikāya Buddhism," etc. (see chap. 2, n. 21).

jātaka: A story about the events of a past life, usually of the Buddha, illustrating the operations of the laws of karma. Compare *avadāna.*

Kaniṣka: The greatest of the Kuṣāṇa emperors, who ruled in the early to middle second century A.D. (exact dates uncertain), and who was renowned in Buddhist tradition as one of the great royal patrons.

Khuddaka-nikāya (P.; Skt. Kṣudrakāgama): The "shorter" or "lesser collection," one of the five nikāyas (collections) that make up the *Sutta-piṭaka* in the Pali canon. It consists of fifteen texts, mostly compilations of various short discourses (*sutta*) and other types of texts, for instance, *jātakas* and *udānas.*

Mahāvastu: A large collection of miscellaneous textual materials, written in Buddhist Hybrid Sanskrit, culled from the *vinaya* of the Mahāsāṅghika-Lokottaravādin school.

mahāyāna: "The great vehicle," the form of Buddhism, generally a later development, that stresses the *bodhisattva* ideal of assisting other beings to attain enlightenment.

Majjhima-nikāya (P.; Skt. Madhyamāgama): "The middle-length collection," one of the five nikāyas (collections) that make up the *Sutta-piṭaka* in the Pali canon, containing the discourses (*sutta*) of medium length.

Middle Indo-Aryan (MIA): The intermediate stage of development of the Indo-Aryan language family, which is the Indian branch of the Indo-European family. The MIA languages include Pali and Gāndhārī as well as many other dialects that are generally grouped under the heading of "Prakrits."

New Indo-Aryan (NIA): The later and modern stages of the Indo-Aryan languages, comprising many languages spoken today in north and central India and in the neighboring nations of southern Asia.

Nuristani: The languages spoken in the remote area of Nuristan (formerly called Kafiristan) in eastern Afghanistan, generally considered to belong to a separate subgroup of the Indo-Iranian group of the Indo-European languages. These languages share some features with the *Dardic* languages.

Old Indo-Aryan (OIA): The early stage of the Indo-Aryan languages, comprising Vedic (archaic) Sanskrit and later, or classical, Sanskrit.

pāda: Quarter-verse.

Pali: The Middle Indo-Aryan language, in origin probably a dialect of north-central India, that became established as the canonical language of the *Theravāda* tradition and is now used as a religious language in Sri Lanka and Southeast Asia.

prātimokṣa: The lists of monastic rules that constitute the basis of the *vinaya* texts.

pratītya-samutpāda: "Dependent co-origination," a fundamental Buddhist doctrinal formula summarizing the conditioning relations among the constituent elements of sentient beings.

Saka (Skt. Śaka): Scythian; ethnonym referring to central Asian nomads of Iranian linguistic affiliation. Various groups of Sakas entered northwestern India from central Asia and were politically dominant there in the first centuries B.C. and A.D.

Śākyamuni: "Lion of the Śākya clan," the honorific title of the Buddha.

Saṃyutta-nikāya (P.): "The combined collection," one of the five nikāyas (collections) that make up the *Sutta-piṭaka* in the Pali canon, containing the shorter discourses grouped thematically.

saṅgha: The Buddhist monastic community.

stūpa (P. thūpa): A Buddhist sacred monument, usually in the form of a mound of stone or bricks, containing the bodily remains of a Buddha or other sacred relics.

sutta or *suttanta* (P.; Skt. sūtra): A text recording one or more of the discourses of the Buddha or occasionally Buddhist teachings spoken by other persons. The suttas as a whole comprise the *Sutta-piṭaka,* one of the "three baskets" (*Tipiṭaka*) of the Pali canon.

Sutta-nipāta (P.): A collection of seventy-two short suttas grouped into five sections; constitutes one of the fifteen texts of the *Khuddaka-nikāya.*

Sutta-piṭaka (P.): One of the three "baskets" of the Pali Buddhist canon (see *Tipiṭaka*), comprising the *suttas,* or discourses. Divided into five nikāyas (collections): *dīgha, majjhima, aṅguttara, saṃyutta,* and *khuddaka.*

Theragāthā: "The Songs of the Elders," a collection of verses (*gāthā*) attributed to the early followers of the Buddha; it constitutes one of the fifteen texts of the *Khuddaka-nikāya.*

Theravāda: "The Doctrine of the Elders," the Buddhist school, generally doctrinally conservative, that is predominant in Sri Lanka and Southeast Asia.

Tipiṭaka (P.; Skt. tripiṭaka): "The three baskets," a term used (principally in the Theravāda tradition) to denote the complete Buddhist canon. The three baskets are *sutta, vinaya,* and *abhidhamma.*

udāna: An inspired utterance, in verse or prose (cf. *gāthā*). Also, a collection of short texts containing such inspired utterances that constitutes one of the fifteen texts of the *Khuddaka-nikāya.*

Udāna-varga: See *Dharmapada.*

vihāra: A Buddhist monastery.

vinaya: "Discipline," the code of monastic laws that makes up the vinaya-piṭaka and is one of the three "baskets" of the Buddhist canon (see *Tipiṭaka*).

References

Archaeology in India. 1950. Bureau of Education, India, Publication no. 66. Calcutta: Government of India.

Bailey, H. W. 1943–6. "Gāndhārī." *Bulletin of the School of Oriental and African Studies* 11: 764–97.

Ball, Warwick (with Jean-Claude Gardin). 1982. *Archaeological Gazetteer of Afghanistan/ Catalogue des sites archéologigues d'Afghanistan*. 2 vols. Paris: Éditions Recherches sur les Civilisations.

Bareau, André. 1955. *Les sectes bouddhique du petit véhicule*. Publications de l'École Française d'Extrême-Orient 38. Saigon: École Française d'Extrême-Orient.

———. 1966. "L'origine du Dīrgha-āgama traduit en Chinois par Buddhayaśas." In Ba Shin, Jean Boisselier, and A. B. Griswold, eds., *Essays Offered to G. H. Luce by His Colleagues and Friends in Honour of His Seventy-fifth Birthday*. Vol. 1, *Papers on Asian History, Religion, Languages, Literature, Music, Folklore, and Anthropology*, pp. 49–58. Artibus Asiae, Supplementum 23.1. Ascona: Artibus Asiae.

Barthoux, J. 1933. *Les fouilles de Haḍḍa*. Vol. 1, *Stupas et sites, texte et dessins*. Mémoires de la Délégation Archéologique Française en Afghanistan 4. Paris: Les Éditions d'Art et d'Histoire.

Beal, Samuel. 1875. *The Romantic Legend of Sâkya Buddha: From the Chinese-Sanscrit*. London: Trübner & Co.

———. 1884. *Si-yu-ki: Buddhist Records of the Western World, Translated from the Chinese of Hiuen Tsiang* (A.D. 629). London: Trübner & Co.

Bechert, Heinz. 1961. *Bruchstücke buddhistischer Versammlungen aus zentralasiatischen Sanskrithandschriften*. Vol. 1, *Die Anavataptagāthā und die Sthaviragāthā*. Sanskrittexte aus den Turfanfunden 6. Berlin: Akademie-Verlag.

———, ed. 1980. *Die Sprache der ältesten buddhistischen Überlieferung/The Language of the Earliest Buddhist Tradition*. Symposien zur Buddhismusforschung 2. Abhandlungen der Akademie der Wissenschaften in Göttingen, Philologisch-historische Klasse, ser. 3, vol. 117. Göttingen: Vandenhoeck & Ruprecht.

———, ed. 1985. *Zur Schulzugehörigkeit von Werken der Hīnayāna-Literatur*. 2 vols. Symposien zur Buddhismusforschung 3.1. Abhandlungen der Akademie der Wissenschaften in Göttingen, Philologisch-historische Klasse, ser. 3, no. 149. Göttingen: Vandenhoeck & Ruprecht.

———, ed. 1990. *Abkürzungsverzeichnis zur buddhistischen Literatur in Indien und Südostasien*. Sanskrit-Wörterbuch der Buddhistischen Texte aus den Turfan-Funden, Beiheft 3. Göttingen: Vandenhoeck & Ruprecht.

———, ed. 1994. *Sanskrit-Wörterbuch der buddhistischen Texte aus den Turfan-Funden*

und der kanonischen Literatur der Sarvāstivāda-Schule. Vol. 1. Göttingen: Vandenhoeck & Ruprecht.
——— (with Klaus Wille), eds. 1995. *Sanskrithandschriften aus den Turfanfunden.* Vol. 7. Verzeichnis der Orientalischen Handschriften in Deutschland 10.7. Wiesbaden: Franz Steiner Verlag.
Bentor, Yael. 1994. "Inside Tibetan Images." *Arts of Asia,* May–June, pp. 102–9.
———. 1995. "On the Indian Origins of the Tibetan Practice of Depositing Relics and *Dhâraṇîs* in Stûpas and Images." *Journal of the American Oriental Society* 115: 248–61.
Bernhard, Franz. 1970. "Gāndhārī and the Buddhist Mission in Central Asia." In J. Tilakasiri, ed., *Añjali, Papers on Indology and Buddhism: A Felicitation Volume Presented to Oliver Hector de Alwis Wijesekara on His Sixtieth Birthday,* pp. 55–62. Peradeniya: University of Ceylon.
Bianchi Bandinelli, Ranuccio. 1971. *Rome, the Late Empire: Roman Art* A.D. *200–400.* Trans. Peter Green. New York: Thames & Hudson.
Bloch, Jules. 1912. "Le dialecte des fragments Dutreuil de Rhins." *Journal Asiatique,* ser. 10, vol. 19: 331–7.
Bongard-Levin, G. M. 1975–6. "New Sanskrit and Prakrit Texts from Central Asia." *Indologica Taurinensia* 3/4: 73–80.
Boyer, A. M., E. J. Rapson, and E. Senart. 1920–9. *Kharoṣṭhī Inscriptions Discovered by Sir Aurel Stein in Chinese Turkestan.* 3 parts (part 3 by E. J. Rapson and P. S. Noble). Oxford: Clarendon Press.
Brough, John. 1962. *The Gāndhārī Dharmapada.* London Oriental Series 7. London: Oxford University Press.
———. 1965. "Comments on Third-Century Shan-shan and the History of Buddhism." *Bulletin of the School of Oriental and African Studies* 28: 582–612.
———. 1977. "The *Arapacana* Syllabary in the Old *Lalita-vistara.*" *Bulletin of the School of Oriental and African Studies* 40: 85–95.
Buddruss, Georg. 1975. "Gāndhārī-Prakrit *chada* 'Ton.'" *Studien zur Indologie und Iranistik* 1: 37–48.
Bühler, G. 1877. *Detailed Report of a Tour in Search of Sanskrit Mss. Made in Kaśmîr, Rajputana, and Central India.* Extra number of *Journal of the Bombay Branch of the Royal Asiatic Society.*
———. 1894. "Further Inscriptions from Sānchi." *Epigraphia Indica* 2: 366–408.
———. 1895. *Indian Studies.* No. 3, *On the Origin of the Indian Brāhma Alphabet.* Sitzungsberichte der philosophisch-historischen Classe der Kaiserlichen Akademie der Wissenschaften, Abhandlung 5. Vienna: F. Tempsky.
———. 1904. *Indian Paleography from About* B.C. *350 to About* A.D. *1300.* Trans. J. F. Fleet. Appendix to *Indian Antiquary* 33.
Burrow, T. 1937. *The Language of the Kharoṣṭhi Documents from Chinese Turkestan.* Cambridge: Cambridge University Press.
———. 1940. *A Translation of the Kharoṣṭhi Documents from Chinese Turkestan.* James G. Forlong Fund 20. London: Royal Asiatic Society.
Caillat, Colette. 1989a. "Sur l'authenticité linguistique des édits d'Asoka." In Caillat 1989b: 413–32.
———, ed. 1989b. *Dialectes dans les littératures indo-aryennes.* Publications de l'Institut de Civilisation Indienne, série in-8°, fasc. 55. Paris: Collège de France.
Callieri, Pierfranceso. 1989. *Saidu Sharif (Swat, Pakistan).* Vol. 1, *The Buddhist Sacred Area: The Monastery.* Istituto Italiano per il Medio ed Estremo Oriente,

Centro Scavi e Ricerche Archaeologiche, Reports and Memoirs 23.1. Rome: Istituto Italiano per il Medio ed Estremo Oriente.

———. 1997. "Pots in Buddhist Sacred Areas: A Study of the Evidence from the ISMEO Excavations in Swat." In Raymond Allchin and Bridget Allchin, eds., *South Asian Archaeology, 1995*, pp. 417–27. New Delhi: Oxford University Press and IBH.

Chanda, Ramāprasād. 1921. "The Jauliāñ Manuscript." In John Marshall, *Excavations at Taxila: The Stupas and Monasteries at Jauliāñ*, pp. 66–75. Memoirs of the Archaeological Survey of India 7. Calcutta: Superintendent Government Printing.

Chhabra, B. C. 1949–50. "Peshawar Potsherds with Kharoshthi Writings." *Epigraphia Indica* 28: 125–9.

Collins, Steven. 1990. "On the Very Idea of the Pali Canon." *Journal of the Pali Text Society* 15: 89–126.

———. 1992. "Notes on Some Oral Aspects of Pali Literature." *Indo-Iranian Journal* 35: 121–35.

Cone, Margaret. 1989. "Patna Dharmapada. Part I, Text." *Journal of the Pali Text Society* 13: 101–217.

Conrady, August. 1920. *Die chinesischen Handschriften und sonstigen Kleinfunde Sven Hedins in Lou-lan.* Stockholm: Generalstabens Litografiska Anstalt.

Cunningham, Alexander. 1871. *The Ancient Geography of India.* London: Trübner & Co.

Dani, Ahmad Hasan. 1960. "Mathura Lion Capital Inscription (A Paleographical Study)." *Journal of the Asiatic Society of Pakistan* 5: 128–47.

———. 1963. *Indian Paleography.* Oxford: Clarendon Press.

———. 1965–6. "Shaikhan Dheri Excavation: 1963 and 1964 Seasons." *Ancient Pakistan* 2: 17–214.

Das Gupta, Charu Chandra. 1949–50. "Shelarwadi Cave Inscription." *Epigraphia Indica* 28: 76–7.

———. 1958. *The Development of the Kharoṣṭhī Script.* Calcutta: Firma K.L. Mukhopahyay.

de Jong, J. W. 1987. *A Brief History of Buddhist Studies in Europe and America.* 2d ed. Bibliotheca Indo-Buddhica 33. Delhi: Sri Satguru Publications.

Diringer, David. 1953. *The Hand-Produced Book.* New York: Philosophical Library.

Dutt, Nalinaksha. 1942. *Gilgit Manuscripts.* Vol. 3, part 2. Calcutta: Calcutta Oriental Press.

———. 1947. *Gilgit Manuscripts.* Vol. 3, part 3. Calcutta: Calcutta Oriental Press.

Dutt, Sukumar. 1924. *Early Buddhist Monachism, 600 B.C.–100 B.C.* London: Kegan Paul, Trench Trübner & Co.

Edgerton, Franklin. 1953. *Buddhist Hybrid Sanskrit Grammar and Dictionary.* Vol. 2, *Dictionary.* William Dwight Whitney Linguistic Series. New Haven: Yale University Press.

Enomoto, Fumio. 1994. "A Note on Kashmir as Referred to in Chinese Literature: Ji-bin." In Yasuke Ikari, ed., *A Study of the Nīlamata: Aspects of Hinduism in Ancient Kashmir*, pp. 357–65. Kyoto: Kyoto University.

Errington, Elizabeth, and Joe Cribb. 1992. *The Crossroads of Asia: Transformation in Image and Symbol in the Art of Ancient Afghanistan and Pakistan.* Cambridge: Ancient India and Iran Trust.

Eskenazi, John. 1995. *Inaugural Exhibition: Images of Faith.* London: John Eskenazi.

Filliozat, Jean. 1958. "L'agalloche et les manuscrits sur bois dans l'Inde et les pays de civilisation indienne." *Journal Asiatique* 246: 85–93.

Finot, L. 1901. *Rāṣṭrapālaparipṛcchā: Sūtra du Mahāyāna.* Bibliotheca Buddhica 2. St. Petersburg: Académie Impériale des Sciences.
Foucher, A. 1905. *L'art gréco-bouddhique du Gandhâra.* Vol. 1. Publications de l'École Française d'Extrême-Orient. Paris: Imprimerie Nationale.
———. 1918. *L'art gréco-bouddhique du Gandhâra.* Vol. 2.1. Publications de l'École Française d'Extrême-Orient. Paris: Imprimerie Nationale.
Frumkin, Grégoire. 1970. *Archaeology in Soviet Central Asia.* Leiden: E. J. Brill.
Fussman, Gérard. 1969. "Une inscription Kharoṣṭhī à Haḍḍa." *Bulletin de l'École Française d'Extrême-Orient* 56: 5–9.
———. 1972. *Atlas linguistique des parlers dardes et kafirs.* 2 vols. Publications de l'École Française d'Extrême-Orient 86. Paris: École Française d'Extrême-Orient.
———. 1974. "Documents épigraphiques kouchans." *Bulletin de l'École Française d'Extrême-Orient* 61: 1–76.
———. 1980. "Nouvelles inscriptions śaka: Ère d'Azès, ère Vikrama, ère de Kaniṣka." *Bulletin de l'École Française d'Extrême-Orient* 67: 1–43.
———. 1982. "Documents épigraphiques kouchans (III). L'inscription Kharoṣṭhī de Senavarma, roi d'Oḍi: Une nouvelle lecture." *Bulletin de l'École Française d'Extrême-Orient* 71: 1–46.
———. 1985a. "Nouvelles inscriptions śaka (III)." *Bulletin de l'École Française d'Extrême-Orient* 74: 35–41.
———. 1985b. "Nouvelles inscriptions śaka (IV)." *Bulletin de l'École Française d'Extrême-Orient* 74: 47–51.
———. 1985c. "A Pedestal Inscription from the Peshawar District," *East and West,* n.s., 35: 143–52.
———. 1989. "Gāndhārī écrite, Gāndhārī parlée." In Caillat 1989b: 433–501.
———. 1994: "Upāya-kauśalya: L'implantation du bouddhisme au Gandhāra." In Fukui Fumimasa and Gérard Fussman, eds., *Bouddhisme et cultures locales: Quelques cas de réciproques adaptations,* pp. 17–51. Études Thématiques 2. Paris: École Française d'Extrême-Orient.
Fussman, Gérard, and Marc Le Berre. 1976. *Monuments bouddhiques de la région de Caboul.* Vol. 1, *Le monastère de Gul Dara.* Mémoires de la Délégation Archéologique Française en Afghanistan 22. Paris: Diffusion de Boccard.
Gandhāra 2: Preliminary Report on the Comprehensive Survey of Buddhist Sites in Gandhāra, 1986. 1988. Kyoto University Scientific Mission to Gandhāra. Kyoto: Kyoto University Press.
Gardin, J.-C. 1957. *Céramiques de Bactres.* Mémoires de la Délégation Archéologique Française en Afghanistan 15. Paris: C. Klincksieck.
Ghosh, A. 1966. "The Relic-Casket from Devnimori." *Journal of the Maharaja Sayajirao University of Baroda* 15: 21–4.
———. 1967. "A Note on the Relic-Casket from Devnimori." *Journal of the Maharaja Sayajirao University of Baroda* 16: 135.
———. 1989. *An Encyclopaedia of Indian Archaeology.* 2 vols. Delhi: Munshiram Manoharlal.
Grenard, F. 1898. *Mission scientifique dans la haute Asie, 1890–1895.* Part 3, *Histoire—Linguistique—Archéologie—Géographie.* Paris: Ernest Leroux.
Gulik, R. H. van. 1956. *Siddham: An Essay on the History of Sanskrit Studies in China and Japan.* Sarasvati-Vihara Series 36. Nagpur: International Academy of Indian Culture.
Härtel, Herbert. 1993. *Excavations at Sonkh: 2500 Years of a Town in Mathura District.*

Monographien zur Indischen Archäologie, Kunst, und Philologie 9. Berlin: Dietrich Reimer Verlag.
Hilka, Afrons. 1910. *Beiträge zur Kenntnis der indischen Namengebung: Die altindischen Personennamen.* Indische Forschungen 3. Breslau: M. & H. Marcus.
Hinüber, Oskar von. 1981. "Namen in Schutzzaubern aus Gilgit." *Studien zur Indologie und Iranistik* 7: 163–71.
———. 1983. "Sanskrit und Gāndhārī in Zentralasien." In Klaus Röhrborn and Wolfgang Veenker, eds., *Sprachen des Buddhismus in Zentralasien,* pp. 27–34. Wiesbaden: Otto Harrassowitz.
———. 1985. "Die Bestimmung der Schulzugehörigkeit buddhistischer Texte nach sprachlichen Kriterien." In Bechert 1985: 1.57–75.
———. 1989. "Origin and Varieties of Buddhist Sanskrit." In Caillat 1989b: 341–67.
———. 1991. "Inscribed Vessels from Buddhist Monasteries in Termez and Salihundam." *Pakistan Archaeology* 26: 120–4.
Hirakawa, Akira. 1990. *A History of India Buddhism: From Śākyamuni to Early Mahāyāna.* Trans. Paul Groner. Asian Studies at Hawaii 36. Honolulu: University of Hawaii Press.
Hoernle, A. F. Rudolf. 1900. "An Epigraphical Note on Palm-Leaf, Paper and Birch-Bark." *Journal of the Asiatic Society* 69: 93–134.
———. 1911. "The 'Unknown Languages' of Eastern Turkestan, II." *Journal of the Royal Asiatic Society,* pp. 447–93.
———. 1914. *The Bower Manuscript.* Reprinted, with additions, from vol. 22 of the New Imperial Series of the Archeological Survey of India. Bombay: British India Press.
———. 1916. *Manuscript Remains of Buddhist Literature Found in Eastern Turkestan.* Oxford: Clarendon Press.
Hofinger, Marcel. 1982. *Le congrès du lac Anavatapta* (*Vies de saints bouddhiques*). Vol. 1, *Légendes des anciens* (*Sthavirāvadāna*). 2d ed. Publications de l'Institut Orientaliste de Louvain 28. Louvain-la-Neuve: Université Catholique de Louvain.
Honigberger, John Martin. 1852. *Thirty-five Years in the East: Adventures, Discoveries, Experiments, and Historical Sketches Relating to the Punjab and Cashmere. . . .* London: H. Baillière.
Humbach, Helmut. 1980. "Hybrid Sanskrit in the Gilgit Brāhmī Inscriptions." *Studien zur Indologie und Iranistik* 5/6: 99–121.
Husain, Javed. 1980. "Shaikhan Dheri Pottery: A Methodological and Interpretive Approach." Ph.D. diss., Cambridge University.
Ingholt, Harald. 1957. *Gandhāran Art in Pakistan.* New York: Pantheon Books.
Iourkevitch, E. A. 1974. "Histoire de l'explorations des monuments kushans d'Afghanistan." *Afghanistan* 27.1: 77–88; 27.2: 46–56.
Jacquet, E. 1836. "Notice sur les découvertes archéologiques faites par M. Honigberger dans l'Afghanistan." *Journal Asiatique,* ser. 3, vol. 2: 234–77.
———. 1838. "Notice sur les découvertes archéologiques faites par M. Honigberger dans l'Afghanistan (suite)." *Journal Asiatique,* ser. 3, vol. 5: 163–97.
Janert, Klaus Ludwig. 1955–6. *Von der Art und den Mitteln der indischen Textweitergabe: Bericht über mündliche und schriftliche Tradierungsmethoden sowie die Schreibmaterialen in Indien.* Jahresarbeit dem Bibliothekar-Lehrinstitut des Landes Nordrhein-Westfalen zur Diplomaprüfung . . . vorgelegt. Cologne: Bibliothekar-Lehrinstitut des Landes Nordrhein-Westfalen.

Jayawickrama, N. A. 1949. "Sutta Nipāta: The Khaggavisāṇa Sutta." *University of Ceylon Review* 7: 119–28. Reprinted in *Pali Buddhist Review* 2 (1977): 22–31.

Justi, Ferdinand. 1895. *Iranisches Namenbuch.* Marburg: N. G. Elwert.

Kawamura, K. 1974. *Abidatsuma ronsho no shiryō teki kenkyū.* Tokyo: Nihon Gakujutsu Shinkōkai.

Kaye, G. R. 1927. *The Bakhshālī Manuscript: A Study in Mediaeval Mathematics.* Archaeological Survey of India, New Imperial Series 43. Calcutta: Government of India.

Konow, Sten. 1914. "Bemerkungen über die Kharoṣṭhī-Handschrift des Dhammapada." In *Festschrift Ernst Windisch zum siebzigsten Geburtstag am 4. September 1914 dargebracht von Freuden und Schülern,* pp. 85–97. Leipzig: Otto Harrassowitz.

———. 1929. *Kharoshṭhī Inscriptions with the Exception of Those of Aśoka.* Corpus Inscriptionum Indicarum, vol. 2, part 1. Calcutta: Government of India.

———. 1931–2. "Kalawan Copper-Plate Inscription of the Year 134." *Epigraphia Indica* 21: 251–9.

———. 1933. "Kharoshthi Inscription on a Begram Bas-relief." *Epigraphia Indica* 22: 11–14.

———. 1935–6. "Hidda Inscription of the Year 28." *Epigraphia Indica* 23: 35–42.

———. 1940. "A New Charsadda Inscription." In Bimala Churn Law, ed., *D. R. Bhandarkar Volume,* pp. 305–10. Calcutta: Indian Research Institute.

Kurita, Isao. 1988–90. *Gandāra bijutsu/Gandhāran Art.* 2 vols. Tokyo: Nigensha.

Lamotte, Étienne. 1988. *History of Indian Buddhism from the Origins to the Śaka Era.* Trans. Sara Webb-Boin. Publications de l'Institut Orientaliste de Louvain 36. Louvain-la-Neuve: Institut Orientaliste.

Legge, James. 1886. *A Record of Buddhistic Kingdoms: Being an Account by the Chinese monk Fâ-hien of His Travels in India and Ceylon* (A.D. *344–414*). . . . Oxford: Clarendon Press.

Lévi, Sylvain. 1915. "Sur la récitation primitive des textes bouddhiques." *Journal Asiatique,* ser. 11, vol. 5: 401–47.

———. 1932. "Note sur des manuscrits sanscrites provenant de Bamiyan (Afghanistan), et de Gilgit (Cachemire)." *Journal Asiatique* 220: 1–45.

Lévi, Sylvain, and Édouard Chavannes. 1916. "Les seize arhat protecteurs de la loi." *Journal Asiatique,* ser. 11, vol. 8: 5–50, 189–304.

Lin, Meicun. Forthcoming. "A Survey of Kharoṣṭhī Texts from China." *Journal of the American Oriental Society.*

Litvinsky, B. A., ed. 1996. *History of Civilizations of Central Asia.* Vol. 3, *The Crossroads of Civilizations:* A.D. *250 to 750.* Multiple History Series. Paris: UNESCO.

Lohuizen-de Leeuw, Johanna Engelberta van. 1949. *The "Scythian" Period: An Approach to the History, Art, Epigraphy and Palaeography of North India from the 1st Century* B.C. *to the 3rd Century* A.D. Leiden: E. J. Brill.

Lüders, Heinrich. 1940. "Zu und aus den Kharoṣṭhī-Urkunden." *Acta Orientalia* 18: 15–49.

———. 1961. *Mathurā Inscriptions: Unpublished Papers Edited by Klaus L. Janert.* Abhandlungen der Akademie der Wissenschaften in Göttingen, Philologisch-historische Klasse 3.47. Göttingen: Vandenhoeck & Ruprecht.

MacDowall, David W. 1973. "The Azes Hoard from Shaikan-Dheri: Fresh Evidence for the Context of Jihonika." In Norman Hammond, ed., *South Asian Archaeology: Papers from the First International Conference of South Asian Archaeologists Held in the University of Cambridge,* pp. 215–30. London: Duckworth.

———. 1990. "The Chronological Evidence of Coins in Stūpa Deposits." In Maurizio Taddei (with the assistance of Pierfrancesco Callieri), ed., *South Asian Archaeology 1987: Proceedings of the Ninth International Conference of South Asian Archaeologists in Western Europe,* 2.727–35. Serie Orientale Roma 66. Rome: Istituto Italiano per il Medio ed Estremo Oriente.

Malalasekere, G. P. 1937–8. *Dictionary of Pāli Proper Names.* 2 vols. London: Pali Text Society.

Marshall, John. 1951. *Taxila: An Illustrated Account of Archaeological Excavations Carried Out at Taxila. . . .* 3 vols. Cambridge: Cambridge University Press.

———. 1960. *The Buddhist Art of Gandhāra: The Story of the Early School, Its Birth, Growth and Decline.* Memoirs of the Department of Archaeology in Pakistan 1. Cambridge: Cambridge University Press.

Marshall, John, and Alfred Foucher. 1940. *The Monuments of Sanchi.* 3 vols. Calcutta: Government of India.

Marshall, John, and J. P. Vogel. 1902–3. "Excavations at Chārsada in the Frontier Province." *Archaeological Survey of India, Annual Reports,* pp. 141–84.

Mayeda, Egaku. 1985. "Japanese Studies on the Schools of the Chinese Āgamas." In Bechert 1985: 1.94–103.

Mayrhofer, Manfred. 1973. *Onomastica Persepolitana: Das altiranische Namengut der Persepolis-Täfelchen.* Sitzungsberichte der Österreichischen Akademie der Wissenschaften, Philosophisch-historische Klasse 286; Veröffentlichen der Iranischen Kommission 1. Vienna: Österreichische Akademie der Wissenschaften.

McDermott, James P. 1984. "Scripture as the Word of the Buddha." *Numen* 31: 22–39.

Miller, Daniel. 1985. *Artefacts as Categories: A Study of Ceramic Variability in Central India.* New Studies in Archaeology. Cambridge: Cambridge University Press.

Mitchiner, Michael. 1976. *Indo-Greek and Indo-Scythian Coinage.* Vol. 7. London: Hawkins Publications.

Mitra, Debala. 1981–3. *Ratnagiri (1958–61).* 2 vols. Memoirs of the Archaeological Survey of India 80. New Delhi: Archaeological Society of India.

Mizuno, Seiichi. 1969. *Mekhasanda: Buddhist Monastery in Pakistan Surveyed in 1962–1967.* Publication of the Kyoto University Scientific Mission to Iranian Plateau and Hindukush. Kyoto: Kyoto University.

———. 1971. *Basawal and Jelalabad-Kabul: Buddhist Cave-Temples and Topes in South-east Afghanistan Surveyed Mainly in 1965.* 2 vols. Publication of the Kyoto University Scientific Mission to Iranian Plateau and Hindukush. Kyoto: Kyoto University.

Morgenstierne, G. 1950. "*Svásā* and *bhaginī* in Modern Indo-Aryan." *Acta Orientalia* 20: 27–32.

Müller, F. Max. 1880. "On Sanskrit Texts Discovered in Japan." *Journal of the Royal Asiatic Society,* n.s., 12: 153–88.

Mus, Paul. 1939. *La lumière sur les six voies: Tableau de la transmigration bouddhique. . . .* Vol. 1, *Introduction et critique des textes.* Travaux et Memoires de l'Institut d'Ethnologie 35. Paris: Institut d'Ethnologie.

Mustamandi, Shahibye. 1970. "Report on Kushanid Studies in Afghanistan." *Afghanistan* 23: 70–3.

———. 1971. "Preliminary Report on Hadda's Fifth Excavation Period." *Afghanistan* 24: 128–37.

——— [C. Mustamindy]. 1974. "Les nouvelles fouilles de Hadda." In *Central'naja azija v kušanskuju èpoxu/Central Asia in the Kushan Period (Proceedings of the International Conference on the History, Archaeology and Culture of Central Asia in the Kushan Period)*, 1.107–12. Moscow: Izdatel'stvo "Nauka."

——— [Chaibai Mustamandy]. 1984. "Herakles, Ahnherr Alexanders, in einer Plastik aus Hadda." In Jakob Ozols and Volker Thewalt, eds., *Aus dem Osten des Alexanderreiches: Völker und Kulturen zwischen Orient und Okzident; Iran, Afghanistan, Pakistan, Indien*, pp. 176–80. Cologne: DuMont Buchverlag.

Nishi, G. 1934. "Ubushnai ni okeru hotchi hi-hotchi kei nado no shoshu no gakusetsu oyobi gakutō no kenkyū." *Shūkyō Kenkyū* 11.4: 564–79; 11.5: 768–89.

Nishimura, M. 1982. "Rokusokuron no seiritsuji." *Sankō Bunka Kenkyūjo Nenpō* 15: 141–56.

Norman, K. R. 1983. *Pāli Literature, Including the Canonical Literature in Prakrit and Sanskrit of All the Hīnayāna Schools of Buddhism.* A History of Indian Literature 7.2. Wiesbaden: Otto Harrassowitz.

———. 1993. "The Languages of Early Buddhism." In *Premier colloque Étienne Lamotte (Bruxelles et Liège 24–27 septembre 1989)*, pp. 83–99. Publications de l'Institut Orientaliste de Louvain. Louvain-la-Neuve: Institut Orientaliste.

———. 1996. "'Solitary as Rhinoceros Horn.'" *Buddhist Studies Review* 13: 133–42.

Pauly, Bernard. 1967. "Fragments sanskrits d'Afghanistan (fouilles de la D.A.F.A.)." *Journal Asiatique* 255: 273–83.

Petech, Luciano. 1966. "A Kharoṣṭhī Inscription from Butkara I (Swat)." *East and West*, n.s., 16: 80–1.

Przyluski, Jean. 1926. *Le concile de Rājagṛha: Introduction à l'histoire des canons et des sectes bouddhiques.* Buddhica, Mémoires 2. Paris: Librairie Orientaliste Paul Geuthner.

Quagliotti, Anna Maria. 1990. "Mañjuśrī in Gandharan Art: A New Interpretation of a Relief in the Victoria and Albert Museum." *East and West*, n.s., 40: 99–113.

Rahman, Abdur. 1993. "Shnaisha Gumbat: First Preliminary Excavation Report." *Ancient Pakistan* 8: 1–124.

Rosenfield, John M. 1967. *The Dynastic Arts of the Kushans.* Berkeley and Los Angeles: University of California Press.

Rye, Owen S., and Clifford Evans. 1976. *Traditional Pottery Techniques of Pakistan: Field and Laboratory Studies.* Smithsonian Contributions to Anthropology 21. Washington: Smithsonian Institution Press.

Sachau, Eduard C., trans. 1888. *Alberuni's India: An Account of the Religion, Philosophy, Literature, Geography, Chronology, Astronomy, Customs, Laws, and Astrology of India about A.D. 1030.* 2 vols. in 1. London: Trübner.

Sadakata, Akira. 1992. "Gandāra no kishin bun." *Bukkyō Gaku* 33: 1–6.

———. 1996a. "Azesu sanjūkyū men no kishin mei." *Shunju*, no. 7: 13–16.

———. 1996b. "Inscriptions kharoṣṭhī provenant du marché aux antiquités de Peshawar." *Journal Asiatique* 284: 301–24.

———. 1996c. "Seihoku Indo no hōzōbu." *Shunju*, no. 10: 20–3.

Sadan, J. 1986. "Genizah and Genizah-like Practices in Islamic and Jewish Traditions: Customs concerning the Disposal of Worn-out Sacred Books in the Middle Ages, according to an Ottoman Source." *Bibliotheca Orientalis* 43: 36–58.

Salomon, Richard. 1986. "The Inscription of Senavarma, King of Oḍi." *Indo-Iranian Journal* 29: 261–93.

———. 1989. "Linguistic Variability in Post-Vedic Sanskrit." In Caillat 1989b: 275–94.

———. 1990a. "A Kharoṣṭhī Inscription on a Silver Goblet." *Bulletin of the Asia Institute* 4: 149–57.
———. 1990b. "New Evidence for a Gāndhārī Origin of the Arapacana Syllabary." *Journal of the American Oriental Society* 110: 255–73.
———. 1995a. "A Kharoṣṭhī Reliquary Inscription of the Time of the Apraca Prince Viṣṇuvarma." *South Asian Studies* 11: 27–32.
———. 1995b. "Three Dated Kharoṣṭhī Inscriptions." *Bulletin of the Asia Institute* 9: 127–41.
———. 1996a. "An Inscribed Silver Buddhist Reliquary of the Time of King Kharaosta and Prince Indravarman." *Journal of the American Oriental Society* 116: 418–52.
———. 1996b. "Five Kharoṣṭhī Inscriptions." *Bulletin of the Asia Institute* 10: 233–46.
———. 1997a. "A Preliminary Survey of Some Early Buddhist Manuscripts Recently Acquired by the British Library." *Journal of the American Oriental Society* 117: 353–8.
———. 1997b. Review of Vertogradova 1995. *Journal of the American Oriental Society* 117: 406–8.
———. 1998. *Indian Epigraphy: A Guide to the Study of Inscriptions in Sanskrit, Prakrit, and the Other Indo-Aryan Languages.* New York: Oxford University Press.
Salomon, Richard, and Gregory Schopen. 1984. "The Indravarman (Avaca) Casket Inscription Reconsidered: Further Evidence for Canonical Passages in Buddhist Inscriptions." *Journal of the International Association of Buddhist Studies* 7: 107–23.
Sander, Lore. 1968. *Paläographisches zu den Sanskrithandschriften der Berliner Turfansammlung.* Verzeichnis der orientalischen Handschriften in Deutschland, Supplementband 8. Wiesbaden: Franz Steiner Verlag.
———. 1991. "The Earliest Manuscripts from Central Asia and the Sarvāstivāda Mission." In Ronald E. Emmerick and Dieter Weber, eds., *Corolla Iranica: Papers in Honour of Prof. Dr. David Neil MacKenzie on the Occasion of His 65th Birthday . . . ,* pp. 133–50. Frankfurt am Main: Peter Lang.
Sawoo, Mangala. 1983. "An Interesting Buddha Image in the Indian Museum, Calcutta." *Indian Museum Bulletin* 1983: 58–60.
Schlingloff, Dieter. 1956: "Die Birkenrindenhandschriften der Berliner Turfansammlung." *Mitteilungen des Instituts für Orientforschung* 4: 120–7.
Schlumberger, Daniel. 1949. "La prospection archéologique de Bactres (printemps 1947), rapport sommaire." *Syria* 26: 173–90.
Schopen, Gregory. 1975. "The Phrase *'sa pṛthivīpradeśaś caityabhūto bhavet'* in the *Vajracchedikā:* Notes on the Cult of the Book in Mahāyāna." *Indo-Iranian Journal* 17: 147–81.
———. 1987. "Burial *'ad Sanctos'* and the Physical Presence of the Buddha in Early Indian Buddhism: A Study in the Archaeology of Religions." *Religion* 17: 193–225.
———. 1991. "An Old Inscription from Amarāvatī and the Cult of the Local Monastic Dead in Indian Buddhist Monasteries." *Journal of the International Association of Buddhist Studies* 14: 281–329.
———. 1994a. "Doing Business for the Lord: Lending on Interest and Written Loan Contracts in the *Mūlasarvāstivāda-vinaya.*" *Journal of the American Oriental Society* 114: 527–53.
———. 1994b. "*Stūpa* and *Tīrtha:* Tibetan Mortuary Practices and an Unrecognized

Form of Burial ad Sanctos at Buddhist Sites in India." In Tadeusz Skorupski and Ulrich Pagel, eds., *The Buddhist Forum*, vol. 3, *1991–1993* (*Papers in Honour and Appreciation of Professor David Seyfort Ruegg's Contribution to Indological, Buddhist and Tibetan Studies*), pp. 273–93. London: School of Oriental and African Studies, University of London.

———. 1996. "The Lay Ownership of Monasteries and the Role of the Monk in Mūlasarvāstivādin Monasticism." *Journal of the International Association of Buddhist Studies* 19: 81–126.

Senart, Émile. 1898. "Le manuscrit Kharoṣṭhī du Dhammapada: Les fragments Dutreuil de Rhins." *Journal Asiatique*, ser. 9, vol. 12: 193–308.

Shih, Robert. 1968. *Biographies des moines éminents* (Kao seng tchouan) *de Houei-kiao*. Bibliothèque du Muséon 54. Louvain: Institut Orientaliste.

Shizutani, Masao. 1979. *Indo bukkyō himei mokuroku*. Kyoto: Heirakuji Shoten.

Simpson, William. 1881. "On the Identification of Nagarahara, with Reference to the Travels of Hiouen-Thsang." *Journal of the Royal Asiatic Society*, n.s., 13: 183–207.

Simson, Georg von. 1985. "Stil und Schulzugehörigkeit buddhistischer Sanskrittexte." In Bechert 1985: 1.76–93.

Speyer, J. S. 1906–9. *Avadānaçataka: A Century of Edifying Tales Belonging to the Hīnayāna*. Bibliotheca Buddhica 3. St. Petersburg: Imperial Academy of Sciences.

Stache-Rosen, Valentina. 1968. *Dogmatische Begriffsreihen im älteren Buddhismus*. Vol. 2, *Das Saṅgītisūtra und sein Kommentar Saṅgītiparyāya*. Sanskrittexte aus den Turfanfunden 9. Berlin: Akademie-Verlag.

Stein, M. Aurel. 1907. *Ancient Khotan: Detailed Report of Archaeological Explorations in Chinese Turkestan. . . .* Oxford: Clarendon Press.

Stwodah, Mohammed Ibrahim. 1980. "Library Condition in the Kushan Civilization (A Preliminary Historical Research)." *Tahqiqāt-i Kūshānī* 3: 1–8.

Taddei, Maurizio. 1983. "Addenda to *The Story of the Buddha and the Skull-Tapper* (*AION*, 39, 1979, 3)." *Annali dell'Istituto Universitario Orientale* 43: 333–9.

Takakusu, J. 1896. *A Record of the Buddhist Religion as Practised in India and the Malay Archipelago* (A.D. *671–695*) *by I-tsing*. Oxford: Clarendon Press.

Tarzi, Zémaryalaï. 1976. "Hadda à la lumière des trois dernières campagnes de fouilles de Tapa-é-Shotor (1974–1976)." *Comptes Rendus de l'Academie des Inscriptions et Belles-lettres*, pp. 381–410.

———. 1990. "Tapa-e-Top-e-Kalān (TTK) of Haḍḍa." In Maurizio Taddei (with the assistance of Pierfrancesco Callieri), ed., *South Asian Archaeology 1987: Proceedings of the Ninth International Conference of South Asian Archaeologists in Western Europe*, 2.707–26. Serie Orientale Roma 66. Rome: Istituto Italiano per il Medio ed Estremo Oriente.

Tissot, Francine. 1985. *Gandhâra*. La Vie Publique et Privée dans l'Inde Ancienne, 2d ser. Paris: Librairie d'Amérique et d'Orient.

Tripāṭhī, Chandrabhāl. 1985. "Saṅgīti-sūtra, Nipāta II, und Ekottarāgama-Parallelen." In Bechert 1985: 1.191–9.

Tucci, Giuseppe. 1958. "Preliminary Report on an Archaeological Survey in Swat." *East and West*, n.s., 9: 279–328.

Turner, R. L. 1966. *A Comparative Dictionary of the Indo-Aryan Languages*. 3 vols. London: Oxford University Press.

Vertogradova, V. V. 1982. "Indijskie nadpisi na keramike iz raskopok 70-x godov na Kara-tepe." In B. Ja. Staviskii, ed., *Buddhijskie pamjatniki Kara-tepe v starom*

Termeze: Osnovnye itogi rabot 1974-1977 gg, pp. 134–59. Moscow: Glavnaja Redakcija Vostočnoj Literatury.

———. 1995. *Indijskaja epigrafika iz Kara-tepe v starom Termeze: Problemy dešifrovki i interpretacii.* Moscow: Vostočnaja Literatura.

Vorob'eva-Desjatovskaja, M. I. 1974. "Novye nadpisi pis'mom *kxaroštxi* iz Termeza." *Vestnik Drevnej Istorii* 1: 116–26.

———. 1983. "Pamjatniki pis'mom kxaroštxi i braxmi iz sovetskoj srednej Azii." In *Istorija i Kultura Central'noj Azii*, pp. 22–96. Moscow: Izdatel'stvo "Nauka."

Waldschmidt, Ernst. 1932. *Bruchstücke Buddhistischer Sūtras aus dem zentralasiatischen Sanskritkanon.* Kleinere Sanskrit-Texte 4. Leipzig: Deutsche Morgenländische Gesellschaft.

———. 1950–51. *Das Mahāparinirvāṇasūtra: Text in Sanskrit und Tibetisch, verglichen mit dem Pali. . . .* Abhandlungen der Deutschen Akademie der Wissenschaften zu Berlin, Klasse für Sprachen, Literatur, und Kunst, no. 1 (1949) and no. 2 (1950). Berlin: Akademie-Verlag.

———. 1959. *Kleine Brāhmī-Schriftrolle.* Nachrichten der Akademie der Wissenchaften in Göttingen, Philologisch-historische Klasse 1959.1. Göttingen: Vandenhoeck & Ruprecht.

——— (with Walter Clawiter and Lore Holzmann). 1965. *Sanskrithandschriften aus den Turfanfunden.* Vol. 1. Verzeichnis der Orientalischen Handschriften in Deutschland 10.1. Wiesbaden: Franz Steiner Verlag.

———. 1968. *Drei Fragmente buddhistischer Sūtras aus den Turfanhandschriften.* Nachrichten der Akademie der Wissenschaften in Göttingen, Philologisch-historische Klasse 1968.1. Göttingen: Vandenhoeck & Ruprecht.

———. 1980. "Central Asian Sūtra Fragments and Their Relation to the Chinese Āgamas." In Bechert 1980: 136–74.

Willemen, Charles, ed. and trans. 1975. *The Essence of Metaphysics: Abhidharmahṛdaya.* Publications de l'Institut Belge des Hautes Études Bouddhiques, série "Études et Textes," 4. Brussels: Institut Belge des Hautes Études Bouddhiques.

Wilson, H. H. 1841. *Ariana Antiqua: A Descriptive Account of the Antiquities and Coins of Afghanistan.* London: East India Co.

Woodward, F. L., trans. 1952. *The Book of the Gradual Sayings (Anguttara-nikāya) or More-numbered Suttas.* Vol. 2, *The Book of the Fours.* Pali Text Society Translation Series 24. London: Luzac, for the Pali Text Society.

Yamada, R. 1957. "Ubu gandāra kei ronsho no tokushitsu." *Nihon Bukkyō Gakkai Nenpō* 22: 283–99.

Zwalf, W. 1996. *A Catalogue of the Gandhāra Sculpture in the British Museum.* 2 vols. London: British Museum Press.

Index

abbreviation formulae (in avadāna texts), 36, 147 n. 17, 165
abhidharma, 158, 158 n. 3
Gandhāran school of, 5–6, 12
texts among British Library fragments, 12, 29, 50, 52, 54, 175
text sample, 29–30
texts surviving in Chinese, 5–6, 6 n. 4, 7, 12, 178
Abhidharma-hṛdaya, 5
aca/aco (problematic word), 72 n. 2, 75–6
Achaemenian Empire, 4, 110, 112
"ad sanctos" burial, 80–1
Afghanistan, 3, 4, 106, 178, 186
Dharmaguptaka school in, 177
funereal jars from, 79 n. 11
inscribed pots from, 187
Kharoṣṭhī inscriptions from, 175–6
Kharoṣṭhī manuscripts from, 20, 57, 59–66 passim, 68
Sanskrit manuscripts from, 171
Afghans, 4
Ājīvika (member of a heterodox sect), 36, 213
Ājñātakauṇḍinya (subject of a pūrvayoga story), 37–8, 44, 49, 174
Alam Bridge, 129
Alexander the Great, 4–5
amulets, 86
Ānanda (subject of pūrvayoga story), 37–9, 49, 174
Anāthapiṇḍika, 36
Anavatapta-gāthā
British Library manuscript of, 23, 30, 43, 53, 162, 166; format, 99; lexicon, 134; morphology, 131, 131 n. 18, 131, 132–3; phonology, 125 n. 10, 126, 127; scribe, 108; style, 138–9; text sample, 31–3, 139
Chinese and Tibetan versions of, 158–9, 161–2, 174
recensions, 163, 174
Andhra Pradesh, 245
Aṅguttara-nikāya
British Library manuscript corresponding to, 23, 48, 54, 91, 132, 164; lexicon, 135; style, 133; text sample, 24–6
Pali, 25 n. 5, 27
anusvāra. *See under* Kharoṣṭhī script
Apadāna (Pali text), 33, 163
apadāna (Pali text genre), 37
Apraca kings, 148 n. 23, 153 n. 27, 154, 180–1
genealogy, 150 (fig. 13), 152–3
territories, 148, 181
Ārā inscription, 116
Aramaic script, 4, 110
Arapacana alphabet, 136 n. 22, 170
Arthavargīya-sūtra. *See* Aṭṭhaka-vagga
Ashkun (Nuristani language), 134
Aśoka, 150, 180
mentioned in avadāna text, 36
rock edicts, 5, 112, 126, 130, 133–4
Aśpavarman (Indo-Scythian ruler), 153–4. *See also* Apraca kings
coins, 145
date, 148–9
mentioned in avadāna text, 37, 141, 145–8, 147 n. 13, 150, 155, 180
territories, 181
Assamese language, 134, 135
Aṣṭavarga-sūtra. *See* Aṭṭhaka-vagga
Atranjikherā, 187
Aṭṭhaka-vagga (of Sutta-nipāta), 27, 158, 159, 160–3. *See also* Sutta-nipāta
auspicious symbol, 232, 234
avadānas, among British Library fragments, 23, 35–9, 43–5, 48, 53, 54, 72, 75–6, 90, 125 n. 10, 147 n. 17, 161, 162, 164
abridged form, 165
colloquial style, 139–40, 140 n. 29, 165
date, 150
historical references in, 141, 145, 145 n. 7, 149, 153, 180

avadānas (*continued*)
Jhādamitra, story of, 145–7, 147 nn. 15–6. *See also* Jhādamitra/Jhādimitra
lexicon, 134, 142
local (Gandhāran) origins, 178
morphology, 131, 131 n. 18, 132, 133
orthography, 122, 123, 127
parallels in other text traditions, 174
scribe, 114, 121
script, 116
text samples, 38–9, 140
Avadāna-śataka, 147 n. 20
Avakhajada (Indo-Scythian individual), 145 n. 6
Azes [I] (Indo-Scythian king), 144, 177
Azes [II] (Indo-Scythian king), 145, 148, 149

Bactria, 4, 169, 177, 187
Bactrian Greeks, 4. *See also* Indo-Greeks
Bahuśrutikas (Buddhist school), 191
Bairam Ali manuscript, 36, 84, 84 n. 20, 165
Bajaur (Pakistan), 148, 181
Balkh, 213
Bamiyan (Afghanistan), 24, 66
Barikot (Swat), 187
Barthoux, J., 63–5, 68
Bāsawal (Afghanistan), 188
Begram inscription, 205
Bengal, 122
Bhagavadgītā, 86
Bhaiṣajyavastu (section of Mūlasarvāstivāda-vinaya), 30, 54, 157
Bhamāla, 186
bhāṇakas, 164
Bhano (character in pūrvayoga story), 39
Bihari language, 134, 135
Bīmārān (Afghanistan), 60 n. 3, 212
birch bark (as writing material), 59–60, 65, 84
conservation, 15–17
fragility, 16–7, 22, 62, 64, 68, 104–6
lenticels, 107, 108
preparation, 106–8
references to in literature, 106–7
sanctity associated with, 86
species used, 106
supply, 68 n. 16
used in central Asia, 102
used in far northern India, 8, 39, 103, 106, 107
used in other parts of the world, 106
al-Bīrūnī, 107
Bodhisattva, 37, 38, 49
Bourdj i Kemri (Kamari), 62
Bower manuscript, 107

Brahmanical culture, 4
Brāhmī script, 3, 4, 57, 67, 77, 84, 85
British Library fragment in, 23, 39, 46, 53, 88, 94
central Asian, 102
coin legends, 113
direction of writing, 112
Gandhāra, adopted in, 107
pot and potsherd inscriptions, 188 n. 3, 225, 230, 240–1, 245
used for Prakrits (except Gāndhārī), 110
buddhavacana ("words of the Buddha"), 156, 157
Buddhavarman (monk mentioned in KDhP colophon), 41
Buddhayaśas (translator), 173
Buddhism
archeological remains in Gandhāra, 5, 7
central Asian, 171, 182
councils, 156, 157 n. 2
east Asian, 7
foreign rulers attracted to, 5
Gandhāran, 5–7, 10, 77, 155, 157, 171
inscriptions, 5, 6
origins and early history, 7, 34
regional centers, 165, 182
sects and schools. *See* individual schools: Bahuśrutikas; Dharmaguptakas; Kāśyapīyas; Mahāsāṅghikas; Mahīśāsakas; Mūlasarvāstivādins; Sarvāstivādins; Theravādins; and Khotan Dharmapada, sectarian affiliation
Buddhist creed, 86
Buddhist inscriptions, 5, 6
Buddhist Sanskrit/Buddhist Hybrid Sanskrit, 7, 133, 142, 230
Burma, 7, 166
Butkara (Pakistan), 188

calligraphic writing
in British Library fragments, 109, 114, 199 n. 16
in pot and potsherd inscriptions, 198–9, 203, 205, 205 n. 24, 209, 211, 218, 227, 228, 238, 242
Cambodia, 7
canons (Buddhist)
Chinese, 7, 13
formation, 9, 182
Gandhāran, 6, 11, 57, 58, 156–8, 163, 165–6
notion of, 11, 58 n. 2, 156–7
oral vs. written form, 11, 163–6
Pali, 7, 8, 9, 156, 157
sectarian, 7
Tibetan, 7, 9, 156

central Asia
Buddhist Sanskrit manuscripts from, 7, 11, 102, 163, 164, 166, 168, 171, 174
Dharmaguptaka school in, 167–8
Gandhāra, relations with, 4
Gāndhārī language, 128
Kharoṣṭhī manuscripts from, 57, 59, 68, 72, 113, 134, 139–40, 167
Kharoṣṭhī script used in, 4
spread of Buddhism to, 10, 180, 182
Chakhil-i Ghundi, 63, 79, 177
Chang-an (China), 5, 113
Chārsada, 79, 145 n. 6, 186. *See also* Pālāṭu Ḍherī
China, 82
Buddhism, spread to, 5
Dharmaguptaka school in, 167–8
Kharoṣṭhī script used in, 4–5, 113
Chinese language
abhidharma texts, 5–6
Buddhist canons, 7, 13
coin legends, 113
translations of Buddhist texts, 5–6, 7, 38
Chinese pilgrims, 177. *See also* Fa-hsien; Hsüan-tsang; I-ching
Chinese scrolls, 88, 102, 103
Chi-pin, 168, 173
Christianity, 9
Chu Fo-nien (translator), 173
Cīvaravastu (section of Mūlasarvāstivāda-vinaya), 54
clay pots. *See* pots and potsherds
coins, 113, 114, 142, 143, 144, 145, 148, 149, 181 n. 14
colophons, 22, 40–2, 87
commander. *See* stratega
commentaries
British Library fragments of, 11–12, 40, 42, 44, 47, 50, 53, 125 n. 10, 132 n. 20, 164, 165–6; sources of verses quoted in, 26–9, 45, 160–2; text sample, 28–9
Pali, 12, 165
Sinhalese (lost), 12, 165
copying of manuscripts, 74, 76, 83, 83 n. 18
Corpus Inscriptionum Indicarum, 112
councils, Buddhist, 156, 157 n. 2
Cukhsa (Pakistan), 181
Cūla-vagga (of Sutta-nipāta), 160. *See also* Sutta-nipāta
Culla-niddesa, 33
cult of the book, 85
Curtius Rufus, Q., 107
Dardic languages, 110, 133–5, 147 n. 19
Darius (Achaemenid king), 4
"dead" books, 82, 85
Dead Sea scrolls, 9, 84
Deccan, 169
Dhammapada (Pali), 26, 27, 45, 47, 159, 160. *See also* Dharmapada (Gāndhārī); Khotan Dharmapada
dhāraṇīs, 86
Dharmaguptakas (Buddhist school), 166–78 passim
in Afghanistan (Bactria), 169
in central Asia, 167–8, 180
in China, 167–8
decline, 10–11
Dīrghāgama attributed to, 168, 170, 173–4
in Gandhāra and northwestern India, 169, 175–8, 181
Gāndhārī language, 167, 169–71, 174
inscriptional records, 168–9, 177
in Iran, 168, 169
Khotan Dharmapada, 170
in Mathurā, 169
patronized by Indo-Scythians, 11, 177, 180
probable source of British Library fragments, 10, 38, 83, 161, 162, 163, 166, 170–2, 174–5
referred to in inscriptions, 21, 151, 169, 175–8, 191, 214, 217, 229, 231, 234–5, 240
relations with other schools, 167
role in Gandhāran Buddhism, 167
role in spread of Buddhism beyond India, 10
texts preserved in Chinese, 7, 168
vinaya, 158, 158 n. 3, 161, 167, 168, 170, 173
Dharmapada (Gāndhārī), 23, 35, 41, 49, 54, 57 n. 1, 58, 75, 90, 159, 160–2, 170. *See also* Khotan Dharmapada
Dharmarājikā inscriptions, 225, 228
dharmaśarīra, 68, 85
Dhoṇa (a brahman), 24–6
didactic verses, 45, 53
Dīgha-nikāya, 147 n. 20. *See also* Dīrghāgama
Dīrghāgama (Chinese), 172
Dharmaguptaka affiliation, 168, 170, 173–4
transcription of proper names in, 173–4
Divyāvadāna, 140 nn. 29–30, 142
drachma (as weight unit), 144 n. 4, 148
Dutreuil de Rhins, J.-L., 57 n. 1, 58. *See also* Khotan Dharmapada

east Asia, 7, 10
Egyptian papyri, 88, 91
Ekottarikāgama, 24. *See also* Aṅguttara-nikāya

eras
of Azes, 144
"Old Saka" or "Indo-Bactrian," 144, 145

Fa-hsien, 81 n. 16, 164
Faiz Tepe (Uzbekistan), 188, 191 n. 9, 240, 241 n. 40. *See also* Termez
Fo pên hsing chi ching, 38, 174

Gadhabadhaġa (character in pūrvayoga story), 39
Gandhāra
as center of Buddhist scholarship, 178–80
cosmopolitan culture, 5
cultural influence on other regions, 4
dynasties, 3
geographical extent, 3, 168
"Greater Gandhāra," 3, 4
literary tradition, 107
local traditions reflected in British Library manuscripts, 10, 12, 23, 37, 165, 178–9
Mahāyāna Buddhism, 178
mentioned in a British Library manuscript, 142, 143
part of Achaemenian Empire, 110, 112
role in spread of Buddhism, 6
Gandhāran art, 3, 5, 103
Gandhāran grave culture, 246
Gāndhārī canon hypothesis. *See* canons, Gandhāran
"Gāndhārī Dharmapada." *See* Dharmapada (Gāndhārī); Khotan Dharmapada
Gāndhārī language. *See also* Kharoṣṭhī script
aspirate consonants, 127–8
Buddhist texts composed in or translated into, 6–7, 27
central Asian dialect, 113, 129, 130
central Asian documents, 39, 41, 113, 114, 121, 123, 147 n. 19. *See also* Niya documents
China, used in, 5
coin legends, 113, 142
colloquial form, 114, 133, 134, 138–40, 140 n. 29
decline, 77, 137
Dharmaguptaka school, used by, 167, 169–71, 174
dialect features, 120
final vowels, weakened pronunciation, 130, 132
inscriptions and their styles, 112–3, 114, 133
intervocalic consonants, 122, 124–7, 152
literary texts, 113
loanwords, 113
local vocabulary, 135

Gāndhārī language (*continued*)
name, origin of, 110
nasal sounds, 120–1
nonstandardization and variability of forms, 114, 131, 136–8, 154
noun inflections, 130–2
original language of Chinese translations, 6, 170
"Questions of Milinda," 5
region of use, 3, 4
role in Buddhist culture, 112, 137
Sanskritized variety, 230
scholastic form, 138
secular documents from central Asia, 113
sibilants, 120, 121
translation of Buddhist texts into, 133, 136, 138–9, 139 n. 24, 165
types of texts extant, 112–4
verbal forms, 132–3, 136, 140
gāthās, 27, 39 n. 49, 41–2, 42 n. 52
Gavāmpati (subject of avadāna), 36
Ghośya (family name?), 233
Gilgit manuscripts, 30, 31 n. 22, 33 n. 28, 54, 82, 84, 86, 107, 132, 139 n. 25, 158, 174
Girdharpur inscription, 169
Gondophares (Indo-Parthian king), 148, 149, 181 n. 14
Gośṛṅga-/Gośīrṣa-vihāra, 58
great satrap, 141, 142, 148
Greek language, 113, 142
Greek papyri, 88, 91, 102, 102 n. 11, 103
Greek script, 113
Grenard, F., 58
Gul Dara (Afghanistan), 188
Guṇṭupalle, 80

Haḍḍa (Afghanistan), 61, 85
Chakhil-i Ghundi site, 63, 79, 177
dating of sites, 181 n. 14
Dharmaguptaka presence, 177
excavations by J. Barthoux, 63
Hellenistic influence, 103
human remains in pots, 77–8, 79–80, 243–5
inscribed clay jars, 153, 188, 190, 209 n. 26, 213 n. 32, 224, 242 n. 42, 243–5
inscription (spurious?), 144 n. 3
Kharoṣṭhī manuscripts, 60, 63–5, 68, 77, 79
name, origin of, 81 n. 16
probable provenance of British Library fragments, 20–1
Sarvāstivādin presence, 177
Tapa-e-Top-e-Kalān site, 79
Tapa-i Kāfarihā site, 63
Tapa Kalān site, 63–4, 78, 79 n. 10, 80
Tapa Shutur site, 65, 103, 177, 188

Hadrumetum (Tunisia), 103
hands (of different scribes), 43–52 passim, 54–5, 74, 114–5, 117, 121. *See also* scribes
Hastināpura, 187
Hellenistic culture, 103–4
Herakles-Vajrapāṇi, 103
Hidda. *See* Haḍḍa
Himalayas, 106
Hindi, 134
Honigberger, John Martin, 61–2, 64, 67, 86
Hsüan-tsang, 24, 58, 81 n. 16, 157 n. 2, 168, 178, 213 n. 33, 242 n. 43
Huviṣka (Kuṣāṇa king), 116 n. 4

I-ching, 167, 168
Indo-Aryan languages, 3
Indo-Aryans, 4
Indo-Greeks, 3, 5, 113, 184–5, 187
Indo-Parthians, 3, 112, 113, 137
Indo-Scythians, 3, 37, 144, 144 n. 4, 145 n. 7, 149, 152, 154–5, 169, 181, 224. *See also* Sakas; Scythians
  as patrons of Buddhism, 10, 11, 177, 180
Indravarman (Apraca prince), 148, 150 (fig. 13), 153, 181
  reliquary inscription of, 118, 126, 149, 152
Indus River, 3
interlinear notations, 71–6
Iran, 4, 5, 168, 169
Iranian languages, 113, 128, 145, 210
Islam, 81–2
Itivuttaka, 26, 27, 160

Jalalabad (Afghanistan), 59
Jalalabad Plain, 20, 61, 65, 68, 80, 153, 177, 186
Jamālgaṛhī stone inscription, 169, 177, 214
Japan, 82
jātakas, 36, 38. *See also* Mahāummagga-jātaka; Vessantara-jātaka
Jauliāñ, 77, 209
Jhādamitra/Jhādimitra (subject of avadāna), 36, 127–8, 145–7, 147 nn. 15–6, 149
Jihonika (Indo-Scythian ruler), 144 n. 3, 148, 150
  date, 143–4, 149, 154
  mentioned in a British Library avadāna, 37, 43, 141–3, 180
  terrritories, 181
Judaism, 81, 82

Kafiri languages. *See* Nuristani languages
Kalasha (Dardic language), 134
Kalawān inscription, 125
Kālidāsa, 106
Kamari, 62
Kaniṣka (Kuṣāṇa king), 10, 115, 117, 119, 150, 156 n. 2, 180, 242 n. 42
Kaniṣka [II] (Kuṣāṇa king), 116 n. 4
Kanjur, 156
Kara Tepe (Uzbekistan), 188, 191 n. 10, 199, 240–1, 242 n. 42, 244, 245. *See also* Termez
kārṣāpaṇa (weight unit), 144 n. 4
Kashmir, 104, 105, 106, 107
Kāśyapīyas (Buddhist school), 170, 177, 191, 191 n. 9
Khaḍgaviṣāṇa-gāthā. *See* Rhinoceros Horn Sūtra
Khaggavisāṇa-sutta. *See* Rhinoceros Horn Sūtra
Kharoṣṭhī script, 110–24 passim
  anusvāra, 120–1, 205, 210–11, 211 n. 28, 228
  Aramaic script, derivation from, 4, 110
  Aśokan form, 115
  central Asian variety, 113, 124, 128, 130
  chart of, 111 (fig. 12)
  China, used in, 4–5, 113
  coin legends, 113, 114
  cursivization, 115, 117
  decline, 77, 112, 137
  diacritic signs, 121–2
  direction of writing, 112
  Gāndhārī language, association with, 3, 4, 110
  inscriptions, 6, 104, 104 n. 12, 114, 139; of Aśoka, 5, 112; in Corpus Inscriptionum Indicarum, 112; geographical range, 113; graffiti, 113, 129; linguistic characteristics, 125, 129, 132; on silver objects, 144 n. 4. *See also* pots and potsherds, Kharoṣṭhī inscriptions on
  literary texts, 113
  long vowels, 199, 230
  manuscripts: from Haḍḍa, 20; from Kotpūr stūpa, 62; from Nandāra, 60, 64; from Pakistan, 57, 67; from Passani, 60, 61
  nonstandardization, 115, 124, 154, 212
  paleographic development and dating, 115–20, 151–2
  pseudo-anusvāra, 120, 205, 211, 211 n. 28, 218, 228
  secular/administrative documents from central Asia, 113, 114
  vowel notation, 123, 199, 230
Khotan (China), 6, 10 n. 6, 58, 102, 242 n. 43
Khotan Dharmapada, 6, 57 n. 1, 91, 113, 135, 154, 159, 174
  additions to, 129, 129 n. 16
  arrangement of text, 99

Khotan Dharmapada (*continued*)
colophon, 41
condition, 106
construction and format of scroll, 92, 96–8, 101–2
date, 10 n. 6, 119, 126
different features from British Library fragments, 91
dimensions, 88, 90, 91
discovery, 58–9, 77, 84–5
orthography, 121, 123, 124, 212
paleographic characteristics, 120, 199
parallels with texts in British Library fragments, 28, 28 n. 10, 28 n. 13, 35, 49, 89–90
phonology, 126, 129–30
place of origin, 57, 120, 130
rolling cylinder, possible use of, 101
sectarian affiliation, 170
style, 139
Khuddaka-nikāya, 26, 33, 34, 159–61
Kohmāri Mazār (near Khotan), 58
Koran, 82
Kotpūr stūpa (Afghanistan), 62
kṣatrapa (satrap), 143, 144, 149, 181
Kṣudraka (section of Dharmaguptaka-vinaya), 158
Kṣudrakāgama. *See* Khuddaka-nikāya
Kṣudrakavastu (section of Mūlasarvāstivāda-vinaya), 241 n. 41, 246
Kucha, 59, 107
Kujula Kadphises (Kuṣāṇa king), 153, 154
Kumārasambhava (poem by Kālidāsa), 106
Kurram relic casket inscription, 67, 85, 117 n. 5, 119, 209, 238
Kuṣāṇas, 113, 115–7, 137, 151, 153, 154, 169
as patrons of Buddhism, 10, 11, 180–1
pottery from time of, 184, 187
rule in Gandhāra, 3, 4, 112

Lalitavistara, 136 n. 22
Lauṛiyā-Nandangaṛh, 67, 80, 85
leather (as writing material), 113
libraries (in Buddhist monasteries), 83, 83 n. 17, 100, 137, 162, 163, 181
Lo-yang (China), 5, 113

Magadha, 213
Mahākāśyapa (subject of avadāna), 36
mahākṣatrapa (great satrap), 141, 142, 148
Mahāparinirvāṇa-sūtra, 59, 168, 171, 173
Mahārāṣṭrī Prakrit, 125
Mahāsamāja-sūtra, 174
Mahāsāṅghikas (Buddhist school)
attested in inscriptions, 170, 191, 191 n. 10, 194, 212 n. 31
Mahāsāṅghikas (*continued*)
Gāndhārī language, use of, 171
texts in Chinese, 7
vinaya, 158–9, 161, 162, 163
Mahāummagga-jātaka, 103
Mahā-vagga (of Sutta-nipāta), 27, 160. *See also* Sutta-nipāta
Mahāvastu, 33 n. 34, 37–8, 170
mahāyāna, 85, 168, 178
absent from British Library fragments, 12, 30, 30 n. 21
Mahīśāsakas (Buddhist school), 167, 173, 176, 177, 191
"mainstream" Buddhism, 178
Mānsehrā Aśokan rock edicts, 5, 112, 130, 133
Marathi language, 134
maṣrugaha (enigmatic word), 142
Masson, Charles, 59–61, 64, 65, 68, 77, 85
Mathurā
Girdharpur inscription, 169
lion capital inscriptions, 118, 118 n. 6, 212 n. 31
Sonkh, 187
Mauryan dynasty, 5
medical text (in British Library fragments), 23, 39, 46, 53, 88, 94
Mekhāsaṇḍā (Pakistan), 188
Menander (Indo-Greek king), 5
Merv (Turkmenistan), 36, 84
Middle East, 4
Middle Indo-Aryan (MIA) languages, 3, 110, 125, 126, 132, 137
Mongols, 4
mosques, 82
Mūlasarvāstivādins (Buddhist school), 163, 174
in central Asia, 168
vinaya, 30, 31 n. 22, 54, 139 n. 25, 158, 241 n. 41, 246
"Muslim invasions," 4

Naḍsur (Maharashtra), 80
Nagarāhāra (Afghanistan), 20, 153, 168, 177, 181, 186
Nāgasena (Buddhist monk), 5
Nag Hammadi manuscripts, 9, 84
Nājigrām (Swat Valley), 67
Nandāra (Afghanistan), 60, 64
Naupur (Gilgit), 84, 86
Navaseas (family name?), 227, 228, 233
Nepal, 7, 8, 122
New Indo-Aryan (NIA) languages, 134
Niya documents, 39, 113, 129, 167, 170. *See also* Gāndhārī language, central Asian documents
Northern Areas (Pakistan), 113

northern black polished ware, 187
"Northwestern Prakrit," 3, 110, 171. *See also* Gāndhārī language
North-West Frontier Province (Pakistan), 3
numerical symbols (in Kharoṣṭhī), 42, 42 n. 53
Nuristani languages, 134, 135

Oḍi (Indo-Scythian kingdom), 153, 153 n. 27, 154
Old Indo-Aryan languages, 3. *See also* Sanskrit
Oriya, 134, 135

Pakistan, 3, 84
  Gāndhārī manuscripts, 57, 67
  inscribed clay pots, 187
Pālāṭu Ḍherī (Chārsada), 79, 80, 186, 188, 228
Pali, 11, 122, 124, 132, 133, 137
  canon, 7, 13
  manuscripts, 8
  Theravāda textual tradition in, 7
palm leaf (as writing material), 8, 66, 101
Pāṇini, 218 n. 37
paper (as writing material), 8
papyrus, 17, 88, 91, 102–3
Pārāyana-vagga (of Sutta-nipāta), 27, 158–9, 160–3. *See also* Sutta-nipāta
Parthia, 168. *See also* Indo-Parthians
Pasai (Dardic language), 134
Passani (Afghanistan), 60, 61
Patna Dharmapada, 160. *See also* Dhammapada (Pali); Dharmapada (Gāndhārī)
Peshawar, 186, 188
Peshawar Valley, 3, 186
Petrovskii, N. Th., 58
Phalura (Dardic language), 147 n. 19
Pitalkhoṛā (Maharashtra), 80
Pliny the Elder, 91
poṭhī (Indian-style book), 101, 104, 107
pots and potsherds
  Buddhist monasteries, found at, 185–6
  decoration, 80, 184–5, 189, 191, 199, 203, 205, 214, 217, 225–40 passim, 247
  drawing on, 80
  human bones buried in, 77–81, 243, 247
  Kharoṣṭhī inscriptions on, 15, 20–1, 68, 78–80, 153, 183–247, 189 (map 3); references to Buddhist schools, 175–7, 188, 190 n. 7, 191, 191 nn. 9–10, 194, 200, 203, 205, 210, 212–4, 217, 229, 231, 234–5, 240; standard formula, 190, 191, 203, 214, 218, 229, 231, 232, 235, 236, 241–4, 247
  manuscripts buried in, 15, 19, 21–2, 69, 76–7, 78, 80, 85, 106, 214, 243, 246

pots and potsherds (*continued*)
  stamped designs on, 185, 191, 198, 199, 203, 226, 227, 228, 231, 235
pradhāna/prahāna (Skt.; = Gāndhārī *prasaṇa*), 24, 91
Prakrit, 3, 110. *See also* Middle Indo-Aryan languages
"Prakrit Dhammapada," 57 n. 1. *See also* Khotan Dharmapada
prātimokṣa, 164, 167, 168, 170, 173
pratītya-samutpāda, 50, 67, 85
pratyekabuddhas, 159
pseudo-anusvāra. *See under* Kharoṣṭhī script
punctuation signs, 72, 73
Puniga (subject of avadāna), 36, 48
Punjabi language, 129, 134
Puṇṇā/Puṇṇikā. *See* Puniga
pūrvayogas, 37, 38, 49, 73, 75, 140

Questions of Milinda, 5
Qunduz vase inscription, 169, 188, 190, 191, 244

Rājagṛha, 213, 213 n. 33
Ramaka's reliquary inscription, 118
Rāṇigāṭ (Pakistan), 188
Rāṣṭrapāla-paripṛcchā, 38
Ratnagiri (Orissa), 81 n. 15
reed pen, 22, 108–9
relics (śarīra, dhātu) and relic cult, 68, 81, 86, 179, 183, 242
reliquaries, 66, 67, 68, 81, 85, 86
Rhinoceros Horn Sūtra (*Kharga-viṣaṇa-sūtra), 23, 33–4, 44 n. 54, 46, 53, 70, 125 n. 10, 162
  format, 98–100
  identified with "Sacred text of the Pratyeka-buddhas," 159
  morphology, 131, 131 n. 18, 132
  orthography, 122
  Pali parallels, 160
  script, 109, 116
  style, 138
  text sample, 34–5
Roman papyri, 88, 91
Rukhuṇakā (Indo-Scythian queen), 150 (fig.13)

Sabrudidrigo (character in pūrvayoga story), 39
Sadaṣkana (Kuṣāṇa prince), 153
Sahrī-Bahlol (Pakistan), 186, 188
Saidu Sharīf (Pakistan), 188
Sakas, 37, 153 n. 27, 210. *See also* Indo-Scythians; Scythians
Śākyamuni, 49, 81

Salihundam (Andhra Pradesh), 245
Sallekha-sutta, 24
Samayabhedoparacanacakra (work by Vasumitra), 167
Saṃghapriya (monk mentioned in inscriptions), 194, 194 n. 13, 198, 225, 226
Sanchi, 148 n. 21
Saṅghaśrava (monk mentioned in colophon fragment), 40–1
saṅgīti (communal recitations), 156
Saṅgīti-paryāya (commentary on Saṅgīti-sūtra), 24
Saṅgīti-sūtra
  Chinese versions, 24, 89, 171–4
  Gāndhārī version, 24, 49, 89, 91, 126, 164, 171–4, 175; text sample, 138
  Pali version, 24, 138 n. 23, 171–3
  Sanskrit fragments, 24, 171–3
Sanskrit, 122, 122 n. 7, 124, 125, 137. *See also* Buddhist Sanskrit/Buddhist Hybrid Sanskrit
  Buddhist texts in, 7, 8, 11, 13, 77
  central Asian manuscripts, 102
  in Gandhāra, 4, 107
  as source of Middle Indo-Aryan (Prakrit) languages, 3, 110
  unique text among British Library fragments, 39, 46, 53, 88, 94
Sārthadāsa (subject of avadāna), 36, 48
Sarvāstivādins (Buddhist school), 163
  abhidharma literature, 5, 6 n. 4
  in central Asia, 168, 180
  Gāndhārī language, use of, 171
  patronized by Kuṣāṇas, 11, 180
  referred to in inscriptions, 21, 21 n. 3, 170, 175, 176, 177, 188, 190 n. 7, 191, 200, 203, 205, 210, 212, 213
  relationship to other schools, 167
  texts preserved in Chinese, 7
satrap. *See* kṣatrapa
scribes, 54–5, 74. *See also* hands (of different scribes)
  preferences and styles, 87–8, 90–1, 108–9, 114, 120, 121, 124, 128, 137, 219, 230
  signatures, 238
  training, 136
scriptorium, 83
scrolls
  construction, 22, 70, 87, 92–6, 100–1
  dimensions, 42–52 passim, 88–91
  division into "volumes," 20, 26, 30, 53, 70, 87, 90–1
  early birch bark manuscripts, preferred format for, 107
scrolls (*continued*)
  found inside statues, 65, 68
  known as "postaka/postaga," 87
  large format, construction of, 70, 87, 92–6
  numbering system applied to British Library collection, 19, 19 n. 2
  number of texts in British Library collection, 20
  original number of, in British Library collection, 19–20
  origin of scroll format, 101–4
  patterns of damage, 22, 40, 46, 69–71, 104–6
  ritual interment, 69, 76–7, 80–1, 82, 84–5, 152, 183
  rolling cylinder, 101
  sewing of margins, 94–6
  size and condition, 17, 22
  small format, 64, 65, 67, 68, 69, 86, 98–100
  storage, 100
  written on one side only, 87–8, 88 n. 1, 90–1, 99
Scythians, 4, 37, 112, 137, 145. *See also* Indo-Scythians; Sakas
Senavarman (Indo-Scythian king), 150 (fig. 13)
  reliquary inscription of, 153
sermon at Benares, 63, 65
Shāhbāzgaṛhī Aśokan rock edicts, 5, 112, 126, 130, 133
Shahr-i Zuhak (Afghanistan), 66
Shaikhān Ḍherī (Pakistan), 151, 184–5, 186–7, 188
Shan-Shan (China), 128, 167
Shevaki stūpa. *See* Shiwaki stūpa
Shina (Dardic language), 134
Shiwaki stūpa (Afghanistan), 61, 62, 64, 86
Shnaisha Gumbat (Pakistan), 104
silk routes, 4, 113
Sindhi language, 129
Sinhala language, 134, 135
Sirkap silver saucer inscription, 148, 149
skandhakas, 164 n. 5
Sogdia, 168
Songs of Lake Anavatapta. *See* Anavatapta-gāthā
Sonkh, 187
Southeast Asia, 7, 8, 165
Sreṭharaña monastery, 176
Sri Lanka, 7, 8, 165
śrīvatsa (auspicious symbol), 232, 234
stater (weight unit), 144 n. 4, 148
Sthavira-gāthā, 161
stotra (in British Library fragments), 6, 53, 99, 100
stratega (commander), 141, 148